Balfour's World

FOR MATT

Balfour's World

Aristocracy and Political Culture at the Fin de Siècle

Nancy W. Ellenberger

THE BOYDELL PRESS

First published 2015

The Boydell Press, Woodbridge

ISBN 978 1 78327 037 8

The Boydell Press is an imprint of Boydell & Brewer Ltd
PO Box 9, Woodbridge, Suffolk IP12 3DF, UK
and of Boydell & Brewer Inc.
668 Mount Hope Ave, Rochester, NY 14620–2731, USA
website: www.boydellandbrewer.com

A catalogue record for this book is available
from the British Library

This publication is printed on acid-free paper

Printed and bound in Great Britain by
TJ International Ltd, Padstow, Cornwall

Contents

Illustrations

Sources: Figs 1, 5, 17 (@National Portrait Gallery, London); Fig. 2 (from *Political Letters and Speeches of George, 13th Earl of Pembroke and Montgomery*, by permission of the Earl of Pembroke); Figs 3, 4, 6, 10 (courtesy of the Earl of Wemyss, Stanway House); Figs 7, 11, 13 (@Illustrated London News Ltd/Mary Evans); Figs 14, 15 (@Mary Evans Picture Library); Figs 8, 9, 12, 16 (courtesy of Nimitz Library, United States Naval Academy)

Acknowledgements

My greatest thanks must go to the descendants of the main characters studied here for their cordial assistance over a number of years. First, all specialists in the period know the debt they owe to the present Earl of Wemyss and March (formerly Lord Neidpath) whose extraordinary preservation and sharing of the Mary Elcho Papers at Stanway have helped scholars interested in the late nineteenth-century political aristocracy for a generation now. In the past I was also fortunate to meet Mary Elcho's daughters, Lady Mary Lyon and Irene, Countess of Plymouth, as well as her grandson the 12th Earl of Wemyss and March. I have always remembered their kind hospitality and generous response to questions.

I am equally grateful to the Earl of Balfour and Mr A. M. Brander for permission to use and quote from the Balfour materials in the British Library and the National Archives of Scotland. The Earl of Pembroke and Montgomery has also been generous in allowing quotation from papers of his understudied ancestor, the 13th Earl of Pembroke. Mr Charles Osborne and the Bonham Carter Estate have kindly given permission to quote from the diaries and letters of Margot Asquith when she was simply Margot Tennant. Paul Chipchase, Nicolas Mosley, the late Earl and Countess of Oxford, the late Duke of Westminster and Lady Diana Cooper also extended hospitality and answered questions. Every effort has been made to contact copyright holders for other references in the text. If any have been omitted, I will be happy to include their names in subsequent printings.

I am grateful to the following for permission to consult their archives, and to the helpful staff whose cheerful professionalism has made research in Britain an exceptional pleasure: the Bodleian Library and Western Manuscripts Department, University of Oxford, especially Colin Harris and Susan Thomas; the British Library Board; the Master and Fellows of Churchill College, Cambridge; the National Archives of Scotland; the Somerset Heritage Centre, Taunton; the Swindon and Wiltshire Record Office; the Hull History Centre at University of Hull; and the Hertfordshire Archives and Local Studies Centre.

My obligations to mentors and colleagues in the scholarly community are extensive, but I would like to mention especially the formative and inspiring work of F. M. L. Thompson, David Spring, Peter Stansky, Stanley Pearson, Peter Marsh, Dorothy Helly, David Cannadine, William Lubenow, Laura Mayhall, Martin Francis, Paul Deslandes, Randy McGowen, R. J. Q. Adams and Gail Savage. Many institutions and professional organisations have also helped to shape my thinking on the recent methodological and historiographical developments that have transformed our understanding of British history. These include innumerable presenters and participants of the North American Conference on British Studies and the Mid-Atlantic Conference on British Studies; the Washington Area British Studies Group, founded and hosted by Dane Kennedy at George Washington University; the Institute of Historical Research, University of London; Dr Brian Loughman and the fellows of University College, Oxford; Dr Gordon Johnson and Wolfson College at Cambridge. The Social Science Research Council kindly provided funding for part of this project. I would also like to thank Michael Middeke and Megan Milan for their flawless support and assistance in working with Boydell & Brewer.

I owe a debt beyond measure to the midshipmen, faculty, officers and administration of the United States Naval Academy for providing me with lessons about professionalism and the ethics of service and leadership that I could hardly have acquired in another setting. The staff of the academy's Nimitz Library have given unending support, as has the Academic Dean's faculty research office, and travel and summer funding programmes. Cathy Higgins found instant remedies for all computer hardware and software challenges. Officer and civilian colleagues in the History Department works-in-progress seminar were an integral part in the evolution of the project, especially Richard Abels, Robert Artigiani, Lori Bogle, Thomas Brennan, David Peeler, Anne Quartararo, Craig Symonds, Larry V. Thompson and Ernest Tucker. The midshipmen in the academy's UK Scholarship programme earn my special thanks for keeping me connected with so many of the scientific, technological and strategic developments of the contemporary world, while a number of history honours students

have written theses over the years that contributed to my understanding of Arthur Balfour's era, especially Justin Accomando, Brent
Cochrane, Joel Hamner, Shannon Martin and Will McGee.

The many personal friends who have expressed enthusiasm for this
project have, I suspect, little idea how much their confidence and interest have meant to me. First, happily, are the best hosts and longest
fellow-travellers, Carolyn Jordan and Alan Webber. Next, tremendous
thanks to my earliest and kindest readers: Fred Harrod and Barbara
Manvel. Cathy J. Raphael, Marylou Symonds, Jane Good, Jim and
Nina Scott, Judy and Leo Pasqualge and Penny Ismay read drafts and
proposals, placed timely phone calls, and otherwise provided friendship in too many ways to list. Finally, of course, Matt and David – the
rocks – and Sarah – the light – of my life.

Abbreviations

NAMES

AB	Arthur James Balfour
GP	George Robert Charles Herbert, 13th Earl of Pembroke and Montgomery
GW	George Wyndham
LT	Laura Tennant (Lyttelton)
ME	Mary Elcho (born Mary Wyndham)
MT	Margot Tennant (Asquith)

PUBLISHED SOURCES

ILN	*Illustrated London News*
LAB	*Letters of Arthur Balfour and Lady Elcho, 1885–1917*, ed. Jane Ridley and Clayre Percy (London, 1992)
LLGW	J. W. Mackail and Guy Wyndham, *Life and Letters of George Wyndham*, two volumes (London, 1925)
LSGP	*Political Letters and Speeches of George, 13th Earl of Pembroke and Montgomery*, two volumes (privately printed, 1896)

ARCHIVES

BP	Balfour Papers, British Library Additional Manuscripts
BPS	Balfour (Whittingehame) Papers, National Archives of Scotland
CP	Chandos/ Lyttelton Papers, the Churchill Archives Centre, University of Cambridge
FHP	Frances Horner Papers, Mells Manor House, Somerset (private collection)

GPP   Earls of Pembroke Papers, Swindon and Wiltshire
        Record Office
GWP   George Wyndham Papers (private collection)
HPP   Herbert of Pixton Papers (Viscountess de Vesci),
        Somerset Heritage Centre
MAP   Margot Asquith Papers, Bodleian Libraries, University of
        Oxford
MEP   Mary Elcho Papers, Stanway House (private collection)
MGP   Mary Gladstone (Drew) Papers, British Library
        Additional Manuscripts
WP   Wenlock Papers, Hull History Centre, University of Hull
        Archives

Characters

BALFOUR OF WHITTINGEHAME

Arthur James (b.1848) Conservative politician and statesman
Gerald (b.1853) Arthur's brother, Conservative MP
Lady Betty (b.1867) wife of Gerald, daughter of the Earl of Lytton
Lady Frances (b.1858) wife of Arthur's brother Eustace, daughter
   of the Duke of Argyll
Alice (b.1851) Arthur's unmarried sister and manager of his
   households

CHARTERIS OF GOSFORD AND STANWAY

Hugo, Lord Elcho (b.1857) heir to the 10th Earl of Wemyss and
   March (m. Mary Wyndham)
Evelyn de Vesci (b.1850) Hugo's sister
Evan Charteris (b.1864) Hugo's brother, suitor of Margot Tennant
Anne, Countess of Wemyss (b.1823) mother of the above, friend
   of Margot Tennant

HERBERTS OF WILTON HOUSE

George, 13th Earl of Pembroke (b.1850)
Gertrude (Gety) (b.1840) George's wife, daughter of the Earl of
   Shrewsbury
Gladys (b.1859) George's sister, Gladys de Grey after her marriage
   in 1885

TENNANT OF THE GLEN

Laura (b.1862) fifth daughter of Sir Charles and Lady Tennant

Margot (b.1864) sixth Tennant daughter

Charlotte (Charty) (b.1858) third Tennant daughter

Thomas Lister, 4th Baron Ribblesdale (b.1854) married to Charty Tennant

Lucy (b.1860) fourth Tennant daughter, married to Thomas Graham Smith of Easton Grey

WYNDHAM OF CLOUDS

Percy (b.1835) Conservative MP, builder of Clouds

Madeline (b.1835) his wife

Mary (b.1862) their daughter, Lady Elcho after her marriage to Hugo Charteris, Lord Elcho

George (b.1863) Arthur Balfour's private secretary, Conservative MP, married to Lady Sibell Grosvenor

PERSONAL FRIENDS

Balfour, Edith (DD) (b.1865) married Alfred Lyttelton in 1892; no relation to Arthur Balfour

Beresford, Lord Charles (b.1846) cousin of Balfour and Pembroke; Royal Navy officer; occasional member of the Prince of Wales's Marlborough House set

Blunt, Wilfrid Scawen (b.1840) cousin of the Wyndhams; founder of the Crabbet Club; poet, anti-imperialist and womaniser

Brownlow, 3rd Earl (b.1844) married to Gety Pembroke's sister Adelaide; minor Conservative Party official; Conservative Party host at Ashridge

Churchill, Jennie (b.1854) American wife of Arthur's rival Lord Randolph Churchill, mother of Winston

Cust, Harry (b.1861) Brownlow's heir; MP and editor of the *Pall Mall Gazette*

Flower, Peter (b.1856) horseman, love interest of Margot Tennant, brother of Liberal peer Lord Battersea

Gladstone, Mary (b.1847) daughter of the Liberal prime minister, cousin of Balfour's love interest May Lyttelton

Granby, Violet (b.1856) cousin of Mary Elcho; artist and sculptor, married to the future Duke of Rutland

Grenfell, Ethel (Ettie) (b.1867) married to William Grenfell of Taplow Court; close friend of Arthur Balfour, Mary Elcho, Margot Tennant and Evan Charteris; noted society hostess after 1900

Hamilton, Sir Edward (b.1847) childhood friend of Pembroke, close friend of Lord Rosebery; permanent civil servant in the Treasury

Horner, Frances (b.1854) married to Sir John Horner of Mells Park; close friend of Laura Tennant; with Pembroke a leader of the Souls

Liddell, A. G. C. (Doll) (b.1847) barrister, civil servant; suitor of Laura Tennant and Edith Balfour

Lyttelton, Alfred (b.1857) barrister; Arthur's closest male friend; married Laura Tennant and later DD Balfour

Lyttelton, Spencer (b.1847) Arthur's college friend; confidant of Margot Tennant

Warwick, Daisy (b.1861) Mary Elcho's cousin; mistress of the Prince of Wales

Wenlock, Constance (b.1852) married to 3rd Baron Wenlock; close friend of Pembroke

White, Henry (b.1850) first secretary at US legation in London; married to Mary Elcho's close friend and confidante Daisy Rutherford White

SIGNIFICANT POLITICAL FIGURES

Asquith, Herbert Henry (b.1852) barrister, rising Liberal politician, Liberal home secretary in 1892; suitor of Margot Tennant

Brodrick, St John (b.1856) Conservative MP; Curzon's close friend; married to Hugo Elcho's sister Hilda

Chamberlain, Joseph (b.1836) Birmingham manufacturer; radical Liberal who abandoned Gladstone over home rule in 1885 and allied with the Conservatives as a Liberal Unionist

Churchill, Lord Randolph (b.1849) Conservative MP, leader of the 'Tory democracy' wing of the party; leader of the House of Commons before his resignation in December 1886

Curzon, George Nathaniel (b.1857) Conservative MP; host of Souls dinners; later viceroy to India

Gladstone, William Ewart (b.1809) four-time Liberal prime minister; advocate of Irish home rule

Harcourt, Sir William (b.1827) leading Liberal politician and front-bench opponent of Arthur Balfour

Hartington, Lord (b.1833) heir to the Duke of Devonshire; leader of Whig aristocrats who deserted Gladstone over home rule, then leader of Liberal Unionists; enters House of Lords in 1891

Lucy, Henry (b.1842) parliamentary commentator for *Punch, Graphic*

Milner, Alfred (b.1854) journalist, civil servant in Egypt, colonial administrator in South Africa; suitor of Margot Tennant

Morley, John (b.1838) writer, editor and politician; Liberal chief secretary for Ireland 1886, 1892-95

O'Brien, William (b.1852) Irish nationalist, journalist, MP; leader of Plan of Campaign and opposition to Arthur Balfour as chief secretary for Ireland

Parnell, Charles Stewart (b.1846) most important Irish nationalist leader of his generation, head of Irish Parliamentary Party and the National League

Rosebery, 5th Earl (b.1847) Arthur's generational rival, Liberal foreign secretary, Liberal prime minister 1892–95

Salisbury, 3rd Marquess (b.1830) Arthur's uncle; Conservative prime minister 1885, 1886–92, 1895–1902; owner of Hatfield House

Smith, W. H. (b.1825) Conservative leader of the House of Commons when Arthur was chief secretary for Ireland

Stead, W. T. (b.1849) newspaper editor, investigative journalist, founder of the *Review of Reviews* in 1890; much concerned with social questions and public morals

Introduction

Arthur Balfour

E ARLY IN 1893, Arthur James Balfour finally sent his friend Margot Tennant some reactions to an essay she had written months earlier about the role that individual genius played in public affairs. Margot was always on the lookout for masterful men, and she shared the Victorian conviction that just as self-help determined an individual's fate, so titanic personalities shaped the fortunes of the world. Truly historic political actors made their own opportunities and placed a personal stamp on their times. The word 'charisma' was not yet in popular use outside its religious meanings, but Margot looked for something like it in her endless scrutiny of the public figures of her day.[1]

Arthur Balfour disagreed. Personal circumstances had long ago convinced him that the most important events in an individual's life were not within personal control. When it came to explaining political success, he attributed most of it to 'sheer accident'. Arthur's own position as leader of the Conservatives in the House of Commons had been the result of a cabinet colleague's unpredictable breakdown in 1887. His subsequent promotion to the post of chief secretary for Ireland landed him a starring role in the most important parliamentary drama of his generation – the Irish home rule controversy of the late 1880s (see Fig. 1). He might have mentioned other fortuitous events of the decade: the self-destruction of his greatest political rival, Lord Randolph Churchill (Winston's father), or the break up of the Liberal Party over the Irish cause. But with characteristic occlusion, Arthur avoided mentioning what might have been pertinent to Margot's argument. Acquiring the highly visible position of Irish secretary had done nothing to ensure that he would display the qualities necessary for the occasion,

Fig. 1 Arthur Balfour in the mid-1880s

much less to become presumptive head of his party within four years.

Arthur's reply to Margot went deeper than what he called this 'extremely trite' nod to the Machiavellian calculus of will versus *fortuna*. 'What you say about "personality" is in a way true', he acknowledged. 'But I do not think you quite realize what a small fraction of what we call personality can really be said to depend upon the *person*. Personality, as you use the word, really means the power of striking the popular imagination: and this is in every case as much due to favourable accident as to inherent capacities.' The need to 'strike the popular imagination' occupied a lot of Arthur's mental energies, surprisingly so for a man – a 'grandee', in the words of his most recent biographer[2] – whose aristocratic connections, inherited income and intellectual abilities made him seem unusually removed from mundane concerns such as public image.

Yet Arthur's generation was arguably the first to worry continuously about the new public sphere being created by Britain's dramatically expanded electorate and vigilant, pervasive press.[3] Ushered in by parliamentary reform bills that more than tripled the number of adult male voters within twenty years, mass democracy in Britain required entirely new skills in organisation and political messaging. Partisan controversy spilled out of the gentlemen's world of Westminster and into the lives of agricultural labourers, mill workers and small property owners across the country. Politicians like Arthur needed to master not only the debating chambers of parliament and, possibly, the cabinet, but the stump speech, the party dinner and the journalists who reported the occasions. By the early 1890s both a young society woman like Margot and a twenty-year parliamentary veteran like Arthur recognised that political culture in Britain was undergoing tremendous change. In Arthur's mind, the 'popular imagination' was the relatively new factor of political life. It rewarded statesmen through a complicated dynamic of its own. Somehow, by the time he wrote to Margot in 1893, he had become its beneficiary.

A decade later, Arthur Balfour was prime minister and leader of the largest imperial enterprise in the history of the world. Younger contemporaries such as H. G. Wells, George Bernard Shaw, Rudyard Kipling and John Buchan began to portray him as the face of Britain itself at the moment of its greatest power and prestige.[4] Liberal and Conservative statesmen would call on his services well into the 1920s, and even today those with no expertise in British political history have heard of the Balfour Declaration of 1917 that pledged the country's support for a Jewish homeland in Palestine. Cool and analytic, equable and courteous, Arthur considered very little of this to result from bending the world to his will. He was always more aware, as were the circles of intimate friends around him, of a feeling of seismic reordering as the forces of global capitalism and mass society destroyed the Victorian world of their youth and created a strange new modern age.

Historians have long abandoned the notion that the late-Victorian and Edwardian decades were a halcyon era of tranquility, an Indian summer, for the British imperial system or the people who ran it. The forty years between Arthur's entry into parliament in 1874 and the outbreak of war in 1914 witnessed material changes and a sense of intensifying human interaction as bewildering to that

generation as the forces of globalisation are to the internet generation of the twenty-first century – indeed, many of the concerns are
shockingly familiar.[5] The public held similar debates about the role
of government in correcting widening disparities of income; there
were similar concerns that finance was displacing manufactures
that had brought the country its greatness, and similar fears of rising foreign competition. In 1886 Irish revolutionary nationalists
planted bombs that wrecked the House of Commons, previsioning
terrorist attacks on London landmarks more than a century later.
Culture wars erupted over moral values threatened by decadent
men and 'new women' who defied religious teachings.[6] Within
these few decades Britain's national elites were transformed. In-
heritors of aristocratic privilege made room for plutocrats buying
up England's great estates and watched anxiously as gifted boys
from the middle classes walked off with university prizes and professional honours.[7] The first great era of advanced, international
capitalism affected every segment of British society, including the
rarified domain into which Arthur was born.

Around the globe small wars of empire proliferated in numbers
and violence. During the two decades (1885–1905) when Balfour
and his uncle Lord Salisbury oversaw the government for all but
three years, Britain annexed Upper Burma without parliamentary
debate, transformed the economic structure of Egypt, launched
a massive three-year expedition to take over the Sudan, fought a
draining guerilla war in South Africa and invaded China as part
of an international coalition. Possibly as many as nineteen million people died of starvation or famine-related disease in British
India.[8] Chartered private companies boasting their own militias
subdued the peoples of modern Kenya, Uganda and Zimbabwe.
British citizens, unlike their European counterparts, escaped con-
scription. But the cultural evidence of empire and the military
action that sustained it infiltrated national life from advertising to
adventure novels, from music hall ditties to the sailor suits worn
by toddlers.

The age of empire and capitalism was accompanied by revolutions in the mental worlds of educated Britons. The modern liberal arts and sciences came into being as universities revamped their
degree fields to meet the needs of new professions. Intellectuals
and career academics spent their working lives trying to understand the forces behind the events they were witnessing – their
discoveries served to amplify the cycle of change. Foundational

theorists in fields from economics to sociology, comparative religion to statistics began their work during these years.[9] Both fiction writers and scientists 'invented the psychological'.[10] Even before the theories of Sigmund Freud reached England, Robert Louis Stevenson and J. A. Symonds were exploring the fractured inner worlds of outwardly respectable people.

Coming of age in the 1860s, during the first wave of reaction to Darwin and the scientific materialism he called 'naturalism', Arthur Balfour engaged with many of the seminal intellectual developments of this protean half-century. He was brother-in-law to the moral philosopher Henry Sidgwick, as well as the Nobel prize-winning physical scientist Lord Rayleigh. Early in his life he thought he might take up an academic career. Even as politics and government consumed more of his time, he wrote or lectured about the epistemological implications of relativity theory, the macroeconomic issues behind money supply and global finance, and the problematic nature of forming the 'imagined communities' that underlie national identity.[11] Everywhere you look in the literature of the fin de siècle you find evidence of 'the mind of Arthur Balfour', like footprints in the voguish new genre of detective stories he loved to read.

Arthur left one of these footprints in 1883, a decade before his exchange with Margot. He was thirty-five, still several years away from being a public name. In 1879 he had published a work on epistemology called *A Defence of Philosophic Doubt*, respectfully reviewed but a non-seller. This new essay was an appreciation of Bishop Berkeley, the early eighteenth-century metaphysical divine whose sceptical approach to the truth claims of science mirrored Arthur's own intellectual position.[12] It was typical of Arthur in these years that he would reveal more about himself in a scholarly publication than in autobiographical confession. When Margot Tennant's sister Laura was first encountering him socially, she wrote that 'Arthur lives with his windows shut and has a few false windows.'[13] But Balfour's appraisal of Berkeley sounds like a remarkably clear depiction of himself, or at least of his own ego-ideal.

Berkeley was a minor philosopher, Arthur acknowledged, crammed between the genius of John Locke and David Hume. His value lay in the portal he provided into the mental and social worlds of his times. The early eighteenth century was an era – like Arthur's – of extraordinary discovery and challenge to inherited beliefs. Arthur insisted that 'Berkeley was NOT a reactionary', stubbornly clinging to 'old ideas with old argumentative weapons'. On the contrary, he shared with Enlightenment contemporaries 'the same impatience of authority in matters of speculation, the same passion for clearness and simplicity, the same dislike of what was either pedantic on the one side or rhetorical on the other, the same desire to clothe his thoughts in an agreeable literary dress'. Berkeley's gifts had been social as well as intellectual. Broad-minded, tolerant and curious, he was the 'best of company', 'a man endowed with the subtlest of intellects, lit up with a humour the most delicate and urbane'. 'Scarce any man of his generation touched contemporary life at so many points', Arthur concluded, an epitaph that might have been written after his own death nearly fifty years later.

This assessment of Berkeley was close to the image that many contemporaries eventually held of Arthur himself. Neither man had the kind of volcanic temperament that Margot referred to. Both brought qualities of charm and personal modesty to a great variety of endeavours, but shone to greatest advantage in the venues of private sociability – the dinner tables and salons of a small, interconnected and privileged world. Yet Berkeley had lived on the Anglo-Irish periphery of an emerging Atlantic empire. Arthur, as he rose to power, had to function at the heart of an imperial metropolis, performing nightly before hundreds of critics in the House of Commons, before thousands in the speeches and lectures of the autumn recess. His challenge was to bring the urbane charms of the intimate and the intellectual into the fiercely contested arenas of an increasingly partisan political culture. That he did, by 1893, 'strike the popular imagination' had more to do with his own efforts than Arthur admitted.

How this occurred is a story of the formative years of the late 1880s and early 1890s in which an intensely private, reserved man of privilege adjusted to being in the national limelight, subject to the interpretation, invective and glorification of a media-saturated culture. The need to perform was not a foreign concept in the competitive aristocratic circles to which Arthur was born. Manners and formal rituals aided the construction of the masks worn in the discharge of social duties, whether to local dependants or to the extended networks of kin and acquaintances that one met a few times a year in high society. But as Arthur moved into the national political scene, the venues and audiences for performance were exploding. Scrutiny was increasingly carried out by strangers for the edification of strangers, and it reached deeper into the private realms of life. It took time for Arthur to learn how to handle his own self-presentation and to manage his image in a political world where 'public relations' was in its infancy and political consultants were non-existent.[14]

He did not achieve this through any kind of bravura self-assertion. Arthur's inclinations were to analyse rather than invent, to convince rather than browbeat. Cambridge-trained and by temperament a problem-solver, he was blindsided initially when he realised how little the mastering of information and argument would suffice in the public world. Nor were the character attributes of a reformed Victorian aristocracy – probity, diligence, disinterestedness – enough to justify deference to power. Arthur needed to show, rather suddenly, that he could sustain a compelling public personality. In doing so he cultivated a temperament that came to define aspects of elite culture after the high Victorians. Informality, flexibility, humour and playfulness characterised the mental outlook of the metropolis in the 1890s. So did evasion. Arthur learned to appear both affably candid and quietly efficient but, unlike the Victorians, neither rigid nor earnestly self-convinced.

This demeanour proved successful in an imperial moment that called for consolidation and management as much as assertion, and in which power was increasingly contested both at home and abroad. Three years after Arthur stepped down as prime minister in 1905, H. G. Wells began to write a fictionalised version of him in his novel about contemporary politics, *The New Machiavelli*. In the same year, John Singer Sargent completed a full-length study of Arthur Balfour (1908), now in the National Portrait Gallery, which so clearly evokes Phillippe de Champaigne's *Cardinal Richelieu* (1637) that it must have been intentional. This was the Balfour of a power that Berkeley never imagined, Balfour as manipulator, master of deception, accommodation and survival.

Even as Arthur was writing to Margot, the social circles he occupied within the national elite began to reflect this new ethos. Neither diary writers nor journalists believed that the private man and the public man were unconnected. The venues of elite sociability formed part of the public's assessment of politicians, as did their preferred recreations – Arthur's autumn holidays with golf professionals in North Berwick revealed as much about him as William Gladstone's tree-felling before crowds of admiring house guests or Lord Rosebery's ownership of Derby winners.[15]

Sociability was not only for escape or relaxation – it sustained the psychological structures of political action among the powerful, both rehearsing and critiquing the venues of more public performance. By the Edwardian years the demeanours that Arthur and his friends modelled became normative for many of those who had public responsibility for an emerging bureaucratic state that was both democratic and imperial. Some of Arthur's best friends – including Lord Pembroke and George Wyndham who figure here – failed at the new accommodations, their disappointments casting light on his success.[16]

When Arthur's social worlds are included in the political history of the era, elite women such as his friends Margot and Lady Mary Elcho become more than the sympathetic 'sounding board' that is a long-familiar role of women in aristocratic political life or 'incorporated wives' performing tasks now done by specialists.[17] The women in Arthur's circles – he remained a bachelor all his life – were integral to the creation of the new psychological milieu that accompanied the political developments of the pre-war years. Margot, for example, first pointed out that new parlour games in which women commanded the floor, outshining men in quick-witted responses, fostered skills of emotional management and verbal acuity that were precisely geared for parliamentary success. Beatrice Webb noticed how the brilliant, wide-ranging dinner conversations of Arthur's circles echoed the cynical superficialities delivered to voters.[18] In a more intimate realm, new informalities in women's lives opened opportunities for self-expression and self-fulfilment. These too required a tempering of emotions and compartmentalising of life that mirrored the bland deceptions practised by politicians. Arthur's women friends were enmeshed in the charm and secrecy, the urbanity and ruthlessness that came to be associated with the Edwardian political elites. As Friedrich Nietzsche argued in these same years, 'to fully accept a set of beliefs is to accept the values and way of life that are bound up in it'.[19]

In the 1880s and early 1890s, Arthur and his friends began to construct a new 'emotional regime' in the world of the British political elites.[20] It is not surprising that changes of the magnitude that Balfour's generation faced would result in different skills, career paths or political alignments. That they might result in the creation of different emotional patterns and interior worlds may be a less familiar idea. But acculturation to the practices of particular social environments is the way that humans learn how to manage the evanescent internal responses they have to all that goes on around them. Familial and social conventions teach individuals which emotional promptings are important to pay attention to, what responses are outlawed or preferred, what behaviours are appropriate.[21] This social conditioning is never complete. Individuals can always surprise with their resistances and eccentricities, and emotional regimes alter in interaction with the social world. Since the 1970s historians have been showing precisely that, positing the emergence of the 'man of sentiment' in the eighteenth century, the autonomous bourgeois individual and the romantic rebel in the nineteenth century and the narcissistic personality in the twentieth.[22]

The idea that historical circumstances condition the ways of feeling and expressing emotions allows for unusual integration of personal, private–social and public–institutional spheres in examining the power relations of a given historical moment. Like all emotional regimes, that of Arthur's world affected the interior lives of individuals themselves, the psychological positions they could sustain as well as the public actions they were willing to undertake. The Balfourian regime acknowledged and conveyed feelings, and in doing so managed them. It was tempered, supple, amiable, animated but self-possessed and, most especially, freed from vehemence. Expressing 'feelings' rather than transcendent 'passions' actually defused strong emotions. These changing patterns help to illuminate what one scholar has called the 'institutionalization of professional classes' in the modern bureaucratic states of the past century.[23] Factoring in emotional demeanour also expands our understanding of political culture. Arthur's cool yet engaged emotionality was a demonstration of what Lionel Trilling called the eclipse of 'sincerity' as a personal and political virtue at the end of the Victorian age.[24] In the sincere self, whose last great public exemplar was Gladstone, the emotions displayed were those that were felt, and these gave policy its moral weight. Arthur's performative outmanoeuvring of Gladstone delivered a different message: if you were truly sincere, your feelings were too simple for the exercise of responsible imperial power.

Virginia Woolf famously proclaimed that, on or about December 1910, human character changed.[25] Her chronological exactitude practically invites contradiction. In terms of the shapers of Britain's imperial political culture before the Great War, a case could be made for the December exactly a quarter-century earlier.

Around Christmas of 1885 the aged Gladstone decided to launch his last crusade on behalf of a clearly moral cause – the aspirations for self-government of the Irish people. He broached the decision with his chosen intermediary to the Tory leadership, Arthur Balfour, the man who would do as much as any other single actor to thwart Gladstone's efforts and bring disappointment to the end of the Grand Old Man's long career. The eclipse of Gladstone marked the eclipse of the Victorians. Without the fierce clarity that Margot might have wished for, the age of Balfour was dawning.

The exploration of Balfour's world that follows reflects a particular choice in historical reconstruction.[26] The narrative often shifts away from Arthur Balfour to describe the lives of five men and women who were among his closest friends in the years when he emerged as a public figure. One of these – his little-known contemporary the 13th Earl of Pembroke – was remarkably similar to Arthur in social standing, tastes and sensibilities. The trajectory of Pembroke's life casts light on the challenges faced by the aristocracy in the fin de siècle when they came unmistakably into competition with the professional and moneyed classes of the late nineteenth century. Two daughters of this new plutocracy are represented by Laura and Margot Tennant. Both were helped in their integration into Victorian high society by their friendships with Pembroke and Balfour, but as outsiders to the worlds of aristocratic privilege they were sharp observers of the manners and mores of their era's elite. The other two characters discussed here – siblings George and Mary Wyndham – were as close to Arthur Balfour as any people beyond his own family. Prolific correspondents, they give greater insight than does Arthur himself into the psychological challenges faced by members of a privileged class who encountered adult realities far different from what they had been raised to expect.

The first three chapters of the book introduce these six subjects in contrasting pairs. Thereafter their stories become interwoven around key episodes and developments of the decade before 1895. With the exception of Pembroke, on whom no substantial work has been done, all are familiar to historians of late-Victorian and Edwardian Britain. The historiography on Balfour is so immense that it has a bibliography of its own.[27] Many of the letters he exchanged with Mary Wyndham after her marriage to Hugo Elcho have been published, and she is a central character in the biography and memoirs of her daughter Cynthia Asquith and in

a new study by Claudia Renton.[28] The Wyndham family printed a
collection of George's letters that has been mined for decades for
its vivid observations. This is supplemented more recently by Max
Egremont's dual biography of Wyndham and his cousin Wilfrid
Scawen Blunt.[29] Margot Tennant made a publishing industry of
herself, full of collapsed chronologies and late-in-life assessments.[30]
She has received a balanced and sympathetic treatment in Colin
Clifford's *The Asquiths* (2002) that largely supersedes Daphne Bennett's *Margot* (1984).

The studies presented here do not pretend to the chronological and multifaceted coverage of the biographies. Instead they
'unpack' key episodes in the characters' early years that are often
given only a sentence or two in a full life treatment. This approach
allows for a depth of historical contextualising not possible for
scholars covering lives that spanned decades of profound change.
It permits a deeper exploration of why an historically obscure man
such as Lord Pembroke was important in his understandings of
friendship, what the experience of combat during a minor imperial incursion meant to the youthful George Wyndham, why
it was dangerous for Margot Tennant to capture the attention
of the Prince of Wales when she was barely twenty years old and
how Mary Elcho faced a crisis of infidelity at a time when scandal
threatened ruin for politicians, to say nothing of the women in
their lives. Arthur Balfour receives extensive coverage of his years
as Irish secretary. Otherwise he slips in and out of other stories as
actor, observer and commentator in the lives of friends who were
themselves autonomous personalities – more than bit players in
the rise of the most famous among them.

As historical genre, then, *Balfour's World* is neither biography nor
collective biography but a braided narrative, one of any number
that might be written with Arthur Balfour at the centre.[31] It incor-
porates different angles of vision from the individual experiences
of the characters and the varieties of written expression they left
behind. This helps in constructing the kind of 'thick description'
of everyday lives that cultural historians have been practising for
several decades, although only recently on elites rather than more
marginalised or 'invisible' members of society. The first section of
the book is particularly concerned with the construction of gendered identities in these privileged Victorian families. The chapters that follow explore the subjectivities developed in venues of
elite sociability, from the drawing room to the party in the country

to the House of Commons. This section uses concepts from social psychologists such as Georg Simmel, Erving Goffman and Judith Butler to show how the 'ritual elements of social interaction' were changing in the fin de siècle. As the narrative moves towards its culmination in 1895, it focuses on forays into outside worlds of electioneering among the masses and engagement with the boisterous world of print culture that prefigured the mass media of the twentieth century. The text attempts to capture something of the lived experience of these subjects. As psychologist Robert Coles observed in his 1977 study of the 'well-off and rich' in late twentieth-century America, privileged lives contain their own problems of agency, performance and self-definition.

Yet the title *Balfour's World* and the framing around the man himself are intended to show that the 'high politics' of an empire and the people who made its decisions form the subtext of the work. Susan Pederson has argued that the search of the 'new political history' for more broadly understood meanings of the everyday lives of political actors should not blind us to the larger structures of state and institutional power in which leadership functioned.[32] Arthur Balfour straddled two transformative traditions in governance. One was that created by Victorian England's public culture of liberal values as William Lubenow describes them – open, tolerant, informed and discursive. The other was imperial capitalism's regime of organisation and efficiency, including the general coarsening of language, behaviours and actions in political life during the pre-war decades.[33] How Arthur Balfour and his friends navigated these conflicting currents of liberal aspiration and Social Darwinian forebodings forms part of the narrative that follows.[34]

1

Men of Fortune

George Pembroke and Arthur Balfour

W HEN GEORGE Robert Charles Herbert, the 13th Earl of
Pembroke and 10th Earl of Montgomery, reached his twenty-first birthday in 1871, the celebrations at Wilton House were stu-
pendous. The welcoming party awaiting his arrival at the family's
ancestral estate four miles west of Salisbury included the mayor of
Wilton, the local rector (a great-uncle, it turns out, of the future
screen actor Laurence Olivier), 150 tenants on horseback, representatives of the Odd Fellows, the Royal Wilton Carpet factory, the
local Friendly Societies and scores of 'mechanics, artisans, and hab-
itants'. Twenty labourers unhooked the horses from his carriage
and dragged it to the great house under arches decorated with the
family's initials and trees planted for the occasion. Like the young
title-holder in Benjamin Disraeli's just published novel *Lothair*
(1870), Pembroke modestly 'thanked them all for the very hearty
welcome which they had accorded to him, and more particularly
so because he had been away a long time, and came among them
almost as a stranger' – an allusion to travels that had taken him
out of the country for much of his adolescence. Everyone cheered
George's mother for her numerous good works since coming to
live at Wilton three decades before. Then the crowds adjourned
for fireworks, choral singing, dances, dining and rural sports. The
festivities went on for a week, engaging a thousand schoolchildren
as well as 'the elite of the town and neighborhood'.[1]

'Younger sons, as is well known, do not come of age', groused
George's contemporary Lord Ronald Gower, himself the eleventh
child of the Duke of Sutherland.[2] An aristocratic estates system
that allowed eldest sons to inherit both public identities and stewardship of a great family and its assets produced such complaints.

George's income placed him among the thirty wealthiest land-owners in Britain.[3] His revenues from farmland in Wiltshire were almost matched by skyrocketing ground rents from property developments in the Donnybrook, Irishtown and Sandymount areas of south-east Dublin. He inherited control of a church living at Jesus College, Cambridge, though he never attended university himself. With a seat in the House of Lords and a father who had served twice as secretary for war, Pembroke was a public personage even in his teens.

Arthur Balfour, although not a nobleman like Pembroke, experienced a similar rite of passage when he came of age in 1869 and inherited the family estate at Whittingehame near the Lammermuir Hills east of Edinburgh. More than five hundred local guests and notables feasted outdoors on the lawns of the great house, the meal interspersed with toasts and raucous cheering. 'I did not much like it', Arthur admitted later. 'There was too much speechifying; and I was shy.'[4] Arthur's paternal grandfather, the younger son of Scottish gentry, had made a fortune through government contracts to provision naval vessels in the Indian Ocean during the Napoleonic wars. The 'Nabob' returned to his native land in 1813 with £300,000, entered the House of Commons and sent his own heir, James Maitland Balfour, to Eton and Cambridge. James married a daughter of the 2nd Marquess of Salisbury and followed his father into the Commons, cementing the family's arrival among the national landed elite that had been forming for the past half-century.[5]

Arthur's inheritance was between £1 million and £4 million (at least $5 million in post-Civil War America). His income of £20,000 a year was only a quarter of Pembroke's vast revenues, but that still placed them both in the top one-tenth of 1 per cent (about 4,300 individuals) of all income earners in an island population of more than twenty-six million people.[6] But the two men shared more than wealth, status and family connections in the highest circles of political society. Their lives ran so in parallel that if it were possible to have a doppelgänger, Arthur Balfour's would be his friend the Earl of Pembroke.

Each grew up in one of the exceptionally religious households that characterised the evangelical aristocratic generation of the first half of Victoria's reign.[7] Each lost his father before reaching adolescence and was deeply influenced by a strong-willed mother whose certitudes were noteworthy even for that conscience-stricken

age. Both families had nurseries full of children, eight born in nine
years for the Balfours, seven born in twelve years for the Herberts.
Arthur and George had mysterious ill-health as boys and undistinguished records at Eton. As adults they tended to be intellectual
and high-minded. Tall, slim, personable and good-looking, in the
early 1870s each moved briefly into the family orbit of the Liberal
prime minister William Gladstone, whose daughter Mary fell deeply in love with Arthur and seems to have viewed Pembroke as a sort
of blockheaded brother.[8] The two men entered parliament in the
same year, 1874, and both published books in their twenties that
explored their generation's crisis of faith and defined their own
religious outlook.

Their political interests evolved in tandem. They were Conservatives, and the divisive issues of Ireland, empire and the condition of the working classes absorbed their public energies for
decades. Despite active engagement in the masculine realm of
politics, however, each acquired a reputation for being unmanly
in terms of the increasingly robust and sporting virility of the day.[9]
They were regarded as too intellectual, too literary, too fond of
friendly, non-sexual companionship with women and not given to
the cruder forms of homosocial bonding that characterised their
contemporaries such as Lord Randolph Churchill or Lord Charles
Beresford.

Their similarities made the differences more striking. When
Arthur died he was one of the pre-eminent statesmen of his age,
not just a former prime minister but the architect of numerous
enduring features of British and Commonwealth policy. When
George died, he rated barely three paragraphs in the *Times* and
the *Illustrated London News*. Obituary writers stressed his attractive
private life and lauded his charitable acts among his neighbours.
Pembroke, who shared so many interests with his friend, was the
shadow Balfour, trailing him through the decades, not quite hit-
ting the mark, never establishing the adaptive and controlled persona that contributed so much to Arthur's eventual success.

In 1885 Adam Badeau, the American consul general in London
through the 1870s, published a book explaining men like Balfour
and Pembroke to fascinated republicans across the Atlantic. In-
terweaving gossipy anecdotes and sociological insight, *Aristocracy
in England* devoted several chapters to describing the fantastic
position of first sons in the British landowning system. Future

heirs, Badeau observed, got special treatment from the moment
of their arrival in the world, not just from servants, tradespeople
and county neighbours but also from family members who knew
the powers they would eventually have. At elite boarding schools
a youth understood to be coming into a title or great fortune enjoyed a protective aura that often spared him the worst indigni-
ties inflicted by snobbish masters and bullying older boys. In the
greater world, public ceremonies monitored by the local or even
national press punctuated the key moments of an heir's life from
birth to marriage to internment in the family vaults.[10]

Arthur and George occupied a particular subset of this privileged group. They were not only heirs, but heirs who were fatherless from childhood. They had neither paternal nor older-brother
role models, and they actually assumed the duties of family heads
as they turned twenty-one. In the 1870s fewer than 15 per cent
of great landowners shared this circumstance.[11] Several figured
among Arthur and George's personal friends, as though early
knowledge of the coming responsibilities of privilege and the incalculable mysteries of fortune formed a psychological bond into
adulthood.

Arthur was aged seven when his father died of tuberculosis
in 1856. He wrote later that he had no memory at all of James
Balfour, though he had spent two winters in Madeira with the
invalid while his mother tried desperately to nurse her dying husband back to health. After James's death Lady Blanche Balfour
suffered a nervous breakdown that lasted several months. Then
she devoted her life to her children, largely abandoning the world
of London polite society and country house visiting to focus her
considerable will within her household and the neighbourhood of
Whittingehame.[12]

Lady Blanche Balfour was by all accounts a formidable figure,
an impression confirmed by the personal letters she wrote to
her greatest woman friend during the years she was raising her
children alone.[13] Lady Blanche had embraced the stern Anglican
evangelicalism that engulfed many of her generation of aristocratic women, not in the form of rigid doctrinal interpretation but
as an internalised sense of guilt and personal responsibility. Her
overwhelming concern with duties to others and the sinfulness
of vainglory made her a paragon in the eyes of pious observers
who recorded the gratitude of servants and villagers for her many
charities. Some biographers described the world she created for

her crowded nursery as a cheerful though disciplined childhood environment, no more given to harsh austerities than was usual for aristocratic families determined to instil character in their off-spring.[14] Nevertheless, memoirs by Arthur's sisters make it sound like no easy regime. Ruthlessly condemning vanity and indulgence in her own nature, Lady Blanche tartly suppressed self-regard in her offspring. Even a sympathetic portrait by the local vicar spec-ulated that she was too powerful a force in her children's devel-opment. Cecil and Alice, next in line after Arthur and his two older sisters, led unhappy lives. Gerald, born in 1853, resented his mother long after her death. The youngest child, mild-mannered Eustace, was an alcoholic by the time he was forty.[15]

Arthur himself stressed Lady Blanche's defining role in his life. Her interests in science, history and literature shaped his intel-lectual outlook, as did her sense of the duties of a great position and the strength of her faith. But Arthur was the luckiest of the children in being able to establish some psychological distance from his mother relatively early. Three years after his father died he went to preparatory school in faraway Hertfordshire, while his sisters and youngest brothers were at home for another decade or more. Kenneth Young speculates that Arthur left for school with something like alacrity, confident of his importance in his mother's eyes but quietly prone later in life to violate many of her precepts about shunning amusement or unproductive use of time.

Although his father had been a reckless lover of the hunt, the sporting worlds of aristocratic males played little part in Arthur's childhood years. He was near-sighted and not athletic, and he learned early to use concerns about his health in order to escape unpleasant situations. During his two years at boarding school, and later at Eton, he received special treatment because of ill-de-fined exhaustion. Masters described him as a dutiful boy, politely good-humoured and able to laugh at himself, but cautious and abstracted. *The Eton College Register* confirms that he left the school in 1866 securely in the middle of the fifth-form examination lists, not elected to the prestigious debating society known as Pop and absent from any prize, sports or activity lists during the years he attended. 'Whether looked at from the scholastic or the athlet-ic point of view, I was quite uninteresting', he wrote with a wry acknowledgement of the increasing importance of hierarchies of performance at the elite public schools of his youth.[16]

George Pembroke was only a little older than Arthur when he

lost his father, the prominent Victorian statesman Sidney Herbert, who died of a kidney disease when George was eleven. The death of his expatriate uncle a year later brought George the ancient Pembroke earldom. As with the Balfours, George and his six siblings were left under the guardianship of their mother. Lady Herbert of Lea, or Elizabeth Herbert as she preferred to be called, was in her own way as exceptional as Lady Blanche, though she was effusive rather than bracing, warm to Lady Blanche's chill. She too was unusually devout, but in a different direction. Her conversion to Catholicism when George was fifteen led to decades of confessional outpourings and charitable work on behalf of the Church of Rome.[17] Before this, however, the two mothers represented the spectrum of Anglican devotionalism of the mid-Victorian era, from the emotional High Church Tractarianism of Lady Herbert to the determinedly self-denying activism of Lady Blanche.

Elizabeth Herbert's attraction to Rome was part of the resurgence of Catholicism among the upper classes in Britain, prompted by the era's intellectual challenges to the foundations of Christian faith. Disraeli, an early admirer of Sidney Herbert, wrote that Elizabeth's 'whole life was dedicated to the triumph of the Catholic cause, and being a woman of considerable intelligence and of an ardent mind, she [became] a recognised power in the great confederacy which has so much influenced the human race'. But Disraeli also described the 'lively and impetuous' Lady Herbert as 'gushing'. She became a figure of fun in society circles, noted for her spirited defence of Catholicism and unflagging pursuit of miracles that she attributed to the faith. 'Her zeal was a proverb', wrote the novelist and social commentator W. H. Mallock in another fictional portrayal. 'Her name was international property.'[18] Queen Victoria privately thought the credulous devotion of the newly converted among the aristocracy 'too ridiculous and disgraceful' on the part of English people.[19]

The aggressiveness of the Vatican's outreach and the conversion of highly placed aristocrats raised considerable alarm in the Protestant establishment of mid-Victorian England. Lady Herbert's embrace of the Church caused enormous strain with her in-laws, including several actions supported by Sidney's old friend William Gladstone that would have made her younger children wards of the Court of Chancery. 'If you have a friend who according to your conviction commits a serious error, or falls into a perilous folly', Gladstone wrote to Elizabeth, 'what would you do? Would you for one moment allow him to suppose that you thought lightly of the crime?' Elizabeth replied with some spirit that she was raising her children in the Anglican faith and that they were surrounded by Protestant servants. When George's oldest sister, Mary, converted to Catholicism in 1873, he was on the receiving end of a tirade from Gladstone warning of the Catholics' 'insidious proselytization' in the great houses of England.[20]

Despite the acrimony, Elizabeth Herbert was never as cut off from society life as her later conversion narrative and her Catholic friends implied.[21] She continued to entertain in London and at Wilton, and Mary Gladstone herself remained friends with Pembroke's two older sisters. Although the youngest offspring were separated from their mother for long periods as they grew up, George probably spent more time in her company than was usual for boys of his age and class, since concerns about his health prevented normal schooling. George abandoned formal education at seventeen, still lodged in Eton's lower fifth form. For months at a time he lived with Lady Herbert on the Continent and travelled with her throughout the Mediterranean, including trips to Egypt, Palestine, Sicily and Spain. Together they survived a hurricane at sea in the West Indies in 1867, and Lady Herbert played a prominent part in the coming-of-age ceremonies in Wiltshire and Dublin in 1871.[22]

These fatherless households gave exceptional scope to strong-minded mothers and capable older sisters in the lives of Arthur and George. They were used to having women determine domestic routines and make decisions with male professionals and employees. Both became adept at navigating the emotional dynamics of a female household, placating and circumventing conflict rather than confronting it with anger or sulks. Dutiful sons and brothers, even as adolescents Arthur and George avoided the risk-taking behaviour – gambling, drinking, carousing – that Lord Lyttelton had in mind when he worried about his eight motherless boys 'going to the bad'.[23] Nor did they transfer emotional allegiance to the all-boy world of boarding school. Other memoirists of their generation devoted chapters of extraordinarily detailed description to schoolmates and boyish escapades, the exactitude of the memories revealing how prominently these years had marked the psychological development of boys removed from their home environments at around the age of nine.[24]

Two vivid anecdotes hint at the contrasting temperaments of

Arthur and George, however, despite the similarities of circumstance. Arthur presented his, related in old age, as the single clear recollection he retained from his first decade. This was during one of the winters in Madeira as his father lay dying, when his Uncle Charles came out to check on the family and took the children sailing. Arthur remembered himself as a small boy – he would have been six or seven – cowering and 'weeping copiously' when a sudden Atlantic squall threatened to swamp the boat that Charles was piloting. 'So far as I remember, little or nothing was *said* by my elders about this inglorious exhibition', he wrote, 'but I was left in no doubt as to what was *thought.*' This singular childhood recollection led historian Judith Hughes to conclude that Arthur learned very young that violent emotions were not only uncomfortable but dangerous, likely to overtax a mother already at her psychological limits with worry and responsibility.[25] In his philosophical publications Arthur often alluded to feelings. Their existence and intensity as human attributes in part sustained his theism. But even more than other Balfours, he resisted showing emotions. As the local vicar observed, one thing that Lady Blanche's offspring learned was self-control.

The anecdote from George's life comes in the form of an 'extraordinary' dream he recorded when he was seventeen. The setting was Wilton, where he found himself in the drawing room surrounded by his father's sisters and their husbands. 'Suddenly some prophesying spirit seemed to come upon me and take possession of my tongue. I commenced saying the most cruel and mischievous things, every word cutting someone like a knife. I was in an agony but I could not stop: some uncontrollable impulse urged me on.'[26] The message was not hard to find. Final words from his dying father that left 'poor dear mama to your care' had placed the teenage boy squarely in the middle of intense family hostilities. George was later described as the best tempered of men, enormously tolerant of the small irritations of domestic life. But, unlike Arthur, he did not always maintain his composure. Throughout his life dogmatic assurance would never fail to spark his emotional outrage.

Eighteen months after this dream, George transcribed into his travel log a remarkably frank analysis of his adolescent personality.[27] One notable feature of his self-examination was its lack of religious tropes. After eight years of buffeting by theological controversy, George did not call on God for help or yearn for

Christian humility. His problems, as he saw them, lay not in a sinful nature but in monitoring the conscious self, learning judgement, perspective and how to control his responses. 'Intensely egotistical, and absurdly sensitive, as most egotistical people are', George began, 'bad tempered, but seldom malicious'. 'Foolishly miserable about small things, careless enough about great ones; tolerably truthful, but given to exaggeration; always veering about between sentimentality and cynicism. Obstinate and argumentative.' The greatest challenges to an emerging autonomous personality, George thought, were his need for affection and his sensitivity to criticism. He was 'usually a shrewd observer of human nature but as blind as a bat when my affections are called into play … very jealous of my friend's affection having a low idea of my power of inspiring it'.

It is impossible to conceive of Arthur, at any age, writing anything as candid as this – even his letters from Eton were amused, controlled and emotionally distanced from anything that touched the inner self too closely. Many of the tendencies George described remained features of his adult personality. A 'ludicrous mix of experience and innocence', as he told Mary Gladstone, George would always convey the sense that he was seeking an inner equilibrium that outsiders assumed to be the birthright of a man in his position.[28]

At Eton Arthur lodged at the residence of the Rev. A. F. Birch, nicknamed 'the House of Lords' for the number of heirs to titles placed there by their parents. Birch was a generally lax supervisor of the ranks of boys under his care. There were a number of 'swells' in the house – extraverted and charismatic adolescents recognised by the whole school as leaders – and a few bullies, but also some quiet, fastidious scholars who avoided the rough-housing and escapades of rowdier youths.[29] Arthur seems to have gone his own way and avoided drawing attention through conspicuously good or bad performance.

One noteworthy aspect of his time at Eton was how little the intensities and emotional confusions of adolescence figured in his story. He was never mentioned as sharing – though he may have observed – the erotically charged world of master–boy favouritism that surrounded his last form master William Johnson, who left Eton suddenly about five years later in order to avoid scandal over his relations with a student.[30] Between the extremes of gushing

sentiment and acerbic sarcasm that characterised masculine interactions at public schools, Arthur tended towards the latter. Both
masters and students used mockery and verbal targeting to provide
psychological boundaries and establish pecking orders. Arthur
may have discovered here the skill at delivering bland put-downs
that would enhance his performance in the House of Commons.
But his later confession that at Eton he began to doubt his own
abilities shows how repressive the boarding school regime could
feel for the unexceptional pupil, neither a scholar favoured by
masters nor an athlete feted by boys, even if he escaped the worst
horrors of bullying.

Arthur tolerated Eton, but at Cambridge he was actually happy.
At Trinity College he made the acquaintance of one of the two older men who would most influence his adult development. While
his uncle, who became Lord Salisbury in 1868, eventually became
a political father-figure, the philosopher Henry Sidgwick provided
the intellectual mentorship that Arthur needed at this time. 'What
most people want in order to do their best is recognition; and the
kind of recognition from a distinguished man of eight-and-twenty
which is most valued by a boy of eighteen is the admission that
his difficulties are worth solving, his objections worth answering,
his arguments worth weighing. This form of conveying encouragement came naturally to Sidgwick.'[31]

Perhaps it helped Sidgwick's rapport with Arthur that the two
shared some important similarities in their youthful psychological
profiles. Sidgwick too had lost his father very young, maintained
close ties to his mother and siblings and suffered from mysterious lassitude that he learned to overcome by exercise. Subject
to a nearly crippling stammer, Sidgwick was shy in social groups
and preferred discussion in intimate settings. But unlike Arthur,
Sidgwick had proved to be a natural scholar. Accolades and prizes
at Rugby preceded first class honours in both classics and mathematics at Trinity. Immediately after completing his degree in
1859, Sidgwick obtained a fellowship at the college, but within a
few years he was abandoning work in classical philology to educate
himself in history, ethical theory and political philosophy. Sidgwick was deeply and personally engaged with the 'crisis of faith'
controversies in the universities of the 1860s.[32] In resigning his
fellowship in 1869 because he could not subscribe to the Thir-
ty-Nine Articles of the Anglican Church, he demanded of himself
a scrupulous confessional exactitude that Arthur did not share

to the same degree. But Sidgwick was a remarkably open-minded searcher for truth in the form of clear analysis of definitions and their logical implications.

Sidgwick was at the centre of a group of young scholar-dons determined to transform education at Oxford and Cambridge to reflect the changed realities of the Victorian era.[33] Their project entailed nothing less than the creation of the modern academic disciplines required to analyse a world deprived of a common religious framework and grappling with the implications of the Darwinian paradigm, the social and economic challenges of industrialisation and a dawning awareness of global imperial responsibilities. During a career at Cambridge that lasted until his death in 1900, Sidgwick played a central role in establishing programmes in economics, psychology, philosophy, politics and history. He was just beginning to appreciate the dimensions of this mental and disciplinary revolution when, under his mentorship, Arthur joined a first group of undergraduates who would read for the moral sciences tripos, a newly introduced honours degree.[34]

Sidgwick's design of the reading lists for the new course of study stressed political economy, logic and political and moral theory since the Enlightenment. Students read the utilitarians, the English positivists and great amounts of J. S. Mill, though Kant and Hegel were both omitted. The course suited Arthur's generalising and systematising mind, allowing him to explore the most contemporary understandings of social change as well as questions of epistemology that occupied him for the rest of his life. At Trinity, Arthur acquired the tools for sustained analytic inquiry and the habit of detached speculation, which were among his most valuable resources for understanding the world and structuring his inner life.

As an undergraduate Arthur's circles of sociability expanded considerably. Only one contemporary from his five years at Eton made it into his memoirs, but the chapter on Cambridge fondly recalled mountaineering and kayaking companions, his tennis buddy George Darwin and musical friends such as Spencer Lyttelton with whom he discovered a lifelong passion for Handel and Bach. Acquaintances recalled Sunday night discussion groups held in his rooms at the corner of New Court, fuelled by an excellent stock of claret.[35] He was inseparable from one young Trinity fellow a few years his senior, the physicist John Strutt, who married Evelyn Balfour in 1871 and two years later became 3rd Baron Rayleigh.

Arthur was already developing an eclectic range of interests and activities, from recreations such as tennis and music to a generalist's informed curiosity about the natural and social sciences.

Arthur was so well-integrated into Cambridge life that it is logical to ask why he was not invited to join the secret, highly prestigious debating society known as the Apostles. Founded in 1820 by a group of friends at St John's College, the self-selecting Apostles (also known as the Cambridge Conversazione Society) had already welcomed such luminaries as Alfred Tennyson, F. D. Maurice and Henry Sidgwick himself. In a later generation John Maynard Keynes, Leonard Woolf, G. E. Moore, Bertrand Russell and Alfred North Whitehead would be added to an exceptional pantheon of Victorian academics, administrators and litterateurs. In the 1860s Trinity men dominated the Apostles, and their Saturday night debates centred on questions that were close to Arthur's deepest concerns – the true sources of knowledge, the foundations for morality in a materialist world, evolving conceptions of human nature itself. Paying higher fees allowed Arthur to sit at the high table with the Trinity fellows. Thus he knew personally many of the Apostles active during his Cambridge years – and they would have known him. It appears that scholars such as Richard Jebb, W. K. Clifford, Henry Jackson, James Stuart, A. J. Butler, Frederick Pollock, possibly even Henry Sidgwick, did not see Arthur as potentially one of their number – Oscar Browning, another Apostle, later said that this was one of the most startling oversights in the society's history.[36]

Some of the reasons probably had to do with academic gate-keeping and professional ambition. Despite Sidgwick's efforts, the moral sciences tripos was still considered a 'soft option' that 'first rate men' avoided because it 'encouraged superficiality'.[37] All five Apostles invited into the group between 1867 and 1869 – the years when Arthur was eligible – studied classics or mathematics. Three of them were academic stars who proved their mastery by being placed high on the honours examination lists.[38] Arthur's avoidance of the long-standing and highly competitive examination fields looked like intellectual laziness. With reliable income and secure social position awaiting him, he was certainly disinclined to grind at unappealing subjects in the scramble for prizes that, for the men of the rising middle classes, ensured opportunities in education, journalism or the civil service.[39] A position among the Cecils – titled and landed since their service to Queen Elizabeth

three centuries before – located Arthur in a different social world
from the bright, driven sons of rural vicars and small-town solicitors who were taking over the ancient universities. Many of the
men he described as his closest friends at Cambridge were or
would be independently wealthy from landed estates – Arthur
Kinnaird, Reginald McLeod, John Strutt and Spencer Lyttelton
among them.

The electors among the Apostles may also have suspected that
Arthur would not enjoy or contribute to the particular ambience of
the group. William Lubenow has described how the Apostles were
not just an intellectual forum, but one of the homosocial venues in
which future members of a national, meritocratic elite established
friendships that replaced the provincial ties of their childhoods.
According to Sidgwick, Apostles were expected to commit to a form
of self-exploration, of open spiritual and personal soul-searching
with fellow members – something that was foreign to Arthur, at this
time and later. The creed demanded 'sympathetic intimacy *and*
truth … conversation that put everything on the line'.[40] Behind
an outward intellectual assertiveness, many Apostles revealed their
moral uncertainty and anguished inner doubts over personal faith
and identity. For Arthur, temperament and upbringing prevented
this sort of exploration. He did not rail, yearn or despair, giving
no evidence of the torrent of passions shown by the Apostles.
There were large areas of human existence that he did not probe
through intimate communication with others, from the reality of
the Christian God to questions of whether one's most deeply felt
personal attachments were to men or women, or both.

Recent scholarship has made clear why Trinity College had the
reputation of attracting not just intellectuals but men who were
either indifferent to women or aroused by same-sex attachments.
In precisely the years that Arthur worked with Henry Sidgwick, the
latter was engaged in a deeply emotional correspondence with the
Oxford scholar and essayist J. A. Symonds over the young man's
epiphany that he could not keep his sanity if he continued to deny
his homosexuality. Sidgwick's most recent biographer describes 'a
mountain of evidence' pointing to Henry's homoerotic proclivities, despite his marriage to Arthur's sister Eleanor in 1875.[41]

The discourses of upper-class masculine friendship were in
flux in the mid-Victorian decades. Older models of sentimental
expressiveness competed with the bluff banter of the man of action and the impersonal blandness of professional collegiality.

That subcultures of homoerotic attraction and experimentation existed within the 'hothouse of seething passions' that constituted Victorian Eton or the Oxbridge colleges was one of those secrets more widely suspected than openly discussed, however. Already the identification of emotional and effeminate qualities in men was shifting from a suggestion of over-refinement or weak character to an indicator of the innate propensities of a newly identified human type, the invert.[42]

There is nothing to suggest that Arthur was part of any of the emotive groups of scholars and educators whose existence has recently come to light, especially among the Cambridge Apostles. None of his personal letters convey the tone of intimacy shared by Symonds and Sidgwick, or William Johnson and Oscar Browning. As his political career took off in the 1880s, however, Arthur's aesthetic tastes and personal associations at Cambridge were used as code to suggest a similarly inadequate masculinity. Journalists noted the care he had taken in furnishing his rooms, his collection of blue china and the excellence of his claret. Supposedly, he acquired the unflattering nicknames 'Miss Nancy' and 'Pretty Fanny'. The sources of these innuendoes about Balfour's sexuality have never come to light, though they could have originated with a political adversary such as the Trinity don Henry Jackson, an Apostle who developed a loathing for anyone associated with the aesthetic movement of the 1870s and whose early support for Irish home rule would have put him in opposition to Arthur in the 1880s. It is intriguing to imagine Charles Stewart Parnell – Arthur's future parliamentary adversary – as the source, since his years at Magdalene College overlapped with Balfour's at Trinity. However, the point is less about the nature of Arthur's private experiences at Cambridge than about his guardedness and the curiosity that surrounded him even as a young man.

One historian of Oxbridge undergraduates in the second half of the nineteenth century found four types by which a largely homogenous student body categorised each other.[43] Arthur might have been grouped with the 'Aesthetes', but he shared qualities of the 'Sporting Man' and the 'Book Man' as well. Ironically, the type most associated with aristocrats – the hard-drinking 'Bloods' given to physical and financial extravagance – was the only character with which Arthur had no affinity. His caution in communicating personal feelings allowed others to speculate about his nature from his external behaviours and interests. It took him decades to learn that he could play with the picture that others projected onto a persona that combined such familiar sociological categories as aesthete, intellectual and aristocratic.

George Pembroke did not follow Arthur into the Oxbridge world of upper-class competitive meritocracy and emerging professionalism – fewer than 40 per cent of hereditary peers of his generation actually did.[44] Nevertheless, he too found a male role model who would take his mind and character seriously. For five years between 1866 and 1871 George was almost continuously in the company of his private tutor, the physician-adventurer George Kingsley, and they remained friends for life. In 1867 the two embarked on a series of sea voyages that took them away from England for months at a time. In a Victorian version of the continental 'grand tour', Pembroke spent his late adolescence exploring the alien cultures of the South Pacific, evaluating the impact of Christian missionaries on native peoples and observing the cruder realities of European colonial expansion. It was an unusual education, introducing the young earl not to the shared high culture of his own civilisation but to the multiplicity of codes and customs held by some of the most exotic 'others' of the nineteenth-century imagination.

It remains a mystery as to why Pembroke's mother allowed him to spend so much of his formative youth in the company of George Kingsley. Kingsley was a younger brother of the famed clergyman and novelist Charles, noted for coining the phrase 'muscular Christianity' to describe the robust, aggressive masculinity emerging after the mid-century. Born in 1826, he had trained as a doctor, then become private physician to a string of British aristocrats including George's uncle, the 2nd Marquess of Ailesbury. Kingsley was about as far from an earnest intellectual like Henry Sidgwick as it was possible to get. A religious freethinker, he was also a vehement anti-cleric, particularly vitriolic when it came to the 'beastliness' of the Catholic Church. His scanty writings mix scientific observation with salacious rumination on the human oddities he found in a lifetime of travelling. Kingsley was well aware of pre-Darwinian evolutionary theories of human and societal development contained in works such as Dumont d'Urville's *Voyage du Pole Sud, Anthropologie* or Robert Chambers's *Vestiges of the Natural History of Creation*,[45] and he was fond of scrutinising the 'coloured races of mankind' for 'fossil' evidence of humanity's physical and cultural progression. Finding such evidence did not temper his disgust

with the representatives of his own civilisation or his irreverence
about all the conventions that a position such as the Pembroke
earldom represented. An extraordinary conversationalist, Kinglsey
was a psychological outsider, his tone detached, misunderstood
and know-it-all – a surprising mentor for George Pembroke, the
fatherless adolescent son of a fervently devout woman.

Perhaps Elizabeth Herbert's in-laws gave her little choice about
her son's travelling companion. At least Kingsley would ensure
against the public relations coup of the Pembroke earldom falling
into the web of the Vatican. But it is also possible that Elizabeth
herself was taken in by the handsome and mysteriously attractive
physician. 'He had a deadly power of fascinating women', wrote
Mary Gladstone, 'and I knew three of his victims.'[46] In sexual matters Kingsley was a Victorian free spirit on the lines of his more famous contemporary Richard Burton.[47] He married his housekeep-
er in 1862 only days before the birth of their daughter, the noted
African explorer Mary Kingsley, and spent considerably more time
away from his family than with it. The reputation of the Pacific
islanders for sexual freedom was widely known by this time, and in
Kingsley's company the adolescent Pembroke would be immersed
in a world of sensuality unavailable outside the most illicit pleasure
houses of Victorian London or Paris. Pembroke's assertion that
he and the doctor kept each other from succumbing to the sexual
temptations of the islands is hard to take seriously.[48]

In a topsail schooner of eighty-six tons called the *Albatross*, Pembroke and Kingsley spent nearly three years circumnavigating Australia and New Zealand, exploring the Great Barrier Reef and New
Caledonia, and in 1869 traversing the Society Islands of Tahiti,
Huahine, Raiatea and Bora-Bora, before sailing for Rarotonga and
Samoa. The archipelagos were not the *terra incognita* that Captain
James Cook had encountered a century before.[49] Protestant mis-
sions were well-established on many of the islands, eliciting caustic
observations from George about the unedifying messages conveyed by rival denominations. Beachcombing dropouts from European civilisation provided local colour, but they were joined now
by settlers hoping to grow cotton or cocoa nut oil for the market,
and by traders and ships-provisioners at the key ports. Though rumours of cannibalism persisted, traditional ruling families on the
more populous islands were trying to establish uniform law codes
and centralised authority. The British had no official protectorates
in the region aside from the New Zealand and Australian colonies,

but within a decade they and the French and Germans would take steps to bring the various island chains under formal control.

George's logs of these trips are full of picaresque detail and astonishment at the strange intermingling of cultures he witnessed. The travellers sound like remarkably good-natured adventurers, happy to test local foods, dress up in strange costumes and make cheerful fools of themselves climbing palm trees. George described oddities of the natural world, attended church services with the natives, exchanged gifts with island royalty and entertained schoolchildren aboard the *Albatross*. The ship's crew was fond of jokes and banter. 'If this goes on much longer', said Mitchell in rough seas, 'I shall bring up.' 'If you do, I shall heave to[o]', replied Kingsley.[50] Voyaging for his health, George recorded neither sickness nor tensions among the crew in all these months. Kingsley's famously volatile temper could erupt over the stupidities of the Europeans they encountered, but never, it seems, in Pembroke's direction.

George's voyages in the Pacific constituted his version of the moral sciences tripos. With no systematic education to speak of, he made lofty pronouncements reflecting economic orthodoxies of the day. One European settler trying to run a cotton plantation groused about the pervasive lack of work ethic among his hands. George accepted his verdict that the locals refused to work because they didn't have to – the basic necessities of life were too abundant. A visit to Tubai prompted a disquisition on migratory labour. Many atrocities of kidnapping and assault could be prevented if the British would station a few small patrol boats to intercept freebooters in human traffic, George concluded.[51] He did not dispute the value of moving Chinese, Cochin-Chinese and native islanders across the seas for work, arguing in apparent contradiction to his other assessment that many of the natives they met wanted the opportunities provided by indentured service. This mastering gaze floated uneasily atop cultural dislocation. George reported views held by Europeans that were jaundiced about the local people's apparent friendliness. One planter noted that he could not speak freely because 'these natives understand more than they pretend to very often, and I might get into trouble'.[52]

Unlike Arthur's Cambridge studies, George's education also involved a crash course in male–female relations. As the *Albatross* plowed its way through the warm seas, each archipelago offered more astounding sexual distractions than the one before. Women swam, bathed and washed clothes in the open streams. Girls broke

spontaneously into the lascivious 'wiggling' dance that George believed to be universal among primitive peoples, including the Irish
of his own day. Ubiquitous orange rum fuelled night-time orgies
on the beach, and island royalty made generous offers of their
subjects' sexual favours. George saw women and men touching
each other's bodies casually, arms around waist or neck, fingers
brushing lips: 'things that would strike you anywhere else as wrong
and degrading, seem somehow only natural and beautiful in those
lovely islands'.[53]

George was clearly baffled by people for whom sexuality was so
open and guiltless. In an agitated letter that he labelled 'rather
smutty', he told his friend Eddie Hamilton of an encounter that
he did not mention in his log. Walking alone one day in Tahiti,
George 'observed a tall handsome well-dressed girl' advancing his
way. When she was within twenty yards, she hitched up her dress
to her shoulders and rearranged her undergarment, 'exposing a
full view of all her charms' before asking for a puff of his cigar and
going on her way. Returning to the schooner, he was 'mobbed by
other pretty girls' and barely got to the boat with the clothes on
his back.[54]

George said that he did not fall for these blatant offers, but
he later wrote about Queen Moe of Raiatea with such intimacy
and admiration that it is not hard to imagine that he had sexual
relations with her. When he learned that Moe's scoundrel husband had been shot, he considered 'whether or not to go back
and propose for her, but reflected that most likely she would have
dried her tears on somebody else's shirt-front'. With enormous
understatement he explained that 'on the whole, perhaps, my
over-fastidious relations might object to the connection'. George
had actually given a pistol to Queen Moe's consort as a gift, and as
Jane Sampson notes, firearms were commonly used by European
men as exchange for sexual favours from native women.[55]

George painted the allures of these tiny jewels of islands so attrac-
tively that nothing else he ever wrote carried the same emotional
conviction. His mind was engaged with sociological explorations,
his psyche falling into the rhythms and mores of island life. In the
end he had to force himself to leave the Polynesians and re-enter
a European culture that he and George Kingsley had been system-
atically condemning for its blinkered devotion to efficiency over
aesthetics, its hypocrisy, intolerance and stultifying respectability.[56]
If his logs are any indication, he also dreaded the London version

of the aristocratic marriage market and the great ladies who would push their daughters his way. But before he had to face this, one more adventure remained. Having been introduced to love in the tropics, George also came face-to-face with death on the high seas.

In the fall of 1870, as the *Albatross* headed homeward through the Fiji archipelago, the ship ran into stiffening winds and rising seas. In the middle of the night of 22 October, the passengers awoke to a great boom and shuddering as the schooner ran aground. 'You may say your prayers now', Pembroke told Mitchell, 'the game's up with us.' 'We climbed on deck and found ourselves in about as awe-inspiring a position as could well be imagined: the vessel lying almost on her beam-ends, the foam flying over her in a white cloud, every sea lifting her up and bringing her down again with a sickening crash, that made the cabin-floor heave like an earthquake, and her whole frame tremble ... The doctor and I said "Good-by!" Indeed, at that moment I don't think anybody but the skipper expected to live ten minutes.'[57]

After an anxious and 'weary' night, the crew discovered at dawn that they lay in shallow water half a mile from an uncharted spit of land. Packing the ship's three smaller vessels with pigs, fowl, tents, tools and lumber, the party established base and waited through eight days of rain and wind for the storm to clear. On 30 October, Captain Brand decided 'we *must* go, or we shall be starved'. As they abandoned their refuge, the boats were so laden that they barely kept above water and had to be roped together to stay abreast in the treacherous shallows. The convoy spent 'an awful night ... pulling and baling in a rough broken sea, wet to the skin and tired to death; listening nervously to the roar of the surf, watching the black masses of water as they charged our bows and shut out the dim horizon'. Sunburned and dehydrated, they reached larger islands the next day, where the locals directed them to a schooner with a Swedish captain who took them to safety.

George did not disguise how terrifying this ordeal had been. The island where they had been marooned was in the Ringgold archipelago, believed to be home to 'the most ferocious cannibals'.[58] Every night a different member of the party awoke screaming in the midst of 'a fearful nightmare' that savages were upon them. Even the phlegmatic Captain Brand succumbed to uncontrollable anxiety, and George lost count of the number of times he thought he would die. In a tragic twist of fate George, just twenty years old, learned on his return to Auckland that his younger brother

Reginald had drowned at sea when the Royal Navy vessel HMS *Captain* sank off the north-west coast of Spain about five weeks before the *Albatross*'s demise.

Within months of reaching home George turned his logs into an extraordinary piece of travel literature, *South Sea Bubbles by the Earl and the Doctor*, which went through seven editions in twenty years. George tried for a jaunty, man-of-the-world tone, presenting himself as an experienced traveller who had gone 'from Panama to Wellington, from New Zealand to New Caledonia, from Auckland to Tahiti, and back again, a fair number of miles'.[59] But this was a pretense, and the structure and pacing of the book were disjointed. Vignettes of cultural oddities jostled with zoological factoids, socioeconomic analysis, lyrical landscape descriptions and anecdotes of personal import. As narrative it represented what J. M. Coetzee calls a collapse of 'systematic discourse' into 'a set of sightings and observations selected from sense-data only on the grounds that they are striking'. The confusion reflected George's growing sense of internal dislocation and alienation from both his society and his faith.[60]

'Is Christianity the only true and useful religion in the world, without which none can be saved?' George asked provocatively at the end of *South Sea Bubbles*.[61] 'Is religion an end, and not merely a means to an end?' His conclusion could hardly surprise readers who had followed him so far, but it must have caused consternation to the religious partisans in the Herbert family circles. Aged twenty-one, with a concatenation of experiences behind him, George found himself joining the 'small but steadily-increasing body of educated men' who could not honestly embrace the basic teachings of their religion. 'Is it not a bold thing to state that the religious belief of one portion only of humanity is a direct revelation of truths from God, while those of the rest of mankind are mere inventions of man, or of that humanly invented bogy the devil?' After he finished *South Sea Bubbles* George wrote two long essays on religion for the magazine *Temple Bar*, which were subsequently published as *Roots, a Plea for Tolerance*. These works publicly announced his agnosticism and incidentally caused the final severance of relations with his father's old friend Gladstone.

Pembroke had come very close to death at sea and in the process looked into what was for him an existential void – that is, the sudden, intense psychological realisation 'that the self is *not* at the center of the universe, master of all it surveys'.[62] His genuine terror during the shipwreck produced no revelation of a loving God who cared about individuals: 'a feeling of want of sympathy is the mainspring of human misery', he wrote. 'In joy and sorrow the stars twinkle, the wind blows, and the sea moans alike. And then from the depths of a man's soul rises the cry that has been the origin of so many great religions: "O God! Give me a sign that I may know that I am not utterly lonely and forsaken" … There is something so terribly dreary, lonely, and forsaken, in that confession.'[63] Nor was he able to adopt the comforting illusion that British civilisation represented the divinely ordained summit of human progress. At times after his return to England he sounded like an embittered veteran driven to distraction by the smug certitudes of people who would never come close to understanding the experiences of his youth.

While George navigated the Society Islands in more ways than one, Arthur received his initiation to love and death in the differently ritualised setting of London polite society. During the social 'season' from February through July each year, wives of the wealthy regulated this realm of amusement, gossip and scrutiny through private entertainments that served the serious functions of matchmaking and patronage.[64] Arthur's mother did not provide him and his siblings with much guidance about the romantic complications and adult relationships that they would encounter in this environment. By the time Arthur went to Cambridge in 1866 Lady Blanche was already exhibiting what Lord Derby described as 'signs of mental eccentricity'.[65] Now, probably suffering from congestive heart failure, she spent most of her time confined to an upstairs bedroom, calling up individual offspring for endless solitary conversations to pass the time. Arthur and his sisters Nora, Evelyn and Alice, in London for the social season of 1870, chaperoned each other and networked through the families of Oxford and Cambridge friends to establish their own circles of affinity.

The most celebrated of these connections came from Arthur's Trinity friend Spencer Lyttelton, one of more than twenty Lyttelton and Gladstone cousins who grew up together at Hagley Hall, the Lyttelton estate in Worcestershire, and Hawarden, the family home of Gladstone's wife, Catherine.[66] Spencer's passion for music and vocal performance cemented his friendship with Arthur. Their Eton association with Hubert Parry, destined to become an eminent composer in the late-Victorian period, reveals one of the ways that George Pembroke's family intersected with the same circle – while George was on his travels, his sister Maude became secretly engaged to Hubert Parry. Despite childhood homes that spanned the length of Britain, the school friendships of the boys and London socialising of the girls created a set of serious-minded young people politically connected at the highest levels and destined either themselves or through marriage for careers in politics, education and the professions.

The group is familiar to historians through the diaries of Gladstone's daughter Mary. Her observations provide the most vivid contemporary glimpses of Arthur after he left Cambridge. They show a young man unused to socialising with women outside his own family, slightly awkward as he explored the proper mix of reserve and self-revelation permitted by Victorian codes of respectability. Shyness was one of the few personality traits that Arthur ever acknowledged about himself. The nervous tension involved in socialising with new acquaintances found release in moments of unguarded mirth. At a small dinner party in February 1871, Mary and Arthur 'talked a good deal of nonsense as usual', and 'he laughed so immoderately as to be forced to starve'. Hosting an impromptu picnic at an Eton–Harrow match, she describes Arthur as being 'in mad spirits, shouting choruses between acts, hatless, with a handkerchief round his head, hair flying all over the place'. Another time, meeting up unexpectedly on a late afternoon ride from Buckingham Palace to Hyde Park Corner, Mary's diary records the Gladstone and Balfour siblings as 'overpowered by laughter as usual'.[67]

Mary also described Arthur at this time as 'the most pitying person in the world', so prone to impulsive gestures of charity that he felt he had to 'sit hard on his sympathies' or risk being overwhelmed by the demands of compassion.[68] Men and matrons saw him as strangely unfocused and prone to wasting time in sedentary activities with the girls. It is hard to escape the impression of a young laird who was not going to be satisfied with a country life on his Scottish estates – and was quietly circumventing his mother's stern injunctions by enjoying the company of sympathetic women and resisting guilt over social problems not of his making. One outlet for these post-Cambridge years was to listen to as much classical music as he could, an activity at which he experienced – and could safely show himself to be experiencing – deep feeling.[69] Another was to explore the wider worlds of elite sociability, a milieu that he would have known mostly through books.

Mary Gladstone remembered that when they first became acquainted Arthur had told her that she and her sister Agnes reminded him of the eldest Bennet girls in *Pride and Prejudice*. Arthur
loved the novels of Jane Austen, rereading them countless times
throughout his life. The emotional drama that followed his introduction to the Gladstones and their cousin May Lyttelton certainly
suggests the miscues and embarrassments of an Austen novel.[70] In
the spring of 1871, while Mary Gladstone fell in love with Arthur,
he was attracted to May. She in turn was swept away by someone
else, the kind of charismatic and roguish interloper who routinely
threatens the true affinity in an Austen romance. May's love object
– Rutherford Graham – was too charming and unreliable to be
acceptable to her family. 'Strong and well-built', wrote a Balliol
friend, he had 'a kind of recklessness, both as regards himself and
other people, which possessed considerable attraction.'[71] Rutherford was also very unlike Arthur in his willingness to convey his
attraction to May immediately and directly, part of what her sisters
thought demonstrated that Graham was a rogue.

Arthur never competed openly with charismatic men, and the
death of his mother in spring 1872 provided another reason to
retreat. Six months later, however, just as May's family appeared
reconciled to an engagement, Rutherford Graham died of diph-
theria. May grieved for nearly two years, then in 1874 came back
into Arthur's life. Around the New Year of 1875, at least by Arthur's account, he had reason to believe that May would accept
a proposal of marriage. Then, in late January, she contracted typhoid at Hagley. After lingering through weeks of illness May died
on Palm Sunday without seeing Arthur again. At a society dinner
more than a decade later, Arthur admitted that 'there were at least
three important things' in his life that he regretted.[72] His dinner
companion did not record what they were – probably he did not
say – but not telling May of his feelings earlier than he did was
surely one of them.

Mary Gladstone's allusion to *Pride and Prejudice* is worth pursuing in order to understand the meaning of this episode in Arthur's
early life. Novels of a specific type – the genre called domestic
fiction – worked to shape not only the understanding but the subjective experience of romantic attachment for Victorian readers.
Though the point is usually made about middle-class women, it is
not hard to see how something similar might happen with those
literate men who found in fiction an avenue for understanding

emotional experiences otherwise limited by their familial and boys'-school surroundings. Jane Austen's world clearly resonated with Arthur. It provided him with a romantic ideal of the early nineteenth-century's companionate marriage, grounded in genteel sociability where polite discourse and emotional discretion nonetheless allowed for the discovery of true affinity in the exceptional couple. Charlotte Brontë condemned such people as 'naturally very calm' with feelings 'moderate in degree'.[73] But Arthur would have learned from Austen that calmness of manner need not mean tepidness of feeling, and he might well have believed that May was exceptional enough to share this understanding.

Two recent historians have presented May as seeing herself, and being seen by others, as different in her generation of genteel young women.[74] She was intellectual in a Balfourish way, genuinely enjoying the mental challenge of reading philosophy and political economy along with her brothers at Cambridge. She was unusually forthright in speaking and apt to defy pointless proprieties in the social life of the young. Whether Arthur knew of the tumultuous emotionality that worried her sisters is less clear. May's willingness to trust her deepest desires to a man whom her family could not accept shares more with Catherine Earnshaw in Emily Brontë's *Wuthering Heights* than with the clear-headed Elizabeth Bennet. But Austen has a heroine like Catherine too: Marianne Dashwood in *Sense and Sensibility*. In the end Marianne comes to the right decision after learning hard lessons about unreliable men and she marries the devoted suitor she had rejected earlier. The fact that Arthur chose such an independent spirit, lost her to a more dangerous type of man, then gained her affection in the end, fits a familiar romantic frame, with Balfour a plausible Mr Darcy in his deep feeling but emotional reticence until certain that the proper moment for candour had arrived.

But this was not how an Austen novel ended. Arthur gave every appearance of being genuinely distraught at May's death.[75] He asked her brother to put an emerald ring belonging to his mother in her coffin. Almost immediately he sought to meet the painter Edward Burne-Jones, who was not showing in galleries in the mid-1870s, and commissioned a series of the haunting, late Pre-Raphaelite dreamscapes in which the artist was privately working through a new imaginary of young men frozen in worship of unobtainable love objects. Though Arthur resumed his social rounds, outsiders observed him to be exhausted, even, according to May's sister

Lavinia, unable to read.[76] He took a restorative trip to the South Pacific in 1876, visiting many of the same places as the *Albatross,* but his reactions were very different from those of George Pembroke. Although he and May's brother Spencer engaged in some strenuous canoeing and horseback camping in New Zealand, Arthur was an incurious traveller and cut the trip short as soon as he found a legitimate reason – by virtue of his sister Nora's engagement to Henry Sidgwick. Spencer, himself a 'shy and introverted' man, told Mary Gladstone that in all their time together he did not talk to Arthur about May: 'neither of us are persons to whom such a thing would be easy or possible, I don't think it would be of use'.[77] In bypassing his planned visit to India, Arthur missed seeing for himself the conditions on the subcontinent where within months his uncle, secretary of state for India, would preside over a horrific famine. He never again visited this region of the world, the centre of Britain's global imperial enterprise.[78]

Arthur returned to his seat in the House of Commons in 1877 and the establishment of new domestic routines with his unmarried sister Alice, now that Nora would be living at Cambridge and his three younger brothers were of age – Frank and Gerald were fellows at Trinity in animal morphology and classics, respectively, and Eustace was pursuing a career in architecture. Arthur's responsibilities in running his Scottish estates did not, Mary Gladstone thought, take much of his time, and in 1878 he assumed undemanding duties as Salisbury's private secretary at the Foreign Office. But during the years after May's death, Arthur became engaged in the most important inward journey of his life, establishing to his own satisfaction the foundations of his theism.

Arthur's first book, *A Defence of Philosophic Doubt,* appeared in 1879, but key chapters had already been published in *Fortnightly Review* and *Mind,* the new Cambridge journal of philosophy and psychology. This work, meticulous in wording and lucid in argument, must have taken him a good deal of time. Despite Arthur's later disclaimers, it was reviewed seriously by established writers in science, religion and ethics such as Leslie Stephen, Edward Caird and F. W. Maitland. *A Defence of Philosophic Doubt* established Arthur's credentials for joining the 'public intellectuals' – many of them Apostles – who had not fully appreciated the seriousness of his analytic quests at Cambridge. In 1879 he was invited to join the Metaphysical Society, though the decade-old discussion group abolished itself the next year, after deciding that its debates over science and religion had reached an epistemological impasse that was unbreakable for the moment.

As Maitland's review pointed out, Arthur's purpose in *Defence of Philosophic Doubt* was to establish that all of the philosophies 'most popular at the present time' were 'thoroughly unsatisfactory' in terms of their ability to demonstrate through reason either fundamental metaphysical truths or epistemologies that were anything other than provisional. In separate chapters he dissected T. H. Green's revival of Kantean transcendentalism, the Scottish schools of 'common sense' philosophy, Herbert Spencer's 'proof of realism' and Mill's *System of Logic,* showing in each case that the underlying assumptions were imprecise, self-contradictory or tautological. His chapter on 'Science as a Logical System', directed against the overconfident scientific naturalism of the day, was both the most persuasive and the most devastating. 'Whether Realism or Idealism be true', he wrote, 'whether either of them or both of them are consistent with Science, this broad fact remains, that the world as represented to us by Science can no more be perceived or imagined than the Deity as represented to us by Theology, and that in the first case, as in the second, we must content ourselves with symbolical images, of which the thing we can most certainly say is that they are not only inadequate but incorrect.'[79] Arthur was not alone in detecting the fallacies in the arguments of the naturalists. J. H. Newman and W. E. Ward were making similar claims.[80] But nearly a century before Thomas Kuhn, Arthur laid out a concept of human knowledge as functioning within paradigms, more or less consistent systems of thought with their own sets of assumptions and rules of evidence and inference. He even speculated, ahead of many physicists, that permanent laws of nature might not exist.

At times Arthur's arguments approached the kind of radical scepticism that fuelled George Kingsley's cynicism. 'It is quite as probable', he wrote in a mischievous jab at Rankean empiricists, 'that all history should be fictitious as that some of it should be true.'[81] Nor could we assume a consistent human nature, allowing past human feelings and perceptions to be inferred from our own. In the face of such indeterminacy, Arthur joined other Christian apologists and intuitionists in concluding that 'each person must, in the last resort, decide for himself whether or not any given proposition is to his mind of the kind I have described ... as ultimate'.[82] Arthur would spend many more years working out why he chose the ultimate realities of the Christian faith, but this original articulation of 'the foundations of belief' had an interesting immediate effect. Arthur came to view human thought and action as occurring in disparate, incommensurable settings – not so much different theatrical stages as separate games, each with its own rules and logic. And though feelings might guide the individual towards their own fundamental grounds of belief, passions were unproductive in mastering games, from golf to logic to parliament. The temperamental and experiential detachment of youth had received an intellectual buttressing that would carry through Arthur's adult life.

In the new Conservative government that Benjamin Disraeli was putting together in the spring of 1874 it is not surprising that he looked for a position he could give to George Pembroke, a prominent young earl with literary flair, forceful opinions and exotic experiences.[83] In the same year that Arthur entered the House of Commons, where he did not give his maiden speech for another three sessions, Pembroke became undersecretary for war with responsibilities for representing the department in the House of Lords. He was completely unprepared for the issues he would have to answer to in debate. 'I am translated into a new sphere, and being thoroughly ignorant of my duties, would appreciate any advice', he wrote to the Conservative politician Lord Carnarvon, a distant relative. 'I had very little time to consider the wisdom of accepting: you were out of town, and I had no one to ask advice of – so I plunged – and hope I may not have to repent my audacity.'[84] As it turned out, the appointment was not a success. A year later Pembroke submitted his resignation, pleading the advice of his doctors. 'He speaks despondingly of himself', wrote his superior at the war office, 'and says "he cannot work at present".'[85]

The evidence is annoyingly scarce, but George seems to have gone through a personal crisis in 1874–75—the same time as Arthur's loss of May Lyttelton – in which romantic and professional challenges combined. Only two months after his appointment he wrote to Eddie Hamilton that he was 'miserable', adding cryptically that it was 'terrible to think that I have spoilt a life that should have been so beautiful and happy. I believe the Devil sent me into this world for the purpose of doing as much mischief as could be done – in the most highminded innocent manner.' George did not admit to the disgraceful conduct of Don Juan, but said that he was 'blessed or cursed with the knack of getting intimate with almost any woman I take a fancy to (a very different thing from genuine love-making) and take my word for it, it is an ideal-shattering demoralizing process'.[86] Then, quite suddenly in August 1874, George married Lady Gertrude Talbot, daughter of the Earl of Shrewsbury, in a private ceremony in the royal chapel of Westminster Abbey.

This was a grand aristocratic match – his wife's sisters were married to the immensely wealthy 3rd Earl Brownlow and the Marquess of Lothian. George was barely twenty-four years old; his wife was thirty-four. The couple never had children, and in later years their relationship prompted much gossipy speculation among their acquaintances.[87] Known to her friends as Gety, Lady Pembroke was devoted to her husband. She nursed him faithfully through his illnesses, fell in with his hobbies and protected him from his mother's meddling in family affairs. She also shared his views on religion. It is difficult to imagine George ending up with someone who was out of sympathy with his agnosticism. More importantly, his wife provided him with a firewall against emotional and sexual anarchy. Whatever it cost in terms of desire and self-fulfilment, George's loyalty to his odd, intense spouse formed a self-imposed duty around which to shape his private life, as his landowning and county obligations in Wiltshire structured his public activities.

It is not clear exactly when Balfour and Pembroke became acquainted, though Arthur is on the list of those sending a wedding gift in 1874.[88] By the early 1880s he was a regular guest at Wilton. He travelled down for a summer house party in July of 1882, knowing that his brother Frank had gone missing while climbing in the Alps, and he was there when he received the wire announcing that the searchers had found Frank's body.[89] The contrasts in the lives of the two men were notable – George's full of adventure, colour, sensuality; Arthur's austere, intellectual and grief-filled. But the two fatherless heirs also had a great deal in common. Absent fathers, the fragile health of youth and a series of emotional shocks had contributed to temperaments that were attractive but cautious. Both men were insufficiently acculturated to the usual venues of upper-class male competition and bonding. At odds with the 'modern regime' of 'actively constructed', individuated selfhood that had been growing stronger since the beginning of the century, many markers of their identity had been settled for them by inherited positions and inescapable responsibilities.[90] By

Fig. 2 George Pembroke in the 1880s

their thirties they shared a sort of internal melancholy and fatalism at odds with the lavishness of their circumstances. 'What is there in the world we know that is not really wrapped in a sad and terrible mystery', George wrote in 1881, encapsulating a fundamental weariness that he was too honest to disguise (see Fig. 2).[91] Two years later Arthur bought Burne-Jones's implacable masterpiece *The Wheel of Fortune* as soon as it came on the market. The painting depicts magnificent male nudes, 'vulnerable and helpless', strapped to the wheel of the blind goddess Fortune as she turns the monumental contraption, indifferent to their fate.[92]

By this time the Liberals had returned to power in 1880's sweeping electoral rejection of the Conservative government of Disraeli. During the five years of Gladstone's administration, members of the parliamentary opposition – including George in the House of Lords and Arthur in the Commons – witnessed plenty of developments in the public sphere to occupy their attention. Irish obstructionists continually derailed the 'mother of parliaments' and led the ministry to a series of legislative concessions to Irish demands. Gladstone stumbled into a takeover of Egypt, then at the Berlin conference of 1884 devised the scheme by which the rest of

Africa would be divided among the European powers without war. The opening of grain markets in North America and the colonies caused a catastrophic collapse in the rents available to the landed classes. For many Tories it felt as though the ground was literally dissolving under their feet. Arthur and George were not among those who retreated to reactionary nostalgia or escapist hedonism. They were forward looking and curious about where the forces of history were tending. But their stance was sceptical and apprehensive rather than buoyant and, in personal as in political terms, they appeared to be stalled, waiting for that giant wheel to lurch forward.

2

Domestic Scripts

Laura Tennant and
Mary Wyndham (Lady Elcho)

L AURA TENNANT and Mary Wyndham met in the early spring
of 1882 in Hyères, a small resort town in south-east France
that had been the most popular Mediterranean retreat among the
British aristocracy for more than a century. Daughters respectively
of a fabulously wealthy Scottish industrialist and a Wiltshire gen-
try-aristocrat, Laura and Mary were there to build up their endurance for the London Season marriage market that they would be
entering when they returned home. Hyères was a safe and relaxed
place 'to learn to be self-sufficient and not depend on others in
little things', Mary's father wrote to her. 'One must learn to manage when with indifferent, if not hostile people – this is hard for
girls who do not leave home until married.'[1] Laura and Mary were
both nineteen, and they were facing the most important period
of decision-making in their young lives. Marriage formed *one* part
of a man's life narrative, a supplement to political or professional
achievements. For a woman it was the dominating reality – the
fundamental choice in this pre-divorce era that would define her
subsequent existence and contributions to the world.[2]

Three years later, when Laura was safely engaged, she described
this period of her life as 'volcanic'. For prosperous Victorian families, female adolescence was fraught with peril as girls abandoned
the innocent romping of childhood, disciplined themselves into
the 'social demeanors' of respectability and sought the husband
who would focus their adult responsibilities.[3] Victorian diaries
and novels chronicled the emotional roller-coaster that girls experienced: feelings of entrapment within boundaries defined by
others, the irritating passivity of waiting to find out how it would
all turn out, fear of being judged as improperly female or too

ambitious, and the inadequacy of religious consolations. 'However much I glory and love being a woman I have come to the sad conclusion after much thinking – that it is very hard being a girl', Laura wrote in the journal she had been keeping since she was thirteen:

> Oh! The whole thing, girls lives, girls proprieties, girls difficulties, the whole thing maddens me – and oh! how I *long* to be finished and done with it all ... Am I very rebellious and unkind and unwise – no – I only long for something broader than I have, away with the horizon and those lines and rules that appear every minute. Can I break loose and be like no other girl, can I be free and pure and broad and loving?[4]

Mary Wyndham kept a much different kind of diary – as Claudia Renton says, one 'of record, not of confidence' – but Laura learned later that she felt the same way: 'I can never forget you, you sitting in my room – saying what you did about Life – and the mystery of living – and the lonely feeling girls have and the terrible fights against oneself and other people.'[5]

The stories of Laura Tennant and Mary Wyndham – Lady Mary Elcho as she became after her marriage – encapsulate the dramas of privileged Victorian girls who faced no imperatives of work or prearranged marriage, only the weighty freedom to choose, from within the circles available to them, the man with whom they would spend a lifetime. Their circumstances in this regard were not identical. Mary was an eldest child, much more susceptible to her parents' guidance than Laura, who was among the youngest of her family's thirteen children. The Tennants were newcomers – outsiders – making their way into the national aristocratic elite to which Mary was born. Material comforts aside, however, Laura and Mary shared a particular attribute: both girls were bookish by the standards of women of their class, more interested in ideas than facts, in values than things. Otherwise there was little in their young lives to suggest that, aside from family members, they would become the most important women in the world of a cerebral intellectual like Arthur Balfour.

Laura, tiny, fair-haired and ardent (see Fig. 3), was a daughter of the Glasgow chemical manufacturer Charles Tennant. One of the richest and most powerful industrialists in Britain, Charles had diversified his grandfather's alkali business and became what would

Fig. 3 Laura Tennant in the early 1880s

now be called a venture capitalist, engaged in enterprises around the globe.[6] In 1879 he entered the House of Commons as a Liberal and strong supporter of William Gladstone. Charles's hospitality during Gladstone's famous Midlothian speaking campaigns of the late 1870s first introduced his youngest daughters to respectable Liberal society. Observers from these established families were quick to note the peculiarities of domestic life at Glen, the baronial estate about thirty miles south of Edinburgh that Tennant had acquired in 1853 and where his younger children were born and raised.

Laura was the eleventh of thirteen children born between 1850 and 1865. Four of the first five never made it to their teenage years, and another succumbed to tuberculosis in 1866 when Laura was four. Still, Laura grew up with three older sisters and one – Margot – fifteen months younger, as well as three brothers who dutifully went off to Eton to make connections among sons of the privileged. The younger members of the family enjoyed an unusual freedom from parental oversight. Charles Tennant spent

Monday through Thursday in Glasgow presiding over the St Rollox chemical conglomerate and his increasingly complicated foreign interests. His wife Emma was a retiring figure, physically and emotionally overwhelmed from incessant childbearing and the trauma of seeing so many youngsters succumb to accident and disease. While Laura and Margot had a much-loved and much-feared nanny, their education was presided over by a string of uninspiring governesses who seldom aroused affection, much less respect.

Charles's adoption of a gentry life actually fostered the girlhood isolation of his daughters. The family was too new to be comfortably integrated into county society in Peeblesshire. They did not know the Balfours at Whittingehame or the Wemyss family at Gosford, both about thirty miles away, until three decades after the move to Glen. In 1878 the girls spent three months in Dresden studying music and German, and a few weeks at a finishing school in London after Tennant bought a house in Grosvenor Square in 1880. Neither produced acquaintanceships of any importance, and there seems to have been no regular circle of friends to replace the family and business ties left behind in Glasgow. In their teenage years, the younger Tennant girls scrambled to construct their worlds from the range of idiosyncratic experiences and cultural influences available to them.[7]

Mothers were often absent from girls' diaries of this period – perhaps they were too obvious a presence to need mentioning by daughters who might also be afraid their journals would be found and inspected. In Laura and Margot's youthful accounts, older sisters loomed much larger than parents.[8] Margot's journal comically revealed the rivalry she felt with Laura for the attentions of Posie (who married in 1875), Charty (married to the 4th Baron Ribblesdale in 1877) and Lucy (who wed in 1879). The elder sisters were eighteen or nineteen when they married. Their fates fulfilled the Victorian model of proper feminine development. Each girl's partner was 'suitable', a man who nudged the family into the landed-professional classes and, with some help from Charles Tennant, provided a secure financial future. Each appeared to be a love match, though Lucy married Thomas Graham Smith very suddenly when she was barely eighteen, partly, it seems, to get away from the stifling emotionality of the female-dominated household. Margot, just fifteen at the time, said that she would '*never* see [Graham Smith] as a husband for Lucy', and her concerns were prophetic, as the marriage was not a success.[9] Laura and Margot interpreted their elder sisters' stories as cautionary, not exemplary. The younger siblings would take their time committing themselves to marriage, but that decision extended the period of dependency and aimlessness that Laura found so irksome.

Eager for the attention of adults and experiences that would help them gauge their abilities in a world beyond the family setting, the younger girls faced a confusing mixture of scrutiny and licence, candour and deception as they navigated the household changes taking place during their teenage years. Their mother and elder sisters admonished improper behaviour such as writing personal letters to boys.[10] But the girls had no difficulty entertaining men as much as twenty years older in their sitting room, which opened directly onto the bedchamber they shared. The house was huge, with shadowy corridors and secluded stairs, private stages where men were met in unexpectedly intimate circumstances. Years later, Lord Rosebery remembered the Tennants as 'little quaint romping girls on the stairs at Glasgow, smuggling themselves to the public meetings and turning up with bright demure eyes in unexpected nooks'.[11] These encounters produced moments thick with unarticulated messages about the most personal aspects of girlhood, which many male visitors found as interesting as did the girls themselves.

With three brothers in public school, eligible young men filled Glen during the holidays. Gladstone's daughter Mary, after her first visit to the house, deplored the 'reckless freedom in bedrooms at night with no sanctuary, no reserves. I should think it would knock the bloom off young girls.' This adolescent rowdiness had little appeal for Laura. 'The house feels like a boy's school', she fumed after the Christmas holidays of 1882; 'Herbert Gladstone [Mary's 28-year-old brother] is such a bear fighter ... the constant locking of bedroom doors, blowing out of candles, booby traps, water jugs upset etc. etc. has a very small charm for me.'[12] Laura was also taken aback by earnest young men who proposed after the shortest acquaintanceship. She described the last lines of one suitor's letter: 'All we that know you gaze on and wonder and worship you, the living personification of an hitherto unreached ideal.' 'Now fancy a man wishing to touch a sensible woman's heart – with that!' she snorted. 'Really the more I know of men, *plus j'admire les chiens* ... I could cry with boredom when I spill through this sort of thing.'[13]

Other encounters revealed how difficult it was for girls to read the signals of courtship. Laura described meeting W. H. Mallock, recently famous for his satirical novel of Oxford worthies *The New Republic* (1877), when she was seventeen and he thirty-one: 'Mr. Mallock has a disagreeable and rather startling habit of pressing your hand and looking into your eyes. When I was alone with him sitting on a seat in the garden he took hold of my hand and I felt quite uncomfortable – and thought he was trying to flirt with me.'[14] The journal makes clear the impact of substantially older men on the girls' dawning awareness of sexuality. The attentions of Algernon West, married with a daughter Laura's age, Godfrey Webb, also born in 1832, or Francis Knollys, forty-six when he obliquely proposed to Margot in 1883, might seem only courtly. Even so, Laura thought that West was becoming 'maybe too friendly' and she was bewildered by his compliments.[15] She was appalled when a distant relative, widowed with grown children, pressed his overtures first in Scotland, then in South Africa where Laura was visiting her tubercular sister Posie in 1883: 'I would rather die. He is intensely pompous, canting hypocritical and conceited beyond measure. May told me some horrid things about him. I wonder he has the face to ask any girl to link her life to his, which is by all accounts none of the best.' While on this trip Laura also experienced an unsettling encounter with her brother-in-law when he came to her room at night, woke her, and collapsed sobbing by the bed: 'He said you know how I love you and respect your opinion … I felt what a struggle it must have been for him to be so humble, so tender, so like a woman … that proud reserved nature begging on his knees for me, ME, to be good to him.' 'I don't want to marry, that's the awful part', Laura wrote a year later. 'It's what men want to do if they love you, and women only want to be still and rest if they love.'[16]

Private journals allowed girls to explore the comic, dramatic and disconcerting moments of encounters that were fraught with intensity and uncertain implications. In a survey of diaries written by New Englanders of Laura's generation and social class, Hunter found their journals performing similar functions.[17] Self-interrogation and chastisement, the diary as a 'receptacle for – and an incitement to – emotional spill-over', writing used to test alternate selves, emotional upheaval expressed in terms of religious guilt or doubt: these aspects all characterised the journal that Laura wrote from her early teen years to the time of her marriage.

The most important discourse in the first years of Laura's journal was religious, as she made 'God' both her interlocutor and her critic for the infractions of being 'rebellious', ambitious, sinful and 'not good'. She worried deeply that her brother Frank and her new brother-in-law Tommy Ribblesdale might not believe in sin as the Church defined it. She attributed her persistent 'state of passive restlessness' to preparation for some divine plan: 'I know all these wasteful years are to mould my soul and strength for something someday. I know though the world is very very wrong and very hardhearted and wise – that God will bring it all square and that He will make it kind and right and simple, and He will purify the clever hearts and bring them through temptation to the cross.' Even at her most devout Laura rejected a punitive deity. In her generation's 'warfare of Conscience with Theology', a message of Christian compassion and good intention superseded thoughtless conformity.[18]

Within a few years, Laura's relationship with an anthropomorphic, evangelical god had transformed into a generalised spirituality felt most acutely through deified nature. 'My Religion is Sunshine and Love', she wrote at about the time she met Mary Wyndham. 'I can't sign the 39 Articles. The faith of my former years is to my present year an impossibility and yet I am nonetheless reverent I hope.' Her writing became saturated with images of light and colour from the northern landscapes to express transcendence of overwrought interior worlds, both architectural and psychological: 'I am reveling in this glorious golden weather and in the glowing green and proud purple of the moors and in the deep blue distances and the hot mists that creep up the hill sides at sunset. I feel almost drunk with the mystic beauty and wondrous waiting of the hills.' Prose passages like this support Mary Gladstone's impressions of Laura's 'weird, far-off, wistful, pale, pitiful, unearthly-mystic' qualities, but they were supplemented by her sly insight and pungent observations that were also emerging. As Laura talked less to God and more to herself, she fumed and moaned, questioned and criticised her way through the perplexities of her late teen years. 'It's better to sweep the rubbish of one's soul into this book', she cheerfully observed, 'than to sweep it into one's daily life.'[19]

Victorian advice manuals recognised that domestic isolation contributed to the difficulties of raising girls in country house settings. They recommended the careful cultivation of female friends as a way to learn about the world outside the home.[20] In her late teen years Laura began to look beyond her family circle for women five to ten years older than herself to provide guidance for adult life.

One of these was a local schoolteacher, Mary Scott Morison, who wrote in 1880: 'It is a very pleasant feeling, to have a new friend … I am a good bit older than you, but it is not a question of age, and I think we have many tastes and thoughts in common.' Mary Morison sympathised with Laura's intellectual aspirations and the fear of young women that they would be labelled too cerebral. She outlined the benefits – that Laura half-envied – of being forced by circumstance into useful employment, even if confined to a small village like Innerleithen.[21]

Through Mary Morison, Laura began meeting with the local Girls Friendly Society, where she prepared readings and discussion topics for neighbourhood working girls. She did similar charity work in Wapping when the Tennants were in London. Laura identified with Dorothea in George Eliot's *Middlemarch* – 'she had so many longings and so do I'. She read diligently, impressed by Andrew Mearns's *The Bitter Cry of Outcast London* (1883) and Henry George's *Progress and Poverty* (1879). In Mary Morison, Laura had a model of the new sort of genteel woman – self-supporting and working for good in a small sphere – that was becoming more prevalent in the last decades of the century. Yet the biographies of Laura's contemporaries Beatrice Webb and Beatrix Potter show how difficult it was for girls in privileged society to adopt such a course of action. At the level the Tennants occupied, it is nearly impossible to find examples.[22] Laura accepted early that she would need to marry someone with secure prospects or risk abandoning her familial and social worlds.

In the early 1880s Laura became intensely attached to another woman, Frances Graham, who would have a deeper impact on her development than Mary Morison. Like the Tennants, Frances's family were wealthy lowland Scots who lived part of the year in London and mingled in the social worlds of the London-based artists and professionals. William Graham's most famous legacy was not his mercantile activity but his patronage of the Pre-Raphaelites, especially Edward Burne-Jones. Frances's life was altered profoundly when she became Burne-Jones's model and confidante in the 1870s, after his tempestuous affair with Mary Zambaco had nearly destroyed his marriage. Letters from this period of their friendship do not survive – Burne-Jones developed the habit of destroying correspondence from women, and Frances burned her own collection of epistles from men just before she married Sir John Horner in 1883.[23]

Frances Horner's memoirs are reticent about herself, and it is hard to form an estimate of her personality when Laura first knew her. 'The *me* that was when I was young', she wrote, had an 'ardent nature', living 'for some strange law of desire of what is beautiful' and dreaming that 'everything is romance'. She described the years of her adolescence, extended longer than she admitted in her memoir, as 'rather stormy', filled with 'love affairs and entanglements' and noted her preference for those who 'rush to meet the unknown', even though 'one has come to grief often by too impetuous a carriage through life'.[24] Frances had rejected her Presbyterian upbringing, and her ruminations on religion reinforced Laura's growing rebellion against guilt-ridden conformity. In April 1884 the two dismissed as 'nonsense' the notion that one should 'try to feel sad in Holy Week and glad at Easter', because the celebration of those events was determined by an arbitrary calendar. Frances had Burne-Jones's habit of telling instructive stories through strung-on sentences that gave an aloof gravity to the lesson: 'do you remember in old days when you were quite little, one used to have a book of stories all about the Commandments, and do you remember how awkward it was when they came to Thou Shall not murder and how they made it mean anything, even being angry with yr brother or sister or being cross and then when they came to the 7th Command how they twisted it about and made it mean thou shall not have two slices of cake, and thou shall not look upon a bathing boy. Wasn't it wicked of them to change it so?' A year after getting to know Frances, Laura decided that the 'things that influence me are more Pagan more Pantheistic perhaps'.[25] About the same time she and her sister spent a night being naughtily 'pagan' in their bedroom. Perhaps this was the evening that resulted in Margot's nude self-portrait found by Mary Gladstone in the drawing room at Glen on a visit in 1882.

Laura's friendship with Frances Graham reinforced the tone of irreverence that she was developing as her experience broadened. Sexuality and its mysterious imperatives increasingly formed the subtext of these passages. Laura's anxieties about a woman's sexual destiny were grounded in hard realities, including her mother's experience. Emma Tennant was pregnant every year from 1850 to 1865. 'We when we grow up find life is different and unreal compared to what it promised to be when we were very young', Emma wrote sadly in 1877.[26] Nearly every family that Laura knew as a young woman shared a similar fecundity: the mid-Victorian

Lytteltons produced 12 children in seventeen years, the Gladstones 8 in fourteen years, the Curzons 11 in sixteen years; Queen Victoria had 9 children in seventeen years of marriage.

Laura never wrote explicitly about sexuality, but a horrified fascination with the physical aspects of love surfaced occasionally. 'Oh! Heavens I wish no one married. I wish the rabbits did the populating. They manage those little trifles so well. I wish one could have friends and nothing more ... I wish all men were as cute as most women.' Some descriptions of women were unselfconsciously sensual: 'Francie has been with me the whole morning and I feel as if I had been to church. I feel so happy, oh! I feel as if her Love, her Soul, her eyes made me happy for ever. She loves me I know and I have the copy-right of loving her as much as anyone in the world. She says so, she was so beautiful and good and kind and let me quite empty myself into her and only stroked my hair and told me what to do and she was so loving and '*sympatisch*.'[27] As Sharon Marcus has shown, intense female friendships could rehearse the emotional passions of heterosexual intimacy for upper-class Victorian women.[28] Laura found in Frances Graham an adult who not only shared her longings and frustrations, but loved her for the qualities that she was most uncertain about – her lofty aspirations, irreverence, silliness and questioning of shibboleths.

Frances might not have been deemed the best model for an impressionable and inexperienced young woman by the advice columnists filling the pages of contemporary ladies' periodicals. Her embrace of the aesthetic movement's 'religion of beauty' not only allowed her to question conventional piety, but also made her the muse of several of the Victorian world's notorious 'girl lovers' – Burne-Jones, Ruskin and Tennyson. These were not sexual relationships, but they contained their own dangers. Girls found themselves in the fixed regard of famous men: literally, when they served as models, and psychologically, as they embodied powerful masculine projections of lost childhood and innocent pleasures that could only be contemplated in distant times or places. The privileging of the immature over the adult, the girl over the sexually aware female, threatened to lock these favoured young women into perpetual maidenhood with the lack of self-defined purpose that this entailed. When Laura was on the eve of marriage, she politely accepted Burne-Jones's compliment that she 'ought never to marry, but to go about being a delight to all'. This was playfully expressed, but the emotional point was real. After more than a decade of friendship Burne-Jones punished Frances when she took a husband, by cutting off contact with her for two years.[29]

Frances actually did prove to be a socially appropriate role model. In autumn 1882, just as Laura turned twenty, Frances became engaged to a Somerset landowner who had been at Balliol with her brother in the late 1860s. Sir John Horner was as far from the troubled aesthetes, poets and sages of Frances's earlier life as it was possible to be. Physically he was an imposing masculine figure, fond of hunting and outdoor life. Intellectually he preferred natural science and history to poetry or art. In personal relationships he was inarticulate, with none of the verbal artistry or emotional flirtatiousness of Burne-Jones. For all her defiance, Frances's acceptance of Horner marked a capitulation to the realities of life for women of her social world, something she tried to convey to Laura. On her first visit to Frances's new home, Laura asked if a woman knew at first glance the man she would marry:

> Frances: well you know I think one talks to him and likes him and one says to oneself 'if he worried me very much to marry him, I might, perhaps' and then if he does, one marries him. It is so rarely that perfect ideal affinities meet ... and then you know it is doing things for people every minute of one's life that makes one love them.
>
> Laura: yes. I often think that the very sacrifice of marrying a man must make one love him, unless of course one hates him.
>
> Frances: oh, yes. It's often like that. It is horrid, and one does it for him and not for oneself, and then love covers the sacrifice and ideal love is ideal sacrifice.[30]

Frances married Jack Horner in January 1883. Within weeks she was pregnant with a daughter born in November. Ensconced in rural duties on the secluded Mells estate in Somerset, she was well on her way to the life of conventional domesticity that Laura in her most rebellious moments scornfully labelled 'jam-pottism'.

Mary Wyndham's father, Percy, was not in the same league financially as the multimillionaire Charles Tennant, but he was an aristocrat and more than comfortably well-off. The second son of the Earl of Leconfield, Percy did not inherit the family estate at Petworth in West Sussex. However, as his father's favourite, he received a fortune of approximately £400,000 on Leconfield's death in 1869. Percy acquired four thousand acres of land in Wiltshire and pursued the life of a substantial country gentleman in his own right. By the late 1870s Philip Webb was building him the much-acclaimed country house called Clouds in East Knoyle, fifteen miles west of Salisbury.[31]

Mary's girlhood shared many features with Laura's in the same years: a spotty education in languages and literature supplemented by holidays on the Continent, much tramping and riding in landscapes of extraordinary beauty, brothers who disappeared into the mysterious world of boarding school, Christmas parties, lawn tennis, amateur theatricals and parents who preferred the arts to the race track. The first of five children, Mary spent time caring for younger sisters, not observing older ones as Laura did. But the mix of material comfort and conventionally prescribed roles was the same.

The similarities in outward forms of privileged girlhood made the differences more intriguing. By any standards of normal child-rearing within affluent circles, Percy Wyndham and his wife Madeline were engaged parents. A country gentleman could spend a lot of time at home, compared with businessmen like Charles Tennant who met in offices, boardrooms and clubs.[32] This was certainly the case with Percy Wyndham, but alone did not account for the attention he lavished on his children. As the oldest, Mary remembered, she was his favourite companion for walks and expeditions. Her diaries recorded readings aloud in the evening while she massaged her father's head. The letters Percy wrote when they were apart are filled with unselfconscious affection and show his familiarity with matters of daily concern to her. Mary's mother Madeline was as great a presence in the family's life.[33] She created scrapbooks with photos, anecdotes, drawings and poetry of her children, supplemented by earnest exhortations to God for their welfare. An artist of some ability, given to endless puttering at the craft tables she placed in the common rooms, she filled her house with guests with whom the children mingled even as youngsters.

'My mother possessed an inner radiance that lit and gave a glow to every room she entered', Mary wrote much later. 'Even as a child I remember noticing how the temperature of the whole house fell when she went away, even for a day.' Mary's youthful diaries provide contemporary evidence for this view: 'Mama not well enough to come down. Everyone feels lost without her.' 'Mama comes, JOY!' Madeline created a family dynamic very different from the emotional chill that pervaded Glen outside the children's boisterous quarters. The Tennants appeared to be spoiled by a lack of discipline and engaged guidance. The Wyndhams were thought spoiled too, but Mary wrote that her parents 'loved us and they indulged us, but we loved them and we always wanted to do what they thought right'.[34]

Madeline's gregarious warmth and Percy's attentiveness accounted for some of the differences in Mary's upbringing compared with the offspring of the Tennants. Equally important were the social positions occupied by the two families. The Wyndhams were born into the country's interconnected aristocracy. They visited dozens of relatives living in hospitable great houses scattered across England, Ireland and the Continent, and they went to London routinely from Mary's girlhood home at Wilbury. The Tennants were moving from provincial to national society during the girls' adolescence; their relatives, with the exception of their in-law Tommy Ribblesdale, did not provide an entrée to established circles. The implications were evident in the diaries. In years when Laura spent the post-London months entirely at Glen, Mary was making a round of country house visits to the Ponsonbys at Windsor Castle, the Duke of Cleveland at Raby, the Wharncliffes at Wortley, Lord Brownlow at Ashridge and the Pembrokes at Wilton. Her mother accompanied her to these homes of long-time friends who greeted Madeline with 'groans of pleasure', Mary noted. On the one occasion when both her parents were absent, a countess known for her rectitude was chaperone: 'Maysie Baring and I were under Lady Brownlow's care' during Christmas theatricals at Wilton.[35]

The years after Mary's 'coming out' in polite society in 1880 (Fig. 4) showed how the marriage market operated in Britain's highest circles. She met scores of eligible young men throughout the year, either in London during the spring social season that coincided with the parliamentary session, at home in Wiltshire or in the country houses of others. At the same time, she was under closer supervision than the Tennant girls experienced. There is no evidence that she had any friends whom her mother did not know about, and it is difficult to see how she would have had much opportunity to pursue secret relationships.

The Wyndhams' introduction of their daughter to the wider circles of polite society included more than monitoring acquaintances. Mary's father, Percy, offered her guidance in navigating the world of gossip and rumour that could damage relationships and

Fig. 4 Mary Wyndham at the time of her introduction to
London society in 1880

restrict opportunities without one knowing it. When Mary was
eighteen he wrote to her from a shooting party at Lowther Castle in Perth hosted by George Pembroke's sister. Gladys Lonsdale
was very young and wild and neglected her guests, who conveyed
to Percy a 'general atmosphere of telegrams about trifles, spor-
tive telegrams by post from bloodish young friends in London in
shocking rhymes' and gossip about women whose misbehaviour in
the Prince of Wales's retinue was becoming notorious.

'I write you this letter to show you the sort of letter it is most dangerous to write except to relations you can trust', Percy told Mary.
'Next to caricatures writing letters makes people most unpopular
and gets them into scrapes. Be very careful of what you say in your
letters to your girl and young women friends. Lord Clanwilliam
carried this so far that when he came to a country house he actually would not even say who he had met in the house he had left.
There is often danger in even doing that.' Percy congratulated
Mary for having kept quiet about a cousin's engagement until it

was officially announced: 'You will be like Mamma who hears many things because she never tells, sometimes I think *disappointing* people who tell a thing to get it told.'[36] Percy's messages revealed a social world in which different generations routinely mingled, and bare acquaintances might share the same leisure activities for days at a time. Uninhibited behaviour with peers and friends would be judged by elders and third parties. It was best not to be talked about – to acquire information about others rather than to provide it about oneself. Only at the end of her life did Mary, in a tone of some bemusement, reveal how stultifying these cautions and social conventions of her girlhood had been.[37]

Mary became legendary for her combination of warmth and reserve, a distance that some people called 'vagueness' beneath her hospitality and kindness. It is not hard to see these qualities emerging in her youthful diaries and letters. Unlike Laura, the record that Mary kept faithfully through her life was not used to vent her feelings, examine her confusions, question the world or dissect acquaintances. Page after page recorded social rounds, expeditions, people met and books read. One can survey months of entries without encountering the kind of communicative ego presented in Laura's journals. Mary frequently reported her days in a plural 'we' that conveyed the collective activity that seemingly defined her adolescent life. While very young she learned to keep secrets about herself and others and, like Arthur Balfour, to hide or deny distressing emotions.

Nevertheless, some of what was on her mind could be inferred from tone and emphases in the diary. Unlike the Tennants, Mary almost never mentioned people who were not part of the prominent families with whom she socialised. If she and her mother engaged in 'Lady Bountiful' activities in the countryside these were not recorded. A major exception occurred in November 1880 when Mary and her governess went for a walk and discovered a family of 'gypsies' along the path:

> We came upon some gypsies, an old man, a young woman good looking with two little girls and a baby and a boy 16 or 17. They looked wretched in the rain with no shelter whatever, the woman was huddled up under a juniper bush, when we spoke to them they said they had had nothing to eat that day; so we went home, and came out again (about 5) in streaming, soaking rain. Mamma took a large piece of felt, I a bottle of milk for the baby and a shawl;

> Madeline, Pamela and Fraulein, bread, tea, sugar, meat etc. They
> were delighted[,] we guided ourselves across the field by their fire
> which was blazing brightly and came up to them from the darkness
> dripping, fancy spending the night crouching round a fire, in a lane!

Laura had a similar experience, while on a night-time walk at
Glen, of meeting homeless women sleeping under the hedges.
With both girls the fascination of encountering the familiar (a
good-looking woman) and the alien (a woman who slept outdoors)
broke through into the daily record, but with Mary it prompted no
rumination on what God intended by such things or how they fit
into her own world.

This is not to imply that Mary gave no thought to the larger
social and political concerns of her generation. She was probably
more comfortably familiar with the national political establishment than Laura was at the same age. The family read contemporary periodicals aloud, including essays on Carlyle and John Stuart
Blackie's pamphlet *Democracy*.[38] Percy's letters were full of allusions
to current politics reflecting the cantankerous, independent Toryism that reduced his parliamentary influence throughout his
life. Mary's account of Christmas theatricals while visiting the
Pembrokes in December 1880 gave an unusual glimpse of the
landed class exorcising political threats through humour in a way
that would not be lost on the young people present. As a supplement to the main play, the house party worked up 'most amusing'
waxworks in the form of scenes that came to life, as automatons
were 'wound up and set in motion'. The first scene enacted the
spiralling violence of the Land War in the Irish countryside and
the arrival of the novel resistance tool of boycotting that was con-
founding Gladstone's new government:

> First Boycott (Sidney Herbert) gazing *fixedly* over his rotting crops at
> the misty future (this first exhibition was true and horrible); on the
> left side of the stage Hugo, looking a most awful ruffian in capital get
> up; squashed hat, coattails *gun* and shillelagh, he shot Boycott in ap-
> proved style when set in motion. Mr Littleton [Alfred Lyttelton] very
> motionless, as Lord Lieutenant was busy carrying out the orders of
> the government in the background, and was lifted by the showman
> still further into the background.[39]

The next scenes replicated 'a group of horrors from Mm. Tus-
saud's' with Mary as Charlotte Corday murdering Marat in his

bath. This was followed by the Sultan of Turkey being forced to give up the Adriatic port of Dulcigno in a border dispute with Montenegro, with Alfred Lyttelton as the British special ambassador 'standing over him in threatening attitude'. A daughter of Lord Spencer, representing the British Admiralty, 'was wound up with a wonderful rattling machine, she jerked and convulsed in the funniest way; rule Britannia was sung from the back of the stage and she opened and shut [her] mouth, the effect was too funny'. Edward Hamilton, George's friend, had known that the Irish sketch was planned and wondered if it was in good taste, given the gravity of the circumstances. A good bit of the fun of such entertainments was in watching friends assume ridiculous roles in public. But they also encouraged a stance of wry amusement at the follies of people fantastically divorced from insider circles. When Mary encountered genuine political enthusiasms she backed off: 'Papa and Betty had a tremendous argument about the Irish question ... it amuses me so.'[40]

The tone of Mary's diary was so neutral that she might have written it so that it could be read by her mother. When she first entered polite society at the age of seventeen, socialising always seemed to be 'jolly' and innocent, with none of Laura's anxiety over proper conduct or Sabbath observance. Madeline Wyndham and her women friends smoked cigarettes.[41] People were not expected to go to church or avoid sports and games on Sunday. At a house party during the Easter season of 1881, the family organised a tennis tournament: 'it was a delightful day, umpires sat on the porch and watched breathlessly, the rest of the lookers on encamped on the lawn which was covered with daisies, primroses, sofas, dogs, armchairs, rugs, balls, books, inkbottles, rackets, frames of work, caps, jackets and prostrate human forms. We were a merrie famileee!'[42] Mary frequently met men who were among the eligibles for her generation: Alfred Lyttelton; Guy Dawnay; George Curzon; Lord Ogilvy, the heir to the Earl of Airlie; and Hugo Charteris (Hugo's name before his grandfather's death gave him the honorary title Lord Elcho, used by the heirs to the Wemyss earldom). But she never mentioned feelings about any particular suitor – and revealed none of the precocious awareness of sexual tension, the psychological disturbance of an exchange of looks with a man, or the illicit kissing found in the Tennants' accounts. Mary's curt announcement of her engagement to Hugo Charteris – 'we settled it all finally' – would have caught any reader by surprise.[43]

Even so, it is possible to discern changes in tone as the years progressed. Mary later described herself as genuinely shy. She certainly had insecurities that she disclosed only after she was safely married. She recalled visits where she had listened 'with silent awe to the flashing repartee, the witticisms, and above all startling aplomb of grown-up conversation. Now I have such an amazing placidity about what outsiders think of me!'[44] The alarm surfaced in a few diary entries: 'drove to Wilton getting there at 5:30 rather sleepy and dazed. The entry into the gallery where what seemed a crowd of people were gathered round the tea table was rather formidable as I could not see who I knew.' She also worried about proper behaviour when not with her family: 'We played round games (cards) and had great fun. The table rocked and there was a good deal of wrangling. I think the Duchess got rather exasperated with us.'[45]

Even more distressing was a session of group gossip of the sort that her father had warned her against: 'After luncheon we sat round the fire discussing the various merits of many people their beauty, cleverness etc., an occupation or want of occupation which makes one despise oneself.'[46] Mary had been making the social rounds for three years by this time. She was only twenty, and, she told Balfour later, 'many wanted me to wife!' But no proposals were reported in the diary, though Mary said later that one suitor of the 'horsey' set had been scared off by her reputation for reading. Other women thought her 'eccentric' for preferring walks to gossiping indoors with ladies who 'looked to me fair, fat and forty, had sloping shoulders and sat all the morning till 2 o'clock doing wool work'.[47] By summer 1883 the prospect of yet another London season of unattached socialising was surely unappealing to a shyish girl who, by her own admission, loathed competition with other women and unkind gossip about absent acquaintances. The sudden marriage to Hugo might spare her that.

By the time of Mary's fateful decision, Laura's search for self-understanding had only become more perplexing. A visit to Cape Town early in 1883 reinforced her social conscience. She was troubled by her relatives' dismissive attitudes towards their native servants and by the jarring contrast between the realities of life in South Africa and the artificiality of the London social 'World' where her future seemed to lie. In a telling rumination she juxtaposed the feminine allures of 'the World' with the hard masculine dictates of conscience and meaningful action:

> Here the World stands up and beckons to me, but oh! she is beautiful, she is luxurious, she smiles she sings softly and sweetly, she tells me to come to her arms, to kiss her, to be kind to her, she tells me I can make her better, and she laughs at my fears, she points to fair women and gems and gloves, she smiles and dances before me and then she prays and soberly bids one pray too ... 'You can be just as good in my arms ... forget those who scorn my Love, hate those who despise my teaching. It is not in my world that ye shall have Tribulation. It is not of me that your MAN GOD speaks when he says He has overcome me! I am still Queen, still Queen of all, without my arm you will fall, you will be laughed at, you will be useless, impracticable, absurd!'[48]

Then, with the 1883 London season over, Laura had another experience that seemed to cast a new light on her possibilities. In September, she was invited to join a holiday trip made by William Gladstone on Sir Donald Currie's 4,000-ton steamship *Pembroke Castle*. The initial tour of Scotland and the Hebrides was suddenly extended to include the Scandinavian coast, where the vacationers gained some notoriety by meeting up with the Danish monarch, the tsar of Russia and a collection of continental royals. Journalists wondered whether a secret diplomatic initiative was under way in Copenhagen, while *Punch* devoted an entire issue to the imagined spectacles.[49]

Most surprising was Laura's inclusion. There were two 'Kings' on board: Gladstone and the poet laureate Alfred Lord Tennyson. The rest of the small entourage included Hallam Tennyson; Algernon West, the chairman of the Board of Inland Revenue; Gladstone's physician; one of the Lyttelton brothers; Lord Dalhousie; and Sir Arthur Gordon, who brought with him a 'Fiji servant, a fine looking fellow in costume, who showed us how to kindle a fire by rubbing two pieces of wood together'. The prime minister's wife and daughter were the only other women reported, and there is no question that twenty-year-old Laura was a hit. Tennyson had numerous private talks with her and called her 'little witch'. After this trip she visited the Tennysons and the Wests, and gained the attention of the seductive politician Sir Charles Dilke ('I think he likes me, at least he said he would put me at the top of his girl list, probably it consists of me and his niece or his old governess's girl'.) Laura began to move in the circle of Balfours, Gladstones and Lytteltons, who had been socialising together for over a decade. 'Arthur Balfour has been talking and tea-ing with me', she wrote. 'He is tall, with a small head and an eyeglass or rather pince nez. The most beautiful eyes I ever saw, brown and like a woman's ... We talked about women and men, Frances Graham and Sir Charles Dilke.' Margot wrote that Laura would have loved Balfour if he had 'loved her but he didn't not even a little only liked her as an intelligent creature appreciates the same in another'.[50]

It is worth asking what was so unusual about Laura that she could win over not just the susceptible Tennyson but the censorious unmarried daughter of the Liberal prime minister. Laura joined the party aboard the *Pembroke Castle* late, and alone, after a travel mishap delayed her arrival. Her nervousness took the form of volubility and bustle. First impressions of any Tennant daughter conveyed a sense that she had not been schooled in the 'repose' of movement and language that was 'an essential indication of good breeding'. Charty's aristocratic fiancé once admonished her saying, 'Well, Charty, you cannot imagine what a bad impression a gushing woman makes on a man', to which she responded pertly, 'Well then Tommy, why did I not make a bad impression on you?'[51] In Laura's case, even the deck crew thought that she might be a loose woman in that her artless enthusiasm looked like boldness and self-display – Richard Kaye notes that only a few years before, Henry James had introduced the American girl abroad Daisy Miller (1878) as one of the first heroines to take the innocently flirtatious behaviour of the *salon* out into public spaces. By the next day Laura's more characteristic patterns of behaviour had asserted themselves and she became, as every account repeated, the 'heart and soul and glory of the whole party'.[52]

One of her future in-laws wrote that there were two Lauras, her public self and the one revealed in tête-à-têtes.[53] In company Laura was a hostess's delight, for she brought an apparently unforced outpouring of energy that sparked others to activity and engagement. She was a willing performer at the piano, on the stage or in parlour games. But she was also happy to share the limelight, could 'strike sparks out of the deadest wood, and make the heaviest natures shine' and at meals 'kept the whole party alive'.[54] Women understood how difficult it was to gear oneself up to this degree of other-regarding interaction. If a girl was comfortably aligned to her social duty of serving others, the self-possessed self-effacement of helping in group entertainment would be entirely natural. If one had not the gifts or desire to enter into this role, socialising would feel torturous, though it should never seem so. Laura had considerable skill in helping to create a companionable atmosphere out of disparate groups that crossed generations, genders and status levels. It was what others meant when they told her that she had 'social genius'.[55]

Laura could rally people to the social work of having a good time in company partly because she was able to establish personal relationships with individual guests very quickly. Victorians called this getting to the 'heart' of someone else, creating a mutual bond that most people experienced only after considerable acquaintanceship. Contemporaries noted that both Laura and Margot would be as confiding with street sweepers or cottagers as with their own family. Perhaps this was easier than breaking down the reserve of people schooled in the cautious repressions of Victorian gender interaction. The stolid, worthy St John Brodrick left an account of how it was done. On a visit to Glen in 1880 the sisters swept him off, as usual, to their sitting room and 'took me over fences till my brain reeled. Had I read this book? Had I heard that Opera? Why was I a Tory? Why not remain at Glen as I was now there, instead of keeping my other engagements? – and the like, till I was forced away, with pledges of undying friendship, which, unlike most of such hasty ebullitions, were kept.'[56] Aboard the *Pembroke Castle* Laura talked to Tennyson for hours about Buddhism, Swinburne and mesmerism, about 'Life and Fame, and Death and Power and the Future'. Mary Gladstone thought she had an 'extraordinarily original and independent cast of thought' in private moments like this. In her youthful aspirations, she was willing to show her inner thoughts and emotions to others to an unusual extent. Her acquaintances experienced this sharing of a 'very transparent' self as a rare phenomenon.[57]

As Margot attempted to evaluate Laura's successes, she noted that her sister 'takes on the form of her surroundings unconsciously', so was 'too adaptable to be quite true to herself'.[58] It is not hard to see this in her letters. Writing about the same experiences on the same day, Laura would be pally with George Curzon, self-deprecatingly girlish with Mary Gladstone, world-weary with Doll Liddell, direct and mature with Mary Elcho. An example of

these different faces to different audiences is evident in two accounts of the *Pembroke Castle* cruise. In a passage written for Mary
Gladstone to see, Laura said that she was 'immensely happy and
having the greatest fun in the world'. Every member of the party –
especially the 'beautiful sonorous pathetic' poet laureate and 'too
sacred' Grand Old Man – came in for praise. A year later, in the
company of Frances Horner and others more likely to scoff at such
sanctimony, the description was different: 'Miss T. told us about
the *Pembroke Castle* trip of last year. Never was such a menagerie on
board a ship. Gladstone and Tennyson the lions, surrounded by a
crowd of doctors, society persons, toadies and bores, all worship-
ping. Into this mixture were suddenly discharged at Copenhagen
three or four kings and their familiars and suites. "The toadies and
society persons had a happy day, and the bores have been borer
ever since".' This sort of insincerity troubled Laura herself. 'I get
to know the sort of things people will think agree with their hy-
potheses of my character', she wrote, 'and I say and do the things
that suit them more or less involuntarily.'[59]

To her journal she again repudiated the qualities reinforced by
her conquest of the social world of the privileged and secure: 'I
have something you people don't see ... I sympathize better with
the poor ... understand vulgarity and wickedness. I sometimes
think a Salon would be the most perfect thing in the world. Then
I feel the Love of the People, of the oppressed, of the wicked, of
the Christless and loveless.' As she turned twenty-one in October
1883, Laura pondered her ability to captivate others. Could she, a
young woman, use these powers for some larger good, for the kind
of 'nobler purpose' that a politician like Gladstone inspired in her?
By Christmas of that year, the answer seemed to be 'not alone', and
not from within the confines of a childhood home centred around
a father's business and political affairs and a woman's society obligations. Without the sanctuary of a stable marriage, girls with lofty
ambitions faced too great a risk of being 'useless, impracticable,
absurd'. If she did not fall in love within a year, Laura decided, she
would give up and marry Tom Carmichael, a friend who had been
wooing her without pressure for three years. They would have a
peaceful life, she wrote, 'I could help him and be happy', for he
was 'sweet, unselfish, sympathetic, obedient to my wish'.[60]

The marriage between Hugo Elcho and Mary Wyndham, consummated in 1883 a week before her twenty-first birthday, turned out

to be so troubled that it is worth exploring how it came about. In worldly terms it was a triumph for Mary. Five years older than his wife, Hugo was the third son in the Charteris family, but by 1874 his two older brothers had died – one from suicide (possibly after contracting syphilis), the other from fever while serving as Garnet Wolesley's aide-de-camp on the Ashanti campaign. By the time he was seventeen, Hugo knew that extraordinary family tragedy had brought him in line to inherit the Wemyss estate of more than sixty thousand acres centred around Gosford in Longniddry, ten miles east of Edinburgh. As long as his mother lived, Hugo felt the burden of comparison with his older siblings.

Early in 1883, Hugo's father inherited the earldom, and Hugo gained the honorific title Lord Elcho. He and Mary were able to move into the family's secondary estate at Stanway in Gloucestershire in the spring after their wedding. Lord Wemyss also bought them a house in Cadogan Square in London. Mary had her own resources as well. Her father had provided her with a settlement of £15,000, mostly in railway stocks, which gave her £400 a year, with another £128 going to Hugo's account.[61]

As a young couple the Elchos were well placed to enter into aristocratic society. They had a country house for entertaining and a London residence to use when parliament met during the season. Hugo was, by this time, a member of the House of Commons. His father had given up the seat for Haddington when he became a peer, but he arranged with the local Conservative committee for Hugo to stand at the by-election required to fill the vacancy. The *Scotsman*, a Liberal newspaper based in Edinburgh, called Haddington 'one of the most magnate-dominated seats in the Kingdom' and accused Hugo of trying to subvert the secret ballot by going door to door and using his position to gain votes. Hugo, supported by his neighbour Arthur Balfour, won the election, having spoken repeatedly at meetings and proven 'an abler candidate' than the press expected.[62]

Benjamin Jowett, Hugo's Balliol College headmaster, confirmed the new MP's potential. Hugo was very quick, very witty – fully able to make his mark as a rising young Conservative of his generation. That the family were 'independent Conservatives' like the Wyndhams provided an added benefit. So did the fact that Mary had known Hugo for quite a while. As early as 1881 the two had nicknames for each other (Hugoman, Cat and Mouse, Hogs and Mogs) and had bet against each other at Ascot.[63] In her diary Mary mentioned no man more than she did Hugo, including a time when they laughed immoderately on a back-row couch at a boring visit to Lady Ashburton's, where J. A. Froude read Shakespeare to the attentive older ladies while their husbands dozed.[64]

Nevertheless there were signs of potential problems. The Wyndhams knew that Hugo's family were 'down upon him', thinking him selfish, undisciplined and cold.[65] The impression was confirmed by letters that Hugo's mother, Anne Wemyss, wrote to him during six months in 1881 when he went to Constantinople in a secretarial position with the Society of Foreign Bondholders. Her farewell letter was a masterpiece of martyred accusation:

> Dearest Hugo, This is just a line to say good-bye – and God bless you – we should have been glad if you had cared enough to spend a day or two with us before you left – but that was hardly to be expected – and for the mere sake of saying goodbye, I think it was as well you did not come … let me tell you what I propose doing during your absence. I am going – as one often has occasion to do in life – to paste down a leaf over the last two years of our home life – and forget all the sorrow and sadness which your want of affection and coldness and reserve have caused me. From this day – and during your absence – all that is blotted out … Meanwhile I indulge myself in the delusion that you have been to me as Franco and Alfred [his deceased brothers] *were* – and exactly as I felt towards them – and wrote to them during their respective absences – so exactly do I mean to think of you and write to you. It will be a very pleasant delusion to me – while it lasts … I only do pray you – to write as often – and as *fully* as may be to your Father. *There* has been the real fruit of the last two years. In my case it may perhaps be of comparatively small moment … but to him the blank caused by your coldness and reserve has been more grievous alas! than you can well think. But I will say no more.[66]

Others of Hugo's siblings had complicated relations with their parents as well, resenting for years the austerity and criticism with which they grew up. Their father, Francis Charteris, 10th Earl of Wemyss – a martinet with his children and inveterate meddler among his military and political peers – was one of the true eccentrics of his generation. His memoirs display an unselfconscious egotism so startling that the Charteris family never had the work published. Whatever combination of forces produced Hugo's flippant, cynical and depressive temperament, he grew up in a household very different from the warmth that Mary had enjoyed.

Given how often Mary and Hugo were brought together from 1880 to 1883, the time it took them to come to an agreement portended problems as well. Other girls were in contention for the eligible young heir. In 1881 Mary's father told her that he did not think Lady Hermione Duncombe, the stunningly beautiful daughter of Lord Feversham, need 'cause us the slightest uneasiness', though as it turned out she and Hugo had a long affair in the early 1890s after she married and then separated from the Duke of Leinster.[67] Equally important was Mary's later revelation that Arthur Balfour 'was the only man I ever wanted for a husband', but he never approached her in that way. Perhaps, she said, if she had been 'as audacious as Margot or Laura' she might have broken through Arthur's reserve, but she was 'too proud and too shy' and herself wanted 'luring'.[68] The Balfour family papers link Arthur's name with that of Mary's contemporary Maisie Baring in 1883, so that Mary may have had concrete reasons to give up hopes of gaining his affections.[69]

Mary's letters from her month-long engagement to Hugo demonstrated her characteristic humour – it is hard to know what is meant seriously. But they contained nothing of the companionate intimacy of a happily matched couple:

> [17 July 1883] Tuesday, 7:30 pm: Dear Lord Elcho: I have hour by hour become more forcibly painfully and unmistakably convinced that when I accepted you a fortnight ago I did *not* rightly understand my own mind. I now feel so perfectly certain that I do *not* love and *respect* you as I feel I should that I feel it my duty my positive and absolute duty to break off our proposed marriage.
>
> 18 July 1883: I think playing 'deers and stags' with one's money to the extent of 700 pounds at the very first onset proves most forcibly that your money ought to be most securely tied up!
>
> 31 July 1883: Darling Hogglindo: as I say I have not been used to being dictated to or *crowed* over, I am an undisciplined creature and you may find me more unruly than you think!!! And that commanding voice may be raised *sometimes* in vain, 'Miss Moggs! Miss Moggs!!! MISS *MOGGS*!!!' However patience! Courage! The task though long is not altogether hopeless! ... I do not doubt but that protracted patience and judicial firmness and above all great circumspection

of *action* will not fail to imbue me with a perfect respect for all your thoughts ways and deeds!

The wedding that followed took place so quickly after the engagement that a special licence was required for its celebration in the Church, and Percy expressed the family's satisfaction that so many people had come despite the lateness of the social season.[70] Mary's diary entry for her wedding day was about as sparse as it could be: 'We went to the Church at 3 and were married. Alan was best man, Madeline, Pamela, Evy and Connie Pelly, and Margaret Burne-Jones and Eva were my bridesmaids. We went to Easton by the 5:23 train and telegraphed when we arrived at 7.'[71]

'Her mother pushed her into marrying Lord Elcho', wrote an acquaintance of Mary's in 1944, 'so one used to be told at least.' Mary said as much to Wilfrid Blunt in 1895, and Hugo's mother clearly blamed Madeline Wyndham for bringing about the marriage despite the hesitations of the couple themselves.[72] The information provides some insight to the forces affecting Mary's decision, especially given Balfour's failure to provide her with a reason to wait for him. Despite Madeline Wyndham's 'life-giving' qualities as a hostess and friend, some contemporaries thought she was ambitious for her children to achieve a national prominence that her shy, quirky husband had not acquired. Scrapbooks at Stanway convey her sense that her family was failing to get the recognition it deserved. A very good marriage in the eyes of aristocratic society was part of her expectations for her oldest daughter. Mary's devotion to her parents corresponded with a strong desire to please them. 'I would rather kill myself than make you miserable and disappointed in me. I *hope* you never will be', she wrote to Madeline in 1885.[73]

Mary was also unconsciously duplicating patterns of her parents' marriage. Hugo had personality traits in common with Percy Wyndham. Both were emotionally undisciplined, impatient and given to enormous outbreaks of temper even in front of others. Hugo's brother Evan Charteris witnessed an example of this during a visit to Clouds when Percy wanted his driver to pull over suddenly: 'Old Percy screamed like a wounded elephant: "G—d—you, *will* you stop" to the regardless coachman.' Margaret Burnes-Jones recorded her astonishment when she heard Percy shout 'God damn your eyes' at his footman.[74] In handling this volatility Madeline, like Mary later, developed an external calmness that combined humour and affection to fend off outbursts and buffer others from onslaughts. Mary would probably not have known that Hugo was a more troubled character than her father, one who did not just explode in anger that dissipated quickly but used sarcasm and sullen withdrawal to convey dissatisfaction. She may have expected that wives played the role of peacemaker, becoming the calm familial centre and masking as much as possible whatever internal turmoil they felt, but without anticipating the toll that this could take.

The first months of the Elcho marriage seemed happy enough. 'Hugo is writing an accumulation of lies to Pamela, I must write The Truth', Mary reported from the honeymoon in Scotland. 'Yesterday and the day before Hugo did not get stags so we drank champagne to cheer our spirits, we drank many toasts and got very drunk each night ... we have a game: gun to shoot with – rod to fish – dog to hunt – Mog to laugh at!'[75] Stanway was not ready for occupancy, so through the winter the couple paid visits to Gosford, Ireland, Paris, Cannes and Monte Carlo. If the tiny serpent symbol in Mary's diary was her way of keeping track of their sex life, it was fairly active, and by the late spring Mary was pregnant.

Six months later, in autumn 1884, the first signs of dissatisfaction appeared. Mary's diary mentioned Hugo's incapacitating headaches, drinking, paying visits without her and failure to write when he was away so that she wasn't sure where he was. Hugo was not attending to House of Commons and Conservative Party business either.[76] Laura met Hugo about this time and gave her impressions: 'Lord Elcho ... is witty clever and unscrupulous. At least so I should judge from half an hour's intimacy. He has a wife that ought to heighten his standard. Unfortunately she is not so clever as he is, let us hope no disillusionment will blacken her life.' Laura had figured out Hugo's *modus operandi* with women – Alfred Lyttelton's son wrote that he was 'rather a scamp, made no bones about his indiscretions'.[77] She was concerned for Mary from this point on.

Laura's hopes and forebodings about her own future were resolved within the year she had set herself in her Christmas resolutions of 1883, though not without considerable drama.[78] After the London season of 1884, during which she became closer friends with Mary, Arthur Balfour and George Curzon, Laura spent two weeks with Frances Horner at Loch Alsh near the Isle of Skye. One of the other guests was Adolphous Liddell, known as Doll but whom Laura called Larry. Doll had been a bachelor friend of the Grahams and the Charterises since the 1860s. He was fifteen years older than Laura and probably sexually experienced with married women. Frances Horner hoped the two would marry and allowed a good deal of unchaperoned time in the hills to supplement the social evenings at home.

Exactly what happened between Laura and Doll is unclear. By one account, he did not go beyond passionate kissing, cuddling and fondling with unmarried girls, and this seems likely to have been the case with Laura. Had full sexual relations taken place she would surely have expressed more guilt than she did. Even so, Laura not only fell in love – for the first time, she said – but experienced the kind of physical petting that made her aware of the power of sexual feelings. In the other-worldly setting of the late summer highlands, without prying elders or suspicious sisters to recall her to her social self, Laura found 'a man who probably understands me better than anyone I ever met and whom I feel is my own personal property in an alarming way. I love him as a bit of myself. We are made of the same bit of oversoul.'[79]

After two weeks of intense companionship, Laura returned home and began a correspondence with Doll. He visited Glen twice in the autumn, and the couple visited Frances Horner at Mells in late November. There also appears to have been a secretive prear-ranged meeting at a train station, perhaps even a lodging house, where Laura went with her compliant brother as chaperone. This rendezvous truly disturbed her. 'I have sinned', she wrote to Doll three months later, 'but I want you to know, and you will believe, that never never did I act before like that – never – and never shall again – so anyhow you must be glad that you know the worst of me.'[80]

Laura's reaction to Doll shows how timid all her relationships with earlier 'pals' and elderly admirers must have been. She had 'made mistakes', she told her journal in October, but had never been so *happy*: 'I had one fortnight this August that will never never come again one dazzling fortnight. I was deliriously happy, savage-ly ruthlessly happy and it cannot ever be like that again.' The prob-lem was that she knew quickly that Doll was not a man she would marry. Although historian Patricia Jalland presented the Laura/ Doll story unflatteringly as one of 'Flirtation and Calculation', it is clear from Laura's letters that she told him immediately that she did not envision marriage, and that they could only be deep and secret friends. 'Oh! Larry, you know we would not suit, we would be too much alike, you would not make me work and I would only want you to be as you are. You must marry someone stronger.'[81] However genuine the passion – indeed, because the passion was genuine – Laura interpreted her time with Doll as transgressive, and she framed her abandonment as return to a childlike state of complete innocence. The world of nature – sky, hills, 'cold passionate streams' – would not judge such 'natural' urgings, but in the social world her feelings could only be accommodated within 'the nursery'. She lapsed into third-person discourse in the parts of her letters that were most intimate, referring to herself by Doll's term 'Bambina': 'Bambina is allowed to be foolish in her nursery but is old enough to know the difference. Yes – she doesn't like coming downstairs – she can't be herself there – what she loves best is to play in her nursery – and have all her toys round her and to feel she can be as baby as possible and not be put in the corner – and downstairs there are more corners than in the dear old nursery.'[82]

Extracts from Doll's diary show a man whose interpretation of what was going on was quite different. Doll's autobiography was kind about Laura. He stressed her fascination, vivacity and repartee, and the 'fund of earnestness and a sympathy which enabled her to throw herself into the lives of other people in a quite unusual way'. In 1884 his comments were more caustic. Laura was an 'able little animal, very smart and flirty', possibly even 'light and of an easy virtue'. According to one later account, it was he who told Laura that he would not marry her; he nonetheless expressed no compunction about the relationship and mused, 'odd things females that she should like all this caressing and not be able to go beyond'.[83] Laura wrote that her most disturbing discovery was that 'I cannot trust myself for I am not a REAL character. I can persuade myself anything, I cannot be sure of the sound of my own heart.' 'No one but Larry' understood her, she wrote, which made his verdict that she was 'hollow' and 'theatrical' all the more frightening:

> He says I look at things from a dramatic point of view, asking more or less consciously 'will this be interesting, how will this go, how will it affect the part I as a prima donna has to play etc.'. It makes me wretched to think I should ever falsify life so much as all this … I don't think I could act a part for long … Altho to outward appearances the footlights would suit my ways, I hope to heaven I am true

to some things and people still and only plain Laura, and not Miss Tennant that odd little creature who makes people in love with her and calmly watches their torture.[84]

It would be hard to exaggerate the extent of Laura's defiance of courtship etiquette at this time. Her letters with their private language, personal names and description of intimate physical moments, such as reading letters in bed or in the bath, were suggestive and indiscrete. So, it seems, was her unchaperoned behaviour. Yet it was not this largely hidden relationship that gave rise to gossip, but one that began at the same time with Arthur Balfour's thirty-year-old brother Gerald in which Laura appears less complicit.[85] Philosophical and other-worldly like Arthur himself, Gerald was equally reserved and emotionally untouched. In October, he paid a visit to Glen that Laura reported to Doll with the mixture of forthrightness and self-deprecation that characterised her letters:

> I have made a convert since I last wrote. I am very proud of him because he was *such* a heretic – and vowed he never could like the Bina [one of Laura's nicknames] – and now he likes her very much – and actually confessed to his conversion. His name is Gerald Balfour! And he didn't used to like me though he didn't know me. Now don't scold the Bina – because she was much too occupied with a houseful to spend much time on him, but it came naturally![86]

Within a few weeks Gerald, despite not seeing Laura again during that time, was on the verge of proposing. Laura was astonished: 'I never thought he was journeying towards that kingdom ... I had no notion he was in love with me. He had kissed my hand but thank Heaven I never was that sort of young woman who because a man gives her a bunch of violets or picks up her fur and pocket handkerchief imagines he is on the brink of be-mine-ism.' Novelist Edith Wharton wrote of the late-Victorian courtship environment as a 'hieroglyphic world, where the real thing was never said or done or even thought, but only represented by a set of arbitrary signs'.[87] Laura and Gerald had clearly not read the signs in the same way. Gerald's fiery sister-in-law Lady Frances Balfour was convinced that Laura had heartlessly planned a conquest, and at Mary's inaugural house party at Stanway in November Laura found Arthur Balfour cold and flippant because he thought she had encouraged Gerald.[88] She felt 'wretched' that she might have 'tumbled down' in Arthur's opinion. There were two more meetings, in London and Glen in December, because Gerald 'begged and begged her to come'. 'He was delightful', Laura wrote in her year-end account of this eventful season, 'and his love for me is the highest and in some ways the greatest offering I ever had laid at my feet.'[89]

Laura found herself the subject of third-party gossip that she did not really understand, which she notes as having been relayed to her by Frances Balfour: 'people I trusted were not true to me and [Frances said] that I could if I chose prevent much being said about me that was said about me. Oh dear! Oh dear! She made me so miserable. What friends have I that are not true to me, what do people say and who are the people!' 'I don't think it is possible for anything to do with me to remain dark', she moaned:

> Things I have never said are raked out into vulgar day and actions I never did. I suppose it is part of the 'kind interest' people take in me, or just disapproval woken in the breasts of the more even breathing and less zigzag. Girls like Constance West are what people call too nice to be talked about. I have often sat opposite her complicated smile and envied her with all my soul... [she] never 'laid herself open' (this medical phrase is what is often applied to me) to people saying she drove horses in London – and wrote letters to men and loved to have people at her feet.[90]

Laura was learning a lesson that Mary Elcho had been taught by her parents. Insider aristocratic circles thrived on transmission of personal information and to be 'talked about' by well-connected strangers could have real consequences for one's future.

Mary's Stanway party of November 1884 was important not only for Laura's story, but because it prefigured so many of the complications of the Elcho's future country house social milieu. Hugo's sister Lady Hilda Brodrick was present with her husband St John and wrote, 'I must tell you that your party is rapidly getting a world wide reputation ... the ordinary country house visit has become quite intolerable. So I find at least from two experiences we have had since – even the people appear to me dull and utterly commonplace.' Both Mary and Laura recorded the unusual liveliness of this gathering that included, besides the Brodricks, Alfred Lyttelton, Arthur Balfour, Lord Vernon, Thomas Anson (the heir to the Earl of Lichfield) and his wife Mildred, and Godfrey Webb. As Mary writes in her diary:

Sunday, 23rd: Bright glorious day – all went to church and stables, walk to pyramid. Hilda, Laura and I came home sooner, garden sitting room. Luncheon. Talk talk the whole time. Laura, Hugo, Arthur, Alfred played lawn tennis in the barn. Hilda and I watched and walked about. I went to her room – tea and splendid talk from 5 pm! Dinner more talk and character game, we wrote sketches of one another's characters.[91]

Laura's letter to Mary Gladstone confirmed the bustle:

It's such fun here – we all quarrel about everything [Mary Elcho recorded that there was quarrelling one night at poker] – we talk up to the top of our bent – we grow hyper-sentimental and blow blue bubbles into the stars and Hugo Lord Elcho comes down upon them with jeers and in pumps and smoking suit. We play games and the piano – we none of us open a book or write a letter – we scribble and scrawl and invent words and language and reasonless rhymes.[92]

Mary recorded numerous walks, tennis games, shooting for all the men except Arthur, a visit to a 'penny reading' in the village where Laura played the piano while others sang, a visit to a jam factory, dancing, whist and an evening when Laura gave a performance from Sarah Bernhardt's hit play about marital infidelity, *Frou Frou*. On the 27th, Mary, Laura and Arthur took a long walk at dusk where they were stunned by one of the extraordinary sunsets that northern Europe experienced as a result of the Krakatoa explosion in 1883. 'Such an Old Testament sky', Laura wrote, 'with the land all rose and madder and great orange belts around the world. Oh! *Wenn es nur immer so bleibe!*'[93]

'One gets an impression of the sheer *douceur de vie* for these young people at this time in history', writes Arthur's biographer Kenneth Young. 'They were gay, they were bright, they were flirtatious, and they were a good deal less inhibited than the majority of their contemporaries.'[94] Young's description failed to note the most interesting aspect of the occasion – that there were no parents or chatelaines of the older generation around. Of the four women and seven men present, Laura and Mary were the youngest at twenty-two. The rest were under thirty, with the exception of Arthur who was thirty-six, and the 52-year-old bachelor Godfrey Webb. A family friend of the Wyndhams, Grahams and Tennants, Webb might have been serving *in loco parentis*, but he was half in love with Laura himself and had already written her a mock proposal of marriage based on the dubious incentive that he would not be around long enough to cramp her style:

> Bewitching maid who played for us tonight,
> A pretty widow to the very life.
> You'd change your role could I persuade you right
> And gain fresh laurels in the part of wife …
> Should discord rise take comfort from my years
> Kind nature soon must snap the galling chain,
> The pretty widow on the stage appears,
> And, smiling, takes the world by storm again.[95]

Mary's Stanway party provided an unusual occasion in which young adults of both sexes could interact without having to heed the household rules and expectations of an older generation. Conversation was freer, behaviour less constrained, the whole ambience less formal and embarrassed than Mary had been used to from visits to her mother's friends. Mary remembered her surprise on the first evening when the guests, 'newly arrived, assembled over the tea table in the big hall and instead of, after a decent interval and with a smothered yawn, saying … that they were ready to go to their bedrooms [to dress for dinner], they remained seated round the table from 5.30 to 7.30 p.m. The conversation never flagged, the ball was never once dropped, everyone said their say, everyone was interested and amused.' Mary credited Laura with introducing her to a new form of entertaining. 'She gave one many fresh ideas and created a new standard in my mind, of what a party of friends should be – full of delightful conversation with light matters treated seriously and grave matters with a light touch.'[96]

It is likely that Laura introduced Mary to another feature of entertaining that would become common at Stanway parties – not the pencil game per se, but the pencil game that involved analysis of other guests' personalities. On the second night of the party when only the Elchos, Brodricks, Laura, Alfred and Arthur were present, the seven of them played the 'character game', later called 'Public Opinion'. As Laura wrote to Doll:

> We played a game tonight calculated to offend the conventional. Each one wrote someone's characters – someone in the house – and then read it out loud no one being allowed to ask any questions – nor to find out whose portrait it was. I wrote my own and Arthur after re-reading it several times spotted it. He wrote a hotchpotch.

Hugo wrote his own – of course I guessed at once from the beginning: 'This is a rare character – all who know it wish there were more
like it.' Alfred wrote a medley too. St John wrote Arthur's and might
as well have tried to write yours.[97]

The game was dangerous because it had the potential to breach
the façade of cautious, impersonal sociability that Victorian politeness entailed. Although character-revealing games were common
in Victorian novels, they were usually confined to family circles or,
when outsiders were included, made into moments fraught with
plot implications. Laura and Hugo played it safe by turning the
analysis against themselves, in Hugo's case with irreverent humour.
Arthur's hodge-podge, in his characteristic spiky handwriting, is
still among the papers at Stanway, and it reveals how such games,
ostensibly harmless ice-breakers, could contain embarrassing
home truths.

Arthur's affectionate description of Mary shows the fundamental stoicism that would form the basis of his long-term attachment
to her: 'Predestined to a full measure of earthly felicity, because
expects nothing more of life than life can give.' About the phlegmatic Brodrick he wrote the unexceptionable line, 'largely endowed with all the solid virtues, but would not like to be told so'.
His vignette on Hugo hit so close to home as to make anyone who
knew the original cringe: 'too self-indulgent to succeed, and too
clever to be content with failure'. And Arthur's depictions of Laura
sound like a not-so-veiled attack on a young woman he found both
threatening and attractive: 'extremely fond of producing an effect,
and comparatively indifferent as to the means by which the effect
is produced', 'seeking after perfection, not because it *is* perfection
but because the search for it is a new and interesting emotion',
and finally, 'fonder of talking about morality than of practicing
it' [*sic*]. St John Brodrick told George Curzon most of Arthur's
composition, but added '*Don't* quote these or know them if you
hear them as A.B. would particularly dislike it.'[98]

A few weeks before this, Laura had written to Mary that 'men
who *won't* undress their hearts have none to undress only a miserable excrescence bulging with vanity and self-importance'. At Stanway, she described Arthur as a man who kept his windows shut.[99]
Balfour was notably resistant to revealing emotions that would give
another person a hold over him. The characterisations of Laura
showed him in a semi-public setting striking where she was most

vulnerable, through charges that she was insincere, theatrical and shallow. Others might convey such personal criticisms in private. Arthur used the cover of a social game to reveal them. It is no wonder that Laura told her diary that she did not feel at home during this visit. On the last day, she dissolved into tears on the tennis court with Alfred Lyttelton, overcome by her uneasy relations with Arthur, uncertainty over whether Alfred himself was a suitor and the prospect of an immediate visit to Mells where she would again meet Doll.[100]

Laura did not know that Mary, the hostess, was grappling with insecurities of her own. Eight months pregnant with her first child, she could not play tennis in the tithe barn with Arthur and the others. Except for walks, she was forced into sedentary conversation with her sister-in-law Hilda Brodrick, also pregnant, and the loquacious, 'driveling' Godfrey Webb. She hoped that Alfred Lyttelton was becoming attached to Laura, but observed closely every occasion on which Laura was alone with Arthur Balfour. She was not the only one who wondered whether Laura and Arthur felt an attraction to each other. Hilda Brodrick wrote to Mary asking whether she thought Arthur or Alfred would win. Doll was so afraid that he avoided reading the newspapers after this visit for fear of an engagement being announced, and Frances Balfour, for all her knowledge of Gerald's devotion to Laura, also believed that Laura was in love with Arthur. Mary's Stanway party inaugurated years of country house entertaining that would follow the pattern revealed here: pleasurable, informal, friendship-building sociability juxtaposed with secret relationships, hidden emotional agendas and stifled anxieties among at least some of the participants.

By the Christmas holidays of 1884, Laura's dilemmas were acute. She half-feared herself to be the soulmate of an older man – sensual but passive, refined but withdrawn and judgemental – of whom she could not approve. The social self that she valued, the one that could attract the Balfours or Gladstones, seemed threatened by rumours and misunderstanding. The house was full of people – twenty-two, according to Margot – many of whom expected private talks in addition to the theatricals, walks, tennis and parlour games of the visit. Laura's engagement to Alfred Lyttelton in the midst of this tumult appeared miraculous, even to her. 'Fortune turned her wheel for me', she wrote Doll, 'and you must be glad that she turned it from evil to good.'[101]

Although they had been acquainted less than a year and corresponded only formally, Alfred and Laura had been aware of each other as potential partners for several months. During a visit that Alfred paid to Glen in October (within weeks of Gerald Balfour's stay and days of the most illicit meeting with Doll), Laura had been so ill that Margot took up most of Alfred's time. Even so, he and Laura had one walk where they 'talked a great deal about everything in the world and about some things that are not in the world'. Alfred was 'sweet and consoling' and 'wonderfully tender and beautiful' about Gerald Balfour, though he did not seem to know how far things had gone with Doll. He himself had to tell Laura that he was ashamed of having misled Margot as to which of the sisters he preferred.

This complication, clear in her journals, had no place in Margot's published account of the Christmas courtship. At the time, her rivalry for the 'splendid' suitor who 'commands the earth and the sun to love him' was intense. When Laura told Margot that she was sure of Alfred's love, Margot with characteristic candour admitted to feeling 'as if I could have bitten her and that my teeth were full of poison like a mad dog's'.[102] Doll was present at Glen throughout this manoeuvring. When Alfred departed an hour after proposing, an exhausted Laura stayed up until three in the morning telling first Doll, then her sisters, that her decision had been made.

Margot's later account of this romance, like much of what she published, involved a conscious reworking of events. She created a highly conventional narrative worthy of a romance novel: the lovers' nervous uncertainty as Alfred waited in the sitting room for Laura to hurriedly don her virginal white gown, the largely inarticulate coming to agreement with gestures because words fail at such moments, a first, dramatic kiss that sealed the vow.[103] Missing was the sheer mayhem of the huge house party, the rival lovers in attendance at the same time and the fluid emotional entanglements. The contemporaneous accounts are actually much more fun, especially competing versions of Laura and Doll, Margot and Alfred, along with other couples, out for blustering tramps in the hills where each group tried to avoid the others while walking the same paths. But Margot's published story allowed the narrative to end in exactly the right psychological moment, with the small, vibrant feminine spirit enfolded in the great arms of her suitor, himself stunned by his good fortune in capturing a prize made all the more valuable because sought by others, and manfully determined to cherish and protect her. She did not reveal that the rejected suitor – Doll – disappeared into a wild and stormy night, though that would have been accurate.

Since this was not a novel, Laura's conflicts did not end with the moment of her commitment. If she had been aware of the framework for understanding her actions – which at this point in history her contemporary Sigmund Freud was in the process of developing – she might have seen her acceptance of Alfred as a bolt from the impulses of the *id*, represented by Doll, to the ideals of the *super-ego*, represented by her fiancé. The temptation of Doll was not just towards sexual pleasure, but towards the mockery, cynicism and demoralised sense of human potential she could indulge with him. Alfred, on the other hand – a nephew of Gladstone, and the youngest brother of Arthur's old love May Lyttelton – epitomised the Victorian gentleman. A rising barrister and a rugged athlete of sunny disposition he was honourable, chivalrous and high-minded. 'How I love to watch him', Laura wrote, 'his great strong figure clad in flannels … He has perfect ease and perfect grace and is delightful to play with because of his fine generous temper.' Alfred epitomised the self-discipline, non-dogmatic piety and acceptance of duty towards others that Laura yearned for. In marrying him she would firmly shut the door on the life that Doll represented: 'too narrow in outlook, too lacking in enthusiasm, too chained to bodily sensations'.[104]

Resoluteness did not eliminate longing and doubts. A month after Alfred's proposal, Laura visited Frances Horner and issued her strongest and most conflicted challenge yet to the supposedly natural destiny of women. Between 28 and 31 January, Laura wrote in nearly identical terms to various audiences – her journal, Mary Gladstone, George Curzon, Doll and Alfred himself – about the discussions she and Frances were having about marriage.[105] The version in her diary gave the argument:

> It [marriage] has few attractions for either of us in that aspect …
> the celibate life has more nobility near it I can't help feeling, tho it
> is the most egotistical too. What we mean is that ANY woman would
> do for any man and some women would do some other things if they
> didn't marry. I for instance might write, Frances might have done
> anything. I don't believe either Alfred or Jack would have died if
> either of us had refused them they would have married some 'sweet

girl' and been quite happy … had I remained unmarried I might have worked for the majority instead of living for the very very minority. Marriage is egotistical, *vous et moi*, not *ils et moi*, and to some women it is the end of womanism, to me it is nothing of the kind.

There were ample confusions in this and the other versions as to which was more egotistical, humanitarian celibacy or other-regarding domesticity, but the conflict between her aspirations and social expectation was clear. In the letter to her fiancé, Laura repeated much of this, but assured him that because she loved *him*, she would not be 'sunk into jam-pottism … some day the world shall hear of her – I swear it shall! Not as the amusing unconventional incautious eccentric LT but as something better wiser truer greater and this she will come to through her Love and her Soul.'

Stephen Kern has pointed out how little acquainted Victorian couples often were before they married. Although Alfred wrote that he knew Laura 'far better than 99 out of 100 know those to whom they become engaged', his moderate responses to her outpourings must have been a relief.[106] He could not, he wrote mildly, agree with Frances that the single state was 'freer and nobler'. He knew that he had 'not a spark of the genius you have', and allowed that Laura should continue to enjoy friends and 'confidences which you will receive from others which I shall have no claim to share'. But as the orphaned youngest son of a minor landowner, he knew something of the hard necessities of the world. 'You will love me a little, darling', he pleaded, 'even if I make no meteors across the sky and you have only to look back at a rather successful early career. I used sometimes to play cricket beautifully and they could never get me out and beat me – and then would come a time when I particularly longed for success because my father was looking on and it would not come. And now perhaps just from the mere "cussedness" of the world when the sweet eyes are bent on her "old boy" and his armour is put on and his limbs strung up and his soul filled with high resolve, some fate may dash away the success which he before attained but which for the first time he passionately desires.'[107]

An appeal like this was irresistible. 'I often feel a passion for reforming the world', Laura once wrote, 'yet an acre of performance is worth a land of promise, and to my mind, if a woman can prevent a man lowering himself, she does a better thing than those who write and think their lives away about what a woman's mission is.' In the last diary entries before her wedding, Laura sounded un-abashedly in love with Alfred: she found her time alone with him 'filling my brain with deep draughts of thought-annihilation and my whole being with a sense I never knew before'. 'I am happier every day and if we go on crescendo at this rate the forte fortissimo will deafen the world.'[108]

A great deal in her social world affirmed the personality that Laura had been revealing and constructing in her writings. She was rewarded with sympathy and affection not for being a sin-gle-minded, integrated, resolute character, but a mysterious 'child-woman'[109] – elusive, mercurial, emotional, questing and desirous of pleasing others. To have a yearning, untamed interior made a woman more fascinating, as long as the important con-ventions were finally accepted. Margot once wrote that Laura was more hard-headed than she herself, more able to take the path necessary for her own protection. In marrying an admirable man like Alfred, Laura indicated her voluntary acquiescence in the so-cial role appropriate to her position in society.[110]

Mary, despite her differences in temperament and upbringing, was developing some of the same understandings as the realities of her situation became clearer. Evidence about the Elchos' marriage during 1885 is too scanty to chart the relationship's deterioration very closely – even Mary's diary for that year has disappeared. Her growing frustrations were apparent from letters to Hugo in which she used the couple's nicknames to refer to herself: '*Don't* say silly foolish vulgar things that you wouldn't like the Migcat to hear, it's *so* commonplace to flirt, so cheap.' 'Don't crush Migs heart with cold and critical indifference attenuated by loathing.'[111] Young, unhappy and unsure how to proceed, Mary discovered an inner re-sourcefulness. She could, she thought, structure a life of her own within the confines of a marriage that was permanent, however im-perfect. She and Laura would develop the girls' club in Wapping, raise their children together and read all the important books that their upbringing had denied them. 'Living with good people and amongst good things and reading sterling stuff instead of trash, help to starch one up', she wrote to her mother.[112]

Laura and Mary thought that they would create a salon of close friends to discuss philosophy, art and the human condition.[113] Arthur Balfour would be integral to the scheme. There is every reason to believe that he would have welcomed it. Sharing ideas about the grounds of faith or the psychology of moral impulse was

Arthur's form of personal transparency, his way of revealing what was most important to him. He was an inveterate conversationalist and belonged to dozens of clubs, academies and dining groups over the course of his life.[114] These were male monocultures, full of experts with positions to defend and staked-out claims to one part of an intellectual field or another. Laura and Mary were different, not only in possessing what Leonard Woolf once called the 'flavour of the female mind', but in their desire to learn and understand subjects that Arthur could explore with them, though without either the assumptions or the moulding of prior knowledge. Laura's aspirations and moral fervour were deeper than Mary's, but the latter's ability to question the exact meaning of phrasing or argument complemented the quest for lucidity that impelled Arthur's non-political writings. Both women had minds that Arthur was willing to take seriously, once marital boundaries around physical and emotional closeness had been erected. In a social world that had already discouraged, even penalised, their reading and speculation, the support of a man like Arthur buttressed Laura and Mary's transition to adulthood.

3

Small Wars

Margot Tennant and George Wyndham

Laura Tennant married Alfred Lyttelton on 21 May 1885. It was a dull and showery Thursday morning, and St George's, Hanover Square, where the ceremony took place, was among the most dismal of London's fashionable matrimonial venues. Nevertheless this was the height of the London season, and the pews were packed with dukes and politicians. Alfred's uncle, prime minister William Gladstone, was there. So were the Duke of Devonshire, Lord Houghton, Lord Acton, Matthew Arnold, the Herbert Asquiths, Mary Elcho and Arthur Balfour. As everyone waited for the bride to appear, George Pembroke's friend Eddie Hamilton cornered one cabinet minister to discuss the political crisis brewing over the war secretary Lord Hartington, another guest at the wedding. Poet, anti-imperialist and philanderer Wilfrid Blunt fantasised about the bride as he did about most attractive young women. Madeline and Percy Wyndham sat mildly distracted by worry for their son George who was serving with the Coldstream Guards in the Sudan. Yet whatever private comedies or dramas absorbed the onlookers, it was still an occasion 'freighted with more good wishes than any one I can remember,' as the foreign secretary Lord Rosebery told Laura's father.[1]

A popular society wedding provided comforting assurance of normality for observers, and this one showed Britain's ruling circles at their best. It offered visible evidence for the openness of an aristocratic landowning class willing to accommodate the forces of change in modern society. Lyttelton forebears had been landowners in Worcestershire since the thirteenth century. Now Alfred and his brothers were making their way in the military, education, the Church and the law, as well as management of the Hagley estate.

The Tennants represented the integration of meritorious business families into the traditional circles of governance through the marriages of daughters and the public school and Oxbridge education of sons.[2]

The match also confirmed gender stereotypes that Victorians saw as essential in a fluid social order. Laura – beautifully dressed after trousseau shopping in Paris – was thoroughly feminine in looks and sympathies. Alfred had been shaped by his athletic successes and the 'sheer mental robustness' developed by practice at law.[3] Laura would soften Alfred's 'leathery heart' and keep him aware of the pathos of those less blessed in existence. As countless letters of congratulation affirmed, he would provide her with 'a rock and a shield and a hiding place'. Laura's moral and spiritual apprehensions, finer because less tarnished by contact with hard realities, complemented Alfred's drive for worldly success, a balance of functions that perfectly fulfilled the domestic romance that both nature and social evolution supposedly prescribed.[4]

The union's final affirmation of Victorian values transcended class or gender considerations. In an age of increasing scientific discovery and religious doubt, Laura and Alfred were earnest in their Christian belief without being rigid or judgemental. 'I have faith that God would not have suffered this to be ... unless there was to result from this a mutual comfort in the Lord', Alfred wrote to his cousin Mary Gladstone, 'that above and beyond the bright genius and the laughter and the tender pathos, there was also the love of things high and noble, and the faculty to draw from me, if I have them, all my best stops.' Laura had written in a similar vein to George Curzon: 'Unless a man and a woman's friendship is built on more foundations than the appreciation of a good story in common ... or even the love of a poet or a novel, it will not stand ... our friendship must be built on one Faith, one Hope, one Love. The Faith is the perfectibility of Man, the Hope of that Perfectibility and the Love of it. Unless we are baptized together into that church it is not much good imagining one's friendship will be a blessed one.'[5] With all the opportunities for pleasure on offer in their privileged world, the favourite moment of the couple's betrothal came when Alfred's brother-in-law, the Warden of Keble College at Oxford, blessed them in the chapel sanctuary.

It is little wonder that their friends welcomed this marriage. Two gifted and well-meaning young people were embarking on a new life together. As far as one could be sure of anything, they would combine privilege with responsibility, light-hearted courage with earnest endeavour, and worthy ambitions with fortitude in the face of mysteries beyond human control. Laura and Alfred demonstrated that the next generation embraced the virtues that would sustain Victorian progress and stability through any challenges that lay ahead.

Like most iconic moments, this one was wishful even as it occurred. Despite Laura's 'terrible fights against oneself and other people', she, like Mary Elcho, was moulding her identity to conventional scripts of respectability and moral duty and learning how to keep at bay any emotional toll that this might take. Their one-year-younger siblings found themselves in darker circumstances. As Laura made conquests among Victorian paragons such as the Lytteltons, Margot was witnessing the ruthless shenanigans of an elite social underworld that her sister never approached, one where *politesse* and privilege masked genuine peril for women. As Mary Elcho sat waiting for the bridal party in Hanover Square, her brother George hunkered among the thorn bushes in heat-stricken Sudan, one small part of an imperial adventure that pitted desperate tribesmen against the resources of the modern state. In some ways he never recovered from the experience. Margot and George were relentless observers and chroniclers. As young people they saw themselves living in danger zones characterised more by conflict than goodwill, more by survival than improvement. Their writings reveal the costs of the small wars of men and women, imperial invaders and metropole habitués, in the decade before the fin de siècle.

In photographs from the 1870s Laura and Margot Tennant often appeared together, dressed identically – small, well-proportioned and agile. Yet no one mistook one for the other. Laura's hair was fair and fine, Margot's so thick, dark and curly that she was nicknamed 'Fluffy'. Laura's face was elfin and piquant. Margot's look was bolder, less melancholy and less enigmatic. Decades later, memoirists conflated the behaviours of the two girls, emphasising the lively unconventionality they had in common. Yet Laura's journal with its Victorian pathos and aspiration seems a generation removed from her sister's. Blunt, forthright, often mocking, Margot's diary was modern in its clamorous self-assertion. By the time she was twenty, Margot observed, she was already known as 'the other one'.[6]

Margot's diary perpetually compared the two. Although Laura occasionally condemned herself for getting angry, Margot described her sister as much more likely to retreat in silent tears, while she herself succumbed to tantrums and recrimination. At age twelve she was regularly getting her ears boxed, storming out of confrontations or moping behind curtains to elicit sympathy.[7] She was physically more daring, climbing walls and staying outside in any weather. The night before leaving Glen for her introduction to London high society, she took Laura to the roof of the tennis court ('where she never would have got on her own') and smoked a cigar as they pondered the social season ahead.[8] Laura presented herself in her diary as responding to the world. Margot attacked it. There is an apt anecdote of her appearing in the drawing room as a toddler, announcing to the grown-ups 'here's me'.[9]

The household that Margot described as a girl was much more volatile than anything Laura depicted. Margot reported being 'whipped like fun' by nurses, loud quarrels between sisters and the troubled adolescence of her brother Frank, who hit Laura, gnashed his teeth and '*hates* mama'. She was candid about her negative emotions, describing herself as 'dark and fierce', 'sullen and horrid', selfish and jealous. Like her sister she worried that she was not good and performed dramatic gestures by falling to her knees with others to pray that they might behave as true Christians. Infractions of behaviour concerned her more than the state of one's soul: Frank sinned by swearing terribly, Tommy and Charty by drawing and playing tennis on Sunday. She was desperate for someone to take her seriously. At fourteen she longed to 'lie down and die and get out of this stupid world where more than three quarters of the people are stupid and wicked'.[10]

Margot was a precocious observer of the family's social advance. She noted the class dimensions of the Tennants' movement from Scottish provincial society to the London-based national elite. She labelled Lady Hay 'not humble' for refusing to shake hands with the governess; *her* family was on terms of jovial familiarity with shepherds and gardeners. She was offended by Edinburgh acquaintances who implied that Charty was 'proud of her title' after she married Lord Ribblesdale.[11] She recorded several instances in which Ribblesdale himself challenged her father, Charles Tennant, with not understanding the practices of polite society, such as when one could appropriately leave a country house party. Laura's attempt to come to terms with the family's liminal status took the form of inner identification with the 'oppressed, the wicked, the Christless, the loveless'. Margot's was to look for slights and challenge the pretensions of those who stood on precedence.

The family worried about Margot's volatile temperament. So did she. But the solution she found herself adopting was perhaps as troubling as the emotions themselves. As young as thirteen, Margot noticed that she had put on 'one of my hardened scornful outsides' when a quarrel erupted with Charty. Later she found that 'however angry inside, I get to all appearances cooler as the argument gets hotter which I find a decided advantage!!' and congratulated herself because she had 'gotten over the horror of being disliked by everyone'. Her siblings observed that she was becoming 'light' and 'hard', and, at age fifteen, this prompted one of the worst quarrels she ever had with Laura, perhaps because it hit their emerging female identities so closely. The discussion began abstractly with an attempt to define the virtues of womanliness. Against three female relatives, Margot argued that virtues were gender-free. There might be qualities appropriate to women, but females should also have virtues associated with manliness such as bravery, generosity and magnanimity. Laura's riposte was *ad hominem*: '*You* need not fear, you will *never* be womanly.'[12]

Several times in these early teenage years Margot noted that 'I am not womanly never shall be.' Her deficiencies were in the qualities that gained Laura her many admirers. Margot was not so concerned with giving others what they wanted that she risked losing her own individuality. She found it increasingly difficult to share the 'softer' emotions, noting that 'I never can cry when other people are crying I don't know how it is but the very fact of them feeling what I feel makes me cease showing my feelings.' She did not hide from herself that she had been born with strong emotions, but learned that these could be hidden: 'if one can act it's alright to other people and only sorrow to *yourself* so nobody knows and nobody cares'. At precisely the stage when her feminine qualities should have been deepening, Margot found that she lacked the sweetness, desire to please and self-effacement that made womanliness not an act, but an expression of the natural self. 'I wish I were a man', she wrote, 'God knows I do.'[13]

Margot's rebellions were partly a reaction to the large number of women in her life telling her what she was supposed to be. While Laura sought empathetic communion with women outside the family to test these messages, Margot looked to men. She dreamed, literally, of the wise older man who would show her what she was really like. When she was sixteen, she dreamed several times of her brother-in-law Tommy, whom she respected and wanted to impress. Charty, Margot's 'Queen', was present in these dreams, but somehow apart. Each time Tommy looked at Margot 'as if he loved me'. This deep exchange of looks that broke down barriers directly into the self disturbed her profoundly.[14] Within six months she had fallen in love with another man ten years her elder, the married Tory squire Walter Long, whom she met when he rescued her after a hunting accident. He was her '*greatest* friend, women and I don't get along'. When he said that she was 'wayward and determined, constant and true', she felt that no one had ever told her anything so accurate and insightful about herself.[15]

During the next two years, between the ages of sixteen and eighteen, the experiences Margot recorded showed her exploring her own nature through her interactions with men – not schoolboy friends of her brothers, but polished and mysterious men whose 'gaze' she found fixed upon her. When some new visitors arrived while she was playing tennis at Glen, 'I sort of felt as if this man was looking at me ... anyhow I felt strangely attracted to him.' She took the married Captain Hay to her room and felt 'hurt, humiliated, humbled and wretched' when he told her that she could 'expect to be talked about' if she violated society's conventions. If she did not take care, she could become 'very wicked'. Alone in Dresden in 1881, she played with this possibility. Writing much later, Margot recounted episodes that she did not record in her diary, in which foreign men mistook her for a prostitute because of her sophisticated dress, easy manner and open gaze.[16] These experiences told her frankly that she had the power to fascinate men. Was her desire to 'conquer people' entirely wrong, she wondered? She was not even sure she wanted to cure her love of the 'reckless happiest feeling' that came when one jumped a fence, smashed a window or gave 'the look or word which you know will settle it for good or bad with a man, I mean that will make him tell you his devotion respect and worship so long and carefully hidden'.[17]

Writing decades later, Margot emphasised the innocence of her isolated border-country upbringing. She claimed that she and Laura hardly knew the meaning of the word 'fast' during that autumn of 1884 when Laura's behaviour with her suitors caused so much distress to the Balfours and Lytteltons.[18] This was extremely disingenuous. When she was barely seventeen the diary showed her evaluating whether she might deserve 'the repulsive word flirt!!' She began a story called 'A Flirt, in one volume', based on her own experiences, as well as observations of the married life of her sister Charty.[19] In the story a youngest sister named Barbara Lister – Margot chose to call her heroine after Charty's newly born daughter – watches a ball where Mrs Langtry and Mrs West, notorious friends of the Prince of Wales, are present. The Listers are 'marrying girls' for tending to find husbands very young, and the heroine knows that in her own case 'nothing under a Duke would satisfy the family'. The girl gazes from afar at the comings and goings of the couples and speculates whether these women paint their faces (a signal that a woman did not care if she was considered improper), but her musings are interrupted by a schoolroom lesson on Schiller. In the next scene the girl is at a concert in Dresden where she becomes aware that an 'interesting stranger' who appears 'slightly dangerous' is looking at her. 'His expression on catching Barbara's eye was anything but agreeable and she fancied he said that which was insulting.'

Margot's story revealed – in a way that the diary did not – her awareness of the world that Charty and Tommy Ribblesdale were entering. Tommy's background was full of interesting scandals.[20] On several occasions during the 1850s and 1860s his father had decamped to the Continent with an equestrienne star he preferred to his wife. He gambled so disastrously that he was forced to economise by renting out the Gisburne estate in Yorkshire and moving his family to France. In 1876, a few weeks before Charty and Tommy became engaged, Lord Ribblesdale committed suicide – Tommy took his seat in the House of Lords only three months before his own wedding. Charles Tennant's great fondness for Tommy Ribblesdale resulted in significant financial help for the couple, but Tennant's business empire was shaky in the early 1880s. Tommy and inevitably Charty scrambled to sustain a life in high society through family connections and sinecures he could acquire as an officer in the Rifle Brigades.

One of these was as an aide-de-camp to Lord Rosslyn, a sporting peer, friend of the Prince of Wales and stepfather of the prince's future mistress, Daisy Brooke, Countess of Warwick. This moment in the late 1870s was a particularly fraught one in the story of Victorian high society. Though the Prince of Wales's marital adventures had been the subject of insider gossip for over a decade, the affair with Lily Langtry that began in 1877 was the first time he had

openly flaunted a relationship with a supposedly respectable married woman.[21] The prince's imprimatur on the notion that an extra-marital affair need not result in social isolation presented every
aristocratic family with the intensely personal quandary of whether
its women were available or not. Anita Leslie, whose grandparents
occupied these circles, said that young married women were 'safe'
from outside overtures until they had produced some legitimate
children.[22] By this unspoken rule, Charty was off-limits until young
Tommy was born in May 1878 and Barbara two years later. Charty
became pregnant again in 1885 with a child who did not survive.
By this time, the couple was increasingly navigating the world of
extra-marital entanglements represented by the Prince of Wales
and his Marlborough House set. Though the details are frus-
tratingly elusive, this was a milieu that Margot and Laura caught
glimpses of by their teenage years. Despite Margot's insistence on
the closeness she and Laura shared, it was a world that the two
sisters experienced differently.

Charting Margot's gradual entry into national aristocratic society is not easy. The published memoirs, seemingly so candid, were
misleading and casual about chronology. Two of her most recent
biographers conflated social conquests that occurred some years
apart and moved them to within months of the court presentation
that marked her 'coming out' in London's polite society in May
1882.[23] This compression made Margot appear more immediately
successful than she was, minimised the extent to which she and
Laura were going in different directions and vastly underrated the
type of influences Margot was under in the early 1880s when she
was eighteen to twenty years old.

Margot made her first independent forays into society through
the hunting scene, a world that Laura never took part in. Her first
day in the field occurred early in 1880 during a visit to her sister
Lucy Graham Smith at Easton Grey in Malmsbury. Over the winter
of 1881–82 she spent enough time with the Beaufort pack to conduct a heavy flirtation with John Gratwicke (Gratty) Blagrave that
resulted in a hilarious brief engagement in the summer of 1882.
When Margot first discovered hunting, she noted that she 'loved
it', but some people thought it 'a sin'.[24] The reasons are not hard
to find.

Hunting constituted an astounding exception to the regime
of surveillance and restraint under which young women in polite society operated in the Victorian period. Public scrutiny was

certainly part of the crowded fields and assembly points of the chase, but Margot's story of her first encounter with the sportsman Peter Flower showed how quickly a couple could find themselves alone out-of-doors. Margot, an experienced rider by the time she met Peter, was mounted on his unruly horse Havoc who proved impossible for her to control. Flower's own mount balked at jumps, and early on they were both thrown and found themselves far away from the pack for a significant portion of the day.[25] Even the train journeys to and from a meet could be unchaperoned except for the maid riding in a different car; Margot's diary makes it sound as though hers frequently were.

The activity of strenuous riding itself upset notions of respectable feminine behaviour. Girls tumbled off horses with deranged clothes, galloped through the woods with 'hair down and streaming out behind' and pulled up at the kill with 'ruby lips' and faces rosy with exertion. 'A woman in the field is a constant object of wonderment or admiration', noted a contemporary expert. 'There is nothing that sets off a nice hunter as her figure does, nothing that adds more to the beauty and interest of the game.' The association of women who hunted with women of loose morals was fading by the late 1870s. Even so, by one estimate only about 10 per cent of riders were women when Margot became involved with the sport.[26]

A certain freemasonry in the field coexisted with its erotics.[27] Riding to hounds was one of the few activities in which women could compete openly with men, winning temporary victories and earning admiration for showing masculine prowess. Hunters were cautioned that safety and fair play required all riders to be treated as equals; a woman must 'take her chances', 'on the same footing' as any sportsman when it came to opening gates, charging gaps, navigating through streams or galloping for position. If a tiny figure seated side-saddle atop a huge horse 'rode like the devil', sailed through footing 'good and bad', and managed animals that would throw a man, she would experience applause that had nothing to do with the sweetness of domesticity. Margot had this kind of courage and skill. It gained her enormous attention as well as a host of injuries, which included an accident that knocked her out cold for two hours in 1883.

Even before Margot gained the adult status of her court introduction, she had had enough experiences with men to ask her diary, 'why should I appear indignant when I am kissed or angry when I am fondled? Its humbug when I like it yes love being cared

about even if it's not the way we call right!' Living within the
strictures set by others was like 'living in a large cage'.[28] Hunting
provided an escape and an absorbing diversion where she did not
compete with Laura, and it gave Margot the social circle that got
her through her first London season. She met Arthur Balfour and
George Pembroke at a dinner hosted by the Duke of Beaufort's
daughter in 1882, though she seems not to have seen them again
for several years.[29]

She must have seen a lot of Gratty Blagrave, the younger son
of a Bedfordshire gentry family whose holdings were below the
thousand acres needed for mention in John Bateman's *Great Landowners of Great Britain and Ireland* (1876). Inexplicably, Margot
managed to arrange an overnight trip to the coast with 29-year-old
Gratty, and her sixteen-year-old brother Jack as chaperone. When
she rejected Gratty's declarations of love – marriage to a daughter of Charles Tennant would have been a very good move for
him – Blagrave went berserk, gnawing his handkerchief to shreds,
biting his arm, berating himself and her, and vowing to sell his
hunters and leave England forever. Margot responded in kind. At
one point she threw herself sobbing to the floor, but mostly she
stood 'in my *black* negligee with my hair on end tumbling over my
face and my hands folded and feeling a thousand years old with
a piteous dumb expression in my eyes (I saw myself reflected in
the glass)'.[30] The theatrics continued the next day as Gratty gave
her the silent treatment while lying dramatically close to a cliff
edge – she ran off to the beach and sat 'screaming at' the sea. Margot presented herself as ratcheting up the drama by using scorn
and reverse psychology, yet she was also half persuaded that Gratty
would take some drastic action if she did not agree to an engagement. She did, if he would wait two years, but time in London to
reflect – combined with family opposition – allowed her to back
out within a few weeks.

In the same months that these events were occurring, Margot
was beefing up her knowledge of romantic relations through her
reading. *Don Juan* and *Tristram Shandy*, she knew, were 'not quite'
the books allowed for girls, 'but must I stick to the Fairchild family?' She and Laura also discovered the Brontës.[31] Margot's cleverly
constructed narrative of the Gratty episode showed the influences. The story was mostly comic melodrama, with hearty hunting
verbiage thrown in: 'By jove, it's harder to fool the family than I
thought!'[32] It also contained the first use of an image that might

have come straight from *Jane Eyre* and that Margot would employ for the next sixty years in describing moments of true attraction and genuine emotion. Always there was a final embrace with the woman's 'little cold white face pressed against his rough coat', as though true feeling required the burying of eyes, eclipse of the interactive social identity of the face and an overwhelmingly dominant male.

A few weeks later Margot was analysing the London season in picaresque terms, categorising social types and flaunting the attention she drew from faceless crowds as she drove her pony alone through the streets. But, during the hunting season of 1883, she moved into circles that would turn her tone detached and cynical. The year was significant for both Laura and Margot. It included Laura's trip to South Africa and the *Pembroke Castle* cruise that moved her into the intellectual Liberal families around Gladstone. Margot's path took her deeper into the hunting shires of aristocratic England where she met quite a different type, not sublimating aesthetes or repressed moralists, but the 'rich tactless tasteless vulgar very kind people' who would form her closest acquaintances for the next three years.[33]

Margot's rebelliousness and emotional volatility were in sharp contrast to the apparently smooth trajectory of George Wyndham's youth. Like his sister, Mary, George was much more accepting of the conventions and guidance of his parents than the Tennant girls were. The differences in his path to adulthood arose less from social position than from gendered experience. If girls remained confined in birth family circles longer than some of them wished, boys of the Victorian privileged classes left home well before their teenage years in order to attend private boarding schools, not only for the education but for acculturation among their male peers and introduction to the 'rules, conventions, and hierarchies' that would define their adult lives.[34]

Whereas the family home was overseen by mothers and shared with sisters – where male and female interests had to be negotiated[35] – boarding schools were overwhelmingly male and the most significant venues for the development of masculine identity in imperial Britain's highest circles. Victorian men who experienced the system of preparatory and public school education were candid about what it was supposed to accomplish, aside from the social networking that would last a lifetime.[36] Individual expression,

personal fulfilment or the cultivation of a private self in boys were
low priorities. Instead, boarding school was designed to shape the
characters of gentlemen who would play 'an honourable part' in
the governance of estate, kingdom or empire. The 'nursery garden
at Eton', wrote one of George Wyndham's fellow students, 'made
an indelible impression on the growing character, the examples of
"playing the game" giving us a natural bent towards straight dealing in after life, and the instinctive good taste which is due more to
our upbringing than to any conscious effort of our own'.[37]

At least partially purged of bawdiness and brutality by a wave
of reforms initiated around the time that Balfour and Pembroke
were at Eton, the great public schools when George Wyndham attended in the late 1870s had become more self-conscious in their
programmes for masculine development. Younger masters related
to their students with less formality than before, but with more
explicit guidance. Team sports enshrined the lessons of submerg-
ing self-interests in those of the group, as well as following rules
and honouring physical, if not intellectual, effort.[38] Older boys retained the enormous authority over daily governance of residence
houses and student activities that they had enjoyed for more than
a century. But now the responsibilities were more explicitly linked
to those they would hold in adulthood. Youngsters who had no gift
of leadership learned to see the value of a place well filled or a role
well played in rule-based hierarchical systems.

Modern historians agree with the Victorians about the powerful
influence of the boarding school in shaping the values and character ideals – the super-ego – of students who spent their most formative years in the system. Personal stoicism, a proper understanding
of duty and playing by the rules, the ability to work collaboratively
with peers, deferentially with superiors and authoritatively with
subordinates suited the careers in politics, law, the military or imperial service that most graduates would follow. Yet a recent body
of scholarship has also begun to explore the implications of this
distinctive system of male acculturation on individual personality,
not just on character. Summing up two decades of literature on
the formation of late-Victorian masculinities, Jonathan Rutherford
provides a vivid listing of personality traits that he finds characteristic of privileged men behind their stiff upper lips: loneliness and
an inexplicable sense of longing; an 'impossibly idealized mother
… encased in a fantasy home steeped in tender love and care';
'misogynistic rejection and emotional need' of women; an almost

feminine fondness towards fathers or father figures; a cult of boy-ishness and sentimental attachment to brotherhoods; a search for identity in nostalgically imagined communities of class, nation or race.[39] Regenia Gagnier's reading of scores of memoirs written by public school boys of Wyndham's generation and later found that two types predominated. In the minority were cynical rebels who went on to spend their lives criticising both the schools and the imperial establishment they buttressed. The vast majority presented the official façade, sentimentally fixated on the value and significance of a process of adolescent toughening that they never challenged.

In George Wyndham's case, six years spent at the Rev. C. J. Chittenden's preparatory school in Hoddesdon and then at Eton reinforced a temperament inclined to adhere to authority, bow to duty and fit in with the standards of the group. Unlike Arthur Balfour and George Pembroke, however, George Wyndham would eventually demonstrate most of the inner traits identified by Rutherford. What fascinated his contemporaries was that he ultimately proved unable to censor the emotional dynamics at work behind the reserve that upper-class men presented to others. His youthful experience of a small war of empire – the Suakin campaign of 1885 – helps to explain the psychological depth and the more obvious struggles with himself that characterised George Wyndham throughout his adult life.

After George's death in 1913, his relatives published a huge collection of his letters instead of the standard official biography. His correspondence with those closest to him served as the place where he revealed outlawed emotions, explored alternate views of himself and passed judgements that would be unwise to air during an ongoing political career.[40] It is a shame, then, that so few of the selections in *Life and Letters of George Wyndham* dealt with his formative boarding school years. George's schoolboy letters contained some of his eye for scene-setting detail, but little about his personal feelings or perceptions. He was, as nearly every letter affirmed, doing 'all right', having 'great fun', 'getting on capitally'.

George's experience of leaving home may have protected him from some of the psychological shock that other men reported about this decisive event in their lives, Winston Churchill most famously.[41] Some boys were sent away from loved ones and familiar surroundings when they were as young as seven and, according to many critics of this practice, never fully recovered from the sudden severing of proximity to their mothers, nannies and sisters who had formed the emotional centre of their lives. They imprinted instead on homosocial environments, coming to see women as alien, inexplicable creatures and reserving emotionality, if not sexuality, for relationships with other men.[42] George did not leave for school until he was eleven, and even then roomed with his brother Guy who joined him within a few months. George remained close to his family all his life and displayed an openness in expressing affection and revealing himself to friends that his contemporaries noted as unusual.

George's school was the same that Arthur had attended fifteen years earlier. Chittenden, writing of Arthur's years at the Grange, presented a picture of the education that was unsurprisingly different from that described by the boys themselves. Arthur – delicate, privileged and excused from games – enjoyed intellectual conversation with adults. Solitary walks with the master both nourished his mind and provided escape from the peer shenanigans that might have got him into trouble. Chittenden's account relayed nothing but gentle humour and kindly feelings as boys were fostered towards adolescence.[43]

Lord Frederick Hamilton, eight years younger than Arthur, provided a different angle of vision, but one partially confirmed by George's letters. He said that Chittenden was a rigorous academic taskmaster, determined that his charges perform well later in life and convinced that inattention – the unwillingness to focus – formed the chief impediment to learning. Slackness and vagueness were punished immediately with 'a piece of heavy leather strap, like a horse-trace, about a foot long and nearly half an inch thick, called the Spatter … It was used freely.' 'You know Bill, who used to play in the Square with us?' George wrote home. 'Well, he's here, and gets spatted regularly, three a day and sometimes more.'[44] The Wyndham children, like the Tennants, were regularly spanked by their nanny, but there was something different about the beatings at school. Memoirs recount the profound impression made the first time a child saw a classmate whipped in public.[45] George's mention of Bill's difficulties may indicate disquiet, but his tone was the expected one of fortitude and acceptance.

George performed well enough under Chittenden's methods to pass into Eton at a higher level than Arthur achieved. In 1877 he took 'Remove' in his three-day exams for admission – a respectable though not spectacular placement given his age. One contemporary explained this new status with a military analogy.[46] Boys in the lower 'forms' were the privates. They had no privileges and served as 'fags', cooking, cleaning and doing errands for boys at a higher level. 'Fifth formers' (usually fourteen or fifteen years of age and above) were officers commanding the services of others. Boys in Remove were the non-commissioned officers, enjoying some freedoms and perhaps only one term away from leaving fag status altogether. Taking Remove meant that George escaped the most intense period of helplessness and disorientation that a younger student might go through on arriving at school. Lower boys, recalled Gilbert Coleridge, could expect to be accosted by bigger boys in the streets and playing fields with abrupt questions, followed by kicks and shoves, according to the mood of the interrogator.[47] 'What is your form?' was one standard inquiry, with reactions dependent on the response.

'What does your father do?' was another regular challenge to new boys, so the problem of rough treatment, if not outright bullying, was probably worse for middle-class sons in the first generation at a school. The unfortunate Tennant brothers appear to have loathed Eton, which they attended at a time when their father's achievements in the business world would have been neither known nor appreciated by status-conscious adolescents.[48] George, the grandson of an earl and son of a Conservative member of parliament, had unchallengeable answers to such questions. He was able to see the room where his father's charcoal drawing of an owl remained burned into a cupboard door, and he learned to swim from an instructor who remembered Percy Wyndham. This sharing of experience across generations reinforced George's attachments to his father and his school, and his acceptance of the values they represented.

George was also fortunate in his parents' choice of residence house. He and Guy shared a room at R. A. H. Mitchell's. Mitchell was in his mid-thirties at the time and had been an Eton contemporary of Alfred Lyttelton's oldest brother, Charles, in the late 1850s and early 1860s. Together they had dominated the cricket scene, serving sequentially as highly successful captains of the school team. When Mitchell returned to Eton as a master his chief interest was the game. He became an unofficial coach to the Eton eleven, and his own house excelled in most sports in inter-house rivalries. Neither an intellectual nor a tyrant, Mitchell had a way with boys. 'To all who knew him, Mike remains a perfect example of the English gentleman, an ideal of all that is wholesome and straight, and of a kindly courtesy that no boy could resist.'[49] Without being a star athlete himself, George had the experience of belonging to one of the houses most respected by the rest of the school. He played football for Mitchell's house, earning his 'colours' before he left in 1880. His letters stressed the atmosphere of games and sports, with accounts of school matches against Harrow, inter-house competitions and injuries ranging from strained hips to broken bones.

By his last term at Eton, George had gained the status of a 'swell', an unofficial in-crowd of senior boys who ambled in together to school events and entertained at specific hostelries in town. He stood second in seniority and achievement among the seventy or so pupils in his house and was elected secretary of the debating society. In the two debates he reported, his views reflected unself-conscious conformity to the largely Tory opinions that dominated the school. On the question whether the Afghan war started by the Conservative viceroy to India Lord Lytton in 1878 was 'desirable at the time it occurred', he voted yes. And in opening a debate on whether corporal punishment ought to be abolished in the army and navy, he argued with the vast majority that it should not.[50] As with his fellows, George's education about contemporary political and imperial affairs came primarily through youthful debates such as this, supplemented by the lectures of visiting policymakers and specialists offered throughout the term.[51]

George left Eton expecting to go to university but needing a spell at a crammer's before he could attempt the entrance exams. This plan proved short-lived. Mary reported in March 1881 that it was 'definitely settled that George won't go to Cambridge'. He would instead spend some weeks in Paris improving his French, and then use an army crammer to prepare for the December entrance exams to the Royal Military College at Sandhurst, where his father had gone thirty years before.[52] George's decision to forego the Oxbridge experience in favour of immediate preparation for the army was one of the few acts in defiance of his father that he ever committed.

Percy Wyndham had always regretted his own lack of university education. He was correct in realising that the decision would be even more important in his son's generation as the professionalisation of British society accelerated.[53] The movement of wealthy middle-class families into the national elites and the expansion of administrative and bureaucratic occupations created a new space for the two pre-eminent universities to serve as gatekeepers to positions in politics, the professions and imperial service. The eldest sons of landed families needed no credentials to secure their place in county life or running the estate. But if they had ambitions on the national stage, matriculation at a university was becoming increasingly important. Nearly all the aristocratic heirs with whom George later associated in politics – Hugo Elcho, Willie Grenfell, St John Brodrick, George Curzon, Harry Cust, Arthur Balfour – attended Oxford or Cambridge. As Paul Deslandes explains, such men entered a 'small world' of relationships, codes, jargon, ceremonies and competitions that made them members of an exclusive club outside of George's experience.[54]

Perhaps none of this was as clear in 1881 as it would have been a decade later. 'A University education', noted one biographer, 'might possibly have given George that scholarly habit of mind which, with all his brilliance and his devotion to literature, he lacked … more likely it would have been a wasted period in his life: he would either have fretted, or given way to idleness.'[55] Hard riding, more than team sports, seems to have been George's obsession in his late teenage years. Like Margot he used strenuous physical activity to stave off restlessness, and there are some hints in the early materials that, without the focus that beginning a military career would provide, he might have become absorbed in his generation's gambling, racing and heavy drinking circles. Percy and Madeline, as attentive parents, acquiesced quickly in the campaign of subtle resistance that George put up – 'I never have felt so depressed since I left Chittenden's; but don't think that makes me dislike the place' – to make the shift from further general education to the military training provided by Sandhurst.

Whatever the Wyndhams might have expected of a university experience, their teenage son's decision on an immediate military career was a clearly acceptable alternative for an aristocrat whose economic resources would place him among the gentry, rather than the great magnates of the landed class.[56] Three of Madeline Wyndham's brothers and four of her brothers-in-law made careers in the military. The southern counties of England where George grew up provided more senior officers than any part of the British Isles except Ireland.[57] Percy's own service had ended in illness during the Crimean War. That had not prevented him from becoming a member of parliament six years later, and he was an enthusiastic participant in the volunteer movement founded by Hugo Elcho's father in 1859. The Wyndhams were a military family as well as an artistic one. Their second son would retire from the Queen's Lancers as a lieutenant-colonel. George's son Percy was killed in France in 1914 while serving with the Coldstream Guards.

With the decision to enter the army settled, George could enjoy his weeks of language immersion in Paris. His letters took the stance of a bemused observer of the human comedy. He described an exhibition at the Salon as 'very funny. The number of perfectly revolting pictures of people with their heads cut off was very large.' He played a lot of lawn tennis and attended the opera where 'being with ladies in evening dress and all that' derailed his attempts to speak French. He amused the family by reporting unusual social conventions, such as the fact that girls were chaperoned even at afternoon tea, apparently unlike his sisters. In letters to Mary he often turned the joke on himself: 'I hired yesterday a very large and aged white horse to create a sensation with in the Bois. I think I must have succeeded. He was very white and all his hair came off on to me in two minutes'; 'I went Monday to Lawn Tennis, but was prevented from distinguishing myself, as in the 2nd game I bust both buttons off my trousers. I finished the set with my left hand gracefully placed behind my back.'[58]

Whimsy, Dickensian depictions of urban spaces and mild mocking of unfamiliar customs were common tropes for privileged young men of George's generation. Funny sketches like those of Phil Burne-Jones, son of the artist and a close friend of Wyndham's, appeared frequently in their correspondence, showing the writer's mastery through humour of situations that might be embarrassing or destabilising. George's letters assumed that the distant family was a psychic community who would appreciate the small dramatic narratives his stories provided: 'I will tell you how I got on amongst the Frenchys; here the proper thing is to take off your hat in your left hand, keep it off and shake hands with your right; it requires some practice to do this gracefully to everybody at a Lawn Tennis party, with a stick and gloves, after having been handed two racquets to choose from.'[59] George's scrutiny of strangers extended to fellow countrymen. Young Lord Castlerosse ('His Mother (?) was Lady Kenmare') erred in not knowing how to spell Wyndham correctly, and another 'unknown' was 'apparently a young man of feeble intellect' for not understanding the theatrical performance he had attended the night before.

Young people in England's highly stratified ruling circles knew the importance of minute distinctions in etiquette and self-presentation based on status. Any encounter with strangers could cause unease as one groped towards correct placement in the rank structure. Mary and George were both aware that they needed to assess people in terms of background and relationship, and openly asked their parents to explain who someone was. George, much like his sister, left deeper anxieties or discontents unrecorded. Only the one line about ladies in evening gowns suggested the sexual implications of a handsome young man on his own in Paris in the early 1880s. A few passing references to loneliness hinted at the disorientation that a seventeen-year-old might feel at encountering a strange city. But mostly George sounded like a well-adjusted young tourist, using his wits, his good looks and his self-deprecating humour to negotiate the mores of a city he would come back to for pleasure and culture throughout his life. Nothing in the record indicated that he was not well on his way to developing the 'autonomous' personality, 'unusually independent and stoical' that David Roberts found characteristic of eldest sons of the landed class, most of whom never showed 'any signs of rebellion, any falling away, indeed any widening at all of the generation gap' with their parents.[60]

Margot Tennant's precocious awareness and scrambling explorations may have been part of her temperament – she certainly thought so – but they were also the product of her failure to identify with the adults in her family. In March 1883, when she had just turned nineteen, she wrote plaintively that she was unfit to take care of herself, but that 'there was no one to do it'. She blamed her own 'very high spirited badly controlled self', not her 'dearest parents' and 'sweetest sisters' in the world.[61] But these words did not reflect the ambivalence about her parents that appeared elsewhere in her writings. Margot presented a highly critical portrait of her mother in *Octavia* (1928), a novel based on her early hunting years. The picture amplified descriptions of Emma Tennant in the published memoirs. Octavia's mother Mrs Daventry, though refined, is 'evasive, irrelevant' and 'not attached to her children'. She erected a 'barrier of reserve between herself and the world' and cultivated 'a feline and disarming small talk which was intellectually depressing'. Emma worried that Charles Tennant's money and social ambition, combined with the unconsidered praise he poured on all his children's endeavours, would produce vanity and indiscipline. To prevent this outcome she, like Mrs Daventry, 'without knowing it ... would in a subtle and disparaging manner check the enthusiasm, dim the glow, and cramp the extravagance of every one round her'.[62]

Censorious, incurious and conventional, a mother like Mrs Daventry could easily produce rebellion and deception. 'There is a charm in constantly keeping one's face [while] always planning meetings and escaping by a hair being found out', Margot wrote when her escapades with Gratty had her climbing railings into locked gardens and enlisting the aid of the servants to cover late-night arrivals. In a scene shocking for the intimacies it implied, Margot once threw her nightgown down to Gratty waiting in the square below.[63]

Her freedom of action was made easier by Emma's lack of knowledge of the families with whom Margot was spending time while hunting, and Charles Tennant was little help. A newly elected member of parliament, he was enjoying his introduction to the London political world. He was also facing worrisome financial problems that undermined his health and attention. In 1883 there was an insider trading scandal in which he sold stock shares ahead of poor year-end results, then bought them back at a lower price. The next year the Mysore Gold enterprise, which had peaked at £8 per share shortly after its offering in 1880, fell to ninepence per share. It recovered by 1886, but Alfred Lyttelton noted later that the catastrophe had coloured the settlement negotiations for Laura early in 1885.[64] Margot knew nothing of the intricacies of her father's business life. He had enough money to buy her hunters, and clothes from Worth's in Paris for the asking. But several accounts indicate that the family atmosphere from 1882 to around 1886 must have been uncomfortable, with both parents distracted for reasons that Margot would not have understood.

Her sisters Charty and Lucy were supposed to be the gatekeepers of Margot's acquaintanceships, but in some ways they were navigating the same terrain. By the early 1880s Lucy's marriage was unravelling. Though the couple stayed together, Thomas Graham Smith's financial troubles and explosive temper led Lucy to involvements with other men. In autumn 1883, Margot noticed that Charty had changed as well. She was developing some sort of intimacy with the 'about as idle as they make 'em' Algernon Grosvenor, and had the 'tone of women *confident*' of their ability to 'kindle the admiration of heaps of people'.[65] Within months Charty was friends with Marlborough House habitués such as Charles Beresford, Christopher Sykes and possibly the Prince of Wales.[66] When Charty visited her sister in South Africa in June 1884, as Laura had done the year before, her new friends chided her for desertion, and she herself 'really *minded* going'. When she returned three months later to the same milieu, Margot said, 'no one has or will say a word or whisper against her', indicating that she knew that women in these crowds were talked about.[67] To Margot's observant eyes, the summer of 1883 marked 'a new epoch in Charty's life – I watch her career apart from my feelings with a great deal of curiosity'.[68]

Margot was herself moving in similar circles, probably with the Ribblesdales as chaperones. She found herself 'made much of' by the Beaufort/ Somerset clan at Badminton, the Wilsons at Didmorton and an unnamed family at Dragcot: 'not good for one at all, beastly conversation, not a nice woman Lady DJ, but very good company'. Margot was drawn to the men of that world for their physical prowess and athleticism; they did not need to pretend to be intellectual or even articulate, but could appreciate her as an untamed creature of the sort they were used to dealing with in the fields and woods. With them she could say 'damn' and smoke cigarettes. Margot thought they would remember her as 'such good company, eccentric, atrocious flirt, cheek of the devil, fond of men and not quite dignified with them but rode very well, had great pluck, really clever … and her conversation to judge by men's faces was very amusing *very much* so'.[69]

Margot tried to present this as an environment of breezy comradeship, but its sexual complications come through. In these circles, her behaviour put her in situations where her body was fair game. She had to fight off the aggressive Mr Wilson ('bear fighting and a nuisance'). She became attracted to Hugh Rocksavage, six years older and heir to the Marquess of Cholmondley. He was manly and tactful and 'just my sort', though 'no denying that he's vulgar … rather jars at times'. On a drive home he kissed her, 'but mind you he's a furious bear fighter and its very hard to prevent it'. Hugh had been married for four years. His pregnant wife had also befriended Margot, who worried that she would be vexed if she heard about Hugh's behaviour. Margot would be miserable, she said, if she made a friend 'jealous of her husband'. At nineteen, Margot was encountering the world of social reputation and women's gossip. She fumed about 'a cat like Mary Hamilton who said I was seen coming out of Penna Somerset's bedroom at 4 in the morning such a d – d lie'.[70] Margot's assertions of freedom sent signals about availability, of which she was only partly aware.

The talk could only have escalated after the famous day at Ascot when Margot and her older brother Eddie secured tickets to the Royal Enclosure and Margot spent hours in the company of the Prince of Wales. Undated in the memoirs, this occurred on 8 June 1883, the day that Wokingham – whom Margot picked to finish – placed fifth in the Wokingham Stakes. Margot got a kind letter and a cigarette case from the prince. A few months later his private secretary Francis Knollys inexplicably proposed – a marriage that would have put Margot in the inner circle of the prince's cronies – but she turned him down.[71]

When she was sixteen, and flirting with married friends such as Walter Long and Captain Hay in the safety of her own home, Margot had blustered against '*les convenances*' of respectable middle-class morality with its mindless prohibitions on girls' opportunities and behaviour. Four years later, she had direct familiarity with a gentry-aristocratic world that had been 'bred' with rather different standards. Late in 1884, she pulled together her various diary entries to draft an essay called 'Women' in which she summed up what she had learned in the previous few years about men and women in polite society.[72] Like the diary speculations, 'Women' was a remarkable document for one so young, and it raised themes and problems that exercised her for the rest of her life.

Margot began by noting that having older sisters 'come out' and marry in high society gave girls a precocious awareness of the 'ball gowns, flirting, fanning, fiddling, flattery, falseness and gardenias' that socialising in privileged circles entailed. In women she observed a universal artificiality of manner as each became a certain type in 'her own way to draw men out': 'some try the religious taking to task, the "do you say your prayers" … others the snubbing banter, "how many people have you said *that* to!" … some the round eyed innocence: "Really, fancy, I'm so glad you think so, I hope its not rude" … others the independent sporting, the "its such a bore to keep down one's petticoats all my governesses hated me".' Though she, as a young woman, probably ought to affect 'blushing' and 'stammering' when courted by a 'clumsy huge creature' with £90,000 a year, she preferred a relaxed, no nonsense approach and had 'a way of acting naturalism which I find very successful'.[73] In an environment where 'every woman is taller, prettier, better known than oneself', one's aim was simply to 'get along with men, not so much from any special delight in their society but chiefly because at the various morning, noon or night gatherings one's women friends are talking to men and do not contemplate being interrupted'.[74]

If women were in palpable competition with each other in these settings, young men appeared baffled by the mysteries of trying to figure out what a woman wanted. Expressing a sentiment that Laura wrote in her diary at the same time, Margot noted that it must be a relief to a man to 'feel a girl he is wishing to get on with will not think he is in love with her if he … kisses her hand … a sense of the ridiculous, a rapid understanding of the unsaid, half thought or suggested … a common sense that clears up trivial misunderstandings puts people at their ease and inspires confidence'. It also had a powerful effect on men. It was so rare to have the genuine 'art of sympathy' that men would truly love, not just fall in love with, the woman who possessed it. But such a girl would inevitably 'become what is vulgarly called a flirt' for having so many suitors at her feet. Thus Margot asserted the practical benefits of an open, forthright, bantering demeanour with men. Like Laura, she worried about the charge of being a 'coquette' for making a man fall in love with her when she was only pretending an interest in him. But both girls condemned men who claimed to love a girl they knew so little that they could not tell how she really felt.

Margot's journal was not as preoccupied as Laura's with the implications of marriage itself. In her essay 'Women' she casually asserted that 'a woman's natural state is marriage unless she has a very decided plan of life', but there was none of the overt railing against domesticity, childbearing and the death of independent aspiration that Laura expressed. On the basis of what Margot observed by 1884, however, her speculations went in a direction that Laura's never broached to consider the ramifications of sexual infidelity. At twenty, she said, she had 'gotten past the vision of the ideal man'. No woman should suppose that 'because a man loves you and marries you … this insures his love and your happiness for the rest of your lives'. 'It is the want of mystery, the soon fathomed however deep affections, and the familiar harmony that damn married life.' To keep a husband's interest, a woman should be sure to maintain her appearance, use charm and humour to remain excellent company, not burden a man with domestic

concerns and, most importantly, play carefully on his jealousy, 'for
you are quite as certain as your husband is to meet some people
who for a short time may interest you as much as your husband'.
A wife must conceal her own jealousy and prove herself superior
to any other woman in her husband's life. These conclusions defied romantic literature and moral prescription, but they reflected
'the London world of now-a-days' and the necessity for a married
couple of 'adapting themselves to their world since they live in it'.
Margot's socialising had drawn her into a different milieu from
the one Laura was frequenting, and her response was more cynical
than anything Laura ever expressed.

In the next few months, Margot moved further into settings that
could have sent her life on a hazardous trajectory. Charles Tennant
had just been made a baronet at Gladstone's recommendation,
resulting in more invitations to court and society functions. Margot regained the attention of the Prince of Wales, who talked to
her privately under the potted palms at several balls. She attended
a dinner party at which she was dressed inappropriately because
she was unaware that the prince would be present. Although she
overheard the other ladies' disparaging comments, Margot was
seated next to the prince at dinner and earned his compliments.
She was, her diary noted, invited to lunch with the prince twice
and to meet him at Ferdinand de Rothschild's new entertainment
mansion, Waddesdon. Laura wrote cryptically to Doll wondering
what it might mean if 'Margot gets into the Prince of Wales set'.[75]

Biographers note changes in the social behaviour of the Prince
of Wales at this time. He was between the strong attachments to
Lily Langtry and the Duchess of Caracciolo of the late 1870s, and
the tempestuous affair with Mary Elcho's cousin Daisy Brooke that
began in 1889. He was enjoying the company of American women
who were 'livelier, better educated and less hampered by etiquette'
than the daughters of the English aristocracy.[76] They brought 'a
little fresh air' to his social rounds, as could the bright daughter
of a rising plutocrat or of an old but impoverished gentry family.
If they were so inclined, such young women could find a marriage
partner in the prince's entourage who would not mind a wife who
received the prince's attentions. Margot had already received a
proposal from the prince's secretary, Francis Knollys, in 1883.

Private lunches with the Prince of Wales and acceptance of an
invitation to meet him at Waddesdon would signal that a girl was
interested in such possibilities. 'Often now, the Prince used the

Fig. 5 Margot dressed as a snake charmer for a fancy dress ball in the 1890s

good offices of the Rothschilds, or his new friends the Sassoons, to accomplish things for him that he could no longer do directly' because of press scrutiny of his private life.[77] In 1896 Henry Asquith told Margot some old gossip from the decade before that hinted at this genteel procurement system. Mary Anderson was a new young American acting sensation on the London stage. Ferdinand de Rothschild approached her manager with an offer of £1,000 if he could get Mary Anderson to meet the prince at Waddesdon. Mary was so angry at what was being suggested that she publicly snubbed Ferdinand's sister Alice and refused all invitations where the prince might be present.[78] His social contemporaries observed that the prince was 'taking to young girls and discarding the married women'. Margot, in her restlessness after Laura's marriage, played on the borders of this 'strange new line' of the prince's, one that might result in his friendship but would firmly establish the type of woman she was in the eyes of respectable families and predatory men (see Fig. 5). Margot's hesitation in advancing relations with the prince beyond sprightly banter in public settings showed

her awareness that, with Laura married into the most respectable
and serious of aristocratic circles, her own life risked taking a turn
into an increasingly visible demimondaine world of the fin de
siècle.

The British Army that George Wyndham entered after a year at
the Royal Military College, Sandhurst was not the one in which his
father had served, however briefly, during the Crimean War.[79] The
inadequacies revealed by that conflict had prompted a series of reforms in organisation, deployment and treatment of enlisted ranks
beginning in the late 1860s. From the perspective of aristocratic
and gentry families, the most important change was abolition of
the purchase of officer ranks and commissions. Admission to the
colleges for gentleman cadets at Sandhurst and Woolwich required
the kind of competitive examination that Winston Churchill failed
twice before squeaking into the pool of those accepted on his
third attempt.

Lodged with a 'military crammer' from July to December 1881,
George worked with a private tutor who helped him through the
mathematics, Latin, geography, English composition and drafting
he would need for the Sandhurst exams. He must have applied
himself, as he ranked eighth of seventy-three taking the exams
for entrance in February 1882.[80] Once there, the most onerous
part of the training appears to have been the sports. Mary's diary
recorded Madeline Wyndham rushing down to the school because
George had received a severe concussion in a polo match.[81] But his
commission into the Coldstream Guards was hardly in doubt. This
regiment of the Foot Guards division was not only his father's old
unit, but in 1883 it contained the highest number of officers from
the peerage and landed gentry of all parts of the British Army.[82]

Many officers in Britain's regular army concentrated their attention on the administrative, training and technological developments that would be needed to fight a major European adversary
such as Russia or France. Increasingly from the late 1870s, however, Britain's 'small wars of empire' dominated the news and determined the careers of military men. Campaigns in Afghanistan,
Zululand and the Ashanti kingdom turned officers such as Sir
Garnet Wolseley and Sir Frederick Roberts into household names,
heroes for the popular journals and boys' adventure novels that
spread as rapidly as literacy in the population at large.[83] In 1882
the theatres of conflict expanded to include north-east Africa. In

that year, despite official rhetoric in opposition to overseas expansion and colonial commitments, Gladstone's ministry found itself forced into a military action in Alexandria that resulted in the de facto takeover of Egypt. While George was at Sandhurst, his future regiment saw action for the first time since the Crimean War as part of a British force that defeated the Egyptian nationalist military leader Ahmad Arabi at Tel el-Kebir. Historians Ronald Robinson and John Gallagher attributed the subsequent wave of 'New Imperialism' to the changes in strategic relations among the great powers inaugurated by this event.[84]

The destabilisation of the Egyptian government provided the context for a revolt by the tribal peoples of the Sudan, who had been subject to increasing interference or outright control by their northern neighbour during the nineteenth century. The leader of this movement was a Sufi religious reformer, Muhammad Ahmad ibn Al-Saiyid Abdallah, who in June 1881 proclaimed himself the Mahdi, the 'Expected Guide' of true Muslims.[85] The Mahdi's followers scored a series of victories over Egyptian forces sent against them over the next two years. In the worst of these debacles an army of close to ten thousand, mostly Egyptian troops led by the British commander Colonel William Hicks, was obliterated near El Obeid on 5 November 1883. Having involved Britain in the governance of Egypt in order to protect the Suez Canal and stabilise revenues for the international investment community, Gladstone's ministers found themselves facing a religious-nationalist uprising in the Sudan that threatened to encourage Muslim opposition throughout the empire. The cabinet decided to abandon the region and isolate the Mahdi. In January 1884 it sent the legendary imperial campaigner Charles (Chinese) Gordon 1,600 miles up the Nile to evacuate Europeans, Egyptians and friendly Sudanese garrisoned at Khartoum. The plan was to stabilise the Egyptian–Sudanese border and concentrate on reform of the more vital territory of Egypt. No one anticipated that within weeks Gordon himself would be cut off from retreat and surrounded by Mahdi forces determined to capture the strategically and symbolically crucial stronghold of Khartoum.

During the year of Laura Tennant's competing courtships, Mary Elcho's first pregnancy and George Wyndham's introduction to the Coldstream Guards, the British public became increasingly absorbed by the story of Gordon's heroic siege in the remote desert regions of the upper Nile. About the time that Laura was meeting

Doll Liddell at Loch Alsh, Gladstone's cabinet reluctantly agreed
to authorise a British military incursion to rescue their beleaguered countryman. Sir Garnet Wolseley, architect of the victory
at Tel el-Kebir, was placed in command of the Gordon relief expedition.[86] Underestimating the poverty of the region, the severity
of the climate and the treacherous nature of the Nile cataracts,
Wolseley took five months to get close to Khartoum. An advance
party reached the area two days after Gordon was killed by Mahdi
forces that had taken possession of the city.

The second Suakin Expeditionary Force, led by Sir Gerald
Graham, was a sideshow to Wolseley's effort to save Gordon.[87] Af-
ter learning of the failure of that objective, Gladstone's cabinet
authorised the incursion to crush the Mahdi's allies in eastern
Sudan and occupy the territory necessary for the construction of
a railway track running two hundred miles from Suakin on the
Red Sea to Berber on the Nile. The adversaries were Hadendowa
tribesmen under the leadership of the Mahdi's local ally Osman
Digna. Graham had fought a bloody six-week campaign against
Osman early in 1884 to secure Suakin and evacuate Egyptian
garrisons along the Red Sea. At both El Teb and Tamai, Osman
encountered British troops operating in classic square formation
and incurred heavy casualties, but he remained in control of the
countryside after the British left. At the time of the second British
invasion a year later, Osman's forces were estimated to be eight
thousand to ten thousand men. Against this foe the mobilisation
committee in London had less than a month to arrange transport,
supplies and support services for some thirteen thousand fighting
men, an equal number of camels, horses and mules and ten thousand non-combatants. After destroying Osman's forces, some of
the troops were expected to stay in the area to suppress guerilla
activity and protect the railroad as it was built.

George's unit, the 1st Battalion of the Coldstream Guards, provided over eight hundred enlisted men and thirty-one officers to
the Guards Brigade, one of two British Army infantry brigades
attached to the expedition – an Indian Army infantry brigade
would join them at Suakin.[88] His father, along with his much more
vocal cousin Wilfrid Blunt, disapproved of the mission – indeed,
Percy had been the only Conservative member of parliament to
vote against the original authorisation of war in Egypt in 1882.[89]
Given the publicity that Graham's first incursion had received the
year before, George's father could have had few illusions about the

nature of the conflict that his son would encounter. On the day George embarked, Percy gave him a letter that showed the mix of reserve and tenderness characteristic of him:

> My own dearest, dearest boy, – I must say once how deeply I love you. I cannot express how I feel that my whole being is filled with *eager tender love for you*. One cannot say this speaking but I should never forgive myself if I had not told you … You know *how* I disapprove of the whole Egyptian business, so like to tell you that I send you, my own dear boy, away quite as willingly as for the justest and most necessary war imaginable. I like you to know that, that I don't think *for a moment* your most *precious* life thrown away, if the worst comes for sweet Duty's sake. We suffer for the sins and mistakes of others, as others in turn (dreadful thought) suffer and will suffer for ours, but judicially we are only responsible for what we do or leave undone ourselves … I wish I could give you, dear boy, the best thing I have, I would part with it myself to do so, my assurance of the *certainty* of life after death, and that you *will* see your loved ones again whatever happens, and if, which God forbid, you pass from this plane I should not let it alter my life but think of you as my dear George, still, whom I shall see again.[90]

Percy also mentioned that Madeline was writing to a 'friend' of George's whom they had not met, but were sure must be lovable, because George loved her. The abruptness of this leave-taking and uncertainty of the future are apparent. Barely twenty-one, George embarked on what turned out to be the adventure of a lifetime (see Fig. 6).

George's experience of small war rates barely a footnote in histories of the British Empire. The second Suakin campaign lasted less than three months before the expedition was called off. George, a captain, left England on 19 February 1885 and reached Suakin on 8 March. Hugo Elcho's brother Alan Charteris was with him, serving as aide-de-camp to Major-General Sir John M'Neill, commander of the 2nd Infantry Brigade. Around the time that their friends back home were celebrating the Tennant–Lyttelton wedding, George and Alan were preparing to return to Alexandria and then Cyprus; they reached home on 11 September. The brevity of this adventure belied its intensity. George participated in several close engagements with an enemy as alien and feared as any the British Army had encountered. He also witnessed the realities of the new wave of high-technology military action against

Fig. 6 George Wyndham, Coldstream Guards, on the eve of the
Suakin campaign

tribal adversaries that would define Western expansionism in Africa, along the borders of India and in East Asia for the next two decades.

The most recent account of this venture indicates the complexity of the operation. In addition to the three brigades of infantry, one brigade of cavalry, a battalion of mounted infantry and various artillery units, there were 'three companies of Royal Engineers (including a Photographic Section), a company of the Madras Sappers and Miners, two Telegraph Sections manned partly by Post Office reservists, a Balloon Detachment, five companies of the Commissariat and Transport Corps and a medical establishment of nearly sixty doctors and 470 men of the Medical Staff Corps'.[91] Logistics entailed bringing infantry from England, Malta and Egypt, as well as native Sikh and Bengali units from India. The forces would consume some thirty tons of food per day and require tens of thousands of items of clothing, ammunition, saddles, harnesses, soaps, oils and utensils. Wood had to be imported from Cyprus and India, meat from Odessa and forage from England. Water, as George often noted, was a particular problem. The humans alone needed nearly four hundred tons a day, supplied by distilling ships in the Red Sea. The challenge of safely storing the output and transporting it inland to the front lines was never fully solved before the expedition was called off.

George's letters home provided vivid and apparently accurate glimpses of some of the novel features of this massive incursion.[92] He noted the arrival of infantry and two artillery batteries from New South Wales, the first time colonial troops were incorporated into a British expeditionary force. He reported that his transport ship had electric lighting and that the *Dolphin*, moored at Suakin, was able to sweep four miles of countryside with spotlights to pick out enemy trying to infiltrate the camps at night. He disparaged the failures of the reconnaissance balloons and was reluctant to use the expensive telegraph facilities (over two shillings a word) except to send news of 'a proper battle'. George never mentioned the automatic weapons that were brought along. The density of mimosa shrub at the location of key engagements, and Osman's refusal to initiate the full-scale assault in open territory that Graham hoped for, reduced the usefulness of the Gardner machine guns that were available. Charles Callwell, the indefatigable cataloguer of lessons from Britain's new 'small wars', explained the problems in employing such weapons in the terrain like that surrounding Suakin: 'In hill warfare these weapons scarcely get a proper chance, as they are not very well suited for picking off individuals, and as it is dangerous to thrust them too far to the front with the small parties which are so much used in operations of this class. In bush warfare also the want of a fair target is unfavourable to them, and when the shooting is at short range the personnel is likely to be put *hors de combat*'.[93] George's company kept the enemy at bay with Martini-Henry rifles and bayonets.

George described other realities of the campaign not amenable to technological solutions. He and his fellow lieutenant James Drummond-Hay conducted an insect hunt in their tent that produced scorpions, three-inch centipedes and a nest of sand-hoppers. White ants that devoured fabric forced him to place his bag on a pedestal of glass bottles, and later in the spring the flies were so severe that 'the traps we set of beer and sugar become tumblers of *solid* black in about an hour. At night, fortunately, they sleep, but, as they cover everything, whenever you touch your coat or blanket a great "buzzing" arises in the dark.' Gearing his letters to the recipient, he told his younger sisters amusing stories of the camp animals and 'natives of all colours, some quite black, much

blacker than niggers' who reminded him 'of penwipers and or-
naments for holding stamps and sealing wax'.[94] Graham was criticised later for over-reliance on pack animals, with the hundreds of
non-combatant handlers necessary to deal with them. Much of the
activity and even the fighting of the campaign involved protecting
these vital logistical components. On his second day in the theatre
George supervised the movement of supplies to the Coldstream
Guards' camp on the few miles of railroad already in place. Even
with that aid to transport, he had to spend fifteen hours pitching
in with three score of enlisted ranks to load and offload the goods.
In his accounts to his parents, he remained, as in Paris, handily in
control of the situation, working hard, maintaining his sense of
humour and reassuring to those back home.

The Coldstream Guards saw combat twice during the campaign,
though they missed the fiercest action at the Battle of Tofrek on
22 March 1885, since they were escorting a supply convey to the
north that day. For an inexperienced unit, their first engagement
was severe enough. On 20 March, two weeks after the Coldstream
Guards' arrival, Graham marched eight thousand of his troops
about eight miles to the west of Suakin to disperse an enemy force
estimated at three thousand and to occupy the hills around Hashin in preparation for later action to the south. While the Berk-
shires and Royal Marines assaulted the elevations, the Coldstream
Guards remained in reserve in the enormous square formed to
protect against attack from any direction, but they were nearly
overrun when their own cavalry and mounted infantry raced into
the corner with the enemy close behind. 'The two coming together
completely rolled up the rear face for some minutes, my company,
No. 6, were practically ridden over, and 5, 4 and 3 were all pushed
together; the bullets began to come pretty sharp and a good many
were hit at the same time.'[95]

Later in the day the Coldstream Guards formed the square's
rear face on the retreat back to Suakin. Since the enemy quickly
reoccupied several of the hills, George's unit came under continuous fire. 'It was a trying ordeal for inexperienced troops', writes
Brian Robson. 'If Osman's men had been better shots, the Guards
could have been in a critical position.'[96] As it was, Graham lost
twenty-nine men and thirty were wounded in a ponderous action
that allowed most of the enemy to escape to the south and took
territory that could not be held in strength in any case. As George
told his father, 'I do not understand how they mean to march us

through this country when they can't supply us with water sitting still.'[97]

George was tired and sunburned enough from this four-teen-hour foray to spend the next day in his tent. The rest of the week was more draining. Two days after the march on Hashin, Graham initiated his major action towards Osman's stronghold at Tamai, twenty miles to the south-west. Along the way he intended to establish the thorn-protected encampments called *zeribas* in order to store water and supplies for a large advance. The first of these was being constructed at Tofrek, six miles from Suakin, with troops under Major-General Sir John M'Neill, when a sud-den attack of five thousand Hadendowa nearly overwhelmed the work parties and partially formed squares. Discipline and steady return fire by experienced Sikh, Berkshire and 28th Bombay Native infantry units prevented a massacre of the British forces. Alan Charteris, in the thick of this action, was speared through the wrist, but managed to kill his attacker and another man before the twenty-minute furore subsided. The British suffered 10 per cent casualties among their fighting forces – some three hundred killed and wounded – as well as more than 150 non-combatant deaths. A third of M'Neill's transport animals were lost, having been caught between the attacking and defending forces. Enemy dead were estimated at 1,500.[98]

The Coldstream Guards came across this carnage a day later and lived in its midst for the rest of the week as they escorted supply convoys half-way to Suakin and back while the *zeriba* was reprovi-sioned. 'When we got near the *zeriba* I had the first taste of what are called the horrors of war and these are nasty', George wrote; 'the whole country round is strewn and reeks of dead camels and bodies; my stomach heaved a good deal.' On 24 March he was himself under attack when the enemy assaulted his convoy 'with our square full of camels':

> I commanded the right half of No. 6 on the right side of the square, on which the Arabs charged. I stood behind two front rank men kneeling who had no rear rank men and got a splendid view. They came straight at my half company, only one reached the bayonets, about fifteen got to within seven yards. I have got the shield of the leader of the charge who rolled over in front of me just as I was going to use my revolver.[99]

To his father George relayed the specific casualties of the

engagement (Beecroft and Gribble, Corporal Bowens, Brigade Major Dalrymple, two Marine officers), and noted that the Coldstream Guards were routinely under fire at night and every time they went to meet a convoy: 'No words can describe what the stink in the *zeriba* was like.' The cold at night was so severe that everyone got up at 2.30 a.m. to walk around until sunrise.[100]

The Coldstream Guards returned to Suakin where they spent a week before taking part in Graham's full-scale advance on Osman's putative stronghold at Tamai. The march was exhausting and uncomfortable but, even at George's junior officer level, rumours had suggested that the enemy would not be found. 'You will have seen by the papers that the great battle of Tamai "as was to be" ended in a fizzle', George told his mother three days later:

> It would have been very pretty if the Arabs had held these ridges and we had carried them one by one, but they did not, cause why! they had all brushed off bag and baggage with the camels and herds and all, leaving only a small force with rifles on the other side of the khor; these made rather good practice at our rear face of the square ... and the bullets came pretty thick. Lambrook in my company was shot through the arm ... One bullet struck between the legs of the man I was walking beside ... We found the huts, threshing floors, goat pens, etc., of what must have been a very great number of Arabs. We found no water so we retired, burning the huts and ammunition in them, and got back at 12 o'clock.[101]

The Coldstream Guards spent another month in gruelling heat protecting the railway supply fort at Handub and chasing down small attachments of the enemy in the surrounding hills. There they learned that the expedition was being withdrawn except for a garrison at Suakin itself. George's youthful summation of the tactical and strategic failures of the campaign indicate that Graham should have begun work on the railway immediately as a way of drawing Osman into the full-scale open attack that would favour British defensive power. Failing that, he should have force-marched a smaller number of troops straight to Tamai after the battles of Hashin and Tofrek: 'It would have looked risky but been quite safe, they would have arrived on the Monday evening (instead of Tuesday week as we did) and caught the defeated army with all its wounded, half of them not having had time to water. All the herds and women were there so they must have fought and the war would be over.'[102] The ponderous and desultory nature of the action resulted in much public criticism for Graham, and his military career never recovered.

George's correspondence from the Suakin expedition provides fascinating detail of a junior officer's experiences in a small war of empire. A young aristocrat wholly outside his normal environment, he was observant, intelligent, able to provide amusing stories of mundane inaction, as well as reassuringly flat narratives of more dangerous moments. Not surprisingly, his letters did not stray far from the genre of military writing that his generation provided in other eye-witness accounts. On the transit to Suakin, George read two recent books to provide himself with the 'textual knowledge gathered before the fact' that characterised savvy British travellers: Josiah Williams's *Life in the Sudan* (1884) and F. L. James's *Wild Tribes of the Sudan* (1883).[103] He sounded disappointed that each had only a chapter on Suakin and its inhabitants. But he would also have been aware of Graham's actions in the same region the year before from accounts such as Bennett Burleigh's *Desert Warfare* (1884) that relied on the author's war correspondence for the *Daily Telegraph.*

Thus George was intellectually prepared for some of what his own letters conveyed: the enemy was a faceless horde of adversaries, nearly inhuman in its ability to withstand hardship and sacrifice lives – including those of women and children – for the salvation promised by ruthless religious leaders. There were hostile tribes and neutral ones, the latter inclined to hang back and even cooperate with the British if it was safe to do so. The native peoples had the advantage in knowing how to live in their forbidding landscape. But the British soldier inhabited a small bubble of rationality, order, discipline, comradeship and logistical support that extended all the way home. For George, the psychic link to normality included his family. From the appalling circumstances of M'Neill's *zeriba* he wrote, 'I think of you all a *great deal* and am sure I feel quite plainly that you are thinking of me. I do not feel at all far away or separated from you in any way and have long talks with you in imagination.'[104]

George did not entirely avoid mention of the horrors of this conflict. When he rode through the area where his own face-to-face encounter with the charging foe had occurred, he 'was surprised at the number of graves, skulls, hands and toes sticking up everywhere. We seem to have killed a good many more that day than we thought at first.'[105] During actions in the northern hills in early May, he reported shooting enemy in retreat and the encounter of one friend with a wounded Arab:

> Austen in the Camel Corps, whom I left on the first hill, was wounded; he went up to an Arab on the ground on the right, – wounded I believe by my men – when about ten yards off the Arab jumped up and went for him. He fired his revolver hitting him in the left shoulder, then on the right side, but still the Arab lifted his spear as he fired his third shot which blew the Arab's brains out. He was knocked over by the spear sticking into his right arm, cutting the artery, however a doctor was near and he is all right now.[106]

But in general the deaths and appalling wounds he must have seen did not figure in George's accounts. He did not mention the gruesome injuries that someone captured by the Mahdi's forces would supposedly face or the fear this engendered. In print, at least, he did not imagine himself into the realities of the Hadendowas's combat experience. Forty years later, a biographer of Osman Digna conducting oral interviews in the Sudan ran across a story from the other side of the action at M'Neill's *zeriba*. After charging through part of one ill-formed British square, Osman's forces fled before the concentrated fire of the Royal Marines in the northern defensive position, including the Gardner gun they had got working. Prostrate behind a thorn bush, one young warrior wondered to a comrade, 'Why do the Inglizi shoot at me and me only? What have I done to draw down their wrath upon me? They must be mad to expend so much energy and so many bullets upon me who am but a dog.' The other replied, 'They do not shoot at us alone, the bullets are everywhere; the whole world is in a blaze.'[107] George did not mention what the destruction of supply stores at Tamai would mean to the families of Osman's tribesmen or the fact that wounded Hadendowa were routinely executed in the field because they might launch the kind of final, suicidal attack that his friend faced.[108] His respect for this ferociously courageous adversary did not, in these letters, translate into doubts about the mission. George always appeared to hope that he would be part of the definitive battle, such as Omdurman provided in 1898, which would crush the opposition entirely.

Safely back in Alexandria and facing nothing more formidable than heat, flies and disease, George told his father that everything he had confronted in his 'little war' was just what he had expected: 'in fact nearly everything in the world has been described so often and so well that travelling is superfluous and writing descriptions ridiculous when you ought to be able, instead, to quote chapter and verse from some book'.[109] Nevertheless, no amount of school toughening, military discipline or literary clichés for understanding the enemy had prepared George for the psychological shocks of this conflict. Letters to his sister in the months after his return documented his restlessness, lethargy and depression. He found nothing satisfying in his old life of Coldstream Guards duties and resigned his commission in 1887 to begin a career in politics.

In an appreciation of Stephen Crane's *Red Badge of Courage* written a decade later, George noted that only the artist, not the descriptive narrator, could convey the emotional truths of combat: the 'stenches that sicken in after-life at any chance allusion to decay … the storms of passions that force yells of defiance out of inarticulate clowns; the winds of fear that sweep by night along prostrate ranks'.[110] Individual soldiers, receiving 'rude and swift answers in the field' to boyish speculations about courage, kept their secrets 'with masonic self-possession'. Throughout his life George would be accused of loquaciousness – but not about his experiences of combat. His attempts to come to terms with his experiences could be found in unpublished poems about 'a captain's death in the desert' or a lonely soldier dying on a far-off battlefield, in repeated metaphors of 'grim eternal Sphinxes', desolate landscapes or the hopelessness of 'some wild tribe' succumbing to 'a higher race'. Four years later he was having nightmares of 'hacking my way … through mounds of men', images that disturbed his sleep at night.[111]

George's reactions conformed to modern diagnoses of trauma. The concrete sensations – smells, sounds, sights – associated with heightened states of anxiety or horror can trigger those emotional responses for years afterwards, undermining the everyday self through the sudden revelation of its lack of control.[112] As he moved into a life of politics, journalism and literary research, George carried these traces with him in ways that most men in the circles he inhabited did not discuss, if they had experienced them at all. Nearly twenty years to the day after his combat in the Sudan, George suffered a nervous breakdown that forced his resignation from the seat he had held in Arthur Balfour's cabinet for the past three years.

Margot Tennant's 'small wars' occurred where they mostly did for women of her class and generation at the heart of privileged society. In the hunting households of some of Britain's highest aristocracy, she gained the attentions for which she had competed so fiercely in her own home, but in ways that identified her with physicality and sexual availability. Men laughed at her quips while groping at her body – her later unpublished essays and story fragments contain recurring tropes of 'leering' aggressive men reaching for girls with great hot dirty hands.[113] Women gossiped about the fact that she put herself in situations where this could happen. When in her teenage years and early twenties she both knew and did not know what she was doing. Her diary shows her narrating and commenting on her own escapades as though she was the omniscient author of some racy society novel, but she was also developing an increasingly brittle and hoydenish demeanour.

George's conflict occurred on a gendered stage as well. He survived the appalling physical perils and atrocities of combat only to encounter threats that were more subterranean – those eruptions of emotionality he could not will away, but that he had to handle alone and interpret as personal weakness. As Janet Oppenheim observes, in this era 'nervous exhaustion brought men perilously close to the feminine condition'.[114] There is no evidence that he was aware of the emerging discourse of these years that was exploring the interplay between shock, emotionality and mental control by articulating the role of the unconscious – and a recent scholar has found almost no discussion of the subject as it related to soldiers or combat.[115] But if Margot was developing a reputation for being hard, George, despite the clear evidence of his courage, was susceptible to the charge that he was soft, lacking in manly control.

Love and violence – passionate attachment and heroic adventure – were two of the most familiar tropes through which privileged young Victorians like Margot and George could explore the inner self in relation to social identities constructed around duty, respectability and family precepts.[116] Yet for them, the realities of desire and danger threatened not only the physical body but the emotional integrity of the self. It is not clear that they were in denial. Both practised a form of self-therapy through writing journals, poetry or private letters that helped contain troubling events by retelling them. But in coming to terms with this 'world of now-a-days', they were increasingly aware of strong emotional responses that felt natural but were inappropriate to the worlds they inhabited. Margot was too defiant and wilful, George too sad and easily agitated. Neither found comfort in the high-minded

Christian discourse that Laura and Alfred used, and both began to adopt the cultural vocabulary of relentless struggle that formed an increasing part of the Western *zeitgeist* after 1870. In this grim worldview, unending strife formed the subtext in all domains of life, from the inner landscape of the individual, to status or re-source competitions within groups, to wars between peoples and nations. At stake, or so both George and Margot thought as they emerged into adulthood, was literally physical, psychological and social survival.

Interlude:
'The Pivot of Politics'

FOR ARTHUR BALFOUR and George Pembroke, the excitements of their friends' private lives played out against the political dramas that unfolded with the collapse of Gladstone's government in the spring of 1885. Three weeks after the wedding of Laura Tennant and Alfred Lyttelton, the ministry was defeated in the House of Commons when the Conservatives forced a surprise division with too few Liberals present to support their own side. Gladstone resigned on 12 June and Queen Victoria invited Lord Salisbury to form the first Tory government in decades without Disraeli among its leadership. With Conservatives still a minority in the Commons, a general election was needed, but this would be delayed for several months while voter lists could be prepared to reflect the franchise and redistricting reforms of the past year. No one knew the implications of the 'new order of politics' that readjusted urban and county constituencies and expanded the electorate by more than two million voters, a quarter of them Irish.[1] Salisbury's cabinet of the summer 1885 through February 1886 ran a 'caretaker' ministry while awaiting the electoral verdict of the new democracy. The Conservatives still managed to annex upper Burma – a territory the size of France – and pass the Ashbourne land act that confirmed the party's commitment to helping Irish tenants buy out their landlords through government-assisted loans.

The manoeuvre to bring down Gladstone was devised at Arthur's London house at 4 Carlton Gardens, a quiet family residence more associated with experiments in psychical phenomena than political or social power-broking.[2] The choice reflected the political role that Arthur had been assuming in the past few years. As Randolph Churchill grabbed the headlines with bravura parliamentary and platform challenges aimed at both the Liberals and the 'old gang' leadership of his own side, Arthur stayed behind the scenes in the kinds of advisory work at which he excelled. In 1881 he had become the youngest of the six-member Conservative Central Committee that allocated funds for the party.[3] The position put him at the heart of struggles between Churchill, Salisbury and the Tory leader in the House of Commons, Sir Stafford Northcote, to reorganise and re-message the party after the trouncing it received in 1880. Two years later he became a trustee of the *National Review*, a monthly journal created to 'present to the nation the various aspects of Conservative sentiment and opinion' on subjects 'not only political, but philosophical, literary, and social'.[4] He and George Pembroke began producing articles almost immediately. Although Arthur had made little impression on the public, he was acquiring an inside knowledge of players and legislative processes for the time when the Conservatives would return to power. His reward came in the change of government in 1885 when Salisbury made him president of the Local Government Board. Randolph Churchill, six months younger than Arthur, became secretary of state for India with a seat in the cabinet.

George Pembroke received no offer that summer, and he confessed to feeling 'rather sore at being so completely ignored'.[5] Despite his friendship with Arthur, his relationship with the new prime minister was not close. His well-publicised religious scepticism made him unwelcome to Lady Salisbury at Hatfield, and in 1881 he had disputed Salisbury's claims to lead the Tory peers in the House of Lords after Disraeli's death.[6] As he wrote later to Lord Carnarvon, 'I have seldom heard him make a speech that did not contain something that was really insulting to the intelligence or the candour of his supporters and I have often felt that if I who was on his side was so much irritated by his insincere and claptrappy arguments, the rubbishness of which he usually scorned to take the trouble to disguise, how exasperating and provocative of contradiction he must seem to others.' George feared that Salisbury's rhetorical abrasiveness would bring retribution on the House of Lords and lose the Conservatives their chance of becoming a 'party of moderation and common sense' that could attract Whigs and independents in combination against the radicals they saw as dominating the Liberal Party. In late 1884, Eddie Hamilton thought that George might lead a cave of young peers in opposition to what they viewed as Salisbury's strategic missteps in challenging the reform legislation.[7]

George admitted that he had not pushed himself forward for one of the minor party positions available in the Lords. Tory leaders might also be forgiven for thinking he was simply unavailable. In autumn 1883, just as he was about to join a royal commission on housing for the working classes, George had a serious hunting accident. His broken leg took months to heal, and a fractured collar bone resulted in bronchitis and pleurisy. In January 1884 he nearly died from convulsions caused by high fever.[8] He missed both the royal commission and most of the parliamentary manoeuvrings over electoral reform. Concerns about his health troubled his friends, as did the sense that he was running afoul of the party's emerging leadership. 'To be left out now means with him I fear practically political obliteration', worried Eddie Hamilton, 'which in the case of a man of such sterling qualities and sound abilities is to be deplored.' George was stoic but pessimistic. 'I am afraid it means being shelved for good and all, for it is difficult to squeeze anyone in when they have once dropped out.'[9]

Nevertheless, George had claims to inclusion among the Conservative 'intelligentsia' that was forming to combat radical initiatives on the great questions of the day. He gave himself a crash course in the readings on political economy he had missed by discontinuing his formal education at seventeen: 'I have a sort of chronic whirl of Mill, Spencer, Humboldt, Fitzjames Stephens and Huxley in my head and cannot get a clear idea about the lot of them.'[10] His conclusions were published by the new Liberty and Property Defence League he had joined after it was founded by Lord Wemyss, Hugo Elcho's father, the year before. He spoke routinely to farmers' associations and local political clubs throughout Wiltshire and wrote letters to the press on subjects ranging from land policy to reform of the House of Lords. During the months of Salisbury's caretaker ministry George was immersed in outreach to the voters of the new Wiltshire South constituency.

When it finally arrived, the outcome of the 1885 election carried messages both hopeful and disconcerting for Conservatives. The Balfour brothers were among the fortunate. Arthur's old 'corrupt' seat for Hertford had been abolished in the redistricting. After initial hesitations, he accepted an offer to run for one of the new Manchester city divisions. The local agents appeared 'to be of the opinion that a taste for Metaphysics & Tennis will recommend me to the Working Men of Manchester', he wrote to his uncle – nevertheless there was 'perhaps a considerable risk' that he might lose.

Gerald became the candidate for Leeds Central, where his sister-in-law doubted his chances: 'He speaks MUCH too fast, drives a subject past its interest, is too minute and consequently dull, and too long ... the exact reproduction of manner which he has when in excited conversation, the same rapid torrent of words especially if he is riled.'[11] Nevertheless, both Balfours were elected – Arthur with 55 per cent of the vote – thus hitching their political fortunes to the emerging 'villa Tory' constituencies of small-propertied professional, commercial and working-class interests that would sustain the Conservative Party for the next century.

In their social circles, however, the negative results seemed more portentous. Rural voters entering the political process for the first time rejected the control of the hereditary great families in a sweeping indictment of relationships that were centuries old:[12] 'Carnage among county Tories was immense. The names of the fallen read like a roll of honour on a memorial to the territorial constitution ... No less than 70 such country gentlemen and sons of peers failed to return to the Commons.'[13] Among them was Pembroke's brother Sidney Herbert, who lost his bid for Wiltshire South. Percy Wyndham had already decided to give up the Commons when his constituency was abolished. Hugo Elcho received only 30 per cent of the votes cast in the family's home district of Haddington. He was roundly beaten by the rising Liberal politician Richard B. Haldane.[14] The message for the new generation of Conservatives was clear: adapt to the broadened electorate or face eclipse as one of the two great parties of the empire.

Complicating the outlook for the next parliamentary session were the results from Ireland. The National League founded by Charles Stewart Parnell to represent the cause of home rule swept the Irish constituencies. Parnellites won eighty-five seats, plus one heavily Irish constituency in Liverpool. Through an astute deployment of their best candidates they even gained seventeen of the thirty-three seats in Protestant Ulster. Neither Liberals nor Conservatives had a sufficient majority to stay in power without propitiating the Irish.

What exactly this would entail became clearer in December. On the 15th, Gladstone paid a surprise visit to Eaton Hall, the home of the Duke of Westminster, where Arthur was staying for a house party. During a private conversation with the young man he had admitted to his family circle so many years before, the Liberal leader seemed to offer the Conservatives a deal – Liberal support for a

Salisbury ministry *if* it would address Ireland's political aspirations. Five days later Gladstone's son Herbert leaked the news that his father, persuaded by the overwhelming mandate that the Irish voters had given, would embrace home rule. This 'kite' – what we would now call a trial balloon – released Salisbury from having to consider a Faustian bargain. The Liberals, with Irish support, would form a new government in February and presumably push for a significant alteration of the political constitution.

As so often in the history of the British Isles, small, impoverished Ireland disrupted English politics in ways that were hardly predetermined. Gladstone's decision to introduce home rule legislation in 1886 split his party. The aristocratic Whig interests led by Lord Hartington refused to support him. So did the radical wing associated with Joseph Chamberlain, his Birmingham caucus and his progressive legislative agenda. The home rule bill was defeated in the Commons in June 1886, requiring another election the next month that would constitute a referendum on Gladstone's initiative. The Conservatives gained more than sixty seats, strengthening their hold on the London metropolitan area and winning back some of the county constituencies lost the year before. The final tally showed that 'Gladstone had crashed stunningly' in thinking he could rouse the English democracy on behalf of a moral campaign for Irish aspirations. The Tories now held 316 seats, twenty short of a majority. They would have to rely on the support of about eighty dissidents from the opposition side, soon called Liberal Unionists. Gladstone had fewer than two hundred supporters, plus Parnell's Irish nationalists.[15]

The Conservative Party would hold office for the next six years and dominate the governing system until the return of a new liberalism in 1906. But it was not the party that Arthur and George had joined in 1874. Over half of the Conservatives elected in 1886 were new to Westminster.[16] Some were 'a younger generation of traditional county Conservatives retaking the ground strewn with the political corpses of their fathers'.[17] Others were men who had made their own way in banking, civil service, law or industry. They were not as familiar to the traditional aristocracy as the Whig grandees whom the Conservatives had been meeting in society and country houses all their lives.

Richard Shannon calls the events of 1885–86 the 'pivot of politics' in modernising Britain.[18] Angus Hawkins writes that '1886 stands alongside 1846 as a moment of dramatic reconfiguration in

British party politics'.[19] Everywhere, from drawing rooms to clubs to party headquarters, strange alliances were forming and old friendships ruptured. All was fluid as new people, new ideas and new behaviours reached the metropolitan heart of empire like an unexpected storm surge that one could not escape, only hope to survive.[20]

4

Strange Friends

Margot Tennant and George Pembroke

A S THE MOST IMPORTANT political realignments in a generation played themselves out in Westminster, Margot went off to Easton Grey to hunt and stay out of the way during the confinement that Laura was expecting after eleven months of marriage. Saturday, 17 April 1886, was a good day for hunting – hot and sunny, Margot recalled – 'and the woods were full of children'. That morning in the field was also the last day of her old life. She was riding through a forest with one of her suitors, separated from the pack. Turning to rejoin the chase, her horse misjudged a jump and she was knocked unconscious when a tree branch caught her square in the face. Her companion scooped her up and took her to a farmer's cottage.[1] Margot had suffered another head injury, but given her sensitivity to women's looks, she was probably more distressed to find her face disfigured by a broken nose and torn lip that required stitches. The accident altered her appearance, and for months her friends noted side effects that would now be seen as typical of concussion. But Margot's uncontrollable moods and inability to concentrate could equally have been the result of an overwhelming grief.[2]

Though Margot did not know it until after her accident, Laura was in dire circumstances in the same hours. The delivery of her baby during the night before had not gone well. According to Lady Tennant, the doctors began giving Laura chloroform on Friday afternoon, but she had been sleepless and in pain for two days before that. 'Laura is so slow', her mother wrote. 'She has not had a smile for a long time, and looks dreadfully worn. I am glad Alfred has been away all day … now past 5 … I feel worn too with anxiety.' After a 'fearful struggle' involving obstetrical instruments, Alfred

Christopher Lyttelton was born in the early morning hours. Telegrams flew across the countryside announcing the safe outcome, and Charles Tennant left the city to spend Easter week in Glasgow. Two days later Laura's condition deteriorated. A 'dreadful bleeding from the liver began, blood coming from her mouth every twenty minutes or so; she became utterly unconscious, and remained so all through Tuesday.' The next morning Laura came to herself, regaining 'even power of speech, and Alfred was able to induce her to take food by appealing to her.' She asked the doctors, 'Shall I get well? Are you sure? Are you sure?' The doctors pronounced her revival a miracle. But the next day she again refused food and became difficult to rouse. 'Alfred's name was I think the last word she uttered' before losing consciousness again.[3]

By this time Margot had reached London. On Tuesday evening when her sister's death seemed imminent, she defied her doctor and took a late train to the city where Spencer Lyttelton and Evan Charteris met her at the station at midnight. On Wednesday she saw Laura who, despite the brief rally earlier, did not recognise her. Margot counted the petals on a daisy by the drawing room window – they told her there was no hope. She spent hours lying on the floor in the corridor listening to the muffled comings and goings of Alfred, Charty, the maids, medical people and clergymen. On Good Friday she refused to go to church with her sister Lucy: 'I was tired – tired of life and death and tired of praying. God knew too well what I wanted – I had offered to be a cripple for life to let Laura live and play with her baby. I had spent my very breath on prayers every second of the day.' Alfred's widowed sister Lady Frederick Cavendish spent the evening telling her 'how all their family had died that week – and she went through the list till I longed to scream'.

On Saturday morning, a week after Christopher's birth and her own accident, Margot was summoned to witness her sister's last moments. In a quiet room, sunlight 'playing on the window-blinds', Laura died in Margot's arms with Alfred kneeling at the bedside. Margot said that the room was full of people, but she mentioned only Alfred's minister brother reciting prayers. Remembering a promise made to her sister weeks before, Margot read out Laura's will with its last words and small bequests to special friends, Arthur and Gerald Balfour, Frances Horner and Mary Elcho among them.

After Laura's death, people made more of her premonitory fears than they had during her last weeks of pregnancy. Perhaps one in two hundred women of Laura's age cohort and social class died in childbirth – considerably worse than the one in several thousand odds faced by women with access to modern obstetrical treatments. Laura's very small frame and the fact that her baby was long overdue were warning signs. 'I am still well alas!' she wrote eleven days before her confinement. 'I never thought I should have an indolent child!'[4] Babies make significant weight gains as time passes after full term, and Alfred Christopher was a 9lb newborn. Though Doll Liddell wrote in his diary that the doctors did not know what killed Laura, her death certificate recorded that she died of internal haemorrhage and exhaustion.

Even her most devout friends could not turn this into the kind of 'good death' piously recorded for Alfred's mother or George Pembroke's father 25 years earlier. Their demises were made to fit an inspirational Christian ideal that dominated conventional discourse through the mid-Victorian era. On this model, the dying remained conscious and aware of impending mortality, weakened but not wracked with suffering. There was time to gather the family, give assurances of reconciliation to God's will and deliver final messages of love and blessing. Laura's death, like May Lyttelton's, was 'harrowing' and hard to idealise.[5] She remained in her own home, but with the Easter holidays beginning the house was a confused mix of people coming and going. She was barely conscious during the last three or four days, and 'the *real* work', as Arthur Balfour wrote to Margot, was done by 'hired Doctors and hired nurses, and done much better'. The final words that Margot recorded from her sister were rending for anyone familiar with Laura's diary, for they showed no sense of a spiritual presence. 'I think God has forgotten me', she murmured, the last conscious sentiment that Margot attributed to her.[6] 'Every shadow seemed to be looking with pity on the silence of that room', Margot wrote, 'the long silence that has never been broken.'

For many of her contemporaries, Laura's fate was meaningless. 'I cannot tell you how this death affects me', Lady Burne-Jones wrote. 'I have never felt the snatching of anybody from life so deeply, except in the case of my very nearest. And, in its circumstances it is a violent death, the very thought of which associated with such a tender creature is shocking. Surely no woman was ever more widely loved.' 'A death like Laura's one *cannot* understand', Mary Elcho told her mother. 'One cannot understand anything that happens or does not happen.' Margot said there was 'a relentless stern almost murderous rapidity about *Laura's* death which I shall never understand – never never'. 'You can but sorrow WILDLY, for a time. Alas! I know it too well', wrote Lady Wemyss, 'the only thing is to face one's sorrows to the full, and endure as best one may.'[7]

Alfred and Margot both said that in this tragedy they found Arthur's letters the most consoling. 'I do not believe – I never will believe', Arthur wrote the day after Laura died, 'that even now and here Love cannot bridge over, though it be but feebly and imperfectly, the chasm of separation made by Death: – those we love and who love us must still be able in some faint and scarcely audible way to whisper to us over the impassable gulf: – but even if not, even if they may not speak, or our ears be too gross to hear, still this is Easter Day: – and who can doubt its message at such a time?'[8] Arthur's search for scientific evidence of the soul's survival after death led to his much studied interest in mediums and systematic investigation of supernatural phenomena. He was among the founders of the Society for Psychical Research and served as its president in 1893–94 when he was opposition leader in the Commons. But neither he nor Margot ever reported the kind of direct, transcendent connection with the departed that could prove that separation was not permanent.[9] Arthur's greatest contribution to his friends was his will to believe otherwise and the example of restrained grief that acknowledged intense emotional pain without succumbing to despair.

'I long for her memory to be kept green amongst those who knew her', Georgiana Burne-Jones wrote. 'Perhaps hers will be the rare lot of being remembered.' The accumulation of artefacts dedicated to Laura reflected the suspicion that these might be the only survival she would have. Frances Horner asked Burne-Jones to design a plaque in Laura's memory for the little church at Mells. He decorated it with a handsome art nouveau peacock and a Latin message, the translation of which read: 'Thou liest in the far north, O most beloved, but here also we who loved thee have set up a stone in token of our inconsolable grief.'[10] The artist also painted her as the mysterious mermaid who drags her drowned lover to the ocean floor in his *The Depths of the Sea,* completed the same year. Two years later Mrs Humphrey Ward dedicated *Robert Elsmere,* the novel of her generation's crisis of faith, to Laura and the philosopher T. H. Green. Frances Horner and DD Balfour wrote her into published fiction of their own.[11]

'She had a unique almost indescribable power of brightening

and making happy those who came across her', wrote George Pembroke, 'a power that her unlimited kindness always delighted to exercise ... Everyone who knew her as a friend, and their name is legion, seems to feel it a personal loss. It is a great testimony to Laura that those who knew her best always loved her most.'[12] Memories of Laura became a nearly mystical repository for an ideal of emotional behaviour in which warmth, compassion and benign intent underlay companionship. To this innocence about motive and reception – naiveté, in the eyes of the jaded – Laura grafted the possibility of a greater candour and expressiveness than many of her friends were used to, with lines of psychological closeness crossing even the boundaries of gender. As the consolations of communion with the divine waned in this generation, the need for sympathetic affect became more compelling. People who had known Laura thought they had never met 'a sweeter or more generous character. She did not know what it was to think ill or evil of anyone ... this made her, with her bright witty mind, a delightful friend. She would have grown in depth as she thought more, and had more experience; charity covers a multitude of sins, and she was genuinely charitable.'[13] With Laura's death, the world of friendship and sociability worsened, a shield having been removed against the competition and instrumental use of others that much in privileged life suggested were as natural and inescapable in social as in biological interaction.

Margot's splendid girlhood diary ended with Laura's funeral. The self-mockingly exaggerated heroine of her own adventures disappeared, not to resurface when she took up diary writing again in the early 1890s. In some ways Margot never got over this death. She spent her life expropriating Laura's memory, correcting perceptions that her sister had been 'goody' or too pure to live and endlessly comparing herself to the lost ideal. After a few months she began to write Laura's name in wavering, underlined capital letters as though the mention alone evoked an ethereal essence. In the 1920s, she used Laura's given name Octavia as the title of a *roman-à-clef* about a young sporting woman torn between different loves; she presented an extended portrait of Laura's brief life in her autobiography and occasionally mixed up her sister's wedding date with her own.[14]

Letters that Margot wrote and received replace the diary to some extent. Those from the summer of 1886 show her seeking

consolation from people who had known Laura. She dined with
the Wyndhams, visited Stanway, entertained at Glen and attended
the Leeds musical festival with an assortment of friends and relations – Arthur Sullivan was not a good conductor, she decided.
'He sits down and looks as if it was rather a triumph coming in
a dead heat with the orchestra.' She loathed the 'cruel philosophy' of Victorian mourning that restricted social life to show the
depth of one's bereavement. Internal grief was far worse than human interaction; it 'drives the iron deeper into one's soul than
anything'.[15] Even her stationery showed how unwilling she was to
eclipse herself for a socially mandated demonstration of feelings.
Within the requisite dense black border she emblazoned a facsim-
ile of her signature 'Margot', boldly alone in the upper corner.
Nevertheless, she was flailing – 'blinded by the fury of passionate
resentment I felt'[16] – and in the process tested the boundaries of
propriety more than ever.

Everyone seems to have known that Evan Charteris, Hugo
Elcho's brother, was unrequitedly in love with Margot, yet she had
to write several apologies for letting him stay late at night in her
room during the Stanway visit in August.[17] In London, she had
a blow-up with her mother who found that she had let Arthur
Balfour's friend Spencer Lyttelton into her bedroom one night
when he was supposed to have left the house. After Spencer's
embarrassed retreat, Margot instructed Lady Tennant on how surveillance would create the behaviour it aimed to prevent: 'I said,
"Mama, you mustn't follow me if you think its too late say so but
never do what you did tonight I won't stand it I'm 22 and if you
don't trust me you'll make me bad and we shan't be friends. I *must*
have friends I thirst for them and even they can't satisfy one's ach-
ing and longing but they're what I like best".'[18] She was defiant
because she felt 'bitter and rebellious' over her loss. But she was
also trying to work through romantic and sexual entanglements
that had begun earlier, now placed in a new context by Laura's
brief marriage and its tragic denouement. One of the not so subtle
messages of Laura's fate was that domesticity could kill.

Spencer and Evan were not the only men Margot met in bed-
chambers at this time. For months she had been in love with Peter
Flower, the 'fascinating out-of-doors animal' she knew from the
hunting scene. Margot gave a thinly veiled account of what Peter
meant to her in *Octavia*, based on an earlier essay still in the archives.[19] In both versions, Margot said that when she first became

attracted to him she invited Peter to her room at night. She met him in a dressing gown and told him to warm himself in the bed while she sat by the fire. 'I did not know the meaning of the word lust', she wrote, 'nor had I ever been ashamed.' Astounded by her innocence, 'Peter taught me his art of love-making' with so much skill and forbearance that he was probably the model for what physical passion should feel like for the rest of her life, though it is likely that they did not have fully consummated sex.

With Peter, if not before, Margot experienced what historians see as a revolution in intimate behaviour between men and women of the European haute bourgeoisie in the late nineteenth century. Disguised behind an open banter that was not necessarily preliminary to a courtship, this new eroticism could involve extremes of foreplay that preserved technical chastity while unleashing sensual feelings perhaps even more intense than those experienced in marriage. Late-Victorian flirtation developed complicated rituals, gestures, signals and signs that would 'shape young love in the West for a century to come'.[20] Specific locations became associated with this extra-marital experimentation – spas, hotels, summer resorts – something Margot might have seen in her sojourns in Dresden and Hyères. Peter taught her what Laura had learned from Doll Liddell in the hills above Loch Alsh. In a mark of the difference between the two girls, Laura had felt sinful in discovering that she had an 'out-of-doors animal' side unrelated to marital commitment. Margot gloried in her physical nature, only rarely expressing guilt over her behaviour with men.

Margot's difficulties in thinking about her relationships arose in the context of a general scepticism about friendship between the sexes, the product of a widely shared assumption that physical proximity and emotional closeness could only be disguise or sublimation of the real and natural motive – physical fulfilment. As John Tosh writes, by this time 'the only context in which easy relations between the sexes were applauded without qualification was the family'.[21] Laura had grappled with this conundrum in her efforts to break down psychological barriers across the gender gap. For her, human intimacies were infused with an older Christian understanding of the passions in which 'higher level' selfless feelings would subsume the promptings of the body through kindness, compassion and shared purpose.[22] She learned the dangers of this stance with Doll, lessons that had 'made me distrust my view of men and women'. 'I hoped there would be no room no necessity for self-control—for grown-up-ism and for all the *triste chimère* that usually stalk the lives of friendships and throttle them. I hoped we would just be completely natural, completely unconventional completely true and good ... Now I see that I was wicked and that you are grown up and I am half grown up and so that to be natural is wrong.' Laura's acceptance of domesticity freed her for higher friendships such as the one she was able to develop with Arthur after she married. In her will, she described him as 'Alfred's and my dear, deeply loved friend, who has given me so many happy hours since I married, and whose sympathy, understanding, and companionship in the deep sense of the word has never been withheld from me when I have sought it'.[23]

Margot's reluctance to marry denied her this protective refuge, and she began to gain a wider reputation for improper behaviour. She added verbal effrontery to her attention-seeking and physical impulsiveness. Her youthful quips were captured eye-witness by the author Marion Crawford when he made her the heroine of his novel *An American Politician* (1885) after a Christmas visit to Glen. In perhaps the first fictional portrayal of Margot ever published, Crawford's Josephine Thornton bluntly informs a new acquaintance that what he has offered as small talk is 'not original', 'not very interesting' and 'inconsistent'.[24] As the book progresses, she is lippy, judgemental and frivolous, and Crawford caught some of Margot's aphoristic speech so closely that he must have been reporting remarks he had actually heard: 'I always say what I think, you know. I cannot help it a bit.' 'I do not know anything, but I can do everything.' 'I do not care to receive confidences. I always forget to forget them.' Margot's own memoirs revel in the zippy retorts she used to fend off insults as she moved through London society in the 1880s. Faced with a 'frontal assault', she advised, 'the only response ... is to be saucy or servile': '"There were some clever people in the world, you know, before you were born, Miss Tennant" ... "Please don't pick me out, Lady Clarke, as if I alone were responsible for the stupid ones among whom we find ourselves today."' Mary Waddington, the American wife of the French ambassador commented on the complicated 'jealousies and rivalries' between women in society circles, resulting in the well-placed 'dig' both given and returned.[25]

In the spring of 1886 Arthur Balfour and George Pembroke warned Margot that they were hearing gossip about her. She responded to Arthur's charge that she was a flirt with a protestation about emotional pretending: 'You surely don't mean to say that I am anything as fascinating as a flirt … a flirt's whole theory is making people think she's fonder of them than she is. I NEVER do I'm sure I put my friends on a healthy level sooner than anyone.' She also tried to explain herself to George, who might have just read A. C. Benson's anonymously published *Memoirs of Arthur Hamilton* in which Margot appeared as a 'fast' girl, 'compromising' to know, 'reckless about what she said and did'. 'You tell me that I am wrong in supposing that you ever make fast speeches', George wrote, 'or lean at all towards what I call Parisianism – that nothing improper ever amuses you, and that I am never to think or say such things again on pain of your displeasure. Well so be it, but attend to my warnings all the same. … The judgment of the world in general in such things is very coarse, and very stupid. I am naturally in a better position than you can be both to know what people say and think about you, and to estimate the danger of it to your life's success.'[26]

Margot was disconcerted by these assessments of her intentions and behaviour, coming from people who hardly knew her. Nevertheless, in the weeks after Laura's death, she began to remove herself from the personal and social dangers of association with the Prince of Wales. In July she told Spencer not to whisper that the prince had paid her a condolence visit alone the previous afternoon. She had not told '<u>anyone</u> but mama and the butler, not even Charty or papa'. In autumn she wrote that the unimpeachable Lady Spencer was going to 'speak to the Princess so that she should not think me one of many of Tum's girl friends'.[27] She was deeply offended a year later when travelling in Zurich to find herself stared at by 'a former MP' for Brighton who told her he had 'heard *much*' about her in London, then proceeded to discuss the Prince of Wales in a way that 'revolted me in every fibre of my being'.[28]

For all her unconstrained behaviour, it was clear to anyone looking closely that Margot needed mentors more than suitors – people who would take an interest in her mind and character instead of her physical attractions. She chose men of ambiguous sexuality, such as the elderly and unmarried Oxford don Benjamin Jowett, the tubercular homosexual essayist John Addington Symonds (Henry Sidgwick's old friend) and Spencer Lyttelton, himself a deeply repressed bachelor. She could literally sit on a footstool at the feet of such instructors – Wilfrid Blunt called them her 'tame

men of learning' – discussing books, eliciting critiques of her
writing and engaging in the safely playful back talk of a younger
relative.[29] A decade later Henry James described this avuncular
type in *The Awkward Age* (1899), where Mr Longdon rescues Nanda Brookenham from the corruptions of a predatory social world.
In the conclusion to the book, Longdon takes Nanda away from
society entirely, ensconcing her out of harm's way in an isolated
country retreat that constitutes a death to 'the World' – rather like
Margot's temporary retreats to Davos or Oxford to visit her elderly
tutors.

These friendships were crucial for her intellectual development
and growing sense of her own mental powers, but Margot was
not interested in a life that would unfold outside of metropolitan
politics and culture. As she charted a path through the heart of
the London establishment she was lucky to be taken up by people
close to Laura, such as Arthur Balfour and Alfred Lyttelton, who
defended her naturalness and generosity of spirit against criticisms that she lacked taste and breeding. George and Gety Pembroke, their relatives the Brownlows, the Elchos and Wenlocks,
Balfour and Frances Horner invited her to entertainments that
challenged the problematic amusements of the sporting worlds
that had previously formed Margot's main exposure to elite society. George Pembroke in particular offered a sort of protective
friendship to girls new to the London scene whose parents were
not reliable guides through the shoals of courtship and social advance among the networked aristocracy – Americans and social
outsiders such as Margot, DD Balfour, Mary Leiter, Violet Maxse
and novelist Amelie Rives.[30] George referred to them jokingly as
'daughters', while they called Gety Pembroke and Addy Brownlow
'the aunts'.

Lady Salisbury once remarked tartly that for a girl 'to be favoured
by Arthur B and Pembroke is much against her'.[31] She was mistak-
en, considering some of the alternatives available to very young
female newcomers. The Pembrokes and Brownlows consciously
asserted forms of entertainment to counter the moral dangers
for young women posed by the ethos of the Marlborough House
set and other 'smart' crowds.[32] They developed different understandings of humour, hierarchy, forms of play and conversational
opportunity as they experimented with a more relaxed sociability
and a 'New Morality' that crossed gender and generational lines.
By 1887 even Arthur was calling this circle of friends 'our crowd'

or 'the gang'. Doll Liddell called them 'the Elect'. A year later, Lord Charles Beresford renamed them 'the Souls'.[33]

'I gather from you … that you're a little sort of set that hang very much together', comments a character in James's *The Awkward Age*. 'Oh yes, not a formal association nor a secret society – still less a "dangerous gang" or an organization for any definite end. We're simply a collection of natural affinities.'[34] The mix of kinship, mentorship and 'elective affinity' represented by a coterie like the Souls was an upper-class version of changes in association occurring throughout Victorian society over the course of the nineteenth century, as geographic and social mobility allowed individuals to supplement local and kinship communities that had largely defined even elite lives as late as the Napoleonic era. People on the move and transcending the circumstances of their birth families produced an explosion of clubs, societies, reading circles and social coteries based on personal choice rather than inherited connections, and on mutual interests and values rather than unavoidable proximity.[35] The same-sex form of many of these new associations have received considerable attention from historians of friendship for the counter they provided to the supposed hegemony of domestic relations in the affective life of the Victorians.[36] Circles of genuinely mixed-sex sociability are harder to locate, however, because of the moral and sexual dangers they were thought to foster.[37]

Sometime in the mid-1880s, Charlie Beresford, a cousin of both George Pembroke and Arthur Balfour, played one of his elaborate practical jokes that showed why sociability in the highest levels of society could be so problematic. The Prince of Wales and his friends were attending the regatta at Cowes – George Pembroke was there the same year with guests on his yacht, *Black Pearl* – and dined one evening with a Mrs Cust. As the meal ended, Charlie insisted that the prince take a tour of the 'really beautiful' house, especially the hostess's bedroom:

> Mrs. Cust was most embarrassed. She could not think what there was in the house worth showing, but Charlie had his way as usual, and our little party, with the Prince at the head, solemnly went on a tour of inspection from room to room. Upstairs we marched, with Mrs. Cust growing more and more embarrassed and puzzled at every step. Charlie led the way, and going to her bedroom door, threw it

open with an air of mystery and triumph. The Prince was actually
standing on tiptoe.

"There, sir!" exclaimed Charlie Beresford, with the magnilo-
quent gesture of a showman.

On the beautiful down bed lay a young donkey, fast asleep, with
a little lace cap tied coquettishly on one side with pink bows!

Mrs. Cust screamed. We all laughed – but the donkey snored
on. Charlie had seen to that, for with his usual kind heart he had
given the donkey a drink of hot milk and champagne.[38]

It would be difficult to exaggerate the ways that this anecdote of
upper-crust fun confirmed the fears of respectable people about
the dangers lurking in the wrong kinds of laughter and amusement
in social settings. Despite the absence of any section on comedy
in Walter Houghton's massive compendium *The Victorian Frame
of Mind* (1957), Queen Victoria's contemporaries did engage in
lively debate over what made things funny. Reluctantly inclined towards the Hobbesian 'superiority theory' of laughter, they feared
that much of what people found amusing was cruel and/or crude
– indicative of 'small minds who are forced to keep themselves in
their own favour'.[39] Those of large soul and right principles either
would not laugh much or laughed from sympathy and affection,
narrowing the distance between self and object. Mid-Victorian delight in the childlike, the eccentric, the nonsensical and the genial
reflected this concern about the potential of humour to promote
unworthy emotions. Even after 1870 when, Robert Martin argues,
wit asserted its prerogatives over sentimental, affective comedy, its
power was seen to lie in the intellectual pleasures of puzzle-solving
rather than the cutting sarcasm that created distance. Coarse and
unkind humour among educated people became associated with
the self-conceit of aristocrats whose lives lacked both the moral
awareness and the 'warm suffusion of the loving, charitable emotions' of the middle classes.[40]

There were deep gender implications in these understandings of
companionable amusement. In 1871 an essay by Virginia Woolf's
father, Leslie Stephen, argued provocatively that 'the humour of
women does not exist'. Stephen writes that, since both nature
and respectable upbringing prevented women from experiencing
the irreverence towards human failings that came 'naturally' to
men, 'many of the most amusing things that have ever been said
in this world are, in one direction or another, such as would be

incompatible with the feminine sense of delicacy'.[41] This message put privileged women in a difficult double bind. If they exercised the derisory wit arising from a superior social station, they were unwomanly for being unsympathetic. If they got the point – or became the point – of comedic shenanigans, they were unwomanly for being vulgar and available.

Sociability in some of the highest social circles, often centred on crude jokes and heavy chaff, confirmed these fears about the class and gender dimensions of amusement. Staged buffoonery established rankings, released the tensions of hierarchy-based protocol and built temporary unit cohesion by exposing one person to ridicule while signalling the vulnerability of everyone else.[42] Stories abounded of aggressive pranks with animals – introducing sewer rats into a house, a bear cub into a tent, a dead seagull in a bed.[43] Food substitutions such as medicine in the wine or shaving cream instead of whipped were found to be hilarious. Consuelo Vanderbilt told of her mother-in-law, the Duchess of Marlborough, putting soap on the cheese platter: 'With tears of laughter still rolling down her cheeks', she said, 'Poor Mr Hope was too polite to spit his out so he swallowed the soap and was violently sick, and, fancy, he never forgave me!'[44] The gentle toady Christopher Sykes entered the historical record not only for bankrupting himself trying to entertain the 'fast set', but for being the butt of physical humour after he failed to protest when his future sovereign poured a glass of brandy over his head: The Prince of Wales went on to invent a way of distracting Sykes while burning his hand with a cigar, and other men imitated the bullying for an easy laugh.[45] The prince both initiated such jokes and approved when others did. They established who could take and dish it out, and allowed the prince to demonstrate his generosity by the placatory gifts he sent later.

In this sphere of privileged leisure, each episode of romping risked moments of overfamiliarity or attempted intimacy for women. Even conversation could be fraught, for sexuality was an accepted topic for innuendo and teasing, as Daisy, Princess of Pless, reported: 'He [Edward VII] was, as always, very delightful, but inclined to chaff too much. He told me he thought I was a humbug (probably because he imagines – goodness knows what, and because I would not be 'nice' to him).'[46] Charlie Beresford's joke with the donkey targeted a woman in mixed company and delivered – on her own bed – its visual punchline about her sexuality.

The ways that women participated in this regime of 'aggressive masculine philistinism' were closely defined.[47] Providing an audience for the jokes of others was essential. Jennie Churchill told of a country house party where a man who had taken sick was informed that he was dying by fellow guests disguised as a doctor and a priest. The other guests listened in on his deathbed confession, convulsed with laughter in a neighbouring room. Many women followed the Princess of Wales in playing the merry *naïf* for whom the physical fun of wild dancing, pillow fights or trying on other people's footwear was permitted under the guise of childlike frivolity.[48] Cluelessly laughing off or not getting the joke in embarrassing moments provided some protection in an environment where 'all men were in search of prey ... and all women expected all men to make up to them the instant they found themselves alone'.[49] Ladies also made jokes that targeted other females, often a good way to raise laughter among men.[50] Women who spent their lives in this section of society seemed variously hard-boiled, coquettishly vacuous or guardedly hostile.

In the face of these social realities, many women in privileged circles conformed to strictures that discouraged them from being uninhibited in behaviour or unguardedly funny in mixed company. As Anthony Trollope had said, the true woman would 'have a great fund of laughter, which would illumine her whole face without producing a sound from her mouth'.[51] They did not amuse in ways that drew group attention, and reserved their epigrams for private letters or one-to-one conversation. Much of the public repartee reported about women took the form of self-defence against a clear attack, like so many of Margot's youthful ripostes. George Russell wrote approvingly of one lady's brilliant comeback when the French ambassador, outraged at Britain's lack of help during the Franco-Prussian War, challenged her in a public setting: 'We always believed that you were a nation of shop-keepers, and now we know you are.' 'And we', replied the lady, 'always believed that you were a nation of soldiers, and now we know you are not.'[52] But even Alice Keppel, Edward VII's end-of-life mistress and reportedly the funniest woman of her generation – fully able to engage in 'sardonic adult laughter' about herself and others – confined her jests to very small settings. Later she feared that her daughter Violet's quick tongue and uncanny gift for mimicry would gain her a reputation for being too clever to attract an eligible man.[53] Eileen Gilhooly has written at length on the 'smile of discontent' with which women of the middle and upper classes encountered the restrictions on their displays of humour in the Victorian era.[54]

At the heart of these dilemmas of sociability lay the question of what women could do and say in mixed company with men who were not relatives or spouses. The correspondence of these years provides a litany of behaviours for which women found themselves suspected of improper libidinal desires for being suspiciously familiar around men: visiting the British Museum with a male friend,[55] co-ed foot-racing at a country house,[56] referring to a man by first name or placing a hand on his arm,[57] a solo dance performance 'in costumes savouring of the Alhambra',[58] drying newly washed hair before the morning-room fire while men moved in and out of the room,[59] saying the word 'voluptuous' at the dinner table.[60] A particular infraction was to go swimming while in mixed company: 'Much against my advice Charty would bathe with Harry, St John, Alfred, Archie and Arthur. She looked nicer than I expected and never lacked courage!'[61] George Pembroke's sister called the Souls 'George's queer friends', a label that points to the anxieties over gender norms, self-expression and leisure behaviour in a world in which women were both freer to move about and more likely to know men with whom their families were not acquainted.

Laughing immoderately, making others laugh and openly taking the floor were transgressive because of the breakdown of reserve that this might permit. In after-dinner drawing rooms, however, the Souls played games at which the point was to be openly funny and intellectually competitive – and where literary parodies, writing contests and guessing games allowed women to shine as well as men. 'Clumps' was their form of 'twenty questions', in which the term to be guessed was an abstraction such as 'alliteration', 'platitude', 'a lost cause' or 'clue'. Margot teamed up with her sister to make Alfred and Arthur guess 'innuendo' and 'quarantine': 'They got quite keen and gave me and Charty "crisis" and I really do think I was rather clever.'[62] In 'Telegrams', the first letters of the message about an assigned topic had to spell out the destination, and in 'Epitaphs', players wrote a short verse about the death of a generic type such as 'the ballet girl'. 'Styles', invented by the Tennant sisters in 1884, required that 'each person writes something – a poem – a sentence – a fragment in imitation of some celebrated author and reads it out loud and the others guess in whose style it is'.[63] Women interrupted, laughed gleefully and capped men

and each other in these contests. Frances Horner and DD Balfour
convulsed a carriage of people when they got Henry Asquith to critique their own poetry under the impression that it was written by
Robert Browning and Matthew Arnold.[64] Charty Ribblesdale was
judged by the other competitors to have composed the funniest essay on 'conversation', even though her husband got his published
in *Nineteenth Century* the next summer.[65]

The Souls also encouraged general conversation among all
the men and women at a party. Victorian dining etiquette actually proscribed this. Guests were supposed to talk quietly to one
neighbour for the first courses of the meal, then turn to engage
the person on their other side.[66] Successful general conversation
required skills on everyone's part in order to avoid degenerating
into a single guest's anecdotal monologue – 'talk composed of stories is not worthy of the name', commented Arthur – or persiflage
among a couple of the quickest wits.[67] Margot reported a party
that put together a menu of topics to discuss at dinner, with Arthur
as chairman. Sixteen people participated and it became 'personal and hilarious. I've never seen anything like it before.'[68] Charty
Ribblesdale once held her own against the entire table while maintaining that men gained more by marriage than women did, and
Betty Balfour reported a visit to Wilton where Frances Horner led
a discussion on which of the traditional virtues should be eliminated. 'Truth was done for, as a virtue which no moral being attempted to practice. Hope was declared a tiresome, weak-minded
thing. Faith followed as a gift you either possessed without effort or
were wrong to cultivate. Charity was left grudgingly. Mrs. Horner
wanted to do away with Justice but Lord Pembroke clung to it.'[69]

Mary Elcho's diary mentions many mixed group discussions of
topics that would be thought, by Victorian standards, quite personal and therefore out of bounds: 'taking things hard or easy and
being reserved or easy to open out', 'telling lies', 'love and matrimony', 'practising virtues if no one sees it', 'repeating things of
your friends', 'ruthless conversation about bores' and 'if any one
of us went mad what form would the madness take'. Other entries
noted 'amusing talk at lunch about depression of spirits' or 'general talk about morbidness'. Games that ranked people by who
was most unselfish, imaginative or bad-tempered, or what flowers,
food or animals someone resembled, flirted with taboo topics that
worked best with bonding humour, suggestiveness and nuanced
expression. Mary's brother-in-law Evan Charteris contrasted this

sort of social entertainment with that of his parents at Gosford where 'there was a sense of formality and observance at their dinners', and people 'conversed quietly in contiguous groups' after they left the table: 'There was less laughter and certainly less freedom, whether of speech or suggestion – taboos were in the air – and restraint guided conversation into safe channels.'[70]

It took courage for young women to speak up in mixed groups on occasions like these, to offer and 'get' risqué remarks and quip without the heavy sarcasm that created distance. They were aided by changes taking place in the metropolitan theatre and print culture. Margot's impulsive physicality had elements of the vaudeville of the 1870s, but during the next decade metropolitan comedy shifted from the antic to the witty, from the crude, childlike or eccentric to the ironic and astute. Mind games created impersonal spaces where feminine humour and eroticism could be decoupled and women could 'play' with less danger of being misunderstood. They were part of an adaptive model of sociability where shared interests and mental acumen could temporarily reduce the erotic distractions of mixed-sex leisure, allowing an expansion of women's mental worlds and the arenas in which they could operate.

These forms of cleverness were also suited to an age that rewarded mental prowess in men. During the year that the Souls were gaining a reputation in London high society, Arthur, in the process of making his parliamentary career, was demonstrating his increasing mastery of the glancing blow, the apt response and the telling epigram. Margot first reported him playing the high-powered parlour games in autumn 1887, precisely when he was establishing his ability to control Irish interruptions on the floor of the House of Commons.[71] He sometimes used discussions with groups of his women friends to test the clarity of his arguments, these interested non-specialists standing in for the backbenchers or essay readers he was trying to reach.[72] His willingness to engage in general conversation mirrored the collaborative rather than domineering approach that he brought to cabinets and administrative offices. Sociability and political performances reinforced each other to encourage demeanours adapted to the wider, non-familial worlds of the late century.

The novelty of the Souls' approach to gendered behaviour on social occasions gained wider attention after George Curzon hosted a dinner for the circle in July 1889. For entertainment he whipped off doggerel verses commemorating each guest. Twenty-six men

Fig. 7 A society lady leads a lively toast, following Charty Ribblesdale's
example, ILN supplement, 23 December 1899

and twenty-two women were mentioned in Curzon's poem, a large
number to assemble in the semi-public setting of the Bachelors'
Club. Daisy White, whose husband Harry was first secretary at the
American delegation in London, confessed initial doubts about
such a self-conscious gathering of the gang, but the party turned
out to be hilariously successful.[73] Waves of laughter and a din of
voices filled the room as Arthur, struggling because he was laughing so hard, read through stanzas like 'America lends,/ Nay, she
gives when she sends/ Such treasures as Harry and Daisy;/ Tho'

many may yearn/ None but Harry can turn/ That sweet little head of hers crazy.' Charty Ribblesdale 'got up and proposed George's health with much grace amidst roars of applause' (see Fig. 7). 'Several men stood on chairs to sing "For He's a Jolly Good Fellow" … Never enjoyed myself more at any dinner', Daisy concluded. 'Never laughed more in my life.'

Curzon's poem and its use of humour had a lot to do with it. Each guest, male and female, was singled out, but none of the comments were unkind. The humour came from the silly groping rhymes and the unexpected things that Curzon chose to compliment in his subjects. Camaraderie and good feeling pervaded the setting, with men, and unexpectedly one woman, cheerfully performing for the common gaze. Curzon found a way to use humour to create group intimacy without emphasising internal hierarchies. Tensions created by social formality and scrutiny were dissipated in empathetic laughter and clever verbal constructions that dwelt on positive aspects of people's appearance and accomplishments. These were forms of humour more typically gendered as feminine, and the fact that they were exercised in such a large mixed group – and by Curzon of all people[74] – marked a change in the relationship between women, humour and public appearance as the fin de siècle began. Far from equating respectable womanliness with witless sentimentalism, the Souls defined humour as a permissible, even essential quality of the attractive female. By the turn of the century, earnest obtuseness would be linked not with womanly virtue but with sexlessness and spinster status.[75]

George Curzon gave Arthur Balfour pride of place among the forty or so guests at the Bachelors' Club dinner: 'There was seen at that feast of this band, the High Priest/ the heart that to all hearts is nearest;/ Him may nobody steal from the true Common weal,/ Tho' to each is dear Arthur the dearest'.[76] By this time Arthur was certainly the most celebrated of the circle, the one most worth knowing for political benefit and social cachet. To the extent that their association reflected something about private selves and intimate sociabilities, however, it could be argued that George Pembroke was the male lodestar of the Souls. At one level this seems a strange suggestion. The many reminiscences and gossipy accounts of parties and performances written at the time record not a single witticism, zinger, conversational coup or game initiative associated with George who, like many women, is more often commemorated by reference to his remarkable good looks. Nevertheless, George's personality, laid out in unusual collections of letters with women friends, helps to reveal the strengths and the limitations of the new sociability between the sexes, and shows how the heedless self-indulgence attributed to this generation of the elites was interpreted and resisted.

George Pembroke was one of those who took Laura's death hard. It coincided with another period of crisis in his life that combined political and personal troubles. In the summer of 1886, after the second general election in as many years required the Conservatives to construct another government, Lord Salisbury failed once again to include him. George began to draw his own conclusions about his potential for life in the national arena. During a cabinet reshuffle six months later, the prime minister finally reached out, offering him the position of undersecretary for the colonies with speaking responsibilities in the House of Lords. Arthur would have welcomed the inclusion of his friend in the daily workings of the government at a crucial time in its fortunes. Despite Salisbury having nearly 90 per cent of British lords on his side in support against Gladstone, he still had difficulties filling party positions with peers both able and willing to undertake steady demands of office and parliamentary attendance.[77]

George, however, turned down this overture, citing unspecified health problems that prevented him taking on official duties. He knew himself to be thin-skinned and susceptible to criticism from other men.[78] With this predisposition, he may have interpreted Salisbury's belated offer as a sop rather than recognition of merit. Nevertheless, the decision was crucial, even decisive, for his future. The holder of the Pembroke earldom might have begun a career at the national level in this ministry, including becoming viceroy to Ireland while Arthur was chief secretary. In the House of Lords, Eddie Hamilton asserted, 'he not only carries weight, but he would command a personal following'.[79]

At the same time there are hints that, twelve years after George's sudden proposal to Gety, he might have fallen in love with someone else, or at least was recognising the restraints that his marriage entailed. The match seemed more or less tranquil, but it was childless and perhaps passionless. Gety was in her mid-forties, deeply involved in the lives of her two sisters Ladies Brownlow and Lothian, whose marriages had also produced no offspring, and a strong-willed organiser of the Pembrokes' Wilton life. Too few letters have come to light to do more than speculate on Gety Pembroke's inner world or the dynamics of the couple's relationship. Her high standards for herself and others, and her impulsive conversational gambits, suggest some reasons why she had still been unmarried well into her thirties. But people with no reason to make harsh judgements of her described an unusual degree of social awkwardness for a woman in her position, and showed how carefully George was navigating relationships between his wife, his guests and members of his own family.

In 1889, Alfred Lyttelton wrote letters to two of his relatives who knew Gety in which he gave his impressions of a two-week yachting cruise he had just taken with the Pembrokes, the Ribblesdales, Harry Cust and several others. He described Gety as having 'honesty and courage and a fine breezy out-of-doors enjoyment of nature', as well as a 'queer originality' in her endless speculations on life and religion. Nevertheless, 'she is selfish and despotic and frankly stupid'. She 'never knows her own mind, but if someone else suggests a plan she finds her mind sufficiently to contradict it, then when it is abandoned and she finds another to which conformity is being made she contradicts herself and upsets it again. In a few days this would bring me to the tomb, but Pembroke bears it with undiminished sweetness of temper and with the high breeding of a perfect gentleman.' 'He behaves like an angel with her', Lyttelton wrote, though the rest of the party 'all suffered terribly at her hands.'[80]

Arthur's sister-in-law Betty illustrated these qualities with a comic little anecdote from her first long visit to Wilton. The guests were at breakfast and getting ready to join the local hunt when Gety asked:

George, when am I to start?
How should I know, my dear …
Please find out, I don't want to settle about it.
Why, you know you won't do what I tell you.
Oh, George, you know I always do what you tell me.
Well, send a message that they are to wait for you till 12.
Why should they wait for us? I am ready to start now.
Very well, my dear, do start now.
No, send to tell them to wait till half past 11.
Exit Lord P and Lady P calls him back to say 'Now don't forget
    George'.[81]

With a wife described as both strong-willed and insecure, it was not surprising that George enjoyed the company of sympathetic and undemanding women like Margot's sister Charty, whom he praised for 'her brightness and tenderness, her simple sincere unconscious graciousness and interest'.[82]

George's emotional turmoil in 1886 was heightened by his conviction that a new 'Epicurean' philosophy of indulgence was spreading rapidly in high society, far beyond its earlier confinement to libertine underworlds of masculine escape. In this year, divorce trials involving Sir Charles Dilke, Lord and Lady Colin Campbell and the Marquess of Queensbury allowed for unprecedented press attention to the salacious details of upper-class misbehaviour – and these weren't even among the Prince of Wales's fast set.[83] For every scandal that actually became news, aristocratic families fended off others that might. During this year Jennie Churchill threatened to bring George's sister Gladys de Grey into the divorce courts for destroying the Churchills' sketchy marital accommodations, and Lady Salisbury gossiped that it might be Lord Randolph who brought action against Jennie, 'whom he accuses of playing tricks with four men!'[84] This was just after Gladys had caused an estrangement between Lord Londonderry and his wife, Gety's niece Theresa, by sending the marquess purloined love letters that Theresa had written to Harry Cust.[85] Charlie Beresford, George's cousin, was beginning his affair with Daisy Brooke. 'Even in the inner circle of one's own friends and relations the dangers arising from errant affections are always lurking', George observed with rueful understatement.[86] He confessed that he could not read newspaper accounts of love tragedies caused by 'intense and overmastering passion' without 'thinking and knowing that but for circumstances the same thing might have happened to me'.[87]

Like many in these circles, George admitted that he had no religious convictions for continuing to observe marital vows that others were surrendering. 'We are both people whose philosophies have for one reason or another rather given way under their feet', he wrote to Lady Constance Wenlock, a desperately unhappy friend who shared his discontents, 'and who are drifting along in a rather rudderless condition clinging tight to everything that may save them from positive disaster.'[88] In another letter he writes: 'How one longs to believe confidently in the divine nature of right and wrong, and the eternal existence of the soul. It would be so easy to choose the higher life, to sacrifice almost anything, if one did;

without it one seems to have no motive power to turn the soul the right way.'[89] Nevertheless, George was deeply committed to marriage as an institution – celibacy was against nature, he wrote to his Catholic mother – and to the standard that spouses should remain sexually faithful to each other. His life-defining experiences in the South Seas had taught him that social lesson, and he identified this aspect of moral behaviour with the structures of civilisation itself. Nor, in the end, could he tolerate the thought of the pain it would cause his wife if he were unfaithful, or the hypocrisies of an existence based on furtiveness and deception. In the face of what he termed 'private and special circumstances' of his situation, George almost certainly resisted the temptations of infidelity at this time and throughout his life.

Rejecting the siren call of individual gratification, George turned to the Stoic philosophers 'to find the rule of life which in the long run is best – and that is in the long run happiest both for self and all those who are affected by what one is and does'.[90] Stoicism acknowledged, George wrote, 'that the world is a hard place in which power of endurance of pain and disappointment is as necessary an ingredient of happiness as any other … It seems to me far more suitable to life as it is than t'other philosophy.' Stoics taught that the self-aware, introspective nature 'would be more likely to attain happiness by not aiming at it directly, but rather making duty its object and benefiting by the discipline that that entails'.[91] This did not require an ascetic existence: 'I believe in the duty of being happy, if one can, of making other people happy, of giving all the affection and sympathy that one's nature possesses to one's friends … to me it's the only thing that makes life worth living.' Admitting that it took conscious effort to absorb oneself in the lives of others 'and feel real sympathy with them', still, George wrote, 'almost all human souls (that are not wicked) are interesting and to some extent lovable if one only really knows them'. Empathetic identification produced friends, and 'no one can be altogether miserable who loves friends and is loved by them …The love of comrades – the sense of comradeship has a virtue against unhappiness itself.'

George's distinctiveness lay in asserting that this comradeship could exist between men and women outside of marriage, and despite the possibility that they might find themselves attracted to each other. Duty and desire often lay in different directions, but both sexes were capable of dealing with that. George wrote to several women correspondents that dichotomies in nature between men and women were not as great as many supposed: 'the differences between their moral and intellectual powers are so slight as to be quite inapplicable in the consideration of individual cases. Seeing how differently they are educated they are astonishingly like, and many of the most striking unlikenesses are purely due to training.' Even among the native girls of the South Pacific, he had found that women responded to invitations to non-flirtatious sympathy: 'It really seems to open up a new life to them when they are talked to as reasonable beings, and nothing more.'[92] Victor Luftig describes this 'universal comprehension' that a man and woman might share – 'an objectless and necessary sincerity of one's innermost life trying to react upon the profound sympathies of another existence' – as a modern, secular addition to the history of heterosexual friendship.[93]

The idea that men and women might be friends, sharing thoughts, feelings, time, perhaps secrets, without succumbing to sexual imperatives was so novel that Frances Horner wrote a sketch called 'The New Morality', describing it as the outlook of the Souls. George Pembroke did not know at first who the author was, but suspected it had to be from among his circle because 'it is full of *my own* views sometimes even my particular expressions'.[94] George's friendships with women such as Frances Horner, Charty Ribblesdale, Constance Wenlock, DD Balfour and Margot Tennant allowed for an openness that was publicly warm and affectionate. George dropped in on women friends unexpectedly in the late morning, went on impromptu shopping expeditions and took them to the theatre without his wife being present. The relationships were so comfortable that people could hardly believe they were innocent. 'You don't quite know the kind of friendship wh[ich] [e]xists between him and his women friends', Margot told Spencer Lyttelton, 'it's *not* really very disturbing.'[95]

This was partly because the 'necessary sincerity of one's innermost life' of this kind of friendship entailed careful emotional management and silences rather than complete transparency. George wrote admissions – often marked 'private' – of intellectual and moral confusion or a sense of inadequacy, but his letters did not extend to candour about feelings or imperatives of the body that would be the Bloomsbury set's contribution to the evolving practice of inter-sex friendship. He assumed that his women friends could show the same acquiescence to duty and temperate consolations of empathetic fellowship that he trained himself to accept. But while he might share feelings, he wrote *about* them, not in the midst of them – especially not those of forbidden passion or angry recrimination – and the innermost secrets of his heart were not written down. Probably they were unspoken, even in private: 'Please understand that I use the word friendship advisedly. If there had ever been love in the man and woman sense, I should not of course be writing to you about it.' As Benjamin Jowett told Daisy White, heterosexual affection between unmarried people was 'no doubt dangerous and required strength of character on the part of both in case the friendship increased into love … the next great thing in such cases he said is to keep it to yourselves and private and not to let the world talk about you and discuss you'.[96] In the eyes of some of Pembroke's women friends, what was missing were vivid realities of passion in either its most destructive or most energising and liberating forms.[97] George might have argued that it was precisely an ability to temper or hide profound emotion that allowed for the new freedoms of contact between the sexes in the first place.

George's personal restraint and his non-sexualised friendships with women threatened to make him a 'man at the margins' in late-Victorian elite society, not a virile patriarch, sporting blood or clubland habitué who used male monocultures as the centre of affective life.[98] Marginal men violated conventions of assertive masculinity in a variety of ways: their concern for niceties of language, their shyness and cultivation of the protections of *politesse* and especially in their unmanly relationships with women, a rejection of 'natural' heterosexuality that Kelly Cannon calls 'precarious, even reprehensible' by the last decade of the century.[99] In a long discourse on different forms of love and friendship sent to Constance Wenlock, Doll Liddell argued that men who were capable of purely platonic or *amis caressants* relationships must either be of exceptionally 'cold and refined temperament' or 'partake somewhat of the female disposition'.[100] Such men existed outside other people's passions, possibly gaining the greater psychological insights of the observer, but marginal to the contestations of power that occurred in domestic and public life when emotions were fully engaged.

Wilfrid Blunt knew George and Gety Pembroke for years. In the early 1880s, Gety had discontinued the Waggers Club parties at Wilton in which Blunt took part because she believed, correctly, that her predatory neighbour was destroying the marital happiness of her sister-in-law Margaret Talbot. A few years later Blunt founded his all-male Crabbet Club for precisely the kind of salacious bonding over masculine sexual prowess that both Pembroke and Balfour refused to engage in. Women were not invited to Crabbet Club, according to Blunt, on the Muslim premise that they lacked a soul and were incapable of rational discourse – a poor subterfuge since no account of these revels describes much besides naked cavorting and risqué verses.[101]

Not surprisingly, Blunt's judgement about George Pembroke was derogatory. There was 'some want in him, in spite of much manly beauty, of full virility'.[102] Others noted George's hesitancy in asserting himself in social settings as well as his extraordinary forbearance with Gety's disorienting inability to read social cues or keep a conversation on topic. But it was a sign of how notions of appropriate masculinity had changed by the fin de siècle that George Pembroke would be a source of gossip because he did *not* betray his wife or use moments alone with a woman to create a sexually charged intimacy. Few in this era would recognise as achievement the psychological protection and space this gave to women who also lived within powerfully limiting constructions of gender relations. The collections of letters that George's friends preserved attest to his importance to them as a source of emotional understanding and personal connection in marriages that had not fulfilled the romantic expectations of youth.

5

Political Performances

Arthur Balfour

L IKE GEORGE PEMBROKE, Arthur Balfour might also have been thought by outside observers to fit the description of a 'man at the margins' in 1886. He too worried that he lacked the qualities to be successful in politics, telling John Morley that 'he had quite come to the conclusion that as a public man he was a failure and that he had no aptitude for politics'.[1] He was also sensitive about charges of unearned preferment. Rather than press his own claims during the government construction in summer 1886, he disappeared to play golf in Scotland, writing to a cousin that he felt 'no natural vocation for being a Great Man's Great Man, still less for being thought to be so'.[2] As it turned out, Lord Salisbury offered Arthur a position as secretary of state for Scotland, a new government office only recently established. Without a seat in the cabinet, the appointment carried no great status, especially since Arthur's rival Randolph Churchill became both chancellor of the exchequer and a very young leader of the House of Commons. Then, six months later, the great wheel of fortune intervened. Arthur plunged forward, transforming himself through his experiences of love and politics in ways that George Pembroke never managed to do.

Arthur was thirty-eight when the surprise announcement came on 7 March 1887 that he would take over as chief secretary for Ireland. The government was in a shambles, rocked by Randolph's impetuous and ill-advised resignation during Christmas week of 1886 – 'one of those exquisite moments', as Morley put it, 'in which excited politicians enjoy the ineffable sensation that the end of the world has come'.[3] Now Churchill's ally Sir Michael Hicks Beach was using the advice of doctors to bow out of the government's anticipated confrontation with the Irish nationalists. Though Gladstone's first home rule bill had failed in the Commons the year before, Parnell and the Liberals were still allied, and the implacable Irish MPs William O'Brien and John Dillon had launched another programme of targeted economic resistance, the Plan of Campaign, in the Irish countryside. Salisbury was committed to addressing some of Ireland's grievances, but he was determined first to enact a range of Ireland-only legal measures that would cripple the organisational tools of the 'revolutionary' movement, including obstructionism in parliament and collective resistance in the countryside. Facing an extraordinary contest for legitimacy and public respect between the Conservatives and the home rulers, even Salisbury called the selection of his untested nephew 'a venture'. Gladstone predicted that the Liberals would be back in power by Easter.[4]

It is easy to overlook how fluid and dramatic was the moment. There had been two general elections and four changes of government in the past two years. The rival programmes of Conservative 'coercion and conciliation' or Liberal 'home rule for Ireland' were becoming surrogate battlefields for a host of political contests engaging the new electorate and the growing labour movement. At stake were the allegiance of the respectable working classes and middle-class 'villa' voters, the fortunes of political parties and their legislative platforms, and the nature of imperial governance as a whole.[5] The number of venues where the new occupant of the Irish 'graveyard of ministers' could fail was daunting, from the cabinet chamber to the administrative offices of Dublin Castle, from the widely reported political dinners of the London season to the provincial speaking platforms of the autumn recess. No setting demanded more at this moment than the intimate stage of the House of Commons, wracked nightly by the interruptions of the Irish contingent and splintered on the majority side among followers of the Whig Hartington, the radical Chamberlain and the gadfly Churchill (see Fig. 8).

Salisbury's biographers have noted how anxiously the prime minister watched the performances of his colleagues in the Commons, helpless to prevent the strategic mistakes or awkward self-presentations that lowered backbencher morale, threatened government majorities and gave fodder to the home rule forces.[6] The vivid, impressionistic reporting of journalists transmitted each nightly triumph or misstep to the reading public, creating stereotypes

Fig. 8 The House of Commons could be an emotional space, especially
when the Irish were involved, ILN, 12 February 1881

– reinforced by brilliant cartoonists – that affected individual careers and rippled through the electorate and across the seas to the
Irish diaspora abroad.[7] As Arthur pondered it in retrospect, this
conjunction of circumstances constituted the moment when luck
intervened to give him the political opportunity of a lifetime.

He left no mention of a second, underestimated agent of change
in the same months, his relationship with Mary Elcho. Since the
long intimacy between these two was revealed by Kenneth Young
in the 1960s, it has often been presented as inherently one-sided,

with Mary the needy pursuer, Arthur the model of mildly irritated forbearance. It is not hard to see why. They were fourteen years apart in age. Arthur seemed so emotionally limited that his own family felt the effects. 'It would be a great gain if the ice were really broken', his brother Gerald wrote in 1883, 'and we could manage to be something more to each other.' Four years later Gerald still found that: 'One has to take his affection on faith sometimes. I dare say I think him colder than he really is.' Arthur's sister Eleanor made the same observation thirty years later: 'He was of course always difficult to know because of his reserve. His inner self has almost always been veiled.'[8] Mary Elcho, on the other hand, was distinguished by her self-effacing warmth and outpouring of epistolary impressions. She asserted her needs for connection more openly, scolded Arthur and complained about the circumstances of their lives, while he did not.

Max Egremont presents a scholarly consensus in describing their accommodations as mostly on Arthur's terms: 'He and Lady Elcho were plain with each other, made a bargain at the beginning and kept to it, and if there was little romance in such a contractual arrangement, that was the way he, with his temperament and needs, preferred.'[9] The interpretation offered here suggests that Mary was something more than a comfortable diversion in Arthur's life of public controversy. She was an integral part of his ability to deal with the contentions of politics and recraft his emotional world in ways suitable to the political realities of the new era.[10]

In the months before her death, Laura had worried about an increasingly open attraction between Mary and Arthur who, she judged, was playing with 'conflagration' by encouraging Mary to fall in love with him. 'Whatever he says, and of course, he will say a great deal and all to the point though not to the base, will not convince me that he is behaving well … What Arthur should do is very easy to see. He should deny himself the gratification.'[11] Alfred Lyttelton, probably the closest male friend Arthur ever had, strongly disagreed that his friend would play with affections in this way. 'Talked endlessly of matrimony', he wrote to Laura after a dinner with Arthur at the Garrick Club, 'of which topic he is very full just now, and he was brilliant':

> I believe you think that his fine and polished intellect overwhelms his emotion, but you have never seen him as I have, swept along by overmastering passion such as a man feels but once in a lifetime, and

which scarcely ever can be repeated ... We found HEARTY agreement in the opinion that tho it is hard to gain anyone's love, it is
bitter beyond words to lose it once gained, and that in consequence
it was infinitely important to make no false pretense, however eager-
ly you might wish to attain the end – better by far would it be to pose
as worse than the real facts warrant. I think that AJB has pushed this
theory to its extreme limits and has sometimes indeed hidden under
a veil of cynicism his tender and affectionate nature.[12]

Mary's diary for 1886 makes clear that sometime in the months
after Laura's death, if not earlier, the couple openly shared their
romantic feelings. During visits to Scotland in late summer she
drew a heart with wings near Arthur's name and kept a sketch-
book that included illustrations of secluded woodland paths and
a solitary overturned dory with the words 'how I wish I could, but
you know it would be impossible' written backwards in tiny letters
along the gunnel. On the back page of the volume she wrote a
poem whose message was barely disguised: 'Oh the black black
shore and the silver sea ... What know they of felicity? ... Greater
bliss can never be/ My love my love – loves me'. A few months
later, a 'small very private and personal incident (gear changing)'
took place in Arthur's study at Carlton Gardens, where Mary interrupted his reading of H. Rider Haggard's new 'male romance'
novel *She*. When Arthur went to Dublin a few weeks later, he left a
message for his sister-in-law Frances to give to Mary in case Fenian
assassination plots were successful: 'tell her that, at the end, if I
was able to think at all, I thought of her'.[13] It is hard to imagine a
greater testament to what she had come to mean to him.

That Mary Elcho, only twenty-four when this relationship began,
was able to keep for herself some good portion of Arthur's 'tender and affectionate nature' for nearly half a century suggests the
uniqueness of her personality. Not least were the still undeveloped
qualities of a mind that others would call 'original', 'delightful'
and 'full of pauses and shadows and leafy places'.[14] Several times
Arthur paid her the highest compliment he could give – that by
nature though not training she was a philosopher, concerned with
the same fundamental questions of meaning and purpose that
engaged him. Mary confirmed that she found details boring or
pointless unless she understood how they related to a larger principle and that she took 'an interest in quite abstract and impersonal things in fact I like them almost best'. During these years, she

organised and actually did the reading for a lecture series in ethics, literature and moral philosophy that the women Souls attended in the midst of the London season – her letters show familiarity with essays by Maeterlink, Romanes, Wallace, Kidd and Huxley.[15] She did not have the time or the self-confidence to write in any depth about her explorations in psychology or social evolution – she always felt unsupported in social terms by having such tastes at all – but it is hard to think of many society women interested to the same degree in the metaphysical speculations of men like Balfour and Haldane. Mary had 'an intense and active intellectuality. She lets nothing conceal itself that can be unravelled', her brother wrote, calling her 'the ferret' for her unwillingness to drop a topic she wanted to learn more about.[16]

Like Arthur, Mary was protective of her deepest emotions. Unlike him, she had spontaneous warmth with other people when alone or in company where she felt unthreatened. As her relationship with Arthur developed it created a private realm that gave them both a kind of psychological assurance in a larger social world where she was the long-suffering spouse of a notable roué and he an ambiguous bachelor. Over time they would come to share the jokes, oblique references, gossip and unspoken confidences of a married couple. But in the crucial year of 1887, at the beginning of the relationship, it is possible to see the new intimacy as helping Arthur to confound the marginal status associated with the childless, celibate and potentially effeminate male. For psychological health and political effectiveness, Arthur needed to discover and contain the emotions aroused by attachment and competition. Mary was integral to this – 'the wall of ice is melting', as his brother put it[17] – and his confidence in her contributed to his ability to navigate the challenges he faced over the next several years.

To say that Arthur had an image problem on the eve of undertaking the most challenging job in Salisbury's government would be an understatement. For decades, middle-class and radical pundits had mocked or vilified Britain's aristocrats as unpleasant anachronisms, tangential to the great forces of modern history.[18] Arthur never fit the pejorative trope of the roistering 'lords of misrule' condemned by Matthew Arnold as 'barbarians', but another stereotype of privilege had more resonance. This was the aristocrat as dandy, an indolent and sneering fop whose refinement itself was unmanly.[19] Hesitations about Arthur's virility had been abroad in London political circles for years, remnants of the unflattering nicknames from Cambridge days. During the 1880s Churchill blithely made him the butt of personal jokes – Winston called it 'harmless and friendly chaff' – and dubbed him Postlethwaite after the lisping aesthete in George du Maurier's *Punch* cartoons, who does indeed look like a Balfour. The *New Review* said the general impression was that Arthur was 'something of a sybarite, an epicurean, a Miss Nancy'.[20]

The Irish nationalist press staked out this terrain of attack the moment that Arthur's appointment was announced. He would, *United Ireland* assured its readers, prove to be the 'weakest and most effeminate of tyrants'. His pale, 'silk-skinned' visage and gangly frame betrayed a 'shattered system'. He needed a gold pince-nez to see, and his shapely hands shook so much that he dropped the notes he needed to get through a speech. 'Delicate nerves' forced him to get fifteen hours of sleep a day, a major handicap as Irish obstructionism kept the Commons sitting long after midnight. Fighting for a comfortable position on the narrow ministerial bench, his slouch was described predictably as 'limp', a freighted visual contrast to the always alert bearing of Gladstone, Parnell and the Irish members.[21]

As nationalists had experienced many times in the English construction of Irish identity, outward appearance encoded emotional and moral qualities.[22] Stereotype images of Arthur conveyed a temperament that was excitable and cold-hearted, cowardly and cruel – thus the cartoon images of his gleeful delight in the sufferings of political prisoners or evicted tenant farmers. 'When Dr. Tanner … calls poor Mr. Balfour "a ghoulish vampire who longs to swim in blood", does he really believe what he says?' asked *Graphic*.[23] He was often depicted as incapable of manly confrontation, instead relying on the 'feline' and 'feminine' weapons of revenge and ridicule.[24] At the heart of such depictions lay the question of whether he had enough fighting spirit for effective political combat. As Salisbury told a Conservative audience on the day the appointment was announced, 'our national fault is that too much softness has crept into our councils'.[25]

Recent scholars on the history of gender stereotypes have established the rising concern among the Anglo-American upper classes that highly educated men would not feel the passions necessary for action in an increasingly competitive world.[26] Men fit to exercise power were not supposed to be devoid of feelings, but rather to possess strong emotions that were controlled through character and humane sentiments. This was one of Parnell's greatest strengths. He gave listeners the impression of extraordinarily intense feelings rigidly and icily held in check. A man of genius like Gladstone not only channelled his own passions in positive directions but was able to inspire the same feelings in others, elevating their emotions.[27] Imagery of Arthur as languid or febrile pertained not just to his physical presence but his emotional register as well.

Stereotypes of Arthur's weaknesses gained traction when they were confirmed by his early performances in the House of Commons. 'Frowned portentously and grew angrily pale', reported Henry Lucy for *Punch*. 'Took everything seriously; trembling with righteous indignation.' His introduction of the government's new crimes bill on 28 March 1887 was 'a terrible fiasco', 'the most elementary want of tact and judgment coupled with an excited manner and a raised voice'. Two young MPs with brilliant careers ahead of them (George Curzon and Henry Asquith) remembered Arthur's debut as 'ineffective', 'hesitating' and 'callow'. Others thought he came near to breaking down.[28] The impressions did not dissipate quickly. London weeklies recorded any number of episodes in the months that followed when Arthur appeared 'rattled', 'cold', 'weary', 'sarcastic' or 'dismissive'.[29] Worst of all were perceptions that he had the feminine trait of petulance: 'Harcourt patronizingly told Balfour to go on. Tried to go on accordingly. Tim Healy on his legs again. Balfour pettishly said if that was the way he was to be received, wouldn't make statement at all, and so sat down. Irish Members laughed to see such fun ... more than ever delighted with this evidence of weakness.'[30] Even after Arthur's implacable and unapologetic defence of police action at the Mitchelstown riot in September 1887, *Graphic* – whose stance was hardly sympathetic to the nationalists – challenged that the ageing Gladstone routinely displayed 'more powers in his little finger' than were contained in 'the loins of the "bloodthirsty Balfour"'.[31]

The sexual subtext of these messages escaped the realm of press innuendo in a stunning piece of parliamentary theatre that occurred when the Commons reassembled in February 1888. By this time Arthur had been governing Ireland under the special provisions of the Irish Crimes Act (1887) for almost six months. Both the Plan of Campaign and Parnell's National League had been proscribed. The editors of newspapers that announced meetings of either group faced prosecution. Nationalists charged that the act itself was creating the criminals, since political activities long permitted were suddenly banned. Just after the opening of the 1888 session, Parnell moved an amendment to the Queen's Speech condemning the government's Irish administration.

Parnell had been absent through illness for much of the 1887 session, so this first real confrontation with the chief secretary was highly anticipated. In a speech dripping with vitriol, Parnell taunted Arthur's efforts as 'puny' and 'impotent'. Contrasting Balfour's supposed failures with the forcefulness of an earlier chief secretary, he concluded with controlled fury, 'Now that was a man.' Even more dramatic was the sudden intervention of the member for North-East Cork, William O'Brien, arriving just hours after his release from three months in Tullamore prison. In a speech that the *Annual Register* described as 'highly effective' and 'highly dramatic', O'Brien charged Arthur with 'hideous and cowardly' acts that betrayed the 'temper of a beaten and angry man, and I was going to say of an angry woman, but I do not want to say it, because it would be a gross libel upon that gentle and tender sex.'[32] Journalists' unease in reporting the episode indicated that even in their eyes some boundary of discourse had been overstepped. *Saturday Review* called Parnell and O'Brien 'foul-mouthed calumniators' for the sexual undertones of attacks made within the chamber.[33]

These insults aired on the floor of the House of Commons itself were not ones that Arthur could ignore. He responded with an extraordinary piece of parliamentary drama of his own. O'Brien's speech was so inflammatory that observers had expected the Irish secretary to leap instantly to his own defence. Instead he waited until the next night – the last of debate – to reply: 'In anticipation of his speech, and the reception it might meet with, the House was crowded in every part. Every seat on the floor was taken, and the galleries were thronged with eager listeners.' At the very opening of his carefully prepared response Arthur chose to address the insults to his manhood. He alluded to O'Brien's charge that his appearance and emotions were akin to women's, and went on to describe a particularly foul slur from *United Ireland* that had said he 'lusted for slaughter with a eunuchized imagination'. He further regaled the House of Commons with nasty things that the Irish had said about former chief secretaries of both parties, the funniest he could find being the characterisation of Sir George Trevelyan as a 'skunk and a cuttlefish'. This was not quite equal to Arthur himself having been called a eunuch, but his willingness to bring

up the most demeaning charges against him, to deflect them by
open acknowledgement and self-assured dismissal, marked a new
stage in his relationship with both his adversaries and the House
of Commons. The London press reported Arthur as 'quite jubilant
in his manner; sharply aggressive; a little flippant; bold, audacious,
uncompromising'.[34]

The ruthlessness and public mockery with which Arthur pursued O'Brien in the next year may have been fuelled by the insult-
ingly personal nature of these early attacks. O'Brien was notably
homophobic and already convinced that the Dublin Castle administration was filled with aristocratic 'perverts'.[35] As *United Ireland*'s editor, he kept the trope of emasculation alive for months.
In the spring of 1888 *Saturday Review* told London readers that
Arthur had been called 'an effeminate runaway' by a nationalist
MP in Dublin and a person whose 'sentiments and principles were
obviously bestial' by a Liberal home ruler in England. Sexual in-
nuendos surfaced again after the press, in response to the new,
highly phallic battering ram used in tenant evictions, decided to
designate it 'Balfour's maiden'.[36] Nevertheless the accusations of
weakness and effeminacy gradually diminished, due to Arthur's
implacable refusal to apologise for his policies, and his spirited
replies to detractors. Whatever else he was, it was clear he was not
cowardly. In 1891 the Irish MP Justin McCarthy framed O'Brien's
confrontations with Arthur explicitly in terms of a contest of manliness and declared Balfour to have won.[37]

The charge that Arthur's responses in the heat of battle were
insolent and dismissive was harder to overcome. Joseph Meisel
argues that 'epigrammatic, sarcastic phrase-making' was Disraeli's
'greatest legacy to parliamentary speech', though arrogant put-
downs were associated with aristocratic male discourse in general.[38]
Arthur honed his verbal banter through years of dinner-table argument with relatives, as well as the rapid-fire parlour games that,
according to Margot, he began to embrace during the autumn
recess of 1887.[39] In the Commons, his facility for pointed repartee
was established more quickly than certainty over what was being
expressed. Intermittently the press took the view of 'average electors' who 'do not understand persiflage, and always exaggerate a
jeer into a sort of insult'. Even Arthur acknowledged that the most
'adventitious aids' to debate were ones that both he and the Irish
relied on: exaggeration, epigram, invective, personal attack. On
the verge of becoming Commons leader in 1891 Arthur could still

be described as too often 'animated by lofty scorn. As you listen to him, you appreciate contempt as a fine art. He has devoted infinite pains to the cultivation of a natural aptitude for treating the other side as almost too absurd for words.'[40]

Arthur needed to create a different effect than this if he wanted to capture the high ground from his most formidable adversaries, Parnell and Gladstone. More than a gladiatorial arena, the House of Commons was an intimate stage, one on which its critical audience regularly participated to express their sentiments. The biggest challenges came in handling the caustic interjections that the Irish excelled at.[41] These were fluid, spontaneous, interactive moments, more like improvisation than following a script. The *Hansard* official accounts are hopeless for conveying this dimension of parliamentary life. Fortunately some very good press observers saw what every backbencher knew, that body language, tone of voice, facial expressions and timing of responses all affected the spoken word, determining whether something came across as emotional weakness or the confidence that allows for self-deprecation, as a defensive lashing out or a legitimate admonishment that earned the agreement of the members.[42]

That the Commons was an emotional theatre as much as a space of rational deliberation was obvious during Arthur's confrontations with the Irish. In early August 1889, while introducing the funding clauses for the Irish court system, he was interrupted twelve times in the course of his presentation, the business of the Commons degenerating into rapid exchange between four or five people across the floor. On the night of 8 August, 'a violent scene took place while the chief secretary was speaking'. E. P. Harrington, 'maddened beyond control' by Arthur's bland dismissal of an accusation, 'pressed forward till he reached the Gangway, striding towards the flushed Chief Secretary ... seemed as if he was about to take off his coat, cross floor, seize Chief Secretary by the throat'. About twenty of Harrington's Irish colleagues crowded in to restrain him.

Arthur's patience under 'the grossest provocation' eventually became legendary, but it was developed rather than innate. He told his sister Evelyn that he survived the fury because, unlike his colleagues Goschen and Chamberlain, 'his mind did not naturally turn to politics. He never thought about them in bed, wh[ich] was the test'. But he had also confided to Morley that he 'never slept well after a rough night ... One's nerves get on edge, and it takes time to cool'.[43] Nevertheless, by the end of 1889, the *Annu-al Register* said that increasingly Arthur succeeded at 'turning the interruptions to which he was exposed to good profit, while never losing either his self-command or the thread of his discourse'.[44] Instead it was Gladstone, the master of parliament increasingly un-able to contain his anger over Balfour's spontaneously delivered jabs, who succumbed to a 'new fury', 'savagery' and 'great bitter-ness' of tone. 'It is sad to see how the once-venerated statesman is gradually sinking to the *United Ireland* level of oratory', lamented *Graphic*. W. H. Smith thought that Gladstone, sitting on the bench opposite him, 'exhibits signs of excitement and anger which would be unaccountable in any other man, and it is difficult to believe that he is completely master of himself'.[45]

Arthur's increasing control of reactions like anger and scorn did not require him to become what he was not – mechanical or stolid. Observers described him as animated and responsive, not an inscrutable Disraelian sphinx or a somnolent Hartington. He was reported leaping to his feet, gloating, chortling, flinging his pencil dramatically in suppressed annoyance and gleefully baiting Gladstone for the fun of it.[46] But he learned to deliver sarcasm in a milder tone and to make a virtue of his own eccentricities by laugh-ing with those who mocked them.[47] The least histrionic of men, he developed an increasingly nuanced repertoire of emotional expression – a toolbox that ranged from pained gravity when he had to rebuke an opposition friend such as Morley, to sorrowful indignation in deconstructing the misstatements of opponents, to empathy in describing people he considered to be victims.[48] Unlike the bludgeoning Harcourt or the 'sledgehammer' Asquith, Arthur used emotional shifts and miscues to surprise listeners. A good example was the bland innocence with which he answered an irate nationalist as to why he had called a particular coroner's verdict 'corrupt'. Arthur apologised profusely and apparently sin-cerely, saying he did not intend to use the word 'corrupt'. What he meant to say was 'incompetent and worthless'.[49]

Borrowing from the Irish themselves, Arthur used humour, ani-mation and emotional dexterity to create fellow feeling or, at least, grudging respect. He gave his Commons audiences what London theatregoers were beginning to experience at the same time, per-formances that had the appearance of observing 'something that was going on next door', not grand gestures or epic drama but natural reactions and impromptu discourse. As George Curzon attested, Balfour's preference for 'more serviceable and extemporized speaking', with less peroration or posturing, would become standard in the Commons in the Edwardian era.[50]

As his Irish administration progressed through the most violent partisanship that Salisbury (of all people) had ever experienced, Arthur constructed the emotional demeanour that would become an enduring part of his public persona. His reputation shifted from the cold-hearted, brittle, insolent patrician, easily rattled and in poor control of his temper, to an amiable, imperturbable, even cooperative colleague and adversary. His sister-in-law noticed the change: 'Arthur has a newly acquired geniality, and the air of a leader of men. When I first knew him he was the young man whose powers had not been appreciated, and who showed a want of reverence to the old, and a want of cordiality to the young.'[51] Whether one agreed with his policies or excoriated them, by 1891 Arthur's ability to project equanimity and sunny reasonableness as he pursued highly contentious political goals was so well-established that it became a significant political asset in its own right.[52]

Arthur's four years as chief secretary for Ireland secured his future. In parliamentary terms his successes were achieved, as the *Pall Mall Gazette* noted, 'over the political corpse' of his rival Randolph Churchill, aided by the lacklustre performances of any other candidates for leadership on the Conservative front bench. Even the 'painfully honest incompetence' of the stolid, likable Commons leader W. H. Smith proved beneficial, for it meant that Arthur fought his parliamentary battles very nearly alone on the nights when Irish affairs were debated.[53] Yet House of Commons mastery, though essential, was not sufficient – Arthur was also administering a law that brought the dark undersides of control over unwilling peoples forcefully to public attention. Along with other Conservative leaders, he had to sell policies of coercion, to be followed later by 'conciliatory' benefits, to a public unaccustomed to hearing so directly the voices of people deeply opposed to what they defined as a foreign rule.

The crimes bill that Arthur enforced contained many troubling provisions for adherents of England's heritage of liberty and due process. For the first time, suspensions of normal laws and procedures applying to Ireland alone were made permanently available to the government, rather than subject to renewal by parliament each year. The executive of Ireland could 'proclaim' districts at will, suppress organisations it deemed dangerous, remove trials to different venues and give magistrates summary jurisdiction over offences such as conspiracies against the payment of rent or encouraging boycotting.[54] The act gave a single government official extraordinary discretion to ban organisations designed to promote political and economic change, in the process qualifying rights of speech, publication and assembly that Englishmen of every rank held dear. The nationalists argued that the act itself created the criminals, as activities long permitted in Britain suddenly became illegal.

In the first two years of Arthur's enforcement of the Irish Crimes Act, twenty-three sitting members of parliament, twelve priests, the lord mayor of Dublin, mayors of Sligo, Clonmel and Cork, barristers and doctors, journalists, poor law guardians, town commissioners and numerous of 'the very best and most respectable' country shopkeepers and farmers – almost two thousand people in all – had been jailed and a nearly equal number prosecuted for offences under the new legislation. Those who went to prison faced the same treatment as ordinary criminals – plank bed, hard labour, convict clothes, frigid cells and bread-and-water diets for disobedience. In the summer of 1888 the Irish nationalist organiser John Mandeville died six months after release from his incarceration as one of the first home rulers prosecuted during Arthur's administration. A coroner's inquest decided that the illness that killed him had been caused by his treatment in prison. The drama was compounded a few weeks later by the suicide of the doctor who had attended him.[55]

The fallout from this prompted one of the most callous replies Arthur ever constructed to the human tragedies of these years. Before a boisterous audience of more than four thousand people in Glasgow, he took two hours to address Mandeville's death, placed in the larger context of the 'ingrained and ineradicable falseness' of the Liberal assertion that 'prisoners detained under the [Coercion] Act were barbarously treated, their health undermined, and their lives in danger'. To rising waves of laughter, he used notes from government agents who had shadowed Mandeville after his release to argue that, only days before succumbing to a sudden illness, the dead man was a hearty, convivial rowdy enjoying tavern life, participating in a 'drunken row' and going about 'the ordinary average business of an Irish agitator'. The most thorough recent analysis of the episode presents Mandeville as a tee-totalling patriot performing his duties as a Poor Law Guardian and National League organiser as best he could during weeks of an illness that sounds like a lingering infection acquired around the time of his imprisonment.[56]

That same summer, the authorities began to use the battering ram and troops of the British Army to carry out evictions of farmers who had withheld rents in accordance with the Plan of Campaign's programme. Sketches and photographs of the apparatus filled the pages of the London weeklies. The government also took the unprecedented step of setting up a special commission authorised by an act of parliament to investigate Parnell's charges that the London *Times* had knowingly committed libel the year before by publishing manufactured evidence linking him to political assassination during the 'land war' years of the late 1870s and early 1880s. Even Salisbury's most recent and sympathetic biographer calls the proceedings a 'state conspiracy trial', as did Balfour's niece.[57] The cabinet selected the commission's three judges, urged its own attorney general to serve as counsel for the *Times* and channelled official information to the newspaper's defence team to make a case against the entire nationalist movement, not just its leader.

Arthur already suspected that the most incriminating documents against Parnell were forgeries, and this was publicly revealed in a moment of high drama in February 1889 when the forger Richard Pigott confessed, fled the country and committed suicide in a continental hotel. Many historians have made the whole dubious proceeding the prime minister's brainchild, but Arthur wrote several times that he had been 'largely responsible' for the format adopted.[58] In his view, Parnell's alleged complicities with revolutionary violence were never the main issue. The goal was to make the public fully aware of the motives and actions of all the men who hid behind an inflamed rhetoric of national oppression in order to gain land from the Protestants of Ireland, power for themselves and the destruction of the United Kingdom.

At each new stage in these unfolding dramas, press coverage of events, speeches and personalities fuelled the conflict over legitimacy. National politicians were increasingly expected to speak across the country – an 'odious addition to the burdens of political life' that Salisbury deplored and attributed to Gladstone – and with an eye to the reporters sitting in the front row just below the podium.[59] Letters to the editor reproved the words reported from public meetings and honorary dinners, where the speakers

themselves recycled their adversaries' wilder claims. Members in
the Commons began to address the House with an outside audience in view: 'What is Parliament?' asked *Punch*: 'A place men may
admire, respect, or hate, Where the Electorate's elect orate to the
Electorate.' As the *Annual Register* reported in summarising politics in 1888:

> Speeches of this sort, brilliant and incisive as they were, only served
> to aggravate the Opposition and to make the breach between Eng-
> lish and Irish more difficult to heal … The only visible result of the
> actual tactics pursued was an increased acrimony in dealings of
> opponents who hitherto had treated each other with courtesy and
> respect and a constant succession of letters addressed to the press by
> ministers and ex-ministers defending their utterances or wrangling
> over verbal differences.[60]

Against this echo chamber of assertion and counter-assertion,
Arthur asked, what did the mere English statesman have? Only
patient explication of fact, corrections of inflamed misinforma-
tion, laws patiently administered simply to prevent Irishmen, as
he wrote to Mary Elcho, from 'picking each other's pockets and
cutting each other's throats!'[61]

If there is one scholarly consensus about Arthur Balfour, it is his
indifference to public opinion, but indifference is not the same
as inattention. The shifting tone of Arthur's letters to his most
trusted Dublin underling, the permanent undersecretary Sir Joseph West Ridgeway, conveys the urgency he felt as waves of press
and platform vilification swept around him.[62] By 1890 a string
of by-election losses had reduced the Conservative and Liberal
Unionist numbers. Demoralised members on the ministerial side
were absenting themselves from sittings, and the government was
surviving on majorities that both the press and the modern historian call 'derisory'.[63] Arthur's challenge as the months dragged on
was nearly unprecedented – nothing less, it might be argued, than
the development of political 'spin', the modern tools of messaging and image control. In Virginia Crawford's assessment, one of
Arthur's underestimated skills turned out to be 'his appreciation
of the crucial role of public relations in politics', especially his
awareness that what he did was less important than how he was
perceived.[64]

*

It took some experimentation before Salisbury's government could be said to have managed the public relations nightmare of the home rule years. The effort it took can be seen through the eyes of one of Arthur's most valuable underlings, his new private secretary George Wyndham. George's life since his return from the Suakin campaign two years before had been full of tumult. Restless and discontented, and fighting a sense of life's futility, within a year he had fallen deeply in love with Lady Sibell Grosvenor, the recently widowed daughter-in-law of the Duke of Westminster. She was eight years older than George and the mother of three children aged seven to eleven, including the young heir to the colossal Westminster fortune. Beautiful, devout and sweet-tempered, Sibell was highly sought after – George Curzon may have had an affair with her even before her acquiescent invalid husband died, and he was one candidate for her hand.[65] She had to overcome family resistance in choosing Wyndham, but in early February 1887 they were married in the private chapel at Eaton Hall. Within a month Sibell was pregnant with George's only child, a son born the next December.

Sibell had a home on the Westminster estate in Cheshire that the duke had given her, with the understanding that she would not move her children elsewhere if she remarried. Thus George Wyndham, not yet twenty-four, acquired a ready-made family, gained access through marriage to one of the most prominent peers of the realm and became something of an appendage in his wife's house. On the honeymoon, he took another leap into the unknown by quitting his military career when he received Arthur's invitation to join his staff. George had no particular experiences to recommend him. As he confessed, he did not even know how much time a chief secretary spent in Dublin.[66] Nevertheless he plunged into the boisterous world of politics with which he would have a love–hate relationship for the rest of his life. Because he was away from Sibell so often, his letters provide a fascinating window on Arthur's years in Ireland.

Initially George found his work environment at the Irish office in Great Queen Street 'very dull and dusty and the view from it foggy and filthy'. He described his duties as those of a 'political aide-de-camp', 'there to receive addresses, sit upon platforms', take amusingly frumpy Irish ladies into formal dinners and play billiards to pass evenings at the chief secretary's lodge in Dublin.[67] Quickly, however, he assumed the role of research assistant. As

Arthur scrambled to rebut the criticisms of his policy, an early
tactic was to expose the inconsistencies between his opponents'
current positions and their former actions. George spent hours in
back issues of *Hansard's Parliamentary Debates* and the *Times*, finding examples where Irish members had launched vitriolic attacks
on English politicians they now called far-sighted statesmen, or
where Liberals had sanctioned legal actions that they now excoriated. As Parnell told the Commons, the chief secretary 'considers
it sufficient excuse, whenever he is accused of excessive tyranny or
mal-administration in Ireland, to point to the Bench opposite and
say "you did the same thing, or worse, when you were in Office"'.
Speaking to a Conservative audience in Battersea, where George
was hoping to be adopted as a parliamentary candidate, Arthur
got good press mileage by condemning Gladstone for denying
that his administration had ever imposed heavier sentences after a
conviction was lost on appeal, when government records revealed
that Liberals had done this much more frequently than the Conservatives. He dismissed Gladstone's pass-the-buck defence that as
prime minister he had not known about it.[68]

George was also responsible for mastering the statistical evidence of rural crime and police activity and distilling it into forms
that could be used in public. The chief secretary relied on quan-
tification to give data-driven authority to government policy – in
Margaret O'Callaghan's view, no people in Europe with the possible exception of the French were as subject to state scrutiny as
the Irish peasantry under Balfour. In a private memorandum for
the cabinet, Arthur admitted that inadequacies in systematic data
collection made understanding realities on the ground in rural
Ireland very difficult.[69] That meant, however, that he could more
easily massage the data to suit his policy needs, arguing either for
improvements that showed government effectiveness or continuing unrest that justified extending coercion.

Arthur's eventual mastery of this type of evidence defied his image as the aristocratic aesthete, and he became increasingly good
at mobilising it after George Wyndham entered the House of Commons in 1889. 'When the Irish estimates are on', George wrote, 'I
sit behind Arthur and note all the speeches as if I was going to
reply to each, and keep going out to his room to refresh his memory on each subject by consulting the official files which are spread
out in three rows across the floor of the room.' By 1890 it was
common to find the press reporting that Arthur's presentations

were of 'extraordinary lucidity' and technical mastery, as well as 'really lively' and 'most aggressive and spirited' in defence of his actions.[70]

Arthur learned quickly, however, as Gladstone had done before him, that political discourse needed more than confusing arguments about contested statistics or parsing of legal distinctions. Vivid anecdotes – concrete and personal stories – made policy debates spring to life. 'What comes home to people's minds are specific examples of gross tyranny', he wrote, in a statement that any nationalist would have agreed with, while differing in the name of the tyrant.[71] *Freeman's Weekly* in Dublin ran a striking series of cartoons centred around events from the front pages that showed Arthur in the guise of diabolical enforcer, beaming and/ or maniacal as he inflicted torments on suffering Ireland.[72] 'Now we have him IN, let us torture and degrade him', orders 'Brave Mr. Balfour' while the imprisoned William O'Brien is forcibly stripped and his head shaved in a prison cell. In 'This Devil's Work', an Arthur drawn in red with cloven feet stands in the moonlit door of a ruined cottage, oblivious to the evicted women, tiny children and elderly man huddling outside. Other Irish cartoonists depicted Arthur, a lowland Scot, with features of the English press's stereotypical Celtic terrorist: snub nose, round glaring eye, ungainly body and fierce exultation as weeping Erin cowers before him. In these visual messages, the Irish nationalists are straight nosed, full bearded, frock coated and upright. It is Arthur, in the sway of vicious passions, who is depicted as using violence in a political cause.

Throughout 1888 George Wyndham was charged with responding to anecdotal calumnies like these with counter-narratives culled from the police reports. Early in his administration, Arthur urged that local officials provide him with 'well established details' of individual outrages as they occurred: 'If I can get this, and I am sure that the Authorities on the spot can easily furnish it if they can be made to understand precisely what is wanted, I should be placed in a very strong Parliamentary position.'[73] The chance was, of course, that the authorities knew how Dublin Castle wanted behaviours and motivations to be interpreted. Personal crimes by the local troublemaker could just as easily be labelled 'revolutionary' or nationalist intimidation.

In a stream of letters to the press that began 'Mr. Balfour has desired me to reply to ...', George combatted nationalist narratives of events by deflating what he presented as their old-fashioned

hyperbole and melodrama.[74] The 'Myth of the Infant Prisoner' de-
constructed how the arrest of one sturdy, rambunctious teenager
had produced 'all the tales of imprisonment of tender children
who intimidate the police, and all the stories of little girls who
only say "boo" to a bailiff'. In 'Mr Finucane's Sentence', George
showed that Finucane was convicted not for listening to a speech
– though he had done that – but for coercing a local farmer into
giving up his tenancy. Compiled into the pamphlet *Lies and Replies,*
George's letters used vivid scene-setting and comic detail to present a loutish, law-defying Irish adversary quite different from the
gallant home rule patriot. 'It required a man with the special gifts
of George Wyndham to pick out the cases to which a telling rejoinder could be made, and to make it with force and hilarity', noted
one observer.[75] In George's letters, an elderly widow whose home
was burned down at the direction of the chief secretary, a man
sentenced to three months in prison for winking at a pig and the
arrest of a typesetter for simply doing his job were all fantastical
misrepresentations that metamorphosed through a kind of anecdotal explosion to reappear endlessly in the ponderous platform
speeches and credulous journalistic accounts of the home rulers.

The welter of individual episodes and confusing denunciations
of these years produced a set of melodramatic encounters that
characterised the Balfour–Irish Nationalist conflict. The court-
house riot, tenant eviction, gentlemanly nationalist's first encounter with prison became fixed in the public mind. While George
Wyndham's letters patiently corrected factual errors, Arthur's
speeches reframed the whole meaning of such events, shifting
the angle of view, redefining who was victim and who aggressor in
every encounter. Evictions were not traumatic ejections of innocent women, children and old men at the hands of weapon-wield-
ing authorities. Instead, sturdy recalcitrants in fortified houses
endangered the lives of agents of the law by assaulting them 'with
boiling water, red hot pokers, filth of every kind, every species of
outrage, injury, and insult'.[76] Crowds who turned up to express
support for a victim of the coercion laws were portrayed as rowdies
courting a police response. The true targets of boycotting were
not egregiously rapacious landlords, but multitudes of common
Irish men and women who wanted to live in their own way within
the protections of British law. Arthur reinterpreted victimhood
by describing how Irish policemen and ordinary citizens suffered
at the hands of fanatics who cared more about their own power

than the daily lives of their countrymen. O'Callaghan leads the group of Irish historians who argue that Arthur's multi-pronged media offensive, which included the Parnell Commission's fifteen months of widely reported inquiry into Irish political agitation, was a triumph in establishing an equation between criminality and Irish nationalism in the mind of the English public.[77]

The Irish replied, though they could not prove, that Arthur followed his own seamy scripts in these years, but his were enacted in theatres of power more shadowy than the highly scrutinised stages on which the home rule advocates operated – it is worth noting that Britain's first Official Secrets Act was passed in 1889. Arthur used a hidden 'black ops' slush fund to pay informants at a much higher level than his predecessors. The Home Office's secret service branch for surveillance and infiltration mirrored the obscure plots of Fenian cells, to the extent of instigating terrorist attacks with the overall goal of discrediting the Irish leadership.[78] From his office Arthur mobilised a private consortium of aristocratic friends to underwrite Protestant estates threatened with bankruptcy through the Plan of Campaign. His 'bland' denials in the Commons of any knowledge of the syndicate are among the few outright lies he can be charged with during these years, but his letter asking George Pembroke to join remains in the archives, along with a statement that his own name could not, of course, be associated with it.[79] The kangaroo court of the government-aided Parnell Commission was as subject to political influence as any Irish jury. A hint survives that, when the commission's report exonerated Parnell to great public acclaim, Arthur might have been involved in keeping William O'Shea from dropping the divorce suit that ended the threat Parnell represented in precisely the months when the government's fortunes were at their lowest ebb.[80] The sheer number and murkiness of the episodes may explain why portions of the public records relating to Arthur's tenure in Ireland remain sealed more than a century after he left the office.

When the ailing and increasingly ineffective Commons leader W. H. Smith withdrew from politics in the summer of 1891, Lord Salisbury did not promote his nephew to the position without consulting key members of the Conservative–Liberal Unionist alliance. Their reasons for backing Arthur were revealing of the political situation evolving in the last two decades of the century. 'We want a personality in the Commons to rally around', one Conservative told Salisbury; 'one who will inspire our Party all through the country with courage – & awake their SENTIMENT', said another. Arthur's only possible rival for the position, the Liberal Unionist chancellor George Goschen, explained why he would withdraw from consideration: 'Balfour', he said, was the only front bench minister who 'had impressed the popular imagination'.[81] The unity of responses hints at qualities that went beyond Arthur's successes in establishing his fighting spirit in parliament, 'framing' his home rule adversaries in the press and wielding the tools of state power. The more inclusive political society that emerged during the late-Victorian decades required leaders who could sustain a 'public personality' and, through this, link voters with the nation's fundamental principles as their party defined them.

With the waning of deference to traditional and hereditary authorities earlier in the century, the connection that popular political figures such as John Bright and William Gladstone made with an expanding electorate came through a Victorian 'code of sincerity' in which politicians spoke 'man to man' with audiences of strangers about their inner convictions as to the common good.[82] In the words of Pam Morris, non-deferential legitimacy had to be 'visible and emotional, because reason alone does not ensure' the feelings of investment and association required for freely given support. In the 1870s Gladstone, 'the People's William', became the master of what Max Weber labelled charismatic, democratic leadership, partly with innovative outreach techniques such as the whistle-stop tour, serial mass meetings and impassioned pamphlets, and partly because he learned to use 'his intense ardour of temperament, like an actor's, which, while he is speaking, makes him seem immensely in earnest'.[83]

An insightful study by D. A. Hamer argues that Gladstone gave the new electorate what it hoped for and what he himself experienced – both a rhetoric and a feeling of 'democratic optimism' about Britain's moral intentions and potential for improving mankind. The rousing affirmation he received from audiences fed his inclination to use emotional connection, sweeping assertion and catchy slogans like 'Remember Mitchelstown' to reach his public, creating a positive feedback loop of declaration and acclamation that supported his own conviction that he was right in his policies. Hamer puts Gladstone's psychological-political profile into an evangelical frame in which an activist God channelled his will through the common people, who conveyed their sound moral judgements in their electoral support of the Liberal Party.[84] Not surprisingly, the Conservative leadership and a great portion of the aristocracy viewed these developments with considerable scepticism. Neither Salisbury nor Balfour, despite their theism, thought it likely that the deity, if he conveyed his will in national politics at all, was doing so through the English or Irish voter. As Arthur impolitely wrote to Gladstone's daughter, 'it is unfortunate, considering that enthusiasm moves the world, that so few enthusiasts can be trusted to speak the truth'.[85]

At a house party in December 1888, Percy Wyndham and George Pembroke had a discussion on the two great political rivals Gladstone and Disraeli. They agreed that Disraeli had been a 'humbug who knows', while Gladstone was a 'humbug who humbugs himself'.[86] Perhaps Pembroke had heard from Eddie Hamilton of Gladstone's statement in the summer of 1887 that there was one thing about which he had a perfectly clear conscience: 'he could honestly assert that he had never said anything in politics which he did not *believe*'. The distinction between the earnest, self-deluded public man and the skilled performer of political sincerity ran through a long discourse on hypocrisy in the Anglo-European tradition, but it gained greater resonance with the arrival of the mass electorate.[87] In the mid-Victorian decades, the 'almost confessional sincerity' of the democratic leader rested on congruence between inner and outer selves, with the ability to 'articulate an impassioned interiority' proving the candour of discourse shared between speaker and audience.[88] The manipulative or 'cynical' politician learned to perform this congruence, wearing a mask of sincerity behind which might lurk other motives and feelings. In terms of political style, many aristocrats, ensconced within the Westminster and Whitehall corridors of power, preferred the sardonic self-fashioning of a Disraeli to the self-deceiving earnestness of Gladstone.

In Arthur's generation, every political figure with potential for national leadership was scrutinised for his solution to the problems of self-presentation and audience connection. Lord Rosebery, for example, established his credentials a decade earlier than Arthur through his astounding ability to reach the crowd: 'Eschewing the thunderous moral earnestness of Gladstone, the cold, remorseless logic of Chamberlain and the vicious invective of Lloyd George, he relied instead on irony, romance, urbane mockery and rich imagery to cast a spell over his audience.'[89] Fifteen months apart in age and with remarkable similarities in the psychological, social

and intellectual forces that had shaped their lives, Balfour and
Rosebery shared a mutual antipathy that has never been fully explained, but this difference in the control of self-display may have
played its part. On his best day, Arthur was not a commanding
presence, a dramatic speaker or a charismatic performer who cast
a spell over crowds. The persona he would come to occupy would
have to rest on something else.

The question of connecting with the public – especially a large
audience of strangers – was clearly on Arthur's mind in these years.
To his sister-in-law he defined the orator as 'a man whose public ut-
terances depended, not upon himself alone, but upon the action
and reaction between himself and the audience he was addressing'. By this definition, he said, no man was more an orator than
he.[90] Arthur's solution to the challenge of public discourse was to
confide in his audience rather than command it. He paid listeners
the compliment of showing his mind spontaneously at work, apol-
ogising when he discovered he had belaboured a point, pursuing
qualifications others might have omitted and acknowledging when
his personal feelings might be affecting his judgement. Arthur's
speeches were conversational, often provoking laughter when he
admitted his own mistakes or responded with raillery to a heckler.
The emotions he revealed were moderate ones hedged in by the
complexity of the issues.

Arthur's public performances, when they worked, contained a
lightness of touch and flexibility that took the press some time to
get used to. The *Saturday Review* caught the new demeanour in 1888:

> If any one looks a little below the surface, he will find no lack of
> seriousness in Mr. Balfour's speech, though the seriousness may be
> clothed with something like that jesting air which made the nincom-
> poops of another day so furiously angry with Canning. Certainly Mr.
> Balfour did not give himself the tragedy airs of Mr. Gladstone. He
> did not say that in serving his country he was prepared for even
> worse sufferings, etc; that his career might be short, but he trusted,
> etc; or that he hoped a good Providence would forgive the wicked
> men who, not knowing what they did, called him names. In other
> words, there was nothing of Pecksniff and nothing of Chadband,
> about Mr. Balfour's manner [references to two Dickens characters
> who embody hypocrisy]; and there are, no doubt, some people who
> are unable to recognize seriousness unless it wraps itself in some of
> the familiar formulae consecrated by these great men.[91]

Fig. 9 Arthur faces down the ageing Gladstone, who whispers with John Morley from the opposite bench, Graphic, 10 March 1894

Arthur's ability to sustain a sincerely held, self-contained emotional delivery reinforced his message that his adversaries were intemperate – so in the sway of passion that they could not be trusted to get the facts straight, admit their own partial knowledge or renounce violence as a political tool. His stance marginalised the vehement and the inspired alike, appealing instead to the common-sense feelings of well-intentioned citizens who could be trusted to follow how a politician's mind worked.

Arthur's form of sincerity avoided the magical 'glamour and grandeur' associated with the spectacle of traditional authority, as well as the messianic simplifications of the charismatic leader. But it also marked a distancing of individual interiority from the self shown in public. What Arthur said in political life was nearly always truthful according to his own understandings, and sincerely meant – he was not a good enough actor to lie blithely. But not all information or feelings that might be considered relevant to the case were declared. An inviolate inner self maintained its secrets in order for the politician to sooth, bluff, entice, compromise and evade as public need required. It is worth pointing out how feminine these traits could appear, though as Norman Vance notes, Arthur's willingness to bring emotional subtlety, lack of dogmatism and 'feline shrewdness' into the public sphere also made him one of the first 'essentially modern figures' in British politics.[92]

Gladstone recognised that a generational shift was taking place (see Fig. 9). In 1891 he told Edward Hamilton that he regretted Arthur's appointment as leader of the Commons because he feared for 'the standard of public life', 'the *morale* of A B, as well as that of Chamberlain and Randolph C[hurchill], was not a high one ... A B was not *straight* enough and too inclined to quibble – indeed, he only stopped just short of telling lies'.[93] As Arthur made his reputation at the expense of both the Irish and the Grand Old Man of liberalism, the virtues of honour, integrity and purity of motivation were disappearing among public men, sacrificed to the qualities that Gladstone saw in Arthur – levity, instrumentality and concealment.

6

———◆———

Country House Party

Mary Elcho and Arthur Balfour

O N 23 JANUARY 1889, Mary Elcho wrote to Arthur that the last of her house guests at Stanway had finally departed. On the whole, she thought the nine-day gathering had been a success, but confessed that she had 'rather counted the days for them to go'.[1] One of the most beloved hostesses of her generation, Mary was sometimes an anxious party-giver, and for this particular one she'd had a lot on her mind. Two weeks before, she and her three small children had barely escaped with their lives when a late-night fire destroyed Clouds, the Wyndhams' newly completed mansion in Wiltshire. She was also midway through her fourth pregnancy in five years of marriage, and out of sorts because she would miss a visit to Dublin to see Arthur before he returned to England in late February. The fact that Mary did not cancel this winter party or even limit its duration attests to the importance of extended visiting for the late-Victorian elites, as well as to the resources that this privileged class devoted to one of its most formative institutions of sociability.

Literary sources provide a variety of approaches for understanding these occasions. Novelists have depicted country house gatherings as scenes of Arcadian retreat, of coarseness and buffoonery, of melodrama or snobbish in-fighting, of Jamesian emotional purgatory or theatre of the absurd.[2] Social historians generally choose a functionalist approach. Leonore Davidoff and Mark Girouard present the rituals of aristocratic socialising as a serious business used to structure elite marriage options, control social mobility and broker politics in an era of dramatic social change.[3] From this perspective, Mary's party served several purposes: the Pembrokes were being repaid for earlier hospitality at Wilton; Lord Elcho,

Hugo, had some game to clear out with a few days of shooting; and DD Balfour (no relation to Arthur) was being introduced to other members of the Souls in the intimate setting of the country house. Yet the novelists' depictions remain compelling reminders of the intricate emotional dynamics and multiple experiences that lay at the heart of this semi-ritualised institution of elite social life. If privately experienced phenomena such as desire, boredom or nostalgia are the creations of history and social circumstance,[4] so too are the intimate encounters of small-scale sociability. As the forms of elite country house entertaining changed over time, the psychological demands of these events were transformed as well. The multiple sources available about this party of Mary's reveal some of the socially manifested, challenged and constructed experiences in the private entertainments of the late-Victorian elites.

Mary Elcho's gathering combined two traditions of aristocratic hospitality that date from the eighteenth century, when new forms of sociability between men and women of roughly equal social rank first supplemented and later supplanted entertainments that had stressed hierarchical display and patronage.[5] One old tradition was the extended visit at which an individual guest became a temporary member of the household, following its routines and engaging in its activities. 'I write an hour or two every morning', noted Alexander Pope on a visit in 1718, 'then ride out a hunting upon the Down, eat heartily, talk tender sentiments with Lord Bathurst, or draw plans for houses and gardens ... At night we play at commerce and play pretty high ... I like this course of life so well that I am resolved to stay here till I hear of somebody's being in town that is worth coming after.'[6] The other tradition centred on country fetes, where house guests along with neighbours and county worthies assembled for a specific purpose such as races, a hunt ball or a coming-of-age celebration. As late as 1859 the author of *Habits of Good Society* still described the 'country party' as one at which neighbourhood hierarchies would figure prominently and conversation would be 'local' and 'unintelligible to you'.[7]

By this time, however, an elision of country house visiting and 'partying' in the country was beginning. Improvements in transportation and communication made the real difference in great house entertaining. People born in the 1820s or 1830s remembered that in their youth 'going into the country was serious business' and 'visitors were few and far between'.[8] By the last decades of the century, Britain's increasingly dense rail networks allowed

hostesses in the remotest locations to invite carefully selected visitors from across the island with some assurance that they could
arrive at the same time and leave when they were supposed to. As
travel became easier, expectations rose that an invitation to a country house implied a 'party' that had been consciously arranged to
bring together people who 'like each other and suit each other
not a little'. Etiquette books began advising hostesses to specify
the time frame of an invitation – a repudiation of open-ended hospitality that showed house parties were no longer serendipitous
gatherings, but purposeful constructions of individuals who either
had existing relationships or who, in the mind of the hostess,
might be expected to form new friendships.[9] Weekends – Saturday-to-Monday as they were known – were just beginning in houses
close to London. This aside, parties with a relatively stable cohort
of guests lasted from five to fourteen days, which was plenty of
time to fill even when hunting, shooting or a special celebration
formed the main activity.

Sociologists of leisure point out a variety of ways that 'spare
time' can be spent: rest and recuperative puttering; attending to
private affairs; 'mimetic' activities from games to hiking, drawing
to performance; and 'sociability' – non-purposeful interaction
with others outside of everyday settings.[10] One of the attractions of
an informal country house visit was the opportunities it provided
for so many of these pastimes. One of the challenges of an extended country house *party* was the focus it placed on sociability and
encounters that lacked the protections of institutional roles or the
anonymity of the modern-day resort. 'Easy mirth', 'general hilarity' and 'playful physical contact' were all more characteristic of
country encounters – Frances Horner's description of the rotund
R. B. Haldane 'looking like a Sunday joint' as he tobogganed on a
tea tray retains its freshness because it arouses such an unexpected
vision of that dignified statesman.[11] Since country house parties
provided the main occasion for extended inter-sex socialising during the Victorian period, their potential for discovery, self-revelation and emotional contretemps was high.

The most famous of pre-war visits remain the massive shooting
and card parties associated with Edward VII. These were highly
formalised occasions, however, and therefore anomalous. Even as
Prince of Wales, Edward was such a stickler for protocols of dress
and presentation that tiny lapses provided endless occasions for
embarrassment and distorted behaviour.[12] In the presence of

royalty, guests could not presume the equality of stating a clear preference or breaking off an encounter by tacit agreement. But as Georg Simmel explained in a sociological study written at this time, at the heart of genuine sociability – the 'play form' of human association – lay the fiction of equality.[13] Whether at games or conversation, inherent in the willingness to interact for the sheer pleasure of it lay the agreement that extrinsic differences of rank, age, wealth, even gender be eliminated and encounters allowed to unfold according to the mutually acknowledged 'rules of the game'. The presence of royalty precluded this fiction and prevented the amiable 'intercourse of persons on equal footing' that extended sociability was coming to represent in an increasingly inclusive and varied social world.[14]

Mary, like most of the hostesses in Balfour's milieu, fostered an approach to country house entertaining that was less hierarchical and male-dominated, more casual and co-ed, than were parties for the Prince of Wales.[15] Activities at which guests could participate on relatively equal terms were common. If shooting showed men in their archaic role as dominators of nature, walking, sketching, conversation, parlour games, tennis and croquet created fields in which men and women were more equal. Mary expected individual interests to be pursued, but her mild insistence on general interaction at dinner and in the evening encouraged the formation of a group *esprit* that itself worked to establish intimacy. In part, she was restoring a focus on pleasures shared among all members of a party that had been eclipsed when mid-Victorian obsession with respectable behaviour and the harsh judgements of others discouraged self-revelation. She was also allowing more opportunities for private encounters than had been common when women, especially, were expected to be visible in the public areas of the house all day.[16] Navigating this new informality posed its own challenges and tests of personality, however, as the restraints on male/female interaction relaxed and the demands of group participation intensified.[17]

Daisy White, the thirty-year-old American member of the Souls, reached Stanway for Mary's party on Tuesday, 15 January, during that cosy early evening interlude when guests were relaxing at tea and before they wandered off to dress for dinner.[18] Although her husband Harry would not appear until Thursday, she found that the rest of the guests were comfortably ensconced. George

Fig. 10 Stanway House, Gloucestershire. The great hall runs between the
lantern window and the large door to its left.

Curzon, an old friend, and Doll Liddell were 'talking alone' in
the drawing room. Hugo was rehearsing theatricals with Gladys de
Grey on an impromptu stage set up in the great hall (see Fig. 10).
At the other end of the room, Mary, the Pembrokes and DD Balfour were 'trying to work up a charade to eke out the amusements
on the acting night'. Also present were Hugo's bachelor brother
Alan Charteris and another couple, the Bourkes, who were distant
relatives of Mary. The guest whom Daisy did not know was 23-year-
old DD, the only unmarried woman present. As usual, Daisy took
care to describe her first impression of a new acquaintance: 'Miss
DD tall fair pale quiet in manner … Lovely long lashes altogether
an attractive girl.'

Daisy's account provides a wonderfully immediate *mise-en-scène*
of arrival at a country house party. Letters and memoirs contain
enough of these moments to indicate the psychological adventure
that visiting could entail. These accounts – with their careful descriptions of the journey to the party, encounters with other guests
along the way, the first glimpse of the house and its setting, the
moments of greeting – dimly echo the tropes of 'adventure quest'
narratives of travel to more exotic imperial locations.[19] The journey itself constituted a liminal domain, as familiar, self-controlled
routines and environments were left behind. In the days before

automobiles transformed country house entertaining once again, visiting involved a temporary abandonment of independence since the guest had to rely on others for timetables and transport. Arthur Balfour acquired a motor car as soon as he could, but in the 1890s he anticipated the mobility it would provide by bringing his bicycle to country house visits so that he could get himself to the train station or go off on solitary rural excursions.[20]

Much of the etiquette surrounding visiting was designed to restore feelings of autonomy even as guests became immersed in someone else's surroundings. Daisy's late afternoon arrival was standard and introduced newcomers to the house at the most structured and predictable time of the day. Everyone had some idea of what tea, assembling for dinner and formal dining entailed.[21] In these hours fellow guests met, determined affinities and set up plans for casual activities. The next day's tour of the house and grounds served to orient first-time visitors to the spaces and resources available to them. By this time, the hostess would also have informed guests of any 'rules of the house', such as when to gather for meals, where to smoke and whether attendance at church or prayers was expected. In 1901, Raymond Asquith reported an alarming 'rule' at Clovelly Court that required guests 'to plunge *en echelon* into the Atlantic Ocean as near the centre of it as may be at precisely 5 minutes before 8 every morning. We are rowed out in purple bathing dresses by bronzed descendants of Armada heroes until there is no land in sight ... and then at a given signal we leap into the blue and bottomless swell and are borne hither and thither like helpless jelly fish in the racing tide.' Mary had no rituals like this. Guests made their own way to the breakfast room as they wished, and even the midday meal was optional. On Sunday, DD Balfour and Doll Liddell returned from a walk to discover that the others had started lunch without them.[22]

The fiction that guests should consider themselves 'at home' in the country house was underscored by the freedom they experienced for most of the day. Proprietors were not expected to be around visitors the whole time: 'the old belief that it was the duty of a hostess never to lose sight of her guests for a moment is now exploded. She sees them comfortably established in the drawing-room, and then departs' for a morning of household arrangements and private business.[23] Though women for decorum's sake might be expected to remain visible to others unless actually ill, members of a house party were advised to read, write letters or

go for walks: 'anything is better than dangling about the house doing nothing all the morning'.[24] Mary's male guests were shooting
on Monday, Tuesday, Thursday and Saturday. Daisy spent her first
morning at Stanway in her room, the next making costumes for
the charades and Friday visiting a friend in nearby Broadway.

At luncheon, a hostess rejoined those members of the party who
were not engaged elsewhere and might suggest 'one or two plans'
for the afternoon. Though she would make herself available for
those at a loose end, she was urged to 'allow them to please themselves' and not insist on their 'doing something'.[25] Augustus Hare,
an inveterate country house visitor, was astounded when he was
not given this flexibility at Streatham Hall in Exeter: 'This is the
oddest house I ever was in! Everything is arranged for you, from
the moment you get up till the moment you go to bed, and you are
never allowed to deviate from the rule laid down.' Frederick Ponsonby noted how guests of the Prince of Wales would plot to avoid
their host's insistence on knowing that everyone had a worthwhile
activity for the afternoon and enforcing something if not.[26]

As nearly as possible, then, a country house visit replicated the
patterns of daily life experienced by the elites anyway: mornings
spent on personal affairs, afternoons that might or might not involve small group expeditions, evenings devoted to social interaction. Mirroring one's daily life in a setting without the normal
responsibilities allowed guests to feel at home and in accord with
their surroundings. Books of advice eerily duplicated the subtext
revealed in letters from this generation. Presenting oneself as natural, not artificial or self-conscious, was admired, but the sort of
'natural' one should be was also constrained. It required being at
ease and putting others at ease, being open and candid but holding in reserve thoughts and emotions that should be expressed
only among intimates. Sociability in the country house reflected
Simmel's goals of good will, harmony, self-regarding and other-regarding sensibilities held exquisitely in balance for the purpose of
enhancing both personal and group enjoyment (see Fig. 11).

The psychic effort to achieve such self-possession was sustained
by the long periods of the day during which guests were left to
their own devices. In Erving Goffman's terms, the 'situational
awareness' demands of extended socialising required times and
spaces where involvement was not expected.[27] As Arthur put it in
a letter from Highclere in 1895: 'I am sitting (1 P.M.) – rather
melancholy – in my bedroom, not daring to go down lest I should

Fig. 11 Casual sociability at the country house party, Lucien Davis,
ILN, Christmas 1892

exhaust the weather, the frost, the prospects of the Government
and the Japanese war before the real burden of the day begins'
– the burden being the effort to appear natural and at ease with
relative strangers, or even friends, from afternoon through the
late evening.[28]

The party as a whole coalesced for tea, dinner and the evening's
entertainments. These were so much the set piece of the day that
fifty years later DD Balfour remembered her chagrin at having to
wear informal tea-gowns to dinner because her best frock was being reserved for later in the week. The most memorable activity at
Mary's party involved the amateur theatricals on Thursday night.
Hugo and Gladys performed their two-person skit *The Happy
Pair*.[29] They had been practising for several weeks and probably
presented it at two other house parties in December and January.
Even so, Gladys was nervous because of her three-page opening
monologue. After this, seven of the party acted the charade that
was being devised when Daisy arrived on Tuesday. The word was
'primrose'. Daisy and Emmie Bourke were prim Puritans in the
first scene, along with George Pembroke and Harry White dressed
as cavaliers. Next Gladys and Pembroke appeared as 'Beauty and
the Beast' to suggest the rose. Finally, the ensemble depicted a

scene from *The Vicar of Wakefield*, whose protagonist is named Primrose. At the end of this, Curzon's high spirits so overcame him
that he 'astonished the audience by seizing his daughter's waist
[this was DD as Olivia] and waltzing round the stage with her –
most unorthodox'.[30] The evening concluded with the house guests
in costume grouped on the steps to the great hall, watching the
moonlight stream through the oriel window as Emmie Bourke and
DD sang – a lovely concert, Mary called it.

Hostesses and their grown daughters bore the responsibility for
evening activities at a country house party, and etiquette books
suggested various amusements: charades, theatricals, tableaux
vivants, seances, parlour games, dancing and music.[31] So many materials from the period describe these group activities that it is easy
to overestimate their casualness. That they figure as dramatic set
pieces in novels, and moments to record in diaries, indicates their
potential for excitement and subversion. The mid-Victorians had
expressed real doubts about the self-display involved in acting, because it might foster skills in deceit and disguise that were dangers
to a society concerned with accurately identifying the character of
newcomers. Theatricals were also a challenge because, under the
guise of playing a part, they might encourage behaviours censored
in ordinary encounters.[32] Performance and competition with
acquaintances threatened embarrassing self-exposures and disor-
dered hierarchies. They could enhance or lower a person's standing and, from the perspective of a hostess, make or break the spirit
of a party. Yet Mary and her circle of hostesses became notorious
for their propensity to push the borders of conventional behaviour
and discourse in the activities they gently foisted on their guests.

According to Jeffrey Franklin, it was a middle-class truism that
aristocrats turned play into tests, with all their anxieties and potential for embarrassment.[33] Competition was inherent in the field
sports and gambling of the country house, and men filled their
letters with boasts and excuses for their performances. Charades
and theatricals also involved self-exposures that were problematic
when the audience was filled with rivals and contemporaries, not
just elderly relatives or country folk never to be encountered again.
Even tableaux vivants, the relatively undemanding performances
that Gety Pembroke and her statuesque sister Lady Brownlow were
fond of staging, required standing immobile for minutes whilst being scrutinised for appearance and fidelity to the scene portrayed.
This was an exaggerated version of the 'libidinal moments' that

all women experienced as their looks and clothes were covertly evaluated and reported each time they went out. The visual framing – and what Stephen Kern calls 'the stunning objectification of womanhood' – that occurred as women displayed themselves in London theatre boxes and carriage windows was thus brought into the more private setting of the country house, where it would be recognised for the 'aesthetically tamed eroticism' it was.[34] Guests at these parties rehearsed and reordered the hierarchies of appearance, prowess and accomplishment through which the Victorians situated themselves and each other, though in settings that might allow the daughter of a merchant or the wife of an American diplomat to outshine, temporarily, a countess.

The activities that Mary and her friends would become famous for went further, however. Games like 'Personalities', 'Public Opinion' or 'Analogies' involved describing other guests' character traits, guessing who had made which judgements about someone else and categorising the qualities of people both present and away. 'We have got a new game (don't shiver and yawn!)', Margot wrote to George Curzon, 'moral and intellectual recipes for mutual friends! – quite thrilling – the friend guessed by the recipe.'[35] Unlike board games or cards, these amusements were not bound by clear rules. They required quickness of apprehension, and discretion in what could be said safely. Literary and psychological pencil games favoured the weapons of the weak – wit, mental agility, humour, the right degree of tact – in ways that could level distinctions of gender and social position. Anyone might be put on the spot to guess, act out or invent, becoming a performer for the amusement of others. The laughter and applause with which they were greeted created more than temporary diversion – they fostered group *esprit* and friendship.[36] When such parties went off well, they became the stuff of social legend, recorded in diaries and passed from letter to letter. Margot wrote that she received eight separate accounts of Mary's party, intimate psychological equivalents of the 'bag counts' and 'lucky bets' of the shooters' and gamblers' correspondence.[37]

Arthur's response to Mary's description of the party hints at the amusement such entertainments could provide even *in absentia*:

> I wish I had seen your Stanway masquerade. That is quite a new development of Stanway gaiety! You do not tell me how *you* were dressed, or whom you looked like. I am mildly surprised at the effect

dress seems to have had on the appearance of yr guests. It is surely odd the H[arry] W[hite] should look like Buckingham who was the *handsomest* man of his day; or that Pembroke should have looked like Rochester who was the most vicious! Dress certainly makes the man![38]

The final quip reveals the gender instabilities in the occasions. For the Victorians, dress was not supposed to make men. Wealth, status and accomplishments did that, and not in settings orchestrated by women.[39] Yet in these high-intensity evening activities, men appeared in wigs and costumes and were directed in their parts by ladies. In the psychological games the personalities of men both present and absent were dissected by women. In literary compositions women's wit might be superior, while in general discussion ladies might demonstrate an 'imperturbable candor' that overturned stereotypes of silliness or emotionality.[40]

The atmosphere of humour, conversation and mixed-gender competition was by no means universally embraced. John Morley, who otherwise liked and respected Arthur, was 'shocked' by his 'social levity – with ladies!' At Wilton just two months before Mary's gathering, guests simply refused to take up Gety Pembroke's suggestion that they devise a charade. On a walk the next day, Gety was 'red hot'; 'she said she had never been so treated in her own house before'.[41] Gladys de Grey may have led that revolt. Just before arriving at Stanway she wrote that she disliked charades, because 'everyone gets so cross and they amuse no one when done'. Her flippant letters imploring 'tear this up!' repudiated any idea of solidarity with a group based on shared experiences or self-revelation. Doll was so moody that no one expected him to participate: 'one tries to forget his presence but one cannot get rid of the uncomfortable consciousness that you are breathing steam from a damp blanket when he is in the room'.[42] His impression of the Stanway theatricals confirms his detachment: 'After dinner they all put on wigs and looked awful ... Miss DD quite spoiled herself in a brown shock' and the great hall suffered in being 'choked with a beastly stage'. Curzon provided his own glimpse of psychological independence on the acting night. His costumed appearance in the Primrose charade prompted him to 'flood out' his psychic energy by grabbing DD and asserting masculine dominance in an impromptu romp, his spirited waltz defying the spectacle the ladies had constructed.[43]

Etiquette books set intimidating standards for hosting country house entertainments like this. 'Her consideration and tact are so successfully exerted that somehow her guests always find themselves doing exactly what they like best and in company with those who are most congenial to them', wrote one advice manual about the qualities of the ideal hostess.[44] Mary approved of this form of apparently casual entertaining, letting guests 'come and go as they liked ... I never feel like Alice [Arthur's sister], a feeling of burden, of duty, a sense of position as hostess, that I must say How de do and Goodnight to them and apologize for this and that', she wrote later in life when she had much more experience.[45] Even at this party she carried it off. 'Where other people fuss and excite themselves you apparently are doing nothing', Gety Pembroke wrote inelegantly in her thank-you note after the visit.[46]

Nevertheless the construction of parties that could sustain the mix of individually pleasant diversion and participatory group amusement was difficult to pull off – 'as hard work as having a playhouse or keeping an inn', Disraeli once wrote after a ten-day party for two dozen people. Mary's children called their mother Napoleon for the extraordinary care she took to anticipate every guest's personal needs while prodding them to join the group.[47] Mary's tepid appraisal of this Stanway gathering reflected the presence of too many guests who could not accommodate the mixture of performances occasioned by long visits like this – 'I thought it an awful bore and effort', she wrote to Frances Balfour, but concluded politely that 'efforts do one good on the whole'.[48]

George Curzon's actions on the charades night show one of the reasons that men of this generation humoured ladies by participating in their games and spectacles: it was the price to be paid for sexual pursuits in which they could engage the rest of the time. Curzon's spontaneous romp with the unsuspecting DD escalated the next morning when she found herself alone with him in the breakfast room. 'When I had finished I got up to go, but before I had reached the door, George got there in front of me, shut it, and kissed me with fervour. I was rather bewildered but not displeased, and got away.' The unmarried Curzon was indeed a 'pouncer', but this physical advance may have reflected DD's outsider status and absence of family members who could take umbrage at his behaviour. As one etiquette manual noted, young women who did not follow the correct chaperonage should 'know that the inference drawn by gentlemen from their conduct is that the restraints of propriety are irksome to them'.[49] After both had returned to London, Curzon kept up a half-hearted pursuit for several weeks. DD was pretty sure his attentions were not serious, since he needed to marry someone with more money than she would have. Nevertheless, they had several spirited exchanges on the propriety of flirtatious kissing and lap-sitting. DD found that she was being labelled a prig for her reserve with behaviours that, for Margot Tennant, were often part of her friendships.[50]

Doll Liddell's diary account reveals that there was an even more sexually charged courtship unfolding at the same time, this one involving DD and himself. The two had met during the 1888 London season, and that summer DD nearly accepted Doll's proposal of marriage. She pulled back because she felt her motive was base. With her father facing a sudden bankruptcy, she feared she might be forced into 'that dreaded Victorian sign of genteel poverty: becoming a governess'.[51] Like Laura Tennant four years before, she was attracted to Liddell physically, but doubted his appeal as a lifetime companion.[52] Nevertheless, on this Stanway visit the relationship intensified. On Wednesday morning, Liddell recorded 'kissing indoors'. By Friday he felt 'such a longing to go to her room but thought I must be mad'. On Sunday, they slipped off for the solitary walk that made them late for lunch, and on Monday morning, talking in the hall, Doll asked if he could come to DD's room. 'Not knowing where these things lead', DD admitted him, dressed in a tea gown and with her hair undone. He 'locked the doors and sat down on one of those old things with sharp edges and striped green covers … I cannot describe those hours.' When they had difficulty meeting up later in London, Doll wrote that 'the Monday morning at Stanway counts for months'.[53]

Neither Curzon nor Liddell seems to have thought their conduct towards an unmarried woman transgressive. Both saw DD as cool, observant and self-possessed. She was intellectual and a good conversationalist, had been raised abroad and spoke French and was visiting without a chaperone. These traits might signal a young woman well past the schoolroom who understood the physical aspects of the game of courtship and controlled the strings of sexual conduct as much as any male admirer. As it turned out, despite Doll's experience with Laura, he was as baffled as DD that he was able to arouse her first feelings of physical passion without an accompanying love. For DD, the renewal of the relationship, though it involved no more than kissing and petting, led to several years of nervous ill-health as she attempted to transform her continuing sexual attraction into the abiding love she thought she ought to feel. The new, uncommitted eroticism that Margot allowed struck DD, as it had Laura, as not only unwise but a violation of a private, inner self.[54]

Andrew St George argues that the increasing conformity in dress and manners that arose as mass society developed in the late century was balanced by a more complex inner landscape. In the Victorian world of 'intensified subjectivity', domestic spaces often became the theatre for personal explorations and enactments of desire.[55] Parties at a 'romantic country house' like Stanway, with its mysterious corridors, mullioned windows and unexpected vistas, provided the ideal location for dramas of courtship and seduction.[56] Mary's party allowed for a host of intimate moments in the breakfast room, the bedroom, behind a baize curtain, in front of the morning room fire. That DD's mother allowed her to pay this visit without a relative indicates she cannot have been aware of the pressures that Doll was placing on her daughter, the informality of this household or what the lack of supervision implied to men.[57]

Private pursuits like this affected the general sociability of a party in ways that the etiquette manuals never addressed. With formal patronage and spectacle no longer providing the frame for country house entertaining, the authors of etiquette books took respectable, companionate domesticity and relaxed 'at home-ness' as the unquestioned base on which informal sociability was constructed. The exclusive absorption in another implied by seduction worked against general interaction, as Mary recognised when she admonished Hugo for 'pairing off with a conk [a woman friend] and having long tête-à-têtes and purely personal conversations'.[58] The possibility for misunderstandings in the arrangement of daytime activities escalated when romantic pursuit was involved. This happened at Stanway on Wednesday when Doll pointedly told Alan Charteris that he was not welcome on a walk with DD. By the end of the week, Hugo and Alan were not speaking to each other, because 'Hugo took Mrs. Bourke away as soon as his Lady de Grey was gone.'[59] Within the informal country house gathering, conflicting goals of private gratification and general interaction were present simultaneously.

Another of the guests at Mary's party was also experiencing the disconcerting juxtaposition of inner and outer worlds on this visit.

On Saturday morning, the day that Daisy White was returning to London, she joined Gety Pembroke for a final walk on the Stanway grounds. Daisy knew the Pembrokes. She had been a guest on the *Black Pearl* for ten days in August and had visited Wilton. During this walk, Gety sensed the depression that Daisy was confiding to her diary and made an earnest 'statement of affection and said always [to] view her as a friend in trouble or sickness'. Daisy's tone in recording this bungled attempt at intimacy was one of surprise and slight affront. She resented the implication that she might need Gety Pembroke's friendship in some older sense of patronage or protection. What she needed was an understanding fellow traveller, someone with whom to share the emotional confusions and sexual temptations she was experiencing. Gety, with her odd oblivious manner and *grand dame* tendency to 'fix' things, was not the person she would have chosen for that.

Nevertheless, Gety was right – Daisy was confronting a personal crisis. She had come to Stanway from Easton Gray where she had been visiting the convalescent Tommy Ribblesdale with whom she was deeply in love. The Ribblesdales were supposed to have attended Mary's party until Tommy's illness intervened. Travelling to Stanway through the darkening afternoon, Daisy felt 'dismal' over leaving the 'friend' whom she saw so infrequently: 'The moon shone all the last part of the long drive. When one is sad the moon smiles upon one coldly and never gives one hope like the sun. She chilled me quite on that drive.' During this week she reported that she could not shake off the worst depression she had experienced in years. Though her diary contains many crossings out and obscure symbols relating to Ribblesdale, it is clear that she was facing a crisis in which she was trying to decide between what she owed her kindly, worthy husband and the fulfilment offered by the 'French morals' in marriage that so many of her friends were discussing. Margot had already noticed this, calling Daisy a woman whose 'mind was not quite in accord', but who was trying courageously to make the best of a somewhat dull spouse.[60]

During the eighteen months covered by Daisy's 1888–89 diary she recorded fourteen conversations – sometimes with a single person, sometimes in groups – concerned with behaviour between men and women, the propriety of kissing someone who was not one's spouse, the importance of virtue in women, and the difference between men and women in approaching love. The relationships of the people at Mary's party make clear how relevant the topics were. Emmie Bourke was known to be unfaithful to her husband. Mary herself, to disguise her relationship with Arthur, had engaged in a flirtation with Tommy Ribblesdale the year before, full of allusions to three-volume novels and Eastern chambers. Hugo may have had an affair with Charty Ribblesdale, who had earlier committed a 'clumsy indiscretion' with George Curzon – only a few months earlier Daisy had had a conversation with Curzon over 'the virtue of women and how far Charty should be condemned for failing in it'.[61] Daisy considered Gladys de Grey a special friend, but she too had shared some degree of intimacy with Ribblesdale. Now it seemed very likely that she was in the midst of an infidelity with her host.[62]

The Gladys–Hugo affair stumbles into the historical record through an accumulation of circumstantial evidence. Gladys, Daisy observed, was at the party without her husband of three years, Lord de Grey (the 'best shot in England' and killer of 370,728 head of game in thirty-three years). Throughout the months that followed this party, Daisy recorded multiple times when Hugo and Gladys arrived at social events together and without their spouses.[63] Doll called Gladys a 'stock and heartless alliance' of Hugo's.[64] Given the two people involved, the relationship was probably one of casual, consensual pleasure. The couple took their theatrical act on the road to other house parties for a number of months, and rehearsing the skit provided perfect cover for moments of private gratification.

The play itself – a one-act comediatta first produced in 1868 – would have constituted a risqué insider joke for those in the audience who knew Hugo. The title – *The Happy Pair* – might suggest the relationship between the actors themselves, and the opening scene introduced a male protagonist remarkably like Hugo. This hero has trouble adjusting to the emotional intimacy of marriage with an attractive, accommodating wife. Silent and dismissive, he sneers at her attempts to bring him to better moods – 'my vital spark can't stand this much longer'. The heroine devises a scheme to lure him back by giving him a dose of his own treatment. She proceeds to out-insult, out-banter and out-criticise her spouse. Much comedic reversal ensues, as well as a frank discussion of divorce-court coverage in the press, before his eventual chastisement.

The obligatory happy resolution was one that no one could have thought the Elchos likely to duplicate. Daisy had noticed the strains between them in Scotland in September. Nevertheless, before Christmas, Mary told Daisy that she would be confined 'again, poor sweet. Evidently rather depressed about herself and does not feel strong. I pray she may get through it alright and never have another.'[65] These unhappy household realities might have been apparent to a discerning guest from the placement of the couple's living areas at Stanway. Victorian convention held that family rooms were grouped together, but Mary's bedroom, just below the nurseries, was in a separate wing from Hugo's, while her day room – where Arthur did so much of his writing – was equally far removed from Hugo's study, placed near the dining room in the 'masculine' portion of the house.[66]

Daisy's diary takes the story of this Stanway party beyond the changing rituals of courtship among the unwed into the world of marital adultery in the setting of the private home. In the circles around Arthur Balfour, country house parties were seething with secrets, jealousies, sexual tensions and grieving hearts in ways that put enormous strain on the public façades of sociability. DD Balfour, whose lengthy treatment of this party in her unpublished memoir attests to its importance to her life, came to her own conclusions. Writing forty-five years later, she told Mary that she had felt enormous pressure on this visit to 'hold one's own among people who seemed so immeasurably brilliant and fortunate and fascinating'. At the time, her verdict was harsher: 'I look around at all my married women friends and there isn't one of them whose life wouldn't make me wretched.'[67] Three years later DD made a love match with the widowed Alfred Lyttelton and combined a marriage of conventional fidelity with a lifetime of contributions to philanthropy, empire service and the arts.

The extent of infidelity among the highest levels of society in Britain has proven notoriously difficult to determine.[68] As Kali Israel cautions, definitions of adultery and understandings of bodily encounters and emotional intimacies were different in the decades before a sexualised interpretation became the dominant way of understanding hetero-social attraction.[69] A good deal of discourse and anecdotal evidence from the 1880s suggests, however, that contemporaries *thought* that privileged wives were experimenting with extra-marital relationships more than had been the case with their mothers in the middle decades of the century, and that they were breaching the spirit, if not always the letter, of the Seventh commandment.[70] Among Mary's friends, marriages that masked tension and unhappiness were common enough that adulterers, male or female, were not necessarily shunned. Friends knew or suspected attachments and sympathised, tolerated, worried or condemned – as the particular circumstances seemed to warrant.

Various strategies evolved that allowed those caught in emotional contretemps to appear candid without having to deliver outright lies. Increasingly, for example, couples went their own ways during the visiting season, a practice that might indicate little more than someone's desire not to spend time at a party centred on activities he or she did not enjoy, while also signalling a spouse's trust.[71] Another ploy was camaraderie between an individual and a lover's spouse (or the spouse's lover). Herbert Sussman notes that it was typical for artistic men to transcend jealousy by the fiction that they were sharing a woman rather than competing for her. The diaries of Daisy White and Mary Elcho show that the same cordiality could exist between women in a romantic triangle.[72] Probably the most common decoy was the masking role of banter and chaff between the sexes, even when seduction was not the goal. For Simmel, flirtation – the 'play form' of actual seduction – was so much a given of leisured sociability that he deemed the indirection, coyness and evasion it implied to be a part of women's basic nature; for them, it was 'natural' to be 'unnatural', innately hiding and altered in manner with men.[73]

The navigation of genuine affairs, seldom preserved in family letters, has been largely neglected in the scholarly literature or, if discussed, presented as an unproblematic feature of marriages never expected to be more than amicable dynastic alliances.[74] But the letters and diaries that have come to light for women friends of Arthur's, such as Ettie Grenfell, Constance Wenlock, Daisy White and Violet Granby, show that infidelity was not a casual indulgence taken for granted by young wives of this generation. That discovery added much thrill to the chase for men like Mary's cousin Wilfrid Blunt. Mary's story in the years that followed this Stanway party shows why another cousin, the Countess of Warwick, wrote that she could not 'remember one friend of mine that was happy' in the supposedly halcyon decade of the fin de siècle.[75]

The mechanics of Mary's relationship with Arthur as he became increasingly prominent provide a course in the logistics of extra-marital attachments, whether physical or platonic, when emotions were genuinely engaged. When both were in London they had an arrangement to meet at 4 Carlton Gardens every

Wednesday afternoon, the day that the House of Commons rose by 6 p.m. Mary wrote that she liked this to be for two hours, only one of which should be devoted to 'business' – catching up on news and plans – as opposed to something more intimate.[76] They met at Clouds over Easter; at Gosford, Glen and Whittingehame during the autumn golfing months that Arthur called the 'East Lothian season'; in Dublin in January; annually for a week or more at Felixstowe or other seaside locations; and often at Bayreuth in late summer for the Wagner festival. To this day the exact nature of their private moments is hidden, and it is hard to find many occasions when wild, uninterrupted romps alone could have occurred. As with most attachments of this era, the couple remained constantly surrounded by servants, relatives, friends and, while Arthur was chief secretary, even bodyguards.

Inevitably they spent weeks and sometimes months apart. They agreed to write at least each Wednesday afternoon – this mostly observed practice produced the great collection of letters available to scholars since the 1960s. Mary's letters from the early years of their attachment have largely disappeared, however. For the fraught period of the early 1890s, Jane Ridley and Clayre Percy published only four, and it is possible that Arthur routinely destroyed them at this time. His were clearly written so that they could fall into Hugo's hands. They were breezier and less personal than they would be later, and when Mary wrote to him about the Stanway party described here, she asked tentatively whether he could 'send me a little P.S. to tear up (inside and separate from the letter)', that would convey 'any little remark' confirming the special relationship that got such cautious reinforcement.[77]

They also had an implicit contract that on social occasions where they encountered each other as fellow guests they would give no sign of any special connection. Ettie Grenfell was astounded at how well Mary managed this: 'Mary E is really too wonderful about Arthur. I CANNOT make it out – she never seems to see him for a moment alone, positively to avoid it – and yet I am sure she is fond of him? If it is all from the "prudence" point of view, I do admire her courage intensely, for life seems too short, opportunities so infrequent that I think most people feel forced and driven into recklessness.' Mary's occasional cries of the heart to Arthur show how little she sometimes had to content herself with: 'I feel I should have been *quite* consoled if you had just *once* looked over the table one friendly look. I know you say it's quite *absurd*

to expect or demand such a thing and yet you often do it quite
naturally – or one look as we left the dining room. I stayed till all
the ladies were left in the hopes.'[78]

In 1886, the same year that Mary and Arthur declared their mutual affection, Rhoda Broughton published a novel in which even
gentle folk in the country neighbourhood know of the bachelor
politician who is the constant attendant of a married society woman.[79] The couple are described as sharing every intimacy short of
the conduct necessary for the divorce courts, but the lady's kindly,
blockheaded husband suspects nothing and has no jealousy in allowing the pair endless private moments together. The possibility
that clever and competitive Hugo was clueless is hard to credit,
unless he saw Arthur as so many others did – too abstracted and
asexual to be a genuine threat. The two men golfed together on
the holidays, with Arthur often taking care to add 'give my love to
Hugo' at the end of letters to Mary that made no such declaration
to her. Hugo engaged in his own pursuits, which, aside from his
amorous interests, included cultivating speculators such as Baron Hirsch in endless attempts to make a financial killing. Mary
and Hugo 'seem *never* to be together', complained Lady Wemyss,
though in the same years Mary was almost constantly pregnant.[80]

Mary was candid about her dislike of the relentless fecundity she
had experienced since her marriage. A few weeks after this party
she wrote to her sister-in-law that she was 'rather a poor creature
altogether and I long for the days to pass by and have no courage
for these last two months; I've been a prisoner in the house for a
month and in bed a great deal, so I feel and look like an elephant!'
When Colin was born on 1 June 1889, Hugo flippantly described
the newcomer as 'the usual hardy annual', and on being 'asked the
sex of the child answered he did not know'.[81] It took Mary weeks to
recover from this confinement and, according to her most recent
biographer, her doctor advised that having another child could kill
her. Sometime in the next few months, the Elchos agreed to dis-
continue their sexual relations, an arrangement that lasted for six
years.[82] The decision reflected the concerns about Mary's health,
but the couple would surely have been able to find contraception
if they had still been committed to each other.

The letters that Hugo wrote to his wife contain enough protesta-
tions of affection to convince some biographers that 'the marriage
rested on deep affection and respect': 'I have no doubt at all that
no one was ever so much in love with anyone else as I am with

you – equally little that no one was ever less in love than you are with me', he wrote in 1888.[83] But Hugo was known among other men for his 'hard, fast pursuit of women' and flirtations that were not going to stay platonic. Willie Grenfell was too worried to make a joke of it when his young wife Ettie began to receive Hugo's attentions in 1890.[84] Hugo's letters to other women share the same subtext of mock deprecation and being the cat's paw of heartless females that he sometimes used in writing to Mary.[85] He was also capable of pre-emptive attacks, accusing Mary of flirting with other men and disappearing without notice in ways more characteristic of him.

One of these episodes occurred in 1890. Telling Arthur of her unhappiness at their leave-taking before another of her convalescent trips to the Continent, Mary wrote, 'Finally before dinner on Sunday, H said he thought you were fond of me (when surrounded only by his family he has more time for observation) and asked me to tell him whether you ever told me so and exactly what you said etc, that chilled me to the bone and made me particularly helpless and nervous all evening and I longed to see you alone and it was bitter parting so … Those sort of questions (by H about you) screw up my entrails! And make me feel quite quivering.'[86]

The timing of this upsetting confrontation was suspicious. The scenario of a supposedly long-deceived husband finally naming his wife's co-respondent in a divorce court was working its way through the legal system at that moment. Four months later it would bring down Arthur's great political adversary Charles Stewart Parnell, foiling Irish political aspirations for another generation. In confronting Mary when he did, Hugo was delivering a veiled threat to both his wife and Arthur that confirms, as Mary's partially destroyed letter went on to say, that some 'uneasy equilibrium' among this trio was breaking down. The source of the change was probably Hugo, more than Mary. A year after agreeing to marital celibacy, he had actually fallen in love with someone else. His affair with the estranged wife of the Duke of Leinster lasted for five years until her death from tuberculosis at the age of twenty-nine.

With the entrance of Hermione Leinster to the story, the polite evasions of 1887–89 were breached. Hermione's sincerity in her newfound love, and her agony at the social situation it placed her in, were poured into a series of remarkable letters to Hugo's sister – and Mary's friend – Evelyn de Vesci, who tried in vain to stem the torrent of passion and bring the lovers back to their moral and social duties.[87] Hermione, a devout Catholic, could not believe that the physical and emotional love she shared with Hugo was not spiritual too, and she was willing to accept any social ostracism that came from what felt like – in its sheer intensity – a natural and selfless abandonment for love of another. Already separated from her husband, she was able to live quietly at Carton in Maynooth, where Hugo could visit without the subterfuge of a large house party, though the press sometimes reported on the movements of Lord Elcho in ways that could raise questions about where he was. The couple were also seen walking the streets of London's West End, hopelessly absorbed in each other. In autumn 1891, Hermione became pregnant with a son who, after the deaths of two older brothers, later became the 7th Duke of Leinster. A year after his birth, Hermione was told she had consumption. Hugo was at her bedside when she died in Mentone in 1895.

Friends and relatives did not take this romance lightly. They reserved most of their condemnation for Hugo, especially for his neglect of 'Sweet Mary' when she was seriously ill with typhoid at Pau in 1890 and for the overall lack of discretion that had made both Mary and Hermione subject to gossip.[88] His mother was especially harsh. Her son, Lady Wemyss told Evelyn, was 'a purely selfish frivolous man' who was 'distinctly deteriorating – more silly pursuits of pleasure, less sense of duty public or private – less idea of sacrifice of any kind' and too often associating with 'Wales'. She called the affair with Hermione 'the hated subject' and 'the whole Hugo chapter – from the very beginning to the very end ... full of bitterness and disappointment'. She did not absolve Mary entirely, finding her daughter-in-law difficult to know and 'not the right sort of wife for Hugo ... I entirely agree as to her cleverness and her real depth, also as to her originality of mind and thought ... but she is in no way *practical* – and never carries out her good ideas ... She is absolutely without influence on Hugo, had she any, it *must* have been for the good.' As it was, wrote Hugo's mother, 'I think Mary's way with him is very much on all fours with that of the Princess of Wales with the Prince.' Lady Wemyss reserved her harshest criticism for Mary's mother, citing the 'great error' Madeline Wyndham had made in 1883 in 'bringing about that marriage when they neither of them cared sufficiently for each other'.[89]

Hugo defended himself to his sister when she urged him to think of the harm he was doing to Mary: 'You say you love her – I know you do. You say you understand her – perhaps you do, but

I think I understand her better. I know I am utterly unworthy of her, but I can appreciate her and do ... and I do know this that she is not miserable, that she is happy.' 'I hardly know what you will say darling', Lady Wemyss wrote to Mary, 'when I tell you that the having "your sanction" – which I have long believed to be the case – is to my mind almost the most terrible part of it all ... you must have reached heights of charity and self-effacement of which I should have been incapable of even dreaming.'[90]

'Tell me', Gety Pembroke asked Frances Horner about this time, 'are you a cynic?' 'I said no except sometimes at a party.' 'What do you think of marriage? I want very much to ask you – are you happy about Mary Elcho and Arthur Balfour?'[91] Over time, the infidelity in which Hugo was so clearly seen to have breached the normal standards of discretion permitted Arthur to show unusual solicitude for Mary and for her to be justified in more open expression of her own attachment. By the spring of 1892 friends were commenting on their fondness for each other. George Pembroke, who had known or suspected the relationship for years, said he was surprised that it 'lasted so hot so long – such a life as his must "*deseche le coeur*" [dry the heart] and strong emotion is so difficult to her'. But he had just spent a week in a country house with them and 'cannot observe the slightest difference. They are as inseparable as ever.'[92] Wilfrid Blunt recorded from a visit to Stanway that summer that his room was next to Arthur's, and he could hear the couple talking companionably with each other – he does not say what hour of the day. He thought that he never saw two people more in love.[93]

Nevertheless, Mary's unhappiness in the early 1890s can be read in her many diary entries about feeling 'low', 'depressed' and overwhelmed with the multiple responsibilities of her separate social and emotional lives. Among these were the hosting of multiple week-long house parties every year, divided between those for the Souls and those for Hugo's sporting friends and, after Hermione Leinster's death, for a succession of mistresses including the actress Mrs Pat Campbell and Lady Crewe. Lady Angela Forbes, Hugo's late-in-life companion for many years, noted that 'domestic troubles are trying enough in any circumstances, but particularly so in other people's houses'.[94] In Mary's case, she might have added, 'or your own'.

*

By the 1890s, unhappy marriages and semi-acknowledged liaisons were a common feature of British aristocratic society. Many
of Arthur's friends lived the settings that Oscar Wilde and Henry
James were describing, ones that mixed 'melodramatic action and
heightened emotion, on the one hand, and the appearance of
rigid public decorum and polite conversation on the other'.[95] The
extended house party was perhaps the largest, certainly the longest, social production in which private desires and social dictates
collided. The psychological demands of sustaining amiability and
urbanity while in extended contact with rivals, ex-lovers, objects of
desire, professional colleagues and old family friends were severe,
as Henry Asquith noted at Glen during an intense family drama
involving several of the Tennant daughters: 'all the time there was
a stream of visitors passing through the house, and the difference
between the surface and the under-current was such that at times
one seemed to be living two lives'. E. F. Benson joked that even a
three-day visit constituted one of the 'diseases which torture the
surfaces of our body without killing us' that characterised society
life in the 1890s.[96]

As a social institution, country house parties of long duration
did not suit a heightened individualism they supposedly helped to
allay. Within a few years, it would become normal for guests to pay
shorter visits than this party of Mary's entailed. A house might be
full, but the combinations brief and rapidly changing. Mary's contemporary, Millicent, Duchess of Sutherland, was so unconcerned
with constructing a genuine party that her guests might not see
her during a visit. They used Dunrobin as a highland hotel for private adventures of their own: 'the castle was full of guests whom my
mother knew but never saw and whom my father saw but did not
know'.[97] Parties lasting long enough for carefully chosen guests
to bond as a temporary family were probably doomed in any case
by the autonomy that automobiles would provide, the decreased
leisure of professional men and anonymous alternatives such as
hotels and travel abroad, and, as Frances Balfour wrote, visits after
the turn of the century were 'too fleeting for them to get into the
home atmosphere'.[98] But this form of entertainment was eclipsed
not just because it was too frivolous and time-consuming, but because it was too intense and involved too much surveillance and
self-monitoring to sustain for long stretches of time. The casual informalities of the late-century house parties encouraged emotions
that they then denied licit expression.

Henry James, a personal friend of Daisy White, was a fascinated observer of these transformations. In *The Awkward Age* he described two kinds of affective expression produced in this social world. One is represented by the charming, evasive Vanderbank who talks happily of friendships where one can 'speak anything', but whose bright chatter avoids conveying anything meaningful at all. Unattractive, kind and wealthy Mitchy represents the other – the relationship in which nothing has to be said because the realities of one's emotional life are already known and tacitly accepted by some of those present. The private encounters and public performances of a house party like Mary's supported both. Superficial, artificial, amusing and performative, one aspect of sociability implied the 'moral evasiveness' of refusing to take anything seriously – 'sincerity is not gregarious', as Nina Auerbach notes.[99] Betty Balfour's sharp-eyed young sister Emily noticed the hectic, effusive, ephemeral humour that the regime of games and conversation could entail – as evanescent as the serial epigrams of the plays that Oscar Wilde was writing. 'Betty is an angel and nothing can spoil her angelic nature', she observed, 'but when she is among Souls she becomes a Soul for the time being, and so spoils herself.'[100] But such performances could also rest on the comfort of having unspoken secrets that others knew and tolerated: 'All these people have lived together through some of the great feelings and experiences of life, they know each other to the very core.' 'Idle chatter', as Wilde observed, 'signals semi-open secrets.'[101]

In personal lives, however, both stances rested on things secret to the uninitiated, with their accompanying evasions, miscues and opaqueness. Sociability consisted of what was not expressed as much as what was – self-monitoring was as great a part of this generation's experience as dissipation or indulgence. In these worlds, interiority – fostered by leisure and culture – was constantly screened, essential truths masked. Perhaps this had been easier to handle when relations with fellow guests were governed by greater formality and fewer expectations of candour. As it was, the worlds of fashionable sociability came to appear to outsiders increasingly brittle and unnatural. As Mrs Cheveley notes in Wilde's *An Ideal Husband* (1895), I 'prefer to be natural' but it is 'such a difficult pose to keep up'.[102]

It is interesting how many of the institutions Arthur functioned in – from the public school to manoeuvring in the Commons to managing news of the empire – could be seen as sharing these qualities of the country house entertainment. Not surprisingly, men often thought of house parties and the London season as the public schools for women.[103] Behind façades of order and reasonable behaviour lay dissimulation and denials that some, at least, might deem relevant to understanding the situation. The question was how to combine the subjective self and the performative self that James Vernon notes as one of the features of the modern personality.[104] Arthur, and eventually Mary, practised the emotionality geared to handling these juxtapositions: temperate, kind, but in the end often appearing distanced and self-protective. Raymond Poincaré, a denizen of a similar world on the other side of the English Channel, warned a married young friend that 'her exclamations and facial expressions revealed too much to the world'; she would expose herself to 'ridicule by revealing too much of her true self'.[105] Mary confessed herself 'haunted' by Hermione Leinster, dead before she reached thirty, who had modelled something different and, in their social circles, more dangerous: 'I wonder where she is now – I'm sure her burning jealousy her loneliness and her miseries Black dogs she called them have fallen from her like a worn out garment and I hope she is serene; she *was* Great of Soul in many ways but had not the Greatness that brings Serenity nor the indifference that can ape it. There was something very wonderful about her intense aliveness – vividness and power for deep emotion.'[106]

Interlude:
Fin de Siècle

I N NOVEMBER 1891, the same month that Arthur became
leader of the House of Commons, he gave an inaugural address
on the occasion of his installation as lord rector of the University
of Glasgow. The title of the printed version was 'A Fragment on
Progress'.[1] It was characteristic of Balfour to call his reflections
on the latest research in science or social theory 'notes' or 'comments' and to pepper his remarks with disclaimers. Yet as his niece
pointed out, these wide-ranging, synthetic ruminations were closer
to his mental preoccupations than almost any other pronouncements he made.[2] While others revealed themselves in letters, diaries and reminiscences, Arthur did so through published essays
that conveyed his thinking about human nature, psychology, religious experience, the origins of social bonds and the prospects
for humanity's future. Four years later, when his magnum opus
The Foundations of Belief appeared, a reviewer for the *Pall Mall
Gazette* noted that in work like Balfour's 'a man must, consciously
or unconsciously, reveal a great deal of his inner self and his habitual habit of mind'. This could not fail to be of 'psychological
interest as a clue to the deepest convictions and motives of one
whose influence upon the political history of the next quarter of a
century seems certain to be so great'.[3] Within weeks, in a strange
conjunction of events, prosecutor Edward Carson would make the
same point about inner selves revealed in writing by using Oscar
Wilde's fictional work as legal evidence of the mental proclivities
of another player with words whose lucidity mystified the public.[4]

Arthur began 'A Fragment on Progress' with his usual ploy of
standing up a straw-man that he then exposed to critical attack – a
practice he disingenuously attributed to 'the controversial habits

engendered by my unfortunate profession'.[5] In this case he took
on the supposedly 'settled belief' that 'there exists a natural law or
tendency governing human affairs by which, on the whole, and in
the long run, the general progress of our race is assured'. The many
historical examples of stagnant societies and extinct civilisations
justified no such assumption, he thought, nor did the major
theoretical models pretending to explain why it would happen.
One of these was evolutionary theory itself. Arthur showed his
familiarity with the most recent thinking about natural selection
by accepting the German scientist August Weismann's argument
that genetic transmission of traits acquired in an individual's
lifetime was scientifically impossible. Thus no one should expect a
rapid alteration in human attributes that had been shaped during
'the vast period in which a blind struggle with the forces of nature
and with each other' had forged the species. Any improvements
in humanity's skills and propensities would have to arise from
'perfecting' the 'manufacture of man', relying on those 'special
aptitudes for social life' – including 'an innate predisposition to
accept a morality without which social life is impossible' – that
enabled humans to learn from each other and consciously adapt
their circumstances.[6]

But here Arthur challenged proponents of the Enlightenment
faith that the importance of environment in shaping human
beings meant that rational actors could plot out rational social
reforms that would guarantee steady progress towards peace,
harmony and self-cultivation for the great mass of humanity. He
had some gleeful fun at the expense of theorists who thought they
could delineate fundamental laws of social behaviour and devise
institutions to guide the outcomes of reform. Without using the
wording of twenty-first-century systems analysis, Arthur articulated
the concepts of unintended consequences, poorly understood
synergies, feedback loops and multi-variant interactions that would
defy the predictions of the most astute social analysts. He had read
Marx's writings in translation in 1885 and agreed with them at least
to the extent of acknowledging that great material forces affected
humans beyond their understanding or control. He rejected the
notion that any system builder had discovered what these were
sufficiently to guide grand agendas for improvement. Even could
such expertise be found, 'a sociologist so coldly independent of
the social forces ... as ... to understand them' would find himself
impotent to control them.[7]

Such were the limits placed on human endeavour that one of the protections of the species was society itself – society not founded upon philosophic models or utilitarian rationality, 'but upon feelings and beliefs, and upon the customs and codes by which feeling and beliefs are ... fixed and rendered stable'. Humans were unable to conduct reasoned analysis of every subject on which they must decide or act. Individually and en masse they were guided by incalculable conjunctions of 'the beliefs, the affections, the passions and the prejudices' of their own time and culture. Without saying it, Arthur was implicitly refuting the recently deceased Oxford idealist T. H. Green, who influenced a generation of Liberal progressives with his arguments that intelligent state action based on reasoned policies could 'speedily perfect the whole machinery by which human felicity is to be secured'.[8]

Arthur called what amounted to blind faith in the mechanisms by which progress would come about 'a great delusion' of his age. In reality, he wrote:

> the future of the race is ... encompassed with darkness: no faculty of calculation that we possess, no instrument that we are likely to invent, will enable us to map out its course, or penetrate the secret of its destiny. It is easy, no doubt, to find in the clouds which obscure our path what shapes we please: to see in them the promise of some millennial paradise, or the threat of endless and unmeaning travel through waste and perilous places. But in such visions the wise man will put but little confidence: content, in a sober and cautious spirit, with a full consciousness of his feeble powers of foresight, and the narrow limits of his activity, to deal as they arise with the problems of his own generation.[9]

Arthur was addressing an audience of undergraduates, and at the end of this piece of deconstruction he tried to anticipate criticism that his message 'was calculated to chill youthful enthusiasm, and to check youthful enterprise'. He gave an unconvincing assurance that 'private virtues', 'energy and disinterestedness in civic life', 'reverence for the past', 'caution' and the careful working of free institutions would suffice to meet the 'problems of our age and country'.[10] Even so, one reporter judged the keynote of the speech to be 'hopelessness', not 'inspiring or inspiriting' to 'ingenuous youth'. The rest of the press joined in a polite consensus that Arthur had revealed himself as 'a more profound student than many were aware of', with a 'singularly wide range' of sympathies and 'remarkable versatility' that made him 'unique' in the tradition of British scholar-statesmen.

'Beware of believing too much or trusting them too far ... and there he left them', summed up the *Dundee Courier*.[11] This was surprisingly close to the position Arthur had reached in a much funnier and more light-hearted way with the students of St Andrews four years before. The topic he chose then was 'The Pleasures of Reading'.[12] He wrote the piece quickly at Stanway after the 1887 parliamentary session, just before travelling to Dublin to spend weeks overseeing implementation of the new Irish Crimes Act.[13] At a political moment when 'the daily and even hourly calls upon me are incessant', Arthur winged it, and produced a piece that comes close to showing the mischievous, unlaboured mind at play that was part of what made his social presence so engaging.

As in 'A Fragment on Progress', Arthur chose a specific target to provide contrast for his views. In this case it was the positivist essayist and educator Frederic Harrison whose specific positions in favour of expanding the role of the state, limiting imperial possessions, granting Irish home rule and rejecting women's suffrage Arthur would oppose in every case. In *The Choice of Books* (1886), Harrison had lamented the explosion of indigestible information and frivolous literature now available to the public. He advocated systematic reading of Western classics, especially great imaginative literature. Arthur noted smoothly that the analogy between the human mind and the human stomach 'engorging' through overfeeding on improper food was 'surely pressed too far', then delighted his student audience by advising them to avoid the 'meagre fare' that Harrison was recommending and embrace 'the enjoyment, not, mark you, the improvement, nor the glory, nor the profit, but the *enjoyment*, which may be derived ... from books'.[14] He urged them to learn the 'refined accomplishments' of skipping and skimming, never to finish a book that had lost their attention, to read for interest alone, to read nothing because of social pressure, but solely, in leisure hours at least, because the work provided pleasure. Arthur said he 'must energetically repudiate' the idea that knowledge ought to be useful, or that superficial knowledge might be dangerous. Any learning was better than none, and the reality was that 'a little knowledge is all that on most subjects any of us can hope to attain'.[15]

The message in 'The Pleasures of Reading' was similar to that in 'Progress'. In a careful jab at the punditry of the increasingly professionalised and middle-class knowledge communities, he urged resistance to the overinflated claims of expert knowledge or theoretical predictive power. Though our own beliefs certainly rested on the 'climates' of opinion of our times, he said, still the individual should have the freedom to explore all imaginative, scientific or moral literature as it personally appealed. But in this essay the tone was buoyant, both the spirit and the mockery light-hearted. 'Has miscellaneous reading all the dreadful consequences Mr. Harrison predicts?' he asked. 'Has it any of them?' Was it really true that excessive reading would dull a man to the finer things in life? Probably not: 'It is true, no doubt, that many learned people are dull: but there is no indication whatever that they are dull because they are learned.' And what was wrong with enjoying the 'huge but undistinguished remainder' of writings that surrounded each generation's masterpieces? Readers could make their own choice whether to 'wade through the lumber of an ancient library, or to skim more than we like off the frothy foolishness poured forth in ceaseless streams by our circulating libraries'.[16] In the end, he writes, 'I am loath to brand any form of curiosity as necessarily idle' or pointless, because anything that 'prompts our wonder at nature or excites our emotions at the works of man' is to be valued as fostering the outlook in which 'nothing that has been done, or thought, or suffered, or believed, no law which governs the world of matter or the world of mind, can be wholly alien or uninteresting.'[17]

If one reviewer of 'Fragment on Progress' thought the essay revealed a politician who was nearly 'unique' in his intellectual breadth, another remarked of 'The Pleasures of Reading' that 'the English language wants a word to describe accurately a mental attitude such as Mr. Balfour's'.[18] It reflected neither 'cynicism' nor practical common sense, but rather a fresh kind of lucidity and playfulness about ideas. Arthur argued powerfully for the role of 'Authority' in guiding belief, but urged each listener to challenge self-proclaimed 'authorities' whenever he found shoddy thinking. He established his own claims to consideration by disclaiming expertise. He made telling points in epigrams. He used the cool tone of logic to assert the fundamental importance of feeling and sentiment as a guide in the many realms where logic was incomplete or inappropriate. And he nearly always concluded a passage of bemused mockery at pretentiousness with a calm *homage* to ennobling virtues that he thought humans as a species were capable of responding to – self-sacrifice, respect for good, reverence for ideals beyond personal aggrandisement.[19] A motto of the Souls, according to Mary Elcho, was to treat 'light subjects seriously and serious subjects lightly'. Arthur tried to bond with audiences by implying that they could figure out the difference.

Arthur's 1887 essay on what and how to read brought the insouciance of metropolitan culture to Scotland's capital of Edinburgh where, according to the press, it was well-received. As Holbrook Jackson pointed out, the late-Victorian generation was self-consciously experimenting with new forms of literature, leisure, social behaviour and opportunities for self-development, to go along with liberating technologies such as the bicycle, phonograph, telephone and electric lighting. 'Wit … is the key to success in such a world, to think quickly and clearly, and to make one's audience laugh, is everything', as Nicholas Freeman says of Oscar Wilde.[20] Arthur's refusal to see most of this innovation as a cause for worry – his trust that the generation after him would do no worse than those before – was one of his most appealing qualities.

'A Fragment on Progress', however, hinted at other and more sombre portents of the time. Some of these were alarmingly mysterious, such as the first truly global influenza pandemics that began in 1889, the recurring famines in agricultural zones and the lingering guerilla conflict that the far-off Burmese continued to wage long after their capital city had fallen. These were symptoms of the interconnectivity of the world's populations, brought about by faster, long-distance transportation as well as the rivalry of new great powers such as Germany, the United States and Japan vying for global influence and the resistance of distant peoples to the subjugations that imperialism was forcing upon them. To an already existing corpus of 'invasion scare' and 'dynamiter' literature, the 1890s would add recurring narratives of national and imperial decline and 'reverse colonisation' by alien forces enacting retribution for Britain's moral and imperial failings. Arthur may have got some of his gloomy imagery of fallen splendors from *She*, the Haggard novel that Mary caught him reading in 1887.[21]

In a throwaway line in 'A Fragment on Progress', Arthur revealed his provisional views on what science was showing about the story of humanity. In relatively isolated communities over millennia of time, 'the great families of mankind … have emerged from the dim workshop where the rough machinery of nature has, in remotest ages, wrought into each its inalienable heritage of natural gifts and aptitudes; – and by these must the character and limits of their development in part be determined.' Arthur, typically, cautioned his listeners not to go too far with this, 'not to think too much of ethnology, and too little of history' or 'attribute to differences of blood effects which are really due to differences of surroundings'.[22] Nevertheless, arguments for scientifically authorised racism were everywhere, and Britain's public sphere embraced a hearty new militarism, accepting the biological inferiority of subject peoples who refused to acquiesce in their own conquest. If the 1880s saw a pivot in political life from aristocratic oligarchy towards a wider, professionalising democracy, the 1890s experienced increasingly public challenges to cultural, social and intellectual assumptions of the high Victorians.

No one in Arthur's circles escaped the questionings of identity and audience brought about by the intensification of mass society in the quarter-century before the First World War. Men who hoped for national – even imperial – influence worried not only how to impress party leaders and insider circles of the metropolis, but how to reach the 'society of strangers' they confronted on platforms and in the mysterious realm of public opinion.[23] Privileged women confronted questions of gender relations and class exigencies for themselves and for daughters being raised in a new celebrity culture. It was not clear what behaviours or attitudes might be criticised, where opposition might come from, what could be expressed, where performance might end and the inner self find some contentment in relation to the outside world. Friendship with Arthur Balfour made these issues inescapable as his political power and personal celebrity grew.

Arthur himself would come to appear curiously above the turmoil. As the 1890s advanced, he structured a daily life around increasingly familiar and supportive settings. Dominant were the corridors of power in Whitehall and Westminster where parliamentary manoeuvring and cabinet decision-making took place. These were supplemented by the relatively small number of country houses he visited regularly, golfing weeks in east Lothian, innumerable men's clubs and societies he could drop in on while in London, and occasional trips to the south of France or Bayreuth. Arthur became notorious among his friends for his reluctance to travel to foreign places or put himself in genuinely unfamiliar, destabilising situations.[24] His greatest psychic adventures played out in the life of the intellect, where he took time to compose his mental response to new discoveries in science, economics, social psychology or historical transformation. He had largely solved for himself – in favour of an intuited theism – the epistemological problems of his generation, and was succeeding in practical fields of administration and political contention. His affective life with Mary Elcho and his brothers' families suited surprisingly well a bachelor with the public responsibilities he shouldered. Sustained by routines, duties and self-constructed coping strategies, Arthur achieved an emotional equilibrium that few of his friends and political colleagues would be able to duplicate as their lives unfolded during the fin de siècle.

7

Terra Incognita

George Pembroke, George Wyndham and Margot Tennant

D URING THE 1890s, Mary Elcho began a practice of visiting the Continent several times a year, often spending weeks at a spa such as Pau in the Pyrenees or Bad Kissingen in Bavaria. While there she went through a regular health regime, caught up on her reading and enjoyed the freedom to do what she wanted without immediate responsibilities – which she praised more than any actual treatment she received.[1] Most in these circles, including Arthur, treated Europe's cultural and geographic attractions as a cross-Channel backyard to Britain itself. They imbibed the art treasures of Italy, risked the gambling casinos of the Mediterranean or cycled through the lowlands. Enterprising men such as Willie Grenfell and Alfred Lyttelton – in the aftermath of Laura's death – went farther afield to experience the grandeur and dangers of US expansionism into the Rockies. Evan Charteris, Harry Cust and George Curzon took round-the-world trips that lasted months, and in the early years of the 1890s as Egypt opened to travellers, both Margot Tennant and DD Balfour visited the sites of the Nile. Ettie Grenfell was intrepid enough to stay with the Wenlocks during their official tour of duty in Madras in 1891.[2]

The letters that these tourists wrote mostly demonstrated and reaffirmed psychic equilibrium by dwelling on home ties and mildly or caustically disparaging the strange worlds encountered. None reported the mental or cultural dislocations that Pembroke had experienced in the South Seas a quarter century before. Margot's journal of her trip to Egypt contained more about the young army officers and British officials she charmed than the local inhabitants, though she did write that talks with the de facto ruler Lord

Cromer and his finance secretary Alfred Milner made her realise for the first time the grandeur of the imperial mission.[3]

Actual social worlds – not merely their mental representations – went with these travellers. Harry Cust and Violet Granby were quite disconcerted when they unexpectedly met Ettie Grenfell in Venice, where they were escaping for a passionate liaison meant to be secret from all back home.[4] Evan Charteris and George Curzon, separately, stumbled across people they knew on the streets of Tokyo. In 1891, DD Balfour found that her association with the Souls had followed her to Cairo: 'there is a "set" in this hotel who hate and abuse our "set", and they call us the Souls and nickname us, and say we are always laughing and that we read Herodotus and those sorts of crimes. They found out I was a Soul because a certain Mrs. Hoare came here, whom I never saw or heard of before, and said I was a Soul and had written something in a magazine.'[5] Increasingly, European hotels, standardised travel opportunities and friends already abroad were allowing members of the elite to take their familiar worlds with them. As the work of Seth Koven has shown, for many it was in fact parts of their own country that were more foreign to them.[6] Britain itself was full of people and locations among whom and where national elites no longer felt at home, as new social groups moved into their familiar spaces and challenged relationships that had been taken for granted by earlier generations.

When George Pembroke turned down Lord Salisbury's offer to join the Conservative government early in 1887, his refusal reflected something more than the health excuse he gave at the time. He was certainly worried about his ability to withstand critical scrutiny and the possibility that he might fail, as he had in Disraeli's government twelve years before. But in establishing where he could make his best public contributions, George was also deciding on his priority of duties as a peer and a landed magnate, one of the grandees at the top of a centuries-old system of title holders, substantial tenants who leased acreage to farm and wage labourers living in estate cottages while working the fields. George's years of stewardship of the vast Pembroke holdings coincided with a quarter century of massive dislocation for this system of rural property ownership and management, as well as for the British agricultural sector as a whole.[7]

In numerous speeches from the 1880s onwards, George showed

his understanding of structural changes in the imperial economy that were transforming rural life.[8] The new technologies of the second industrial revolution allowed staple foods produced more cheaply in the peripheral settlements of the Anglo world (Canada, Australia, the United States) as well as India, Egypt and parts of Europe to undercut the prices that England's agricultural producers could obtain. The change was not slow and progressive, but seismic and abrupt. By the mid-1880s, rental income for British landowners with tenants engaged in arable farming had dropped by one-third within about a decade. The price of wheat reached its lowest point in two hundred years.[9] George thought that the tariffs keeping French and Belgian small farmers afloat were not politically possible in Britain after the triumph of the free trade doctrine in the middle of the century. He was not even sure that protection would be desirable, due to the burden it would place on all wage earners in the form of higher food costs. By the 1890s, in his part of southern England, he saw 'a grave state of things – of loss of capital, of buildings falling into disrepair, of land going out of cultivation, and of labourers being driven away from the country by lack of employment'.[10] George witnessed in his own lifetime the shift away from rural living that continues to this day across the global economy.

Two decades later, David Lloyd George would lead a sustained assault against the traditional landowners by arguing that the existing system of agricultural production channelled too much revenue into the conspicuous consumption of sport and lavish living by 'unemployed' aristocratic owners. Well before this, proprietors were resisting legislation that would enable voluntary, much less compulsory, breakup of great estates into smaller holdings – precisely the solution that Arthur Balfour and George Wyndham would bring to Ireland after the turn of the century.[11] More radical reformers advocated ownership of the land by local authorities who would lease it out to enterprising, self-employed farmers. The landed interest sought – and after the Conservatives returned to power in 1895 attained – some relief from the local taxes that owners paid by pushing to have the central government assume more of the costs of socially necessary functions such as schools, prisons and poor relief. But even these changes, George believed correctly, would not prevent the end of the territorial landed system as it had existed for centuries before he came of age. For now, he and many of England's capitalist landlords who had other sources of income tried to provide the investment monies for estate housing, agricultural improvements and rent abatements by subsidising their rural holdings with revenues from mineral resources or urban property development like his in Dublin.

Historians note that the 1880s and 1890s marked a general 'nadir' in morale among English peers like Pembroke, with 'perennial references in private diaries and correspondence' to the 'threats' that democratic electorates, confiscatory socialist solutions and the competitions of a global market posed to the landed system. When George decided to forego the national political arena in 1887, he still hoped that sacrifice and care by good landlords would weather the crisis. He became part of a conscious effort among peers to shore up the traditional fabric of English rural society by spending more time in residence on country estates and reconnecting with the surrounding population.[12]

This did not mean inattention to affairs in the House of Lords. George joked that the Lords met 'for an hour every few days and did a little business', while 'the House of Commons sat for nine hours every night and did none at all'.[13] But the lords did not now constitute much in the way of a deliberative assembly. After Gladstone's home rule conversion, a huge majority of peers were Salisbury's to command, and business was conducted by the handfuls of front bench officials of the two major parties. George attended the House of Lords regularly, though he spoke seldom, and avoided the small number of government or party positions that required an uninterrupted presence in London. His story shows the time and attention that the obligations of the conscientious landlord could entail. On a typical morning, he wrote, he had at least forty estate or community-related matters to deal with before he could think of turning to anything else.[14] His duties in Wiltshire and Dublin gave him as much work as he could handle.

From the moment of coming into his inheritance, George had headed what might be seen as a very large family enterprise: 42,000 acres of farmland in Wiltshire, over 2,000 of urban land in Dublin and numerous dependencies and responsibilities relating to the properties and to other family members. He consulted with dozens of white-collar specialists – solicitors, bankers, accountants, surveyors, estate agents – who provided the legal and financial services needed to manage these concentrations of property.[15] He met periodically with the substantial tenants who employed the labourers. Wilton House alone required scores of gardeners, gamesmen, coachmen, grooms, kennel keepers, a personal attendant for shooting, a clerk of the works, foremen and hands in the saw mills. Household staff took care of the nearly 300-year-old mansion, as well as substantial town houses on Carlton House Terrace in London and Mount Merrion in Dublin. A captain and chief engineer maintained the *Black Pearl.*

George's inheritance also contained two-thirds of Dublin's Ballsbridge, Sandymount, Ringsend, Donnybrook and Irishtown areas, created as the Pembroke Township by a private Act of Parliament in 1863 and governed by a board of commissioners until 1899. George visited several times a year to consult on urban development that was transforming the properties into upscale residential neighbourhoods and bringing in revenues nearly equal to the Wiltshire acreage that was about twenty times larger.[16] By the late 1880s, these monies were helping to sustain the hospitality and country pursuits – grouse shooting, hunting and harrier packs – that allowed a magnate to entertain friends from afar and meet local farmers, tradesmen and village professionals 'on terms of neighbourly friendship and acquaintance'.[17]

The Pembrokes took seriously the responsibilities in local philanthropy and governance that accompanied a position like theirs.[18] They gave funds to support clothing and fuel drives for the indigent, and built trade schools for local children. The current Ringsend College in Dublin laid its foundation stone as a technical school in 1893 with George presiding. Its goal was to teach local children practical and scientific knowledge of navigation, fisheries and boat crafts that might restore livelihoods for residents of the decaying 'seaside parish'.[19] Gety and George volunteered time as well as money. George reached the rank of colonel in the Wiltshire Rifle Volunteers, was elected to the new Wiltshire County Council in 1889 after serving for years as a magistrate and sat on municipal charity boards. These were not sinecures but were for those who took the work seriously. After his death, councillors and town officials noted with 'considerable feeling' the loss to Wiltshire of 'a most able magistrate, beloved and respected by everyone' for that 'kindliness of feeling which characterized his whole life'.[20]

Gety and George were also organisers of the Conservative Party interest in south Wiltshire. With over three thousand members, Gety headed one of England's largest rural 'habitations' of the Primrose League, the new Tory organisation created to mobilise cross-class, cross-gender and cross-generational support for the causes associated with modern conservatism.[21] With George's help, the Wiltshire Tories acquired a local newspaper to provide 'a course of political instruction' for the 'millions of new voters', and he helped create a branch of the Conservative and Constitutional Association where upper-class and working-class men could learn each other's 'opinions and wishes'. The goal was to integrate society's traditional leaders with the 'new and more educated generation of labourers' in their districts.[22]

Every year at about the time that parliament opened, George provided the Constitutional Association with a substantial survey of the legislation that would be pending and his views on the opposition's arguments. Here he gave his assessments of the state of English agriculture, a subject that he knew was of concern to his audience, but also national issues such as money supply, naval building, imperial defence and Irish home rule. He was unstinting in support of the government's Irish policy, calling Arthur 'a great friend of mine' who was 'very bold and singularly clear-headed', but as 'kind and gentle and wide-minded a man as he was brave and spirited'.[23] George demonstrated the change in party outreach that Joseph Meisel attributes to these years in which members of both parliamentary chambers shifted from flattery and local anecdotes when addressing neighbourhood audiences to pointed discussions of national and imperial issues.[24] George often apologised for forcing remote subjects on his listeners or addressing them as he would the House of Lords. But it was important to the country, he said, that they understand the arguments of different sides as they talked with their neighbours and made up their minds at election times.

However much Arthur Balfour cherished his home and the landscapes of east Lothian, he paid nothing like this attention to the local affairs of Whittingehame and its neighbourhood. By the late 1870s he was dividing his energies between Westminster and the academic intelligentsia of Cambridge and London. In 1891 he sold the 70,000 acres of unremunerative Scottish highlands that the family had owned for over half a century, despite the heartbreak it caused his sister Alice who had come to know Strathconan's inhabitants personally.[25] Arthur was convinced that the estate could never be anything but a drain on income and, like equally remote parts of Ireland, a place that inhabitants were better-off leaving. George Pembroke agreed on the importance of assisted emigration from really unproductive land, but Arthur was more willing to see the Celtic fringes depopulated than George was to abandon Wiltshire.[26] George argued that in regions amenable to farming, the relationships established around great estates like his constituted the foundation of England's national identity. Through feelings of hereditary obligation they induced conscientious aristocrats to invest capital into rural areas and, unlike finance or manufacturing, kept 'rich men' personally connected to the lives of common people.

This was an argument of aristocratic paternalism that the landed interest had used since the industrial revolution began, but it was not merely cynical. George tried to live it, as did others of his friends in this generation of aristocrats such as lords Carnarvon, Cowper, Brownlow, Windsor, Wenlock and Bath. Asked once why he did not publish more literary works, George said that 'it is really much more important that all the people that a man in my position has to do with should get their business promptly attended to, their letters promptly answered, their complaints inquired into … and that relatives and friends who are dependent on one in any degree for their happiness should get the full benefit of my services when they want them, than that a little more literature … should be given to the world.'[27]

Historians are divided on whether the decades after 1880 should be seen as a time of aristocratic political resurgence or corporate collapse of this patriarchal landed society. Martin Pugh and Andrew Adonis stress the effectiveness of activities like George's in maintaining the influence of the peerage as a whole, as well as the status and influence of individual magnates. Others see no uniform pattern, only diverse families scrambling to adapt to circumstances as best they could. But, at a personal level, George's story shows how forced the supposedly organic relationships based on deferential interactions were coming to feel. George loved Wilton and its inhabitants, but his responsibilities did not bring the kind of affective identity that Mary Elcho, for example, eventually found in the Stanway community. Gety Pembroke described county duties as 'tedious affairs', and when W. T. Stead called George a model landlord, he responded that he never felt he did enough to extend hospitality to tenants, parish clergy, schoolmasters and village tradesmen in the neighbourhood.[28]

As for political outreach, George shouldered this duty as well, but said that sometimes it was 'to me very distasteful work … preaching politics to scanty and uninterested country audiences

who only listen to me at all out of a sort of personal kindness'.[29]
The speeches collected after his death show care for argument
and clarifying issues, but they have a tone that is mostly instructive,
with little of the colour or humour that would imply a common fellowship with his audience. From Mary Elcho's house party of 1889,
Doll Liddell reported what a meeting like this could feel like: 'went
down to Stanway, where I found a large party. Our host [Hugo] is
standing for the County Council, and some of us went to one of his
meetings. The room was crammed, parsons, doctors, farmers and
their wives in the front row, rustics behind. The speech excellent,
but monotonous in delivery. I watched the rustics, and could not
trace the faintest reflection of assent or dissent in their faces, nor
did any of them utter a sound.'[30]

Margot once wrote that George Pembroke did 'not have quite
enough to do to make friendship a recreation, it becomes an occupation'.[31] She was not in much of a position to judge, but George's
letters do sound as if the country house parties and yearly *Black
Pearl* cruises with intimate friends were where he felt most contented: 'I don't know what we all did exactly. I never *can* remember but we were all very jolly and went to Salisbury Cathedral and
Longleat, and galloped to Stonehenge in a snowstorm … I lost
my temper one night about pencil games and AJB one morning
about the devil knows what.'[32] The yachting accounts in particular
have the same sort of 'ship of fools' quality as the *Albatross* journals, describing a self-sufficient body of comrades – on *Black Pearl*
with mixed rather than single gender – enjoying good-humoured
adventures as spectators of strange other worlds. But this did not
make George's adult life idle or indulgent. The habitual melancholy others observed in him arose in part from the changes he
was witnessing that made it hard to identify with the position he
inherited, or to connect with rural inhabitants in ways that would
help to secure it.

The evidence that survives shows how private and domestic
George's life – focused on the country estate – was coming to appear.[33] With all his 'rare mental gifts', 'great personal charm' and
humility about his own merits, he was a steward, not a progenitor
or leader of men.[34] He acknowledged himself to be 'lamentably
deficient in the instinct of competition' that characterised the
'new regimes of social worth' of the emerging professional and
political classes.[35] Testing oneself through active engagement in
some chosen field was the proving ground for men. When his

brother Michael pondered leaving the Foreign Office over a minor personnel issue, George argued strongly against it. People would forget the reasons for your action, he advised, and 'treat you as a failure and with half-contemptuous tolerance'. 'I only quit because I had no choice – and I had peerage and large estates which give position and occupation. Even so I've felt loss of status.'[36]

The visible arrival of the manufacturing and financial plutocracy and service professionals needed to sustain cultural, state and imperial power structures coincided with the crisis in patrician economic power to threaten both the privileges and the self-appraisals of those like Pembroke who inherited their positions. Psychological dislocation characterised a number of peers in this generation.[37] Some of George's aristocratic friends – his brother-in-law Lord Brownlow, Lord Cowper, Evan Charteris, Lord Windsor, Tommy Ribblesdale, even George Curzon – would eventually use positions on the boards of Britain's great universities and national arts institutions to assert a final, inbred claim to the nation's 'cultural capital' that might replace their waning political clout and local identities. Family traditions of learning and patronage allowed them to challenge the judgements of professional administrators and subject area specialists who relied on acquired expertise to assess the relationship of culture to Britain's heritage.[38] George made no claims in this area either. But he certainly discovered that the conscientious performance of duties as the local lord no longer brought the psychic rewards it once had. His Wiltshire neighbour Walter Long – often associated with the county-gentry landowning interest – largely gave up involvement in his estate so that he would be available for cabinet positions in the governments of Salisbury and Balfour.[39]

Nor did George find himself able to answer the question of what type of men now spoke for the interests of Britain as a whole. They did not seem to be the independent-minded and disinterested Victorian gentleman he consciously tried to be: a man whose 'excellencies though great and rare … are negative rather than positive. I should find it difficult to define him and yet know perfectly well what he is like. I see him as plain as a pikestaff whenever I am tempted to say or do certain things which he would rather die than say or do. I doubt by the way whether he is *altogether* appreciated in the present age.'[40] George himself seemed to accept that adherence to duties and the restrained conduct of the older generation of gentleman made for an insufficient male life story for his era.

The 'man who achieves nothing is nothing', he quietly observed when a correspondent tried to assure him that his services to family and friends, employees and county residents were achievement enough.[41]

The summer of 1892 brought a general election in which the Liberals emerged victorious, though with a margin of only forty votes. Gladstone formed his fourth ministry and pledged to bring in Irish home rule legislation once again when parliament assembled the next February. Arthur welcomed the change in government. It would give him time to write *Foundations of Belief* and the chance to lead a party in opposition – easier, for him, than to be the one in power.[42] Nevertheless, many Conservatives were demoralised by the electoral support that had produced another opportunity for social reformers and Irish nationalists to pursue their dangerous legislation.

Spectator ran an article called 'Conservative Languor' trying to explain why Tory members of both houses – such as George Pembroke – appeared too dispirited to show up, much less mobilise for the next great fight to protect the union.[43] They had 'put forth all their energies during a seven years' war of no ordinary severity, and were beaten', the author wrote, referring to the kinds of local outreach that Pembroke had been doing since 1885. 'To see their landed property undergoing depreciation, their social station attacked, their influence rivalled or even exceeded by that of professional politicians' showed that 'the old order is changing so rapidly and so completely that they … hardly recognize the world of their youth in the world of their manhood.' Until 'a race of Conservatives has grown up which is refashioned in the mould of the democracy', no one should be surprised at 'the sense of weakness and lassitude' in the Conservative ranks. Whatever energy there was in the opposition forces available to Arthur Balfour, the *Spectator* thought, would come from the Liberal Unionist alliance and the forward thinking of the restless Joseph Chamberlain.

At just this moment, however, others were actually detecting the emergence of the new crop of Conservatives that the *Spectator* said was needed. Fifteen years or more younger than the party leaders, many of these men were aristocrats from among the Souls and included, for example, George Curzon, St John Brodrick, Alfred Lyttelton and Harry Cust. Others were related to the 'Hotel Cecil' of Salisbury relations: Arthur and Gerald Balfour, the future

Lord Selborne, Lord Percy and Salisbury's son Lord Cranborne. University educated, hard-working and conscious of the unprecedented competition they faced in crafting political careers, they were increasingly convinced that aristocrats who wanted a life in national politics 'must become professional politicians, i.e., live for Politics, as an Engineer lives for engineering, or an Actor for Acting'.[44] None of Arthur's young protégés tried harder to understand what this meant than the author of the words themselves, George Wyndham.

George was barely twenty-six when he entered parliament in summer 1889. In an uncontested by-election he secured the seat for Dover, a solidly Conservative constituency of retired military families that would never present him with much in the way of re-election worries. He was so untested that the worst observers could say was that he was too good-looking to be taken seriously – 'dark, swarthy, dreamy, light of build, graceful, with a head of hair which the Romans might have adorned', an Apollo of parliament, a 'ready-made Romeo'.[45] The next caution was that George already had an Irish contingent gunning for him as Arthur's 'devil', the writer of all those sarcastic letters debunking nationalist stories of oppression. He entered the Commons just in time for the August debates over funding the chief secretary's administration, and said that 'the Irish are continually making side hits at me for my letters, for fetching papers for Arthur etc'.[46]

On Arthur's staff George was the loyal factotum and interested observer of politics. Once he joined parliament, he was his own actor in venues and with people almost as new to him as the dervishes of the Sudan – and those at least he had been able to view through the clarifying lens of armed combat. Like Arthur a few years before, he had qualities to suggest that the learning curve could be steep. In appearance he was both handsome and fastidious in an aristocratic way. He was imaginative and loquacious, ornate and convoluted in speaking. He smoked cigarettes rather than manly cigars, liked the French, wrote poetry and was cousin to Oscar Wilde's lover and nemesis Lord Alfred Douglas. All, by the early 1890s, were markers of elite refinement calculated to compound the impressions of nepotistic advantage arising from his closeness to Arthur.[47]

Having never attended university, George Wyndham had little familiarity with the men of the professional and business classes who were forming an increasing portion of the Conservative party

'out-of-doors' as well as inside the Commons. 'Don't you agree
with me that, setting Happiness aside as an unattainable mark for
every-day archery, the best way to be comfortable and "enjoy life"
is to live in harmony with your surroundings', he wrote to his sister
Mary in 1886, 'in the country to be a bumpkin, in London to live
for society and enjoy art; at a country house party to play the fool
agreeably, and in a castle alone to be a hermit?'[48] The absence
of professional male venues was suggestive. It became a standard
lament of concerned friends and criticism of party task-masters
that George stretched himself in too many directions, but with associations more like the aristocratic amateur than the professional
politician that the coming century would require.[49] As the fin de
siècle progressed, George identified himself variously as the bluff
soldier-adventurer, poet-dreamer, linguistic scholar, hedonist, journalist and prophet of the people, but not, as it turned out, an administrator or handler of routine. He brought to politics the same
personal, high-stakes emotionality with which he approached the
other aspects of his life – and in part because he was so often away
from his wife, he reported it more extensively than most political
men of his generation.[50]

George's letters from the early 1890s show how hard he worked
to establish himself with the leadership and among the scores of
backbenchers in the Commons, a noteworthy contrast to the neglect that his brother-in-law Hugo Elcho demonstrated in these
years. No one, including himself, knew whether he could speak
under the forbidding conditions of the lower chamber:

> Addressing the House of Commons is like no other public speaking
> in the world. Its semi-colloquial methods give it an air of being easy,
> but its shifting audience, the comings and goings and hesitations of
> members ... the desolating emptiness that spreads itself around the
> man who fails to interest, the little compact, disciplined crowd in the
> strangers' gallery, the light, elusive flickering movements high up
> behind the grille [where women viewers sat], the wigged, attentive
> weary Speaker, the table and the mace and the chapel-like Gothic
> background with its sombre shadows, conspire together, produce a
> confused, uncertain feeling ... as though I was walking upon a pave-
> ment full of trapdoors and patches of uncovered morass.[51]

In this 'most critical assembly in the world', George confessed to
tremendous stage fright: 'All anti-speech symptoms are very pronounced so am curled up in my den with tangled hair and blear

eyes and stomach-ache and all the rest of it, in the black despair of composition … I wonder if anybody hates the day before as much as I do.'[52] He spent weeks researching a single speech, preparing so extensively that he made the beginner's mistake of belabouring background material while losing his main points. 'Handsome Mr. Wyndham delivered platitudes in a loud and monotonous voice', noted the press, prompting George's admission that 'that is the shape my nervousness takes in the House'.[53] He worked up topics for which he had no affinity – bimetallism or pub licensing – because Arthur wanted someone ready to speak on the subject, then chafed when he failed to catch the Speaker's eye at the right time or found his arguments pre-empted by someone else.[54]

Political work outside the Commons was arguably as time-consuming as anything that George did inside its walls. Balfour's young Tories were all writing for periodicals, but none engaged with the same entrepreneurial zeal as George. 'We must accept journalism as a force in the life we have got to live here and now … and *positively* to mould and direct it', he wrote in 1897 as he prepared to launch a new weekly called *Outlook* that survived until 1928.[55] By then he had already spearheaded the investment consortium that kept W. E. Henley's *National Observer* afloat until 1893, after which the group bought and served as the editorial board of the monthly *New Review*.[56] These periodicals, along with the *Pall Mall Gazette* that Harry Cust was editing, were central to the emergence of Conservative imperialism of the 1890s, but also to the unusual subject areas and irreverent perspectives that contributors such as George Bernard Shaw, H. G. Wells, William Butler Yeats and J. M. Barrie were adding to the 'New Journalism' of this decade.[57] As Wells explained it in *The New Machiavelli*, the goal was to place the best of modern literary stylists alongside expansionist imperial visions of an Anglo-organised and dominated world that would make the new century an era of global progress. The words might have come from George Wyndham himself.

Even more onerous were the speaking engagements that established a newcomer's willingness to do the slogging work of constituency development wherever it was needed. 'I must speak at Kennington on Saturday and Monday, and 19th Manchester, 20th London, 23rd Manchester, 27th London, 30th April in Lancaster, and two in May in Ayrshire', he wrote to his wife in 1889. On another occasion he described in minute detail a thirteen-hour, 300-mile rail journey to tiny Helmsley, forty miles north of York, to give a speech of eleven minutes, followed by a failed attempt to unlock the door to the new Conservative club building that he was dedicating. In the few weeks of the 1892 election, George travelled almost 2,500 miles to speak in Birmingham, Battersea, Worksop, Farnham, Bourne, Ashford and Litchfield, in addition to his own constituency.[58] Political life introduced George to parts of Britain far removed from the great houses, London drawing rooms and county sports scenes of the national elites. His letters from these years sound as though his greatest mental dislocations came from these new exposures to his fellow countrymen.

This was certainly true of the desperately impoverished people he encountered in remote parts of Ireland during a tour with Arthur in October 1890 – the first time either man had been west of the Shannon River.[59] Arthur undertook the trip in aid of three initiatives designed to alleviate the extreme poverty of Connaught and west Donegal. Most immediate was provision for relief of what threatened to be the worst food shortage to strike the western coast since 1847, partly through direct government aid, but also through public works projects on light railway construction that parliament had authorised the year before. Arthur was also planning to create a Congested Districts Board in the land bill to be introduced in 1891, with the goal of fostering long-term agricultural improvement and economic development in regions neglected by government and landlords alike.[60] These 'conciliatory' gestures to the needs of fellow countrymen were applauded by the local priests and officials that the travellers met throughout their two-week journey. But always behind Balfour's shoulder loomed Conservative contingents that deplored expansion of state responsibility, encouragement of dependency on the part of aid recipients and anything that looked like legitimising nationalist complaints. Arthur's rhetoric in both public and private echoed these suspicions. Typically, his pronouncements came across as harsher than his policies, through rhetorical alignment with the recalcitrant rather than humanitarian impulses of British policy and arguments that stressed feasibility and efficiency over appeals to the heart.

George Wyndham's responses to what he saw were quite different.[61] He described the extraordinary beauties of the landscape, the 'silence and perfect civility' of crowds that gathered as they passed, the 'quickness and savoir vivre of which England knows nothing' of a young nationalist they spoke to – 'what a pity such men are against us'. On a day when he and Arthur had to buy gloves to protect against the intense cold, he marvelled at young women riding in carts with bare feet and legs. As the tour progressed from Mullingar to Ballycastle his accounts darkened. At Costello on the Galway coast he saw:

> a far greater depth of misery than any we have seen or I had imagined. It really made one sick to think of the extreme wretchedness of these people living on a few potatoes growing in the mud and water between the rocks, their houses standing in morasses. For the first time the people looked pinched and yellow and *frightened* ... you cannot conceive the poverty of this district ... The majority have never *seen* a *plough* or a *harrow*. There is no mill nearer than twenty miles. They never eat meat, and are always on the brink of starvation. I do trust we may be able to help them.

He told his wife that 'I have learnt more since Thursday of the West, than in all the rest of my life.'

George's family omitted the letters about the 1890 expedition from the collection published after his death. They may have feared that the vivid, empathetic impressions would confirm criticisms from his later political career that he was too soft-hearted about the ungrateful Irish. George was not much older than Arthur had been when Mary Gladstone observed Arthur quelling his emotional responses to distress among the highland poor. This was never so easy for George Wyndham. A decade later when George was himself chief secretary, he told Mary Gladstone that he could not write what he really felt about the condition of the Irish peasants lest he be thought a 'sentimental idiot'. At the same time Curzon's wife was telling her husband that Wyndham *was* a 'sentimentalist' who 'hasn't the hard sense to do strong things'.[62] Throughout his years in politics, George needed to use emotional commitment to boost his political energies, but it took him time to learn that compassion was an emotion that should not be expressed publicly.

George's reactions to the equally unfamiliar provincial and municipal middle classes he met around England were less understanding. Richard Shannon describes how rough and uncultured the rapidly expanding 'party out of doors', overseen by the Conservative central office and hundreds of party agents, could appear to traditional elites in these years.[63] During the annual autumn speaking circuit, George was repelled by carriage processions through interminable city slums 'enwrapped and shrouded by

... cold coal fog', by the garish decorations and strange smells of
meeting halls, by the yowls and hoots of rambunctious audiences
and the 'atmosphere you could cut with a knife' of dinners with
local worthies.[64] Like Arthur's brother Gerald in the same years,
George was astounded at the narrow concerns of self-made men,
busy about their local affairs and oblivious to the great aesthetic traditions or imperial visions that absorbed the metropolitan
elites.[65] In the Commons, MPs from these social groups shared the
electorate's parochialism, earning the labels 'small', 'mean', 'vile'
or 'petty' in George's moments of greatest frustration over public
affairs. That parliamentary life consisted not of heroic achievements such as helping the starving Irish or colonising Africa, but
of long rail journeys, 'pens, ink and paper, ugly rooms, exhausted
atmospheres, commonplace people, and sordid details' became a
continuing refrain of his letters about politics.[66]

Throughout the 1890s George worked hard to overcome his difficulties connecting with professional and business-class Conservatives in Westminster and among local activists. Increasingly the
self-presentation of political men needed to avoid class markers of
dress and demeanour – 'anything that appeared to betray a sense
of social superiority undermined' the fictions of egalitarianism of
the new democracy (see Fig. 12).[67] Friends and well-wishers urged
George to simplify his speech and writing, reduce his literary allusions and make his points with fewer digressions. 'The quality
which most clearly defines masculine language practices ... is the
quality of restraint', writes one scholar of the language changes of
the period. The masculine writer 'curtails "flights and fancies" in
the interests of efficiency. His linguistic restraint mirrors the other
forms of restraint by which he might equally be expected to live
his life.'[68]

Over time George's political writings became tortured into
self-conscious brevity and organisational exactitude in his attempts
to develop a serviceable professional prose – L. P. Curtis called
it writing like 'Balfour's star pupil'. George would have difficulty
falling into the more conversational rhythms of spoken discourse
that Arthur and the Irish were pioneering in the Commons and
on the platform, and came across as nervous and grandiloquent.
As Mary Elcho tactfully cautioned him, 'people *might* think you
are lecturing them', causing needless irritation.[69] He deeply resented criticisms that he squandered his time on aristocratic sporting and aesthetic pursuits and promoted himself as one of the

Fig. 12 A gentleman politician losing control of his audience,
Harper's Magazine, September 1893

conscientious plodders among the new men in politics: 'The 'igh
Society talk won't really wash. I never go into Society. I fought in
the Sudan. I have been a railway director for ten years. I plugged
at the Irish Office through all the scrimmage; I am plugging away
now. You know that.'[70]

Perhaps most troubling was George's inability to contain the
emotional reactions he had to the events and people of the political
environment. Wells's *New Machiavelli* is chronologically confused,
but its narrator hero seems to have been trying to establish himself
in the same 1890s political world as George, with whom he has a
lot in common. Wells knew George in these years through their
joint work with Henley and with Cust at the *Pall Mall Gazette*. Wells's
hero demonstrates the 'ostensible' daily, active self of George, fig-
uring out how to gain the attention of the Commons, participate
in the political press and speak to audiences of strangers. But he
is also one of those 'rarer men' of artistic temperament who has
an active internal life – a private 'hinterland' of ideas, visions and
emotions that he is continually trying to reconcile with the external world. George was acutely aware of this inner self – he called it
an endless 'monodrama' that constituted for him an independent
reality coexisting simultaneously with the actual events of each

day. Even a routine night in the House of Commons unsettled this inner self: 'Listening to Debate tires me more than [it does] the phlegmatically indifferent … I mark, approve or resent not only every word of the speaker, but every change in the attitude of his audience; snorting inwardly with disgust when they do not see or applaud … I mean to be callous but get engrossed in the game.'[71]

John Tosh has argued that many boys of the middle and upper classes of this and following generations inculcated codes of emotional repression so severe that 'even the awareness of inner feeling became incompatible with a masculine self-image'.[72] George was forthcoming in private letters about the intense feelings of the subjective self: the buoyancy of romantic attachment, the fondness he expressed with intimate friends, the pain and indignation of perceived injustice. Reviewing his writings three decades later, the modernist poet T. S. Eliot thought the letters revealed the self of 'a peculiar English type, the aristocrat, the Imperialist, the Romantic, riding to hounds across his prose, looking with wonder upon the world as upon a fairyland'.[73] George admitted to being a romantic in both the 'abandonment to love' and the 'action- adventure' senses of the word, and found these qualities hard to integrate into a modern political career. But the letters that the family chose *not* to publish show him less likely to use images of fairyland than of battlefields to describe public life, metaphors where combat was inevitable or even desirable, stakes were high, heroes fell and dreams were shattered as often as they were fulfilled. George tried to keep these highly dramatic responses confined to the hinterland self. They did not seem welcome in the overscheduled, mindless routines of the professional politician. But as the decade progressed, he was clearly looking for a cause that would unite the emotional and ostensible selves into an effective political actor who could reach the experts, professionals and strangers who filled the democratic landscape.

The new venues and participants in the late nineteenth century public world affected the lives of women in political circles as well.[74] The memoirs of Arthur's sister-in-law Lady Frances Balfour present a sharp account of how much had changed in these exclusive spheres during the last thirty years of Victoria's reign. Frances's mother, the Duchess of Argyll, had been part of the extended Whig-aristocratic cousinhood that dominated inner circles of national politics in the middle decades of the century and formed one of the main strands of the Liberal Party as it emerged in the 1860s. She had died in 1878, aged fifty-three, after bearing twelve children in under twenty years. Frances described her mother as deeply but unassertively religious, well-read, and acquainted through the duke's active public life with all the important people of London political society. But the list of restrictions defining her existence astounded her daughter.

The Duchess of Argyll lived her whole life without being in a situation where she was not surrounded by people she knew – in other words, where she had to deal alone with a stranger. She never bought a train ticket, shopped at a store, took a carriage by herself, ate in London outside the home of an acquaintance or ventured to 'go forth to help the down trodden' through charitable works beyond her family's doors.[75] The wives of political men of her generation networked through private functions in London or the country house, where they engaged in a 'politics of personality', serving as 'wielders of patronage, as confidantes, and as go-betweens'.[76] Part of the duchess's seclusion was personal preference. Widows like Arthur's mother had little choice but to assume some of the 'masculine' tasks of household management, while more extroverted women might cultivate important London editors or provide the kind of connections for a favoured newcomer that make up the story of Anthony Trollope's Irish MP in *Phineas Finn* (1869). But women like the duchess did not campaign among the electorate, speak in meeting halls or write for popular consumption. The three great innovations of expanding democracy – press, platform and petition – were largely closed to them, to say nothing of the vote itself.[77]

Much of this would begin to change after the electoral expansions and local government reforms of the last decades of the century. As late as 1882, Frances Balfour, in her twenties and already married, found herself criticised by relatives because she had spoken 'publicly to a group entirely of women'. Three years later, she was appearing on behalf of her brother-in-law during his hard-fought election for Central Leeds – though mostly, she admitted, as an 'ornament'.[78] She had begun to serve as president of a metropolitan Travellers' Aid Society designed to protect women and children stranded in London, and was active in organisations for her life's work, women's suffrage. From her London home west of Holland Park she rode omnibuses and shopped in stores. Her life was hardly less centred around family than her mother's had

been – for nearly half of every year, Arthur's two married brothers
and their families lived at Whittingehame. But Frances had five
children in about fifteen years to her mother's eleven in the same
time span. She travelled the long distances between London and
her Scottish homes with greater frequency and, as Margot noted
in the same years, was often in the midst of very large crowds of
strangers, whether at an election site, a volunteers' review or a music festival.[79] She had her own friends and associates, both male
and female, who had little connection with her husband. By the
early 1890s, she was also beginning to frequent the halls of parliament to watch her male relatives there and talk to people who
might help her causes.

On 25 February 1888, only a week after Arthur's vigorous defence of his masculinity in the face of those Irish slurs, the cartoon-
ist Harry Furniss devoted *Punch*'s 'Essence of Parliament' graphic
to the news that 'increased facilities are now provided for Ladies
dining, etc, with Members' of the House of Commons. Circled
around a resplendent young woman in evening dress, he drew
tiny montages of Gladstone eating chops in his study with his female relatives, Irish members dancing jigs with bonnie lasses while
brawling with each other, a man and woman engaged in cosy private dining, William Harcourt basking in feminine adulation, even
a willowy Arthur performing some sort of legerdemain before a
rapt group of beautiful ladies. In *Graphic*'s view five years later, all
these visions had come to pass.[80] The cell-like Ladies Gallery with
its iron grille was filled every night with curious women observing
each other and the men on the floor below. The peephole next
to the chamber entrance was so backed up with lady viewers that
members returning for a vote could hardly get through the door.
Corridors echoed with rustling silk and female laughter. During
the dinner break from 8 to 8:30 p.m., women actually entered
the chamber to lounge on the front benches, experiencing an
especially thrilling *frisson* 'if the seat selected be guaranteed to be
Mr. Balfour's'. *Graphic*'s commentator was well informed. A lot of
the women making incursions into this most masculine of settings
were Arthur's friends – Margot Tennant, Charty Ribblesdale, Violet Granby, DD Balfour Lyttelton, Frances Horner and his own
sisters-in-law.

George Curzon and Edward Hamilton were not alone in thinking there were 'petticoats everywhere', which in their eyes detract-
ed from the business and dignity of the assembly by sexualising its

Fig. 13 In the Ladies Gallery above the House of Commons, Max Cowper,
ILN, 10 March 1906

ambience.[81] *Punch* and *Graphic* treated this new development as a
kind of comic reversal, with imperious, beautifully attired ladies
turning the gaze around to become spectators of the ridiculous an-
tics of men – possibly sharing jokes about the acres of bald heads
so apparent from above (see Fig. 13). The journalists neglected
to mention, because it was the default situation, the innumerable
daily occasions in which men at the heart of power met alone in
their convivial huddling around the dinner table after the ladies
had departed, the proliferating men's clubs that excluded women,
the many official or associational male-only dinners of the London
season and the party organisations where women volunteers had
hierarchies of authority separate from the men's.[82] In fact, longer
hours and heavier sessions of parliamentary work for ministers,
undersecretaries and shadow leaders reduced the ability of political hostesses to arrange evening occasions where important guests
could be sure of attending beyond the truncated dinner hour. The
restorative 'Saturday-to-Monday' in the country further complicated the social planning of wives who did not have retreats close to
the capital.

One way for parliamentary men to continue seeing their female
friends and relatives was to bring the society conviviality into the

political setting. Women's ability to roam the hallways, dining rooms and terrace of the Commons depended on a member's invitation. The prolonged bachelor status of men such as George Curzon, Harry Cust, R. B. Haldane or Arthur himself made these evening arrangements appealing, as they were for married men like Henry Asquith or John Morley whose spouses did not participate in political society. The interest of the women in attending can be seen as another aspect of the spectator sport that national politics was becoming, as well as the desire to meet the rising men in each party. The development revealed the subtle ways that sociabilities were changing as an earlier aristocratic control over the social aspects of high politics waned.

During the 1891 London season, Pembroke and Curzon noticed the 'new fashion of the women running after the men' among the Souls. Curzon coined the term 'Cosquiths' to indicate how a cultural icon like Oscar Wilde, a visiting eminence like the American jurist Oliver Wendell Holmes and an emerging political star like Henry Asquith were receiving fawning invitations to social get-togethers that before would have been restricted to the original 'Gang'.[83] Grand aristocrats like the Pembrokes had fostered the inclusion of charming upper-middle class women into their social circles. Now those women were extending the courtesies to able middle-class men. Margot Tennant took exception to the idea that this was either 'lion hunting' or a shallow pastime to ward off the boredom of frivolous lives. She said that it was a conscious attempt to reduce the social ostracisms that political society was suffering as a result of the home rule controversies. She and her friends entertained Gladstone and Salisbury, Lord Randolph Churchill and Lord Spencer. They were the most attractive group in society because they welcomed robust discussion of varied points of view, as long as it was done with civility and humour by people who had something worthwhile to say.

As with so much of Margot's reminiscence, she had a point, but not exactly the one she was making. There is no evidence that anyone's hostessing initiatives changed long-established social patterns among the Salisbury–Gladstone generation. Moreover, the unpublished diary of the Liberal MP John Morley shows how much inter-party entertaining continued anyway during the most vicious political controversies of the late 1880s. Morley, ten years older than Arthur Balfour, was a paradigmatic Victorian liberal: disciple of Mill, editor of the *Fortnightly Review*, unvarying supporter and later biographer of Gladstone. He was a relative latecomer to parliament, having given up journalism for election to the Commons in 1883, but he served as chief secretary for Ireland during the short home rule session of 1886 and would do so again when the Liberals returned to power in 1892. Morley was mysteriously estranged from his wife by the 1880s, so he was making his way into metropolitan political society on his own during years of exceptional political antagonism. Nevertheless, his diaries show him at many social functions not only with Gladstonian stalwarts, but often with the minister directly opposite him on the front benches – Arthur Balfour, with the fiercely partisan Conservative hostess Lady Londonderry, with George Curzon, George Wyndham and Salisbury's son Lord Cranborne.[84]

The initiatives of Margot Tennant, Charty Ribblesdale and Frances Horner in the early 1890s were important, however, in introducing the younger Liberals H. H. Asquith and R. B. Haldane to the inner circles of the political aristocracy as represented by men like Arthur Balfour, Lord Cowper or George Pembroke. These university-trained newcomers were familiar with male-only conviviality that encouraged general discussion of differing views – part of the informal 'liberal public sphere' during these years that William Lubenow has described.[85] But the Souls' liking for this sort of engagement in mixed company, and the demeanours appropriate to it, was less familiar to these Liberals. As Frances Horner observed of Haldane, intellectual men often had trouble handling 'the bewildering maze of female conversation'.[86] At a party of the politician and arts patron Cyril Flower, Morley thought Arthur 'very flippant and dandiacal amid a bevy of dames ... more noisy levity than I ever saw in him before'.[87] It took these men some time to appreciate the purposes that women might serve through open inclusion in the socialising at the heart of the modern political elite.

This was not done through participating in explicit debates over policy. Even before Arthur's career took off, his family thought his aversion to discussing political issues on social occasions went too far: 'Arthur was in his very best form and we had a most delightful evening, talking somewhat of politics, but mostly on the subject of Arthur's views of conducting general conversation, and his care to keep all serious discussion out of it. We all attacked him from various points, and he defended himself well and with great brilliancy and humour, tho he did not manage to convince us.'[88] Arthur relaxed

in conversation about those less immediate topics that earned the
Souls their name – ethical dilemmas, changes in modern social
relations, the difference between historical fashion and fundamental truths. When John Morley first got to know the Pembrokes, he
disapproved of time spent this way. Nothing about 'agreeable idle
talk … displeases me more than futile cleverness about questions
essentially insoluble, or wrongly propounded … whether if you have
done a wrong thing[,] confession or persistent refutation is the
proper course: if you try to repair without confessing, you are living
a lie, etc'.[89] Aside from neglecting how women who had received
little education might be genuinely interested in questions of ethical
responsibility or constructing a moral stance in the world, he was
underestimating the intangible contributions they provided in such
settings, contributions to which Arthur was alert.

Julia Bush points out how much of the work of women in political society can be understood as psychological. They were
intelligence-gatherers, drawing men out, discovering their characteristics and providing insights on their qualities. As Charty Ribblesdale wrote to Harry Cust, 'we have invented a splendid new
game, writing conversations and guessing who the conversers are.
It is most amusing and gives such scope for insight into character.'
She also noted that often men 'with any reputation' only listened
when confronted with such drawing room activities, their refusal to participate as revealing in its way as actual performance.[90]
Astute operatives like Arthur and Henry Asquith were inveterate
gossips – to put it another way, seekers of information and impressions of other men's capacities. Women provided points of view
outside those acquired from a politician's own observations. Even
John Morley in these years admitted that he wished 'I knew some
femme de monde, with good brain, and knowledge of politics,
who could play Egeria.'[91]

The presence of women could also soften the starkly binary
constructs of political opposition. Mary Elcho was adept, Beatrice
Webb noted, at serving as 'a bridge' between aristocrats, artists,
anarchists, bureaucrats and bourgeoisie.[92] Informal conviviality
helped reduce the sting of publicly enacted rhetorical assaults and
complicated the emotional simplicities of partisanship. Mixed-gender socialising across the political divide – attending the same balls,
dining in the Commons, relaxing at Daisy White's rented house at
Ramslade – helped Balfour and Morley cooperate on the functioning of the new Irish Congested Districts Board, whichever man

held office. It also conveyed how political vitriol could be part of a game done for outsiders to observe, but for insiders to understand as the self-conscious, less-than-transparent spectacle it often was.

As the arenas of politics 'out of doors' multiplied beyond country houses and London drawing rooms, elite women began to make contributions farther afield in the service of enhancing their relatives' and friends' political impact. Within less than a decade, Conservative women in the Primrose League undertook activities that party managers thought essential in enlarging the Tory voter base for the 1892 and 1895 elections by organising local events and boosting turnout at the polls. Liberal women followed suit, and Margot's draft essay about electioneering for her brother in Glasgow in 1892 shows how exciting this could be.[93] She enjoyed the door-to-door canvassing among working-men: 'handsome, manly, intelligent; most of them in their shirt sleeves, reading the papers, full of argument and tolerance, civil, but not emotional!' Shouted at by a huge crowd to speak on a mass platform, she presented herself as a tiny figure courageously piping out the appropriate encouragement in a 'high, clear voice' before burying her face in the rough coat of Asquith standing behind her. As the Edwardian era progressed, Balfour's sisters-in-law on behalf of women's suffrage, and Violet Cecil and DD Lyttelton in the name of imperial service, developed more fortitude in their ability to speak publicly on behalf of causes they embraced and their party leaders supported.[94]

By 1900, Jon Lawrence argued recently, women were apparent everywhere in the public sphere through their work in political and electoral organisations, aside from the much studied activities associated with the suffrage movement itself. Yet these new engagements did not imply an equality of authority with men, especially for friends and family members of nationally recognised political figures. By the elections of 1910, perhaps one-third of parliamentary candidates could count on their wife's visible participation in a campaign – nearly double from 1895. Even so, a woman actually spoke on the platform at only 8 per cent of meetings. Increasingly sophisticated understandings of how to reach voters found that the 'lady bountiful' persona of a *grande dame* like Gety Pembroke could alienate more than attract male electors and their wives.[95] More visible among strangers than their mothers had been, their authority still rested on service roles in support of the party causes of male relatives and friends.[96]

Margot's initiative in autumn 1892 to create a quarterly journal 'by women for men' shows how she was experimenting with and ultimately misjudging the limitations.[97] Her memoir says that she lined up nearly all her friends – male and female – to contribute to the venture, along with members of the cultural and intellectual worlds such as Edward Burne-Jones, Ellen Terry, Benjamin Jowett, J. K. Stephens and Lionel Tennyson. It was an impressive roster and surely could have supplied the half-dozen numbers she envisioned, with illustrations provided by her sister Lucy and Violet Granby. Suggestions for the title of the journal show that the focus was supposed to be the women's point of view on public life. References to Eve, Mrs Grundy, petticoats, pinafores, sphinxes, veils, masks and idle ink fill the list. But the tentative 'programme for the first number' reveals a singular uniformity in what would be offered. 'Tomorrow' – the title eventually chosen – was going to be overwhelmingly dedicated to character sketches, gossip, anecdotes and ephemera of the sociopolitical scene. In addition to a regular leader on 'Persons and Politics', other columns were to be called 'The Social Zodiac', 'Occasional Notes', 'Men and Women' and 'Conversations'.[98]

Margot's autobiography provides her 'Persons and Politics' leader for the first issue, the same essay that prompted Arthur's speculations about the role of luck in politics referred to in the introduction to this book. As Margot put it in her anti-Arthur stance:

> In Politics the common opinion is that measures are the important thing, and that men are merely the instruments which each generation produces, equal or unequal to the accomplishment of them. This is a mistake. The majority of mankind desire nothing so much as to be led. They have no opinions of their own, and, half from caution, half from laziness, are willing to leave the responsibility to any strong person. It is the personality of the man which makes the masses turn to him, gives influence to his ideas while he lives, and causes him to be remembered after both he and his work are dead.

Her signed article went on to describe the 'diffuse and ineffective personality' of the retiring home secretary Henry Matthews, the 'invincible indecision' of George Goschen, the 'lifelike imitation of a strong man' that constituted William Harcourt, the 'over-delicacy of nervous organization' of John Morley and the lack of any 'trace of genius' in Lord Spencer.

Henry Lucy made a living from this kind of insider observation.

His snippets are still used by historians to illustrate the essential traits of political figures. But he was a fifty-year-old established male journalist, Margot a thirty-year-old female upstart. She had been getting a lot of reinforcement for her 'masculine brain' – though not masculine nature – from male friends and mentors who encouraged her to write down her impressions on the important people and events she was well placed to witness. But for her to present them openly to the public was a step too far for this generation.

Harcourt's quip that he was not interested in the 'souls' of Arthur's women friends but in their bodies encapsulated the mockery that persuaded Margot to give up the idea of having women publicly advise men on their political strengths and weaknesses. Over the next two decades, the women in Arthur's circles remained notably split in their attitudes even towards suffrage. The Balfours supported 'votes for women', the Lytteltons signed the famous 1889 appeal against it, for example, and Martin Pugh has made the counter-intuitive assessment that, at the highest levels of the political elite, the Conservative leadership was always more supportive of women's access to legally established voting rights than were the Liberals.[99] But women at the centre of political power generally needed to keep a low profile. They could be open, attractive and humorous with mixed company, competing with each other to score points and show their greater insights.[100] But to take an independent or combative course risked losing access to the very information and personal connections that made them interesting and useful to the men in their lives.

The geographies and spaces available to privileged Britons were multiplying rapidly in the late nineteenth century. Experiencing these as consumers of culture, goods and adventures signalled the material and psychological resources one had available to transcend the routines of elite life. Being *required* to participate in unfamiliar worlds on terms even partially constructed by others was something else, however. Falling into circumstances where one's place and pedigree were unknown, or worse, known but unadmired, threatened to reveal the ways that one might not be the master of all situations. Arthur was not drawn to personalities brash, assertive or oblivious in the face of these realities, but to people who privately admitted their sense of dislocation and might even interpret it as personal inadequacy. As the 1890s progressed, however, it was becoming harder to escape the evaluation of strangers and still maintain place and power in the national arena. Increasingly true in everyday interactions, it applied even more to that expanding and intangible sphere called public opinion, and the burgeoning print discourse that fed it.

8

---◆◆◆---

Celebrity and Scandal

Margot Tennant and Arthur Balfour

A RTHUR BALFOUR'S rise to prominence was one of the defining features of public life in the 1890s. His duels with Gladstone and the Irish, leadership in the House of Commons, even the widely caricatured high forehead, side whiskers, lanky frame and ubiquitous golf club made his name and image recognisable far beyond friends and colleagues. Gety Pembroke acknowledged this new pre-eminence when she wrote about the annual house party she was planning at Wilton over the 1890 Easter recess: 'the great A. Balfour is coming ... he is a wonderful man. It is funny to look back to when he used to come here quite quietly and nobody thought anything of him except us – now – he is like a standard and the whole world wish to come and meet him.'[1]

What Gety meant by the 'whole world' was actually the 'world' as the aristocracy had traditionally understood it – the national political and social elites, the habitués of metropolitan society and professional life most interested in governance. As Arthur's social cache rose, his friends had inevitably found themselves the subjects of gossip and chaff by this 'shamelessly inquisitive' conglomerate. Gladys de Grey reported a sporting gathering at Riddlesworth in Norfolk where 'the old Soul joke continued from the beginning of dinner until we went to bed. They even condescended to "jeux de mots" about fried Souls and other cheap witticisms that bring tears to the eyes.'[2] Early in 1891, when Lord Wenlock arrived in Bombay on the way to his new position as governor of Madras, the *Pall Mall Gazette* reported that an Indian newspaper had described the Wenlocks as Souls, members of a society as 'secret as the Masons', according to the anonymous London correspondent.[3] The private sociabilities of London were reaching newspaper readers in India, to say nothing of the English provinces, then recirculating back to the city as more news.[4]

Prominent families already knew something of this. As national elites formed in Britain during the Napoleonic era, aristocratic families had begun to use print media to convey information to far-flung acquaintances. The Court Circular column in the London *Times* reported the entertainments and movements of important people across the country and abroad, starting with royalty but including prominent title-holders as well. In an 1884 example of this, the Pembrokes put a notice in the *Times* announcing that George had survived the crisis of fever and pneumonia that had threatened his life in the previous few days, not as an item important for a general readership, but as a way to reach the large circles of friends, relations and associational contacts that were had by a man of Pembroke's position.[5]

By this time, however, the 'great printing revolution' that began in the 1860s was accelerating the problems of publicity. What Matthew Rubery calls the 'age of newspapers' helped to create a 'public sphere accessible largely through print media' with press articles and commentary that confronted prominent figures with an image of 'the self as seen by the outside world'.[6] In Antony Trollope's Palliser novels of the 1870s, the prime minister wants to read press opinion of his policies, but finds himself inundated with stories of his private life and tastes. At first such reporting was largely confined to a metropolitan readership in proximity to Fleet Street, Westminster and London clubland. Through chitchat columns, insider gossip and the new profession of journalism, newspapers and men's clubs were the 'kindred institutions of print capitalism' that paved the transition from the 'World' as understood by the manageably small aristocracy and its metropolitan observers to the world of modern public awareness.[7]

Technological innovations of the1880s expanded and transformed this public sphere. Thirty years before the advent of radio, national news could be brought to country towns within hours via telegraphs and railways. 'The model London letter of today', said Henry Lucy, 'telegraphed nightly to the provinces, serves up, hot and fast, the news of the hour', so that distant regions might even be a day ahead of London 'in matters of personal or political intelligence' (see Fig. 14). Revolutions in paper manufacturing and mechanised compositing dramatically lowered the cost of weekly magazines and daily papers. By the end of the 1880s, photographs

Fig. 14 The urban public devours the latest news,
L'Illustration, 7 December 1872

began to supplement artists' renderings of people and faraway events: 'Now one's peers, one's monarch, their women and even their playthings could be recognized and turned into the subject of comment which was based on far more specific information than hitherto.'[8]

Whole new readerships of women, workers and children emerged during the last third of the century, along with the consumer products whose manufacturers would pay to advertise in periodicals geared to these audiences. In the process, information was increasingly delivered in the form of entertainment, a change that David Reed calls 'something quite new' to the periodicals of the 1880s.[9] 'Fashionable intelligence' that focused on the lifestyles and private worlds of the rich and privileged, including their womenfolk, took up ever more column space. The *Spectator* deplored this development in 1890 in a piece called 'Fashion and Democracy'. The now endless minutiae of weddings, clothes, guests, balls and high society events was not provided 'for the benefit of the few people concerned', but as 'a matter of absorbing interest to a multitudinous public'. It was a 'melancholy' and possibly dangerous sign that 'the lives of the great mass of people are so empty, so utterly devoid of interest, that they are driven to find amusement in reading of the lives of a select few, of interests that they cannot understand, and of pleasure that they cannot share'.[10]

If the fin de siècle marked a high point for the print devoted to political debate, it also began to see the construction of celebrated personalities known less for specific achievements than simply for 'well-knownness'.[11] The 'world' of people who thought they understood something about you but with no first-hand knowledge mysteriously expanded. Modern celebrity was being created during the years of Arthur's rise, complicating the relationships between information, reputation, private lives and self-understanding in this generation of the privileged. Of all his friends, no one was more affected by this development than Margot Tennant.

As the fin de siècle decade began Margot Tennant was turning twenty-six. She was still unmarried, almost completely in charge of her own activities as well as her parents' entertainments in London and Glen, and she was gaining the notice of the press. 'I wonder what poor AJB thought about the paragraph', Margot worried when a rumour arose that Balfour, then chief secretary for Ireland and a bachelor, was courting her.[12] In February 1890, the *Dundee Advertiser* ran a fluff piece on 'Sir Charles Tennant's brilliant daughter' that described how she had danced solo at a charity bazaar in Glasgow while her father was running in a by-election there. It also raised the possibility of a romance with Balfour who had recently visited Glen, and Charles Tennant was asked at a public meeting what would happen if his daughter married the Irish secretary.[13] 'Miss Margot's dancing has outraged the Glasgow proprieties!!', Arthur wrote to Mary Elcho, clearly feeling no need to defuse the courtship speculation for her benefit: 'Sir Charles's tongue and Miss Margot's heels are powerful allies of the Unionist cause.'[14] Margot danced in public again for an amateur charity opera at the height of the London season in June. This 'bizarre novelty' was attended by six duchesses, six marchionesses, eight countesses, the Prince of Wales and Princess Louise. A year later, press reports linking her name with the recently widowed Rosebery were the talk of high society in Washington and New York.[15]

The real attention began in autumn 1892 – around the time that Margot was floating her journal idea – with a cluster of articles in the metropolitan and provincial press about the Souls. In November 1892, the *Birmingham Gazette* announced the dissolution of the group of 'kindred spirits' supposedly started by Arthur Balfour and George Curzon 'for purposes of high thinking'. Three days later the *News of the World* picked up the story in nearly identical words. An avalanche of press items followed, with 'snippety gossip' in the *Glasgow Herald, St. James's Gazette, World, The Hawk* and *Truth*. *England* published a long 'Interview with a Soul' naming both male and female members of the 'select and most private coterie of distinguished and brilliant men, and of beautiful and accomplished women, whose main object in association is mental and literary pleasure and improvement. Their union is purely spiritual. They read and recite to each other, and indulge in sweet converse generally.' Arthur Balfour and George Pembroke were mentioned as promoting the 'Platonic and harmless association of men and women', Harry Cust for a snobbish dislike of admitting newcomers to the circle, and George Curzon for leading a double life by pursuing more ribald amusements elsewhere.[16]

Shortly afterwards, the censorious conservative pundit W. H. Mallock raised the stakes with a poem dedicated to 'Miss M__' that served as leader in the *Fortnightly Review*'s December edition. Under a guise of flattery, Mallock accused Margot and her women friends of decorative vacuity combined with shameless self-display. The piece was prefaced with an explanation that 'Miss Margot Tennant' had prompted his remarks herself by writing to the *St. James's Gazette* to defend her friends from charges of cliquishness and frivolity. Margot denied that she had publicly intervened in this way. With characteristic impulsiveness, she had simply fired off 'an irritable private letter only I never put private on it' responding to a woman who had written asking her to explain the Souls. This may have been a wily subterfuge set up by the *St. James's* itself, for Margot's response was immediately in print. 'It's too beastly this mad spirit of journalism isn't it', she wrote to Spencer Lyttelton after learning how her private letter had become fodder for Mallock's pen. 'I shall be *very* careful to say nothing about it to a human living soul and mind you are careful not to let them talk more than you can help.'[17] To be named in gossip-column ephemera was one thing, but a long poem in the *Fortnightly Review* mocking one's rarified existence and personal immaturity took too far the status of being a woman 'talked about'.

Margot's attempt to let unwanted publicity die by ignoring it was thwarted more seriously several months later. On 19 May 1893, the *Times* reported the 'publication today' of a two-volume novel called *Dodo: a Detail of the Day*. The author was E. F. Benson, the 25-year-old son of the Archbishop of Canterbury, for whom the unexpected sensation of this first book launched a long career as an Edwardian novelist, essayist and social observer.[18] The first edition of *Dodo* sold out within a month. By December, the book was in its twelfth run, including a one-volume version that reduced the price more than two-thirds from a sovereign to six shillings. Publisher advertisements for *Dodo* touted glowing reviews. The *Guardian* called it 'an unusually clever and interesting novel'. 'The story [is] told with charming grace and much power', raved the *Speaker*, 'a feast of epigram and paradox'. The *Spectator* devoted two long columns to the 'delightfully witty sketch of the "smart" people of society as it is in the Row and the "house-party" of the day … Dodo incarnates in a brilliant and charming fashion a new type – woman as she has become since she cast herself loose from the customs built up during so many centuries.' Methuen promoted *Dodo* as 'the Novel of the Season', an accurate assessment of its unexpected money-maker.[19]

The title character of Benson's novel is indisputably Margot. She dances in public with unusual grace and an unselfconscious abandonment to the music. She visits factory girls in the East End (for a little while, because it is 'the thing to do'), displays a skull in her sitting room to remind her occasionally to think of life's profundities, rides a 'vicious brute' of a horse and energises others with her 'inexhaustible fund of vivacity'. Dodo is surrounded by a group called 'the apostles' or 'the disciples' who meet together in London and country houses to flirt and outdo each other in glib conversation. Occasionally they mention philosophy and play games of 'marking people for beauty, and modesty, and cleverness, and so on'. Dodo is a brilliant outsider to the traditional circles of polite society, with a deep ambition to be 'admired and amused by clever people'. 'All these people must know who I am', she proclaims, as she decides to marry a moneyed peer she only pretends to love. The word 'vulgar' appears as often in Dodo's discourse as in Margot's. To be vulgar was to be common, to be what unthinking, unoriginal people were.

Some of Benson's throwaway lines have actual precursors in the letters and anecdotes of Margot's life. Arthur's famous quip in response to the 1890 press speculation that he might marry Margot

– 'No, that is not so. I rather think of having a career of my own'[20] – is recycled in the novel when Dodo describes the good man she has married as not doing very much, but 'then again he's married – to me, too. That's a profession in itself.' One admirer's description of Dodo's 'hidden depths and unexpected shallows' sounds like a line from H. H. Asquith's courtship letters to Margot, raising the interesting prospect that she had shared them with others, an infraction for which she frequently had to apologise.[21] When Dodo comes close to confessing that she plans to marry without love, her admission sounds like Margot's own self-interrogations as she debated her marital choices: 'Oh, my God, I don't know what to do. It isn't my fault that I am made like this. I want to know what love is, but I can't—I can't.'

Benson's biographer argues that his achievement lay in letting his heroine present herself 'through her speech' rather than authorial explanation.[22] The reader's first meeting of Dodo is set in Hyde Park where she tells her old suitor and now comfortable friend Jack that she has accepted Lord Chesterford's proposal. The scene is dominated by her stream-of-consciousness prattle:

> Jack, come and see us this evening; we're having a sort of Barnum's Show, and I'm to be the white elephant. Come and be a white elephant too. Oh, no, you can't; Chesterford's the other. The elephant is an amiable beast, and I am going to be remarkably amiable. Come to dinner first, the Show begins afterwards. No, on the whole, don't come to dinner, because I want to talk to Chesterford all the time, and do my duty in that state of life in which it has pleased Chesterford to ask me to play my part. That's profane, but it's only out of the Catechism … Who wrote the Catechism? I always regard the Catechism as only a half-sacred work, and so profanity doesn't count, at least you may make two profane remarks out of the Catechism, which will only count as one.

Punch lampooned this artless, preposterous self-presentation in a take-off called 'Bobo' where the heroine soliloquises at the breakfast table with her husband Cokaleek and a friend called Bill: 'You're not eating any breakfast. Put the mustard-spoon in his mouth, Bill, if he insists upon keeping it wide open while he stares at me. Ain't I fascinating this morning? … Here, somebody, see if my spur's screwed on all right. "I wish your head was screwed on half so well", said Bill.'[23]

H. H. Asquith wrote that on his first meeting with Margot, in autumn 1890, she appeared to him 'abominably frivolous, and talkative, and irresistible'.[24] Any reader of her letters grapples with the breathless pace and non sequiturs, to say nothing of lack of punctuation, of Margot in full stride. Dodo talks enough like Marion Crawford's Joe Thornton, the character based on Margot in *An American Politician* (1885), and like Pen in Julian Sturgis's *The Folly of Pen Harrington* (1897), to recognise the similarities described by these authors who were casual acquaintances of the original. Their fictional accounts are as close as it is possible to get to Margot's spontaneous conversation, with its manifestations of what one reviewer termed 'the genius of fragmentary wit'.[25]

Benson was both lionised and abused for his close portrait of such a recognisable society woman – 'all her bad points and none of her good ones', as Arthur's sister-in-law put it.[26] It would have been hard for readers to separate the externals of Margot-like speech and behaviour from the overall personality of Dodo, and equally hard to find the character attractive. She and her friends 'cultivate emotions' – 'I would walk ten miles any day in order to have an emotion' – and freely discuss their feelings as part of their social games. Only apparently confessional, they are actually cold-hearted and incapable of empathising with others. Dodo does not feel much affection for her infant son or much grief when he suddenly dies. She stops trying to hide her boredom with her amiable husband and treats him with either irritation or a 'passive tolerance that is very hard to bear'. Why can't they, she wonders, accept their marriage of convenience and simply 'go on living together as fifty other people lived – being polite to each other, and gracefully tolerant of each other's presence'. When her husband dies in a hunting accident, she experiences a jolt of remorse that passes quickly. Breezily entertaining, she is 'pitiful in her incapacity for any emotions except those which her "play-acting" provides for her'. *Graphic*'s reviewer was singularly unimpressed by 'a girl without even a rudimentary heart or soul, coarse in mind, vulgar in manner, and selfish and licentious from hair to heel, yet with some mysterious charm about her which every man, woman, and child who has to do with her experiences, with the sole exception of the reader of her story'.[27]

Dodo reflected a storm of 1890s fictional and journalistic discourse about the febrile, enervated emotionalism overtaking Britain's highest social groups, possibly indicating the degeneration of the nation as a whole.[28] Benson gave his anti-heroine an outlandish, cautionary fate. After her husband's death, Dodo accepts an offer of marriage from Jack, the long-time suitor and faithful friend who loves and understands her restless nature. But she jilts him on the very day they are to get married and betrays all her social aspirations by running away to the Continent with a mysteriously masterful, charismatic foreigner who collects women like trophies. It is clear that once the conquest is made, he will abandon her to one of the unpleasant fates that generally awaited the era's 'bad woman'. Her actions appear inexplicable to herself and the reader because Benson gives no guidance to the inner life of Dodo, only to the thoughts she blurts out to others. In some ways like Margot, she is a 'pre-psychological' personality who endlessly parades self-descriptions but has no self-understanding, attributing her actions simply to a 'nature' she was born with and cannot control.

Benson's inability to imagine another future for his heroine exacerbated Margot's own doubts about where her life was going. Just before the unexpected appearance of *Dodo*, she had visited Paris with her mother and Daisy White. As the world looked at her through Benson's eyes, she watched Pembroke's sister Gladys de Grey who had taken up residence in the city. Margot often behaved like and was taken for a Parisian *mondaine*, but she was appalled by the life she saw there. The de Greys did not even pretend to a conventional marriage. Superficially, Gladys appeared to be a liberated woman, surrounded by beautiful objects, food, music and an entourage of charming, aimless men – including Ribblesdale's brother Reginald Lister – to take her on endless rounds of amusement. Nevertheless, Margot found herself saddened and depressed by an environment where 'you *see* the wickedness more [than in London] … it hardens a vague impression to hear horrid things said and it accustoms the flame of one's soul to draughts which might blow it out'.[29] 'No manly man would stand Gladys's mode of life or undisciplined monopoly', Margot thought. 'She neither desires nor deserves to attach men nobly to her, and she has not the passion or the power to retain them immorally.' Her courtiers had 'civility', but no 'reverence' for women and nothing to talk about beyond erotic suggestion. They were always 'sooner or later ridiculous'. Gladys's Parisian world was where Benson imaginatively placed Dodo at the end of his novel – a glittering prominence, but empty of dignity or purpose.[30]

In midsummer, as the Dodo sensation raged, Margot wrote that she did not 'mind what he says about my character, but I am so sick of hearing it, it is so stupid and so vulgar'.[31] But clearly she did mind. Her life had escaped the bounds of inner-circle chitchat to become part of a wider public image in which her personality served as the lightning rod for a generation's anxieties about female character and behaviour. Celebrity for her was closer to notoriety, resting on the 'rather dangerous life' she had lived so far and her anomalous position as a woman whose actions courted public attention without a husband's protection.[32] Can you, she wondered, 'prove you to yourself as a woman of courage and nobility instead of a woman who is talked about and who is often in reality very wild and self-indulgent'?[33] Charty warned her that 'if you are not very careful no decent man will marry you'.[34] In August 1893 Margot retreated to Glen, battered and depressed, to sort out her life. As Evan Charteris put it, 'a crisis has come to you … brought more from without than within I do believe, but none the less undeniable in its demands on your character and courage'. 'The reckoning is coming upon her', Doll Liddell echoed ominously. 'She has played so recklessly with love and passion that she has got into a sort of hysterical state, and her cool head seems to have entirely left her'.[35]

Benson defended himself from the critics of his too-close fictional portrait of Margot in an article in *Nineteenth Century* titled 'A Question of Taste'.[36] He explained that he had used superficial, external traits of 'one original' to clothe a character that he saw as a modern social type, more complicated than either heroic or sentimental fiction provided: 'The majority of us are no longer satisfied with pictures which, however splendid and noble, do not, as a matter of fact, bear much resemblance to the people among whom we live.' *Dodo* was Benson's youthful, anxious attempt to engage with the changing worlds of courtship and marriage of the fin de siècle, settings in which flirtatious behaviour had shifted from a stage in wooing – a socially observed but private exploration in creating the romantic feeling and erotic compatibility for marriage – to a generalised game among men and women, wed and unwed, in arenas of leisured life surrounded by observers.

Richard Kaye's subtle explication of nineteenth-century discourses about flirtation rejects the idea that changing notions of coquetry reflected mainly the rebellious assertion of 'new women' determined to explore permutations of desire that were before only available to men. Both the behaviours and their fictional representations were, in his view and that of the authors he studies, part of the formation of a modern personality characterised by a more practised emotionality, heightened self-awareness of individual dissembling and performativity, and a correspondingly more baffling and 'opaque' inner life.[37] These impulses could characterise men as well as women, expanding the domains of interaction beyond the domestic for both sexes, but complicating the task of understanding relationships in all aspects of life. This was presented by novelists as new terrain in Balfour's world, occasioned not because more people suddenly had secrets, but because the possibilities of being observed and judged by strangers had changed the circumstances in which knowledge of the self was acquired.

If Margot's dilemmas show these developments acting on a woman, the simultaneous drama that Harry Cust was experiencing uncovered a contemporary male flirt and the responses he aroused as he pursued a course of seductions and betrayals.[38] In 1893 Cust was thirty-two years old and had just learned that he would be heir to his distant, childless cousin, the 3rd Earl Brownlow.[39] Widely considered a brilliant and rising political star, he was the sitting member for Stamford in Lincolnshire – a seat in which Brownlow held an historic interest – and had recently become editor of the *Pall Mall Gazette* under its new proprietor, William Waldorf Astor.[40] He was a member of Wilfrid Blunt's Crabbet Club and a youthful lothario, having had an unknown number of affairs with titled wives including at least Theresa Londonderry and Gladys de Grey, and he was still entangled with Margot's sister Lucy Graham Smith and with Violet Granby, the future Duchess of Rutland. The Harry and Violet affair produced a daughter, Diana – Violet Granby's second child by a man other than her husband – who was born at the end of August 1892.[41]

Until this time, Harry Cust's philandering was amusingly tolerable because it appeared to be confined to married women. In these circles, bachelors delaying marriage for financial and professional reasons might well have mistresses or occasional encounters – George Curzon, Evan Charteris and Alfred Milner all did in these years.[42] Harry, however, stepped over the line of tolerated behaviour when he had sex with an unmarried woman of respectable society, Nina Welby-Gregory, the distantly related daughter of a gentry landowner in Lincolnshire. Evan Charteris had noticed Harry pursuing Nina to the extreme alarm of her father, who was 'savagely hostile to the innovating morality and tone' of the 'younger bloods' that these men represented.[43] In the summer of 1893, Nina wrote to Harry that she was pregnant. It was rumoured later that he shocked a crowd of men at the country house where he got the letter by mocking her missive aloud, though a recent scholar disputes this as one of several possible canards of this murky tale.[44] Nina's disclosure, however, did prompt Harry to become engaged – but not to her. His betrothed was Pamela Wyndham, sister of George and Mary, whom he had also wooed with hopes of marriage for over a year.[45]

The events that followed disillusioned many 'pretty tough and experienced men and women of the world', as George Pembroke put it.[46] Harry's infraction was doublefold. He had not confined himself to sexually awakened upper-class wives who knew the risks of illicit romance, but had seduced a maiden from an established family. He then knowingly put himself in a position where he would either have to jilt the trusting Pamela or abandon the tainted Nina. George Wyndham urged his sister's claims during hurried visits to the Brownlows at Ashridge and in sleet-drenched Scotland, but it is not clear how much of the whole story even he knew. 'I can only say that I am fighting for Truth, individual liberty of judgment, and essential verities, as against sheer and mere worldliness so mined and corrupted by intrigue and lying that for its very rottenness it gives no purchase to the honest hand', he fumed, as gossip swirled around the protagonists.[47] Harry maintained that Pamela was the love of his life, and he may have urged Nina to get an abortion.[48] Violet Granby, reputedly willing to share her lover with Nina,[49] consulted Arthur Balfour, who had also been informed of the story by George Curzon. Arthur urged Harry to marry Nina, in which case he would continue political support.

Harry dithered for weeks before accepting the inevitable. 'We did not know until the very end whether the marriage would go through', Lady Welby confessed after the ceremony in Paris on 11 October. The *Times* published a tiny, cryptic announcement, prompting Curzon to tell Arthur that Harry Cust's friends should put out a story saying that the sudden match had been a case of 'passionate elopement' – a fiction that 'if industriously circulated may shut the mouths of the public'. The saga did not end at the altar, though, turning what might have been plotted as farce into something closer to personal tragedy. Within a fortnight Nina suffered a miscarriage. Speculation surfaced immediately that she and Violet Granby had concocted the pregnancy claim, while news of the jilted and miserable Pamela became more widely known. Pamela and Lucy Smith fled, separately, on recuperative voyages to India, and Lord Brownlow made it clear that he would not support Harry for the Stamford seat in the next general election.

'Full of passion, disappointment and hate', Harry did not behave well. He led people to believe that he thought the pregnancy had been a fiction and 'overwhelmed' his wife with 'reproaches about his ruined life etc'.[50] Within weeks he was importuning Lucy Graham Smith to take him back. 'He bombards her with letters telegrams and messages begging to see her. Surely someone can help to stop this', Margot complained to Curzon.[51] The Custs never had children, and Nina remained a mysterious and melancholy figure. 'Her extreme calm, and absence of all emotions, good or bad, and her utter indifference to any consideration except that of what Harry's feeling towards her for the moment may be, are very disconcerting', Frances Horner observed. In 1894 when the furor was still fresh, DD Lyttelton feared that Nina, through shame, would will herself to die: 'I don't want her to, though I generally feel it to be the only solution.'[52]

Of all the onlookers to this crisis, no one was more disillusioned than George Pembroke. He had penned an impish poem about the fiasco in October showing that, despite his relationship to the Brownlows, he was a latecomer to many of the details:

Nina Welby, you may well be,
Rash to marry, wicked Harry;
Still I trust, if you must,
You will break him, mould him, make him,
Till the Devil wouldn't take him
And with virtue so endow him, that his friends will hardly know him
And he grows for all to see, very near as good as me.

A few weeks later, George could only write with bemusement of the 'corruption, heartache, dissension and bitterness of spirit that pleasant fellow whom to know was to like has been in our small circle of friends the last five years'.[53] George had often written amusing snippets of gossip about women falling victim to Harry Cust, but he seems to have genuinely believed that most of these were platonic emotional connections. That Harry had managed to bring about so many co-running physical conquests shocked him profoundly, in part because of what it implied about the women in his circles. 'I have not got a really great friend among women whom I do not believe to be a good woman (in the sense of a moral one), and I rather doubt whether I could have, the difference it makes to me is so great.'[54]

This innocence about women's behaviour – 'Pembrokism' according to Asquith, 'mawkish sentimentalism' in the eyes of Hugo Elcho – meant that George framed the Harry Cust fiasco in terms of gendered moral categories and allocations of blame.[55] Several decades of divorce-court coverage of male abuses had resulted in a significant shift in opinion on where the fault most often lay in sexual misconduct.[56] In keeping with this, Pamela Wyndham was an innocent, undeserving of anything but sympathy and protection. Nina was too, unless she actually had been Harry's mistress for two years, as some asserted, in which case she had brought social ostracism on herself. Violet Granby was 'a bit of a goose' and may have acted emotionally after the crisis of the pregnancy arose. But Harry was genuinely 'wicked'. He was 'so depraved' and had 'so completely lost all sense of honour and morality ... [that] he has not the 15th part of a gentleman in his composition'.[57] Pembroke could hardly believe that he had been so misled by a man he thought he knew well.

Nevertheless there were people of both sexes who had sensed something off-putting about Harry even before this debacle. Margot, Frances Horner and DD Balfour kept him at arm's length. As young children visiting Escrick in the late 1880s, Constance Wenlock's nieces found Harry faintly sinister as he and other artistic male guests such as Doll Liddell coolly appraised them while they posed half draped for portraits by Constance, Violet Granby or Gladys de Grey.[58] When Alfred Lyttelton spent a week with Harry Cust on the *Black Pearl* in 1889, he came away thinking him 'the most excessive person I ever met. When he works he reads himself into headaches of violent character. He eats mountains of meat and swills sherry like water – he smokes cigarettes to such an extent that his hand trembles and his companions grow headachy. When he is fond of anyone he imposes his company upon them for hour after hour. He has the want of control of a poet and some of his imagination with the body of a materialist.'[59]

The relatively few anecdotes that survive from contemporaries show Harry Cust as a man well able to ingratiate himself with both sexes.[60] Was he a deliberate, cynical manipulator, using bonhomie and sexual conquests to establish his prowess in men's club smoking rooms, whatever the wreckage left behind? Was he a sensitive poet endlessly seeking a romantic soul-mate and finding her in woman after woman? Did he know? In 1886, the well-connected novelist Rhoda Broughton made 25-year-old Harry the model for a central character in a surprisingly daring piece of fiction titled *Dr Cupid*.[61] Her antagonist – the feckless, poetic heir to a great estate – is a relentless arouser, then casual betrayer of women's affections. He plays with the wives and daughters of men of his own class, taking no responsibility for the broken hearts and marital havoc he causes. But he is something different from a Victorian rake because he is never masterful, but, in ways usually gendered as feminine, cajoling and manipulative. Evan Charteris once said that being around Harry Cust in the proximity of women 'brought on headaches, dramatic attitudes, and insidious ways' – he meant on the part of Harry, not the women. Broughton's character also succumbs to crippling headaches, lounges in dark rooms, reads letters and poetry in the garden and seeks every moment to be alone with his object of interest. He breaks promises with charming, unanswerable excuses and explains it as some mysterious part of his nature – or alternately some compulsion from outside forces – that requires him to abandon commitments without notice and show up again without warning, full as ever of blandishments.

Fin de siècle fiction saw the emergence of increasing numbers of characters like these – male as well as female – who don't know what compels their unending urge to lay claim to others' affections by asserting exclusive psychological connection and unique intensity of feeling.[62] Broughton's anti-hero has all the new vices of plausibility, apparent sincerity and infinitely flexible self-justification that Harry Cust would show in his romantic relationships. George Pembroke, with his stoical rejection of libidinal impulses and refusal to enact deep emotions in order to beguile others, could not understand Harry, whose behaviour made George fear that the Darwinian theorists of sexuality were right – there existed a 'sort of sexual warfare, a sort of hardness that often astonishes in kind natures, a sort of acknowledgment that we are in the region of natural war where the strongest must win and the weakest go under and the luckiest escape and the unluckiest perish'.[63]

Harry's own voice and the stories he told himself or others about this transforming moment in his life's trajectory are largely missing from the historical record. There is no single tapestry of firm threads to be woven, only dense, shifting and oblique portrayals

produced by multiple participants, knowledgeable contemporaries, 'truths' transmitted to subsequent generations and to the historian.[64] The recorded world of the privileged also includes openly
fictional accounts like *Dr Cupid*, in which Broughton disapproved
of the Harry she created well before his semi-public scandal, but
she refused to deliver what Beth Newman calls 'narrative punishment'.[65] At the end of the book the protagonist's most innocent
victim dies of a broken heart, while he sails off on an exotic ocean
adventure like a new personality – the modern narcissist – set afloat
in the world. In this fictional guise Harry was closer to Benson's
out-of-control Dodo than was Margot. This story of a male flirt
and careless young women formed another part of the cautionary
background to Margot's marital decision-making in the autumn
of 1893.

The problem that Margot faced as the fin de siècle decade began
was Peter Flower – 'it has always been Peter'.[66] He had returned
to England in the late 1880s, to the hunting life of Leicestershire
and the racing rounds of Newmarket. The eroticised friendship
between them was renewed, probably with many nights spent together at country houses during the hunting season, most probably without full sexual consummation. Her friends and family believed that this luckless man hung around Margot so long because
he thought her father would be willing to sustain a son-in-law's life
of sport and travel. As Margot presents it, their relationship was
full of dramatic quarrels, furious displays of jealousy and temper
and teasing psychological games. Peter lived out the reckless, untamed, unthinking nature that Margot cherished in herself but increasingly had trouble fitting together with her other social worlds
and aspirations.

Margot wrote that she spent eight years trying to get Peter to
adopt some occupation that would provide him with the income
and purpose he needed for her to marry him. In 1891 she made
one last attempt to secure his prospects by arranging a chance for
him to make his fortune in Britain's new South African empire.[67]
Peter had a model of hand-to-mouth adventurism in his friend
Moreton Frewen (nicknamed 'Mortal Ruin'), whose sister-in-law
Jennie Churchill had already provided Peter with solace for the
technical celibacy Margot imposed.[68] The expedition to Masho-
naland that he joined by selling his hunters for £2,000 shows the
bizarre intersection of hard-living high society, casino finance and

colonial adventuring that lurk behind scholarly phrases such as 'gentlemanly capitalism' and the 'scramble for Africa'.

A small collection of letters that Margot preserved provides a fragment of the largely vanished voice of Peter Flower.[69] Those from South Africa are breezy, unselfconscious, full of 'boy's own adventure' detail. He survives a sudden brush fire by rallying the native bearers 'with a big whip which I laid on freely'. Alone he heads off to visit ruins of the 'lost kingdom' of great Zimbabwe where no guide will take you for fear of reprisals from outraged tribesmen. Different groups of the expedition get separated from each other, while wagons founder in muddy riverbeds, pack animals die and old Boers regale him with stories of 'this sort of guerilla warfare'. Hundreds of miles north of the Tuli River, Peter comes to realise how remote the settlements founded the year before actually are; the logistical difficulties and approaching storm season raise fears of famine for the Europeans perched on this forward edge of colonial expansion. Within weeks, Peter wishes 'with all my heart I'd never heard of the Syndicate'. He was seeing first-hand what other investors and geological experts would establish. Great mineral bonanzas in the new Rhodesia were unlikely, and agricultural development would be slow until someone built a transportation infrastructure. At Salisbury, 'prospectors, diggers, and local police think the Chartered Company is out of money. Don't tell this.' Peter returned to England early in 1892 having lost the money he fronted and more in debt than ever. Margot told him that she could never marry him, though the decision was agonising, and she continued to use what she felt for him as a means to test her other relationships.[70]

In the meantime, while she firmly laid to rest the hopes of the future South African consul Alfred Milner, her life became complicated in another way.[71] For nearly a year Margot had been friends with the barrister and parliamentarian Herbert Henry Asquith (known as H. H. Asquith, or Asquith), engaging in the kind of tutelary correspondence that she enjoyed with other men who could not possibly be suitors. Momentously, however, in September 1891, Asquith's wife Helen – thirty-five years old and mother of his five children – died of typhoid in the midst of a family vacation in Scotland. Helen's death changed everything. Within weeks, Asquith was making it clear that he wanted to marry Margot – that he had seen himself loving her both physically and spiritually even before his wife died. Margot was deeply upset at this abandonment of their non-sexual frame. With characteristic tactlessness, she told Mary Elcho and Ettie Grenfell that she wished she had imitated them by wedding a sexy, sporting love object first, and then forming an intellectual friendship with a more impressive man to supplement a husband's deficiencies.[72] As it was, there was no reason now why she should not consider the rising star of the Liberal Party as a potential spouse. No reason, except that she was not physically attracted to him and, because of Peter, she knew the difference.

Margot prided herself on seeing 'people and things pretty much as they are'.[73] The apparently forthright picture she presented in multiple accounts of these years described a nature torn in two directions – between the physically passionate but self-centred existence she would have shared with the deeply loved Peter, and the life of mental engagement and other-regarding obligations she would assume as Asquith's wife and the stepmother of his children.[74] She barely mentioned the third possibility, Evan Charteris – possibly because he was still alive when she was infuriating and beguiling the public with her autobiographical writings in the 1920s.[75] Peter, about whom she wrote over and over, had died in 1902, and was so disregarded in society at the time of his death that only local newspapers concerned with the Midlands hunting scene mentioned his passing.[76]

Nevertheless, Margot's choice involved a triad, rather than a dyad of suitors. On the day she married Asquith, she wore a piece of jewellery that Evan Charteris had given her, attached to a locket with Peter Flower's hair inside.[77] Evan's letters, along with Asquith's, were the only sustained, intimate correspondence from men that she preserved from the great bonfire to which she consigned the missives of George Pembroke, Spencer Lyttelton, Lord Dudley and many others during autumn 1893. The perspective provided by Evan's letters during these troubled years, later depicted as her glorious youth, casts light on the psychological trajectory of Margot's life and the expectations that were shaping it. If Peter represented the sportsman-adventurer and Asquith the public-minded professional, Evan was a modern aristocratic connoisseur for whom, she wrote, she felt 'hunger as of the forbidden fruit and who and what forbids him to me?'[78] Neither she nor Evan could figure that out.

Is it 'unfair to remind you how much I love you and how much you love me?' Evan asked Margot while she was making her decision. 'To make you feel again *how* happy we are together, and what sunlight and warmth we bring to one another?'[79] They were within days of the same age, both conscious of having raised themselves at the tail end of many older siblings who dominated family attention. Friends for years, they shared more interests and acquaintances than Margot did with Asquith. Evan loved and excelled at country pursuits. He had a discriminating taste in art and literature, a sardonic wit and a gift for writing. Although his ambitions were not political – he had to earn money and began a successful career at the parliamentary bar in 1891– their marriage would keep Margot within the same circles of friendship and intimacy she already enjoyed.[80] Since 1885 Lady Wemyss had been a surrogate mother, cautioning her about raising Evan's hopes, but secretly wishing the match would come about.[81]

Evan's letters to Margot are direct and personal. By the late 1880s, they are devoid of the clichéd fantasy worship he used later in his long intimacy with Ettie Grenfell.[82] He had pulled back during the years that Margot was in love with Peter, using humour and gossip to distance his feelings. Nevertheless, while her indifference had 'driven me more than once to petty infidelities, in not one of them have I ever forgotten or denied that I loved you more than any woman that ever has been or will be for me'.[83] Evan knew Margot's bewildering bundle of personality traits as well as anyone by this time, and they shared a physical attraction that went as far as hers with Peter. He addressed her as a psychological equal with whom he could see himself sharing his life. When she told him in late November that she had decided to accept Asquith, he wrote, 'It beats in on me with strange insistence that we have left the most unsaid, that there was still so much that we had left to learn from and impart to each other, so many discussions to hold, so much humour and passion to exchange, and so many joys and amusements to share … oh darling, what have you done?'[84] Even if she could not see her way to marrying him, he would rather she stayed single than tie herself to a man she neither knew nor loved as well as himself.

Later in life, Margot strongly condemned the martyred foot-dragging with which she faced the prospect of marrying Asquith. At the time, she shared her hesitations so freely that her friends were alarmed. 'Your letter of tonight makes me very miserable', Lady Wemyss wrote. 'I think it means that you are *reasoning* yourself into a decision and that your heart has no say in it.'[85] The logic behind choosing a respected cabinet minister over a chronically indebted horseman escaped no one, but as Margot reached adulthood her rejection of Evan spoke to her deeper uncertainties about gender and personal identity.

The criticism that Evan resented most from Margot was that he belonged to the 'weaker generation of men as you mean it'. For if young women of the 1890s were becoming more assertive, their male counterparts could appear self-conscious and malleable, ironic and unfixed – what George Pembroke called 'those unreal restless self-appraising unselfrespecting young men that seem so common nowadays'.[86] Evan assured Margot repeatedly that she had given him steadiness of purpose, 'shown me that life to be profitable must be serious' and convinced him of the importance of moral commitments. But he saw none of this as requiring him to abandon his conviction that selves could be understood as con-structions, indeterminately related to the shifting imperatives of an inner life that was in constant re-creation through engagement with the external world.

Evan was clearly aware of the views Oscar Wilde was articulat-ing in 1891 that authorised the unstable, performative self and the impossibility of genuine unselfconsciousness in modern life. Responding to a suggestion that Margot's sister Lucy was an 'in-tentional humbug' in her relations with men, he wrote, 'if I really believed her a humbug, the addition of the "intention" would save her to my mind. I respect anyone for successfully being what they mean to be – it's the people who are at the mercy of their own du-plicity that one contemns.' Echoing Evan's sentiments, his friend Ettie Grenfell wrote that it would be pleasant if one could try out identities sequentially – nihilist, idealist, hedonist, materialist – but modern life was too complex for that. The impulses existed together, and had to be negotiated continually in relation to the worlds of others. 'It is the astonishing number of alternatives now-adays spying out all one's ways that drive one to seek compromise and eschew conviction ... as it is one is like a novice in a signal-box surrounded by handles, with no time to learn their significance yet compelled to seize one – knowing that 9 out of 10 of them at that particular moment mean disaster. If it wasn't so exciting it would be intolerable.'[87]

Both Evan and Ettie were consciously performative in a way that Margot now repudiated. In her early diaries, she had shared this sense of the need for nimble interaction but now she could hardly have disagreed more. Complexity, she asserted, was 'a modern illness … it is emphasized by modern conditions – studied – written of and encouraged'. But 'such self-consciousness is very unsympathetic to me', a 'disease of the mind' that she had not yet acquired.[88] 'I long to be a whole person', she wrote, a unitary character who influences others through the force of grand and passionate engagement with important public concerns. J. A. Symonds wrote once that for all Margot's defiance of social conventions she was actually very conservative and very 'good'.[89] She had no vocabulary for understanding the 'psychological self' that might explore and explain emotional states, and as she showed in her correspondence with Arthur, she believed in noble characters and unconflicted personalities who took control of the world.[90] In marriage she sought a man who would make her what she was 'capable of being and was intended to be, a force which would inspire great men to do great things'.[91] Margot said at the time and later that she married Asquith because he was her superior in education, intellect and character.

Doll Liddell, quietly observing from the outside, thought that the 'constant pressure of a steadfast man of strong will is crushing her rather' and forcing her hand in his favour.[92] She was still deeply apprehensive, disclaiming any real interest in motherhood and cautious about her fitness to be a political wife. Her ambivalence at the idea of being possessed or mastered through matrimony remained unresolved. But Asquith's tremendous persistence in the face of the obstacles she put in his way seemed to prove his patience, reliability and devotion, as his rapid political rise showed ambition to make an impress in the public realm. Marriage to a man who was closer to a psychological equal was available to her with Evan, but she did not trust either him or herself enough to risk that. The Brocks may be correct that Margot's choice of Asquith showed the middle-class origins and assumptions of both.[93] Evan, with his philandering relatives, attractiveness to women and clever aestheticism might have seemed too much like the charming, unreliable aristocrats she knew. With him, she risked having to muddle along, accepted as she was but responsible for determining her own direction. Evan, she wrote, would be in *her* life; a marriage with Asquith would ensconce her in *his* already existing bundle of domestic and public responsibilities. With him, she was certain she would not share the fates of Dodo or Gladys, internally lost as they succumbed to ill-considered impulses, selfish desires and public notoriety.

Nevertheless, if Dodo's proclamation that 'all these people must know who I am' still held, that at least was assured by Margot's acceptance of the Liberal home secretary. 'Everybody who is anybody' attended the wedding on 10 May, including five past, present or future prime ministers. The extensive press coverage devoted itself as much to the bride as to the groom, despite his cabinet status. 'Miss Tennant has made a reputation for herself in London Society by her exceptional ability, her wit, her vivacity, and her good looks', wrote *Graphic*. 'It is scarcely going too far to say that amongst the younger women of our generation she is one of the most prominent and the most popular.' 'There was about the whole occasion something interesting and sincere', noted an observer for the provincial press, 'an atmosphere of cordial good-will to both bride and bridegroom which removed it out of the ordinary category of "fashionable weddings".'[94] Margot had been 'cruelly caricatured' in *Dodo*, wrote the *Leeds Times*. While indeed 'the whirl, the rush, the fever of this electric age possessed her whole being', she nevertheless retained a 'deep inner reverence and earnest and strenuous religious convictions'.[95] As far as celebrity goes, this was more like it.

A vague and, surely to many readers, opaque rumour of Harry Cust's misadventures reached as far as the *New York Herald Tribune* four months after his wedding to Nina Welby, reported by Alfred Lyttelton's golfing friend Horace Hutchinson: 'the friendships are supposed to be Platonic, and the male and female Souls are sinless: but a small cloud that appeared on the horizon a few weeks ago has assumed such thunderlike proportions that the Souls are in much doubt about themselves'.[96] But it was Arthur's promise to support Harry's political career that threatened to elevate the tale into a public scandal capable of joining the increasing number of exposés of misbehaviour among aristocrats and politicians before the First World War.

Historian John Garrard argues that scandal of the sort that Harry faced is a product of modernity.[97] The Habermasian 'public sphere', able to appropriate private behaviour for collective appraisal, required the creation of mass media, concentrations of people with access to the same news and a democratised citizenry expecting a voice in evaluating the conduct of authorities. Not every modern scandal is political and not every political scandal is about sex. In John Thompson's typology, financial corruption

Fig. 15 'Voyeurism/Journalist': an enterprising newsman gets scandalous
details, Roubille in *Le Rire*, 18 November 1905

and official abuses of power are the other most common forms of
malfeasance that will exercise the polity.[98] But sex scandals have
had enormous staying power since the eighteenth century as a
means of ruining public figures and attacking the legitimacy of the
larger social or political group they represent (see Fig. 15). They
are barometers to changing behaviours and the social attitudes of
the times in which they occur.

Sex scandals involving public persons have been unevenly dis-
tributed over time, arriving in clusters like their economic counterpart, financial panics. Theorists argue that they are characteristic
of periods of exceptionally rapid and contested change in public
values and power relations. One such period certainly occurred in
fin de siècle Britain. A single decade, 1885–95, saw media storms

over the Charles Dilke and Lord Colin Campbell divorce litigations, the Cleveland Street male prostitution exposé, the country
house gambling uproar that brought the Prince of Wales into the
courts, the adultery crisis that destroyed Parnell and, finally, the
Oscar Wilde case, which may or may not have contributed to the
collapse of both the prime minister Lord Rosebery and his Liberal
government in the spring of 1895.[99] As will be seen, Harry Cust's
misfortune was not allowed to reach this stage of public spectacle,
but it too showed the complicated interplay between private behaviour and political fortune at that time. Nina Cust recognised
the connection: 'It is terrible enough to have to feel that I have
destroyed his happiness', she wrote to Arthur two weeks after the
shotgun wedding, 'I could not live with the thought that I had
ruined his career also.' The envelope of materials relating to the
events lies among Arthur's papers in the National Archives of Scotland, with unfulfilled instructions handwritten on the front – 'Mr
Balfour says burn eventually'.[100]

After Lord Brownlow withdrew his political backing for Harry
Cust in 1893, Arthur felt bound by the commitment he had made
to find another constituency. Local organisers in Manchester
agreed to adopt Harry for the northern district on Arthur's assurance that the candidate's only impropriety had been the 'mere
seduction' of a young woman whom he then married – even in the
eyes of the vicar of Leeds, this was not a disqualifying infraction for
a bachelor in public life.[101] Then, early in 1894, the suffragist and
women's advocate Millicent Garrett Fawcett got wind of the larger story. She tried to reach Arthur through his sister Alice, then
wrote to contacts in Manchester of the much wider dishonourable
behaviours of the man that they would have to support in the next
general election. After several weeks of fact-finding, both wings
of the Conservative-Unionist alliance voiced deep concerns about
Harry, who ended up leaving parliament after the dissolution in
1895. He came back as MP for Bermondsey in 1900–06, but as a
spent force and acknowledged failure. 'Admitting every fault, can
you imagine a life less "fortunate" than mine', he wrote to Margot.
'Every time I am offered a constituency 1893 is, in two days, flung
in my face.'[102]

Scholars coming across the story have described a 'doctri-
naire' hounding of Harry by evangelically inspired social-purity
campaigners of the 1880s and 1890s. The alarm is presented in
bemused tones as the triumph of judgemental prudes, obsessed

with other people's sex lives and projecting their own moral panics onto an electorate not particularly concerned with the marital problems of their representatives.[103] The letters between Arthur and Millicent Fawcett surrounding the event were more complicated than this implies. Millicent began the exchange by rehearsing the facts as she understood them and defending herself against charges that she had traduced Harry and spread gossip about other participants such as Pamela Wyndham without warning either the party leaders or Harry himself. She had in fact been in communication with Harry first, and his response had been so insulting that she had refused to see him without a solicitor present. Arthur replied calmly and at length, with Millicent's final letter providing a nearly point-by-point rebuttal of his case. The record shows curious missteps on Arthur's part – he did retreat eventually by advising Harry to withdraw his candidacy – as well as a glimpse of political and social forces at work.[104]

Couched in his usual cool and lucid prose, Arthur's position constituted a multi-pronged attack on Millicent Fawcett for an unjustified interference into Harry's attempt to stay in public life. In keeping with his general views on the fragilities of human understanding, he argued that the truths of this case were impossible to determine since they involved the conflicting perceptions and accounts of so many people. Millicent Fawcett, he said, had alerted the Manchester authorities to information that rested on rumour. The spillage of these uncertainties into the wider sphere hurt mostly Nina Cust and Pamela Wyndham – the victims in the case – without securing any clear resolution of the depth of Harry's infractions. Millicent replied tartly that Harry's own male friends, hardly models of middle-class propriety, were calling him an 'infernal scoundrel' and 'a cur'. As George Pembroke put it in a private letter, 'the most immoral men in Society were quite longing to beat him with sticks'.[105] Millicent also told Arthur that he seriously underestimated how talk about Harry had already spread beyond the confines of London clubs and drawing rooms. She was right. In November, several newspapers had made suggestive allegations about Harry's absence from the country and one stated that Pamela Wyndham was supposed to have been his fiancé. A joke was going around that '30 young ladies drew lots for Harry Cust and that 29 of them are going to have illegitimate babies'.[106] Given this climate, Millicent said, Harry was the one bringing his wife and Pamela Wyndham into the spotlight by his decision to seek another parliamentary seat. If he waited four or five years, behaving as a model spouse in the meantime, she thought the stigma might be overcome.

Arthur's second major argument was one familiar to this day. The private actions of politicians, he thought, should not be brought 'gratuitously' into the public sphere unless they had reached the level of legal or 'other' certainty strong enough to 'shock the moral sense of the community'. In this regard, the Balfour family, from Lady Frances to Gerald, thought that the working men of the constituency Harry would stand for rather liked the roguish behaviour of gentlemen. In most cases, the facts of private life 'never can be properly understood, even if they are correctly stated (which they seldom are)'. Individuals and the public interest were best served by discrete management of moral malfeasance, and forthright denial of gossip when unproven and harmful to innocents. Powerful men could be trusted to do their own quiet policing of conduct among themselves.[107] Millicent Fawcett's clever rebuttal smoothly asserted her interest in saving the Conservatives from themselves. How could party leaders even consider putting up a man who would be laying foundation stones for churches, defending religious values on the platform and handing out prizes at school fairs, while many in the audience suspected his own moral code? Nor, she thought, would a woman's organisation allow Mrs Cust to speak for the Primrose League or a local parish event.

Arthur's letter brought up, in order to pre-empt, this question of flagrant hypocrisy between public and private selves. If you were to start in on the moral rectitude of public men, he thought, there would be 'many offences' as bad as Harry's 'of which it is impossible and because impossible, therefore undesirable, to take public note':

> What say you to the man whose frigid cruelty and undeviating selfishness remorselessly kills every possibility of happiness, or even of colourless contentment, for his wife: the man who uses his domestic power to torture from day to day his helpless victim? He is probably eminently respectable: but is an infernal scoundrel nevertheless, and one who in your own words 'strikes at the root of all that makes home and marriage sacred', worse effectually than a dozen H Custs. Are you prepared in the interests of public morality to pry into the private life of such an one; to collect the gossip of his 'friends', to publish the current anecdotes about his behaviour?

In his off-handed hypothetical example, Arthur was unusually re-vealing. The domestic tyrant he described closely fit the behaviours of Hugo Elcho. In acknowledging that character flaws might be *endemic* in the Commons, however, if that indeed is what he meant to say, Arthur was countering the common view of his colleagues that abusive male behaviour was exceptional among men of their class, only prevalent among lower orders who could not control their behaviour.[108]

Millicent Fawcett's position that Arthur misunderstood the pub-lic relations impact of the talk about Harry Cust was confirmed by letters from men whom Arthur held in high regard. His old friend Edward Talbot, vicar of Leeds, Arthur Lyttelton – whose brother Alfred had already told Arthur 'gently' that he should not have forwarded Harry's name[109] – and Manchester officials he knew personally all wrote indignantly about the candidacy of Harry Cust. Arthur was informed that he had seriously underestimated the ex-tent of general knowledge about Harry before Millicent ever took action, as well as the religious and moral concerns of working-class voters and the indignation of local party workers in having such a man shoved down their throats. A final, thinly veiled accusation was that the Manchester leaders were beginning to suspect that Arthur had knowingly lied in assuring them that Harry's only fail-ing had been to marry a young woman after he got her pregnant. As Edward Talbot wrote, 'the point seems to me this: that this is not the simple case of private morals disqualifying for public duty. It is a case of aggravated and complicated villainy such as that if the facts came out C's candidature would be impossible (which a 'mere seduction' would not necessarily involve) … [and] you will be put in the position of having vouched what was not true.' These men would have shared Arthur's assumption that public figures were under no obligation to offer the whole of the private self to the outside world, but what *was* offered should not be known to be false.

Arthur's mistake in thinking that he could put Harry Cust be-fore the new voters and clamorous journalists of the 1890s reflects how rapidly the political and media environment was changing. His own motives in helping Harry were not difficult to decipher. Arthur had a broad tolerance for men he could use in the party in-terest, and he was loyal to those who did the work required. Harry was having impressive success as editor of the *Pall Mall Gazette* in attracting new readers to a daily paper that was meant to appear

independent and unaffiliated, while pursuing an overall conservative line: openly partisan papers, Arthur had told Harry, were 'of
no earthly value to a party in the way of making opinion, as their
criticisms are a foregone conclusion'.[110] In this role and as an MP,
Harry was part of the new generation of able, energetic young aristocratic Conservatives that Arthur fostered.

In addition, Arthur's enjoyment of casual gossip kept him immersed in a continuous buzz of potential libels, slurs, near-misses
and minor litigations that rippled through these social worlds.
Daisy White and Violet Granby faced servants who tried to blackmail them for alleged indiscretions. Both William Gordon Cum-
mings, at the centre of the country house gambling scandal, and
the Duchess of Manchester were known to cheat at cards even by
people who never associated with them.[111] George Curzon's biographer has marvelled at his 'foolhardiness' in having mistresses
temperamental enough to take him close to public exposure as his
political career took off, problems for which his fellow politician St
John Brodrick served as confidant.[112]

Challenges and libel actions resulting from election campaigns
were rising too, starting with the 1892 polls. Both Brodrick and
George Wyndham got involved in one of these cases, against Arthur's advice, when George's close friend Charles Gatty accused
his Conservative opponent of a smear campaign that cost Charles
the election. The courts awarded him £5,000 in damages for opposition flyers that said Charles had been sent down from boarding
school for immoral conduct at the age of thirteen, although his
family affirmed they had withdrawn him because of bullying. Two
years later, an Act of Parliament allowed removing a member from
his seat if convicted of slandering an opponent in this way.[113]

Many of these stories shared the quality of the mysteries that
Arthur loved – contradictory accounts, obfuscations, lack of concrete evidence, partisan motives for exposure. Arthur knew legal
professionals who advised friends on how to deal with threats to
reputations, and so many were resolved without exposure that he
overestimated the insider world's ability to avoid public access to
such news. As a result he seems to have missed how quickly journalists were now able to pick up the gossip generated in men's
clubs and social luncheons, derailing attempts to establish spin
before rumours could reach a wider audience. Harry was already
a public figure, the editor of a major metropolitan newspaper and
a member of parliament. Curzon wrote to Balfour that he was

inundated with questions 'in the Club and in the street' on the day that the small *Times* announcement of Harry Cust's marriage appeared, and he urged the Conservative leader to help spread a plausible story. But the ways that 'news' could breach the bubble of the metropole were multiplying, as were the interests of the public constituted by the new electorate as it was organised and informed by party activists. The Marquess of Hartington had hesitated to take on leadership roles urged on him by Liberal Unionists and Conservatives alike because he feared the exposure of his long affair with the Duchess of Manchester – as the 1890s began, Irish nationalists debated making the matter public in order to show the hypocrisy behind the reactions to Parnell's loving but adulterous relationship with Kitty O'Shea.[114]

In the case of Harry Cust the transmitter of news was a politically active woman. When Millicent Fawcett was told that the committee of the Manchester Liberal Unionist Association would not respond to her cautions, because 'men do not like women to interfere in things of this kind',[115] she approached the women's branch. Even without the vote, women had networks of party association, and they had reasons to be concerned about the character of the candidates the central organisations put forward, as Millicent so clearly pointed out to Arthur. Men at the centre of local organisational efforts could not risk alienating the increasingly important women campaign workers.

But the success of W. T. Stead's moral purity campaigns in the *Pall Mall Gazette* of the 1880s should have given Arthur grounds for thinking that the male electorate might also be concerned.[116] Arthur's reluctance to admit this aspect of Millicent's argument rested on a Victorian definition of what public responsibility and informed public opinion entailed in the parliamentary system. Governance at the national level concerned affairs of the state, and these were matters for reasoned discourse and policy analysis in arenas separate from the tastes or behaviours of an MP's personal life. But as recent work by James Thompson has shown, 'public opinion' about imperial policies was understood to involve careful weighing of reasoned assessments by different constituencies trusted to have valuable points of view.[117] The claims of newly enfranchised working men for inclusion in such debates rested on their character as productive workers, householders and family providers – in other words, self-controlled and reflective men. The character of candidates mattered for the most politically engaged

of these men. To be brazenly self-indulgent was an insult to their
manliness incompatible with the status of custodians of the country's future.

That Arthur was willing to put a man like Harry Cust before the
party activists and voters of North Manchester shows the levels of
duplicity he accepted as inevitable in public life. His education in
this regard had come during his battles of image manipulation
and media spin with the Irish nationalists. He had no expectation
of fair hearing or discretion from the press or from adversaries on
the platform. The solution was either to have nothing in public
or private life to hide – a rare phenomenon, as his letter to Millicent Fawcett indicates – or to develop the cool temperament and
skills of emotional management that would minimise the chance
of exposure. Arthur certainly had a genuine personal aversion to
dramatic emotional expression. He wrote to Mary Elcho with a
distressed account of Lord Londonderry's explosion of temper
when unexpected delays in a Lords' debate prevented him from
speaking when he had expected to: 'The scene really was a very
painful one:– I hate seeing my friends make fools of themselves: …
his conduct was so unmeasured and had in it so large an element
of personal pique that I was quite shocked. It is an episode that
I mean to forget as soon as possible.'[118] But the ability to control
one's actions and reactions assumed new proportions when the
inability to control them could come under the scrutiny of so
many strangers with the power to vote and manipulate the public
imagination.

These circumstances explain some aspects of the Conservative
Party's 'Hotel Cecil', the incestuous ministerial clump of family
members and insider friends for which the Salisbury–Balfour
governments of 1885–1905 have long been criticised. Andrew
Adonis explains why, beyond sheer class solidarity, aristocrats were
so over-represented in the highest levels of government long after the expansion of the political nation. As long as the House of
Lords was an equal participant in legislation (that is, until 1911),
all governments operated on the 'principle of equilibrium' that a
roughly equal number of members from both Lords and Commons
needed to be present in cabinets and government positions.[119]
The Tory leaders certainly looked within the traditional landed
class for these officials, but among relatives and friends whose
characters they trusted to avoid open scandals. These scions of aristocracy were, unlike Salisbury and Balfour, not brilliant – indeed

they were often considered stolid – but they were hard-working, reliable and, equally important, not promiscuous: men like Lords Midleton, Lansdowne, Selborne, Windsor, Brownlow and indeed Devonshire, after he was able to marry the widowed Duchess of Manchester. Andrew Roberts notes that Salisbury would not invite Harry Cust to his house even before the episode described here, just as he would not entertain the Prince of Wales unless the Princess of Wales was included in the party.[120]

In her final letter to Arthur, Millicent Fawcett argued that now was the moment when an equality of treatment in the sexual infractions of men should require some of the same consequences as those unleashed on women: 'If we don't level up we shall have to level down. I want to level up.'[121] As Arthur would have anticipated, her hopes for the private behaviour of public men were not fulfilled. Charles Dilke might have lost the chance of the premiership through the seamy and extraordinarily graphic details of his exposure in 1886, notes Kali Israel, but his political career continued until his death. Only the party leader was considered by these men to require a spotless reputation – and Mary and Arthur corresponded about the tiring press scrutiny he was under after 1902. But, within the next decade, even a prime minister could have a mistress – for the first time in half a century – if he knew how to handle himself, his womanly attachment and the press.

The men Arthur worked with most closely shared a habitus – a system of demeanour and deportment – that reflected the challenges of the increased responsibilities and exposures of the time. In Martin Jay's view they fostered a British 'culture of secrecy' inherited from an aristocracy that had managed to retain control of the state for the past two centuries through a system of norms and confidences operating behind façades of politeness and candour.[122] This might result in compartmentalised lives, but it was not hypocrisy, because it recognised its own deceptions and the 'noble lies' required to maintain the stability that only successfully managed power produced. Secrets, need-to-know information and judicious caution in deciding where responsibility for events should fall lay at the heart of public as of private life. Among such people, mild irony, coolness and emotional opacity were invaluable, as well as the civilised expressions of fondness, cordiality, temperance and patience that Arthur practised. None of these qualities characterised Harry Cust, something that Arthur should have known by this time even without reading *Dr Cupid*.

This represented professional as much as aristocratic elitism, however, and it helps to explain the phenomenon that David Cannadine has noted as a decline of both talent and political ambition on the part of aristocrats in the generation that came of age in the late-Victorian period.[123] What was the point, George Wyndham once mused, of seeking the leadership if it meant he would have to 'give up romance'? Men of the privileged classes either learned the patterns of deception that Arthur represented or abandoned the political arena in favour of the frenetic amusements and sexual opportunities of the new century. Before the First World War, British aristocrats were already dividing between those who could adjust to the new performances of political responsibility and those more akin to modern 'celebrities' – people of personality rather than character, flamboyance rather than reserve and social cachet rather than public power.[124]

9

<hr>

1895

WHEN GLADSTONE's second home rule initiative passed the Commons in 1893, only to be defeated by the most lopsided vote in the history of the House of Lords, the Grand Old Man of Victorian liberalism finally retired after sixty-one years in parliament. His reluctant successor in March 1894 was Arthur's contemporary and Scottish neighbour Lord Rosebery. Temperamental, a victim of insomnia and fractious colleagues, he lasted hardly more than a year. A general election in summer 1895 returned the Conservative–Unionist alliance to power for the next decade, and with Lord Salisbury's health and faculties weakening, Arthur would take on significant new responsibilities as his deputy. In 1902 Arthur became prime minister himself.

Only two years after Arthur's reflections to Margot Tennant about the role of chance in political life, he might have been excused for wondering how so many of his generational rivals had been removed so fortuitously. Rosebery never re-emerged as a viable national figure. Parnell was dead. In January, Randolph Churchill's funeral took place, with Arthur making a hasty trip from Scotland to attend: 'It was very impressive and pathetic', he told Mary Elcho. 'Rosebery, Harcourt [the other contender to succeed Gladstone] and I sat together, Harcourt in the middle, and I could not help speculating which of his neighbours he liked the most, or perhaps I should say the least!'[1] Ten years later a sudden, incapacitating stroke removed Joseph Chamberlain just as he looked poised to challenge Arthur for leadership of the Edwardian Conservative Party.

Arthur, not yet fifty, was reaching the pinnacle of power at a moment when national and imperial affairs were intersecting in

unforeseen ways. The year 1895 was so fraught with portents of
the new century that a recent scholarly study by Nicholas Freeman
made the year itself the protagonist.[2] Month by month, Freeman
charts the developments in commodity culture, leisured consum-
erism, revolutionary aesthetics, imperial adventures and public
discontent that revealed to contemporaries 'the drama, disaster
and disgrace' of late-Victorian Britain. Freeman reports the 'national success' of Arthur's *Foundations of Belief* and his opening
speech to the new parliament elected in the summer: in the House
of Commons Arthur expressed cautious optimism that now, with
home rule laid to rest, parliament would have a period of tranquility to deal with long-neglected educational and social reforms for
the next generation of Britons. Like the Prince of Wales, Henry
Asquith, Joseph Chamberlain and H. G. Wells, in early January,
Arthur was also present at the opening night of Oscar Wilde's last
play *An Ideal Husband*.

Wilde's plot devices of 'indiscretion, secrets, compromising
letters, imperiled marriage, outraged aristocrats and eroticized
blackmail' seemed ripped from the headlines and club gossip
of the previous few years. The play also notoriously previsioned
the author's own fortunes in the coming months of courtroom
defeat and incarceration, during which George Wyndham took a
tangential role through a hurried visit to Wilde the night before
the arrest to urge him to flee the country.[3] Wilde's complicated
examination of the interrelationship between the fabricated and
the actual, between banter and panic, caught many of the realities
of Balfour's world at the end of the century. The same could be
said for the lives of his friends, who were experiencing changes in
their own circumstances that caught some of the complexities of
their generation.

Among the Souls themselves, the sense of threats and transition
was brought home personally by the death of Lord Pembroke.
George gave his last public speech – to the Constitutional Association at Wilton – in early February 1895. With parliament just
convening, he addressed the obvious weaknesses of Rosebery's
government and his belief that a general election could come at
any time. Shortly after this he had another severe attack of the
mysterious gastrointestinal illness he had been fighting for nearly
two years. On 7 April, in a pencilled letter to Constance Wenlock,
George Pembroke said that he had been near to dying three or

four times in the past six weeks. 'A mere skeleton' and 'too weak to stand', he was leaving for Bad Nauheim, the health resort north of Frankfurt that was beginning to specialise in hydrotherapy for the kind of heart condition that a new German doctor had told him was the source, not the result, of his other problems.[4]

In fact, the medical community never did figure out the cause of George's excruciating, drawn-out decline. Was it having 'the heart of a man who should be six inches shorter'? A progressive reaction to a severe bout of dysentery acquired years earlier in Palestine? An intestinal form of the tuberculosis that killed his brother a decade later?[5] Sir William Broadbent, a widely honoured physician to aristocratic society and the royal family, infuriated George's wife, Gety, by suggesting that her husband's symptoms were those of 'an hysterical patient'. No diagnosis could be more insulting in an era when 'shattered nerves' and inexplicable lethargies in men suggested character flaws, rather than organic agents poorly understood by medical practitioners.[6] But this illness went far beyond the psychosomatic, and it made George's final year an agony. In a farewell letter to Margot, he said that he might have 'another attack at any time, and I … have not the strength to stand the exhaustion or the necessary treatment … nor can I bring myself to wish to go through again and perhaps again what I went through the other day … I feel full of doubt whether I shall see any of my beloved friends faces again.'[7]

Attended only by his wife, the Brownlows, the German doctor Theodor Schott and the same faithful servant, Charles Mitchell, who had been with him on the *Albatross* three decades before, George died in Bad Nauheim on 5 May. In two months he would have turned forty-five. His brother and heir Sidney brought the body back to England for burial a week later. In an eerie reversal of the coming-of-age ceremony, mourners assembled in the court-yard of Wilton House to escort the deceased earl back down the drive under its canopy of maturing trees to a final resting place in tiny Fugglestone Church. Over two thousand people, including girls from the Wilton Park School and an honour guard of the Wiltshire Rifle Volunteers, lined the procession of tenants, mayors, corporation officials, estate workers and household servants. They were joined by 'honored guests' such as Arthur Balfour and Charlie Beresford who had arrived on a special train from Waterloo for the service. Among the other notables were personal friends from the Souls – Doll Liddell, the Ribblesdales, George Wyndham, Evan

Charteris, Frances Horner, the Grenfells, Betty Balfour and Spencer Lyttelton. Twelve barrows of floral offerings 'literally filled the air with fragrance'. They came from the Asquiths, Mary Anderson, Violet Granby, the Sisters of Charity Blind Asylum, the fishing and smack-owners of Dublin's Ringsend district, Princess Louise, the gardeners and workmen of Mount Merrion. Mary Elcho, Charty Ribblesdale, Frances Horner, Daisy White and Evelyn de Vesci had all paid their last visits to George in the final months of his illness.[8]

Despite this evidence of the regard in which he was held, George had faced his mortality with the same fundamental sense of aloneness that characterised his outlook since the South Sea voyages. This self-positioning was clear from his choice of burial place. The family vault of the Herberts lies in Wilton parish church, which George's parents had helped to restore in grand style in the 1840s and where a monument commemorated his brother Reginald's death at sea. The local newspaper hinted that George's burial at Fugglestone was Gety's selection, a final brick in the barrier that she was thought to have built between George and his family.[9] But it is nearly impossible to believe that Gety would have violated her husband's wishes in such a matter. Something about resting at Fugglestone appealed to George's sense of his appropriate place in his spiritual, social and generational worlds.

George lived long enough to read *Foundations of Belief* before his final crisis, yet despite his friendship with the author, he was not persuaded. 'Arthur Balfour's book has been received with general delight. To be told on such authority and with such logic that one may believe whatever one likes, and that the more one wants to believe it the more likely it is to be true – is just what humanity likes. Whether such a doctrine tends towards truth in the long run I am doubtful.'[10] Arthur's assessment that both reason and emotion suggested the existence of a 'personal and moral God', a loving order to the universe that was beyond human comprehension, struck George, and many other doubters, as little more than a willed faith.

To the end George refused to align himself with a humanity that had 'debauched its mental and spiritual tastes with the strong meats of supernaturalism and superstition till it can barely do without them'.[11] He retained the rueful agnosticism that had overtaken him in the South Seas – spiritually inclined, but unable to feel connection with a creator who had placed so many limitations on human happiness or failed even to meet the standards of amiable tolerance of an English gentleman. 'As for telling my Deity that I hope I've done nothing to offend him and am sorry if I have – I don't feel somehow on those sort of terms or attitude', he wrote to his sister:

> I think it's extremely unlikely that He has ever allowed himself to feel annoyed by my action or shortcomings … and feel that if I took that line he would say, 'Please don't mention it' … I did not at all want to die, when it seemed that I had to the other day. Parting with all those whom one loves perhaps forever is and must be very bitter – I felt it bitter and very much the worst part of death. There is no doubt that the religious believer has a pull at such times but those who haven't got a definite belief of God and his views and the supernatural must do without.[12]

The Bishop of Salisbury, noting how cooperatively George had worked with him on parish matters over the years, could only comment that he hoped now the veil had been lifted on mysteries that George had grappled with all his life.[13]

George's dislocations were not solely a product of a religious scepticism that seemed to grind through the intellectual controversies of the mid-century until his final days. He was also disappointed in his attempts to exemplify the landed way of life and the model character of those responsible for it. Several times George wrote about recognising himself in the eponymous hero of Robert Louis Stevenson's novel *Prince Otto* (1885).[14] It was a revealing identification with a strange and not entirely convincing personality. Stevenson called Otto 'a sweet party but as weak as paper', and wrote the novel as he worked through his own ambivalences about aesthetic, possibly decadent individualism and acceptance of conventional measures of social and professional performance.[15] The ineffectual ruler of a Zenda-like East European principality, Otto is the object of mockery and eventually revolt by his subjects because of his self-effacing relationship to devious courtiers and an ambitious wife who is widely, though wrongly, believed to be having an affair with his chief adviser. Otto is a decent man, determined to remain honourable as those around him connive and betray. He rejects attempts at seduction by a forceful countess who schemes to replace the princess and instead vows to continue faithful to his wife despite her reputation.

Stevenson does not mock this hero who tries to adhere to the myriad public and private responsibilities of a position he had

assumed at birth. Crippled by his inability to assert himself in relation to others, Otto ends the book having regained his wife's love
but otherwise dispossessed. He remains an attractive character,
but free-floating, psychologically unanchored by either social role
or the sense of direction provided by some other guiding commitment. In an almost exact description of Prince Otto when the
reader meets him at the beginning of the novel, Edith Olivier's
chief memory of the Earl of Pembroke of her childhood was his
long solitary walks around the Wilton environs, stopping for brief
chats with those he encountered, but clearly more comfortable
with a solitude that took him into landscapes rather than social
engagements.[16]

On his rambles, Otto has the misfortune to overhear his subjects'
critical remarks about his failures as a head of state. Whether or
not this happened to George, he nevertheless told Edward Hamilton at the end of 1892 that 'he had a good many estate troubles:
it was the worst harvest since 1879 and in some parts of the estate
where he had done the most for his tenants and the labourers,
there was a good deal of difficulty, fostered by agitators'.[17] Duty
and consideration could not reverse the fortunes of a system of
landed society that was dying. George's death made Wilton the
first great estate subject to the new 'Harcourt death duties' enacted by parliament the year before. Sidney would owe £100,000 in
inheritance taxes and in order to raise the revenue would have
to lay off household and estate workers, cut back on employees
at the timber yards, close wings of the great house for a few years
and significantly reduce contributions for the local charities. F. M.
L. Thompson's study of the Wilton finances shows that by 1896
'the estate expenses exceeded the income'. The earls of Pembroke
were living 'on the growing bounty of Dublin ground rents'.[18]

Five years later, Arthur unveiled Alfred Gilbert's bronze statue of
George Pembroke that stands outside the Wilton gates.[19] The in-
scription provides an unusual evocation of personality, rather than
a list of manly achievements: 'fearlessness, singleness of soul, the
will always to strive for wisdom, opened hand and governed appe-
tites and piety and love of lonely study, humbleness, uprightness,
heed to injure naught which live … a contented heart'. The last
was surely the contentment of fortitude, rather than fulfilment.
'In all he says there is a gentle melancholy, which attracts me, and
makes me wish to give him one's mite of sympathy', Betty Balfour
wrote. 'I suppose it is partly due to physical lack of vitality, fortune

and nature, living in the lap of luxury, surrounded by all that is beautiful, with rare mental gifts, and great personal charm, and yet to feel that life for him has been a "might have been", and nothing more.'[20]

Arthur, who at the unveiling of the statue called George 'one of his oldest and one of his best friends', would not have agreed that it was a life of might-have-beens. Both men sought to live up to obligations inherited in a Victorian world where deference and privilege were repaid by the kind of personal restraint and attention to duties that George had demonstrated. Both were temperate and conciliatory – not gigantic personalities intent on reshaping the world or dismissing its claims as beneath considera-tion. The circumstances of George's youth ill-prepared him for the bonding rituals and competitions of male peers, while enhancing his feelings of personal responsibility for the privileges he had received. He was neither the boisterous rake nor the decadent sensualist that his South Seas experiences might have produced in a privileged man of different temperament. Instead he identified himself as a consciously dutiful holdover of Victorian courtliness, but found this guise poorly aligned with both the bludgeoning and the tactical flexibility of modern public life. Unlike Arthur, George never found the ability to construct workable façades for public performance that kept people guessing about his meanings and motivations. He remained candid, transparent, unable to speak the partial or equivocal platitude in which he did not believe. He retained this beleaguered ego until his death, hardly crediting how rare his kindness and reluctance to stand on rank had seemed to those who knew him personally.

Margot was one of the few friends absent from George's funeral. After a year of marriage, she was apprehensively expecting her overdue first child. She survived the long and difficult delivery on 15 May, but only because her doctor, unlike Laura's a decade earli-er, sacrificed the baby. Margot was bedridden for weeks afterwards. Though she gave birth to a healthy daughter two years later, 1895 marked the beginning of a decade of reproductive hardships. Mar-got experienced five full-term pregnancies in this time, but three of the babies died within hours of birth. Her former energy and high spirits were undermined, inaugurating years of severe insom-nia, nervous anxiety and very low weight. She was also doing her best to raise the children from Asquith's first marriage, three of whom were not yet teenagers. She had five fewer hours a day, she said, for the private reading and letter-writing that had helped her keep composure before. Her biographers agree that Margot came to love Asquith deeply and loyally – that she was generous to her stepchildren, devoted to her own offspring, beloved by servants who stayed with her for years, and capable of much unsolicited thoughtfulness towards friends when they most needed help. Nevertheless, this marriage probably did not evolve in the way that either of the partners expected.[21]

During their long courtship, Asquith had given Margot multiple pictures of the personal qualities he cherished in her and never wanted her to lose. The most important of these was her tender and vulnerable inner 'soul – your real true self – the self that I recognized a year ago … [that] is like a star and dwells apart'.[22] This was an aspect of personality that Laura had been able to reveal to many people – male and female – and that formed a large part of the legendary impression she made on her generation. Margot reserved it almost entirely for men, during the courtship years several men, and probably neither she nor Asquith knew how fragile it was. Behind her façades of social self-possession, Margot became increasingly sensitive to perceived slights, disloyalties, neglect or fears that she had fallen lower on the kind of priority lists of affection that she assumed everyone compiled as endlessly as she did. Before her marriage, she had presented this 'dwells apart' self as a plucky, tender and untamed child. As her family responsibilities grew, she would conceive it in terms of a quintessentially female nature, showing her exceptional femininity through the extremes of pain, grief, devotion, worry or indignation that she felt. Margot had long used the heightened language of melodrama to describe her psychic dislocations – a language that gives voice to the distress of the powerless and vulnerable.[23] Her diaries and the anecdotes of friends show her behaviour, not just her language, giving way to uncontrolled emotion that worsened if she encountered sangfroid in response.

For fifteen years before her marriage, Margot had been able to compartmentalise her life, finding her different attributes affirmed in different – mostly male – locales of hunting, political society, Oxford, stage performance, tentative forays into literary criticism or publishing. By the turn of the century much of this had stopped, with the demands of marriage, childbirth and political hostessing concentrating her mental and emotional energies into a narrower helpmate frame. She had always been competitive with other women, a judgemental hostess or guest, and reliant on the approval of men. Now she became a grim parody of Victorian womanly qualities that she just as often condemned as showing the inferior nature of her sex as a whole. Margot's misogyny was occasionally virulent, especially after Asquith's deep opposition to 'votes for women' made him a target of the suffragists, who Margot despised for being irrational harridans whose actions proved women's disqualification for the political equality they sought.[24]

Margot's deeply emotional investment in Asquith's career conformed to the Victorian prescript of wives sharing values, interests and public identities with their husband. But he had told her early on that he did not want a fierce advocate as a wife, but someone with an independent mind who could act as a trusted sounding board and provide more balanced perspectives that he might miss in the flurry of day-to-day contention.[25] Margot's recently published war diaries show her trying to keep to this role and just as often failing. She fired off private letters to public men she did not know well, Asquith's Liberal colleagues especially, admonishing and instructing them as though there were reasons that they should follow her guidance. She could not keep her opinions to herself or resist making provocative comments in public settings such as the Ladies Gallery of the Commons.[26] She never abandoned the practice she had begun long before her marriage of passing on confidences – even letters – that her informant had assumed to be private. In this way she was untrustworthy, needed careful handling by Asquith's staff and colleagues and justified the exclusions she most feared.

If, as Ben Griffin suggests, tranquil harmony was integral to the 'domestic ideology' of public men of this era, Asquith did not experience it.[27] Within three or four years he was quietly seeking refuge in other women – usually much younger than himself – partially for sexual foreplay, but also for the undemanding listener he had thought he would have at home. When George Curzon's wife made a trip to England in 1901, she quickly learned of Asquith's 'amorous interest in various people ... Can you conceive of anything more grotesque than Henry as a lover of girls?'[28] As Martin Pugh observes, Asquith chose women 'essentially as amiable companions and uncritical supporters', much like his first wife Helen, but with greater interest and knowledge about the world of politics than she had felt.[29] Margot had coolly anticipated this phase of marriage in her 1885 essay 'Women', but when it happened she was deeply hurt.

Little of this was known to the wider public. Because of Margot's longtime friendships with so many Conservatives, she and her husband stayed immersed in the worlds of high society socialising that seemed incomprehensibly bipartisan. Traditional Liberals condemned her for corrupting Asquith's moral compass in politics, over-taxing their joint income and enabling his drinking. Margot became a stand-in for the narrow elitism of British political leadership before the First World War, and her public face of lavish entertaining and strenuous leisure was highly criticised for distracting important men from their important purposes. But among political insiders she was atypical of the behaviour and demeanours of the groups around Arthur and Mary Elcho.

Margot certainly identified with power structures and powerful actors, but she was also conflicted about what this meant. Sometimes she claimed men's prerogatives – in her writing, her willingness to court attention, her sharp criticism of male performance, her celebration of her physical courage. Just as often, she presented herself as completely averse to seeking male authority through public speaking or valuing women's open participation in public affairs. If Margot had been a caricature of upstart 'wild woman' misbehaviour in the early 1890s, she would become a figure of mockery in Arthur Balfour's political world, always capable of those outrageous zingers, but an outré eccentric, tolerated as a touchstone for others to measure their own greater self-control and insider savoir faire. Frances Horner wrote that it broke her heart to see Margot in the Edwardian years, compared to when she had first known her in the 1880s.

Lord Salisbury's third ministry, confirmed by the general election of July 1895, was the first in which the Liberal Unionists accepted open partnership with the Conservatives. Five of the most important, including Joseph Chamberlain at the colonial office, took cabinet positions.[30] The need to accommodate the rising men in both parts of the alliance complicated the prospects of younger politicians. St John Brodrick, in the Commons since 1880, and George Curzon, a member since 1886, were able to secure undersecretary spots at the War Office and the Foreign Office that augured well for their future careers. George Wyndham, despite all his willingness and hard work, was not given a spot. Salisbury reportedly said that he did 'not like poets' – shorthand for those eccentricities of discourse and temperament that bedevilled the young political aristocrat.

George Wyndham managed to restrain his disappointment, partly because Arthur Balfour assured him of his continuing support and partly because he had something of a literary triumph in the same months. For several years, George had been immersing himself in the poetry of the French and English Renaissance, and in 1894 he began work on an introduction to Thomas North's 1579 translation of Plutarch's *Parallel Lives of the Greeks and Romans*, part of a Henley series of reissued 'Tudor Classics'. Phyllis Rose has noted that Victorian men often turned to Plutarch to 'learn about the perils and pitfalls of public life'.[31] George was not expert in either ancient or Tudor history – his own research tended in the direction of etymology as an aid to translating poetry. But he clearly used Plutarch as Rose suggests, and his long introduction to the volume told as much about his own preoccupations as the times in which his subjects were writing. His impressions of the dramatic lives of the ancients served as commentary on popular politics in his own day and a working out of his approach to the new conditions.[32]

As he made his way through North's Plutarch, George was struck by the centrality of 'the State' – the imperial polity – as the only worthy arena for men of ambition and noble character in the Greco-Roman world. His descriptions of these actors served as admonishments to himself and the politicians around him. The ancient societies rewarded strong, bold, masculine characters who uncomplainingly accepted the game of power in their own time, sometimes risking life itself in a single throw of the political dice. They had been extreme in action and careless in how they justified it – not for them compromises that were 'delicate and effeminate' or the 'fluent earnestness', over-vehemence, irritation, contempt and emotional assertion that constituted the weaknesses of his own political action. The Roman statesman did not react to external pressures, but to reasons 'self-gathered from within', the exact opposite of the modern politician's brooding calculations of how the self was coming across to others. There is no indication that George was aware of Friedrich Nietzsche's writing, but his depiction of the 'natural grace', independence, casual forbearance, courage and soldierly courtesy of Plutarch's subjects sounds like the German philosopher's aristocratic type.

George did find one ancient model that translated into the modern day. This was the Athenian trickster Themistocles: 'this day, deceiving his friends, the next overawing his enemies; with effrontery or chicane, with good-fellowship or reserve; but ever with infinite dexterity, a courage that never falters, and a patience that never wearies: he keeps the shuttle of his thought quick-flying through the web of intrigue. And all for the fun of weaving!'[33] In the early 1890s George frequently used images of jugglers or navigators to describe this master politician who transcended attacks and setbacks and accepted the wily stratagems needed to subdue chaotic forces of mass politics and insider intrigue.

George experienced a flurry of political activity like this himself in the spring of 1893, when Gladstone refused to delay consideration of the second home rule bill despite the fact that Arthur – leader of the Commons opposition – could not attend because he was felled again by influenza. Just returned from his own bout with the illness, George served as intermediary between the bedridden Conservative chief, party whips, depleted opposition front-bench and potential Unionist speakers: 'these are days of the most intense excitement hinging upon delicate and confidential issues in which I find myself playing a most interesting and complicated part ... I tried hard to speak last night, rose five times, and had three good points to make, but no luck. This I do not mind, the new excitement of another pitched fight has nearly cured me of my influenza.'[34] George's contemporary political model was, of course, Arthur, whose flexibility and insouciance masked the inviolate inner self that George was trying to achieve. Wilfrid Blunt blamed Arthur for fostering a superficial cynicism and social Darwinian callousness in his young cousin.[35] For more than a decade George would try to impersonate this canny tactician and patient political operative.

After his failure to gain a position in 1895, George decided that he needed to establish himself as the Commons expert on some important contemporary issue, as George Curzon had become with his Eastern travels, to impress the leadership and enhance his contributions to debate. He found his cause in the surge of imperial activity taking place in South Africa. This arena of freebooter enterprise hit the headlines in December after the failure of Leander Starr Jameson's raid on the Transvaal. The incursion – of dubious provenance, quixotic and easily foiled – was meant to spark an uprising for increased political rights among foreign mine workers in the Boer republic. George arranged to meet Jameson when he returned to England for trial early in 1896. The next summer he founded the Imperial South Africa Association with Jameson and four others as a political action committee to promote awareness of British interests in the lower continent.[36] This was followed by an extensive trip through the Cape Colony and into the new territories of Rhodesia. In the view of his friend and private secretary Charles Boyd, the experience 'made a new man of him'. In these frontiers of action and conquest, George thought, 'there may be two or three centuries still ahead of the glorious indiscretions and rapt visions of youth'. He was both echoing and contributing to the decade's growing prescription for Anglo-Saxon racial renewal through empire.[37]

George returned home to join the parliamentary inquiry that obfuscated the roles of Cecil Rhodes and Joseph Chamberlain in the Jameson raid and exonerated Salisbury's government.[38] His efforts were so persistent that he became known as the 'member for South Africa'. After he was appointed undersecretary of the War Office in 1898, he carried out the most successful intrigue of his own career by supporting Alfred Milner's aggressive agenda to establish British sovereignty over the Boers: 'The Press are ready and under complete control', he told Milner. 'I can switch on an agitation at your direction. The French and German shareholders of the [mining companies] are in line ... [we] are in your hands and we shall wait and be patient, or charge home, just as you decide.' If the South African war that broke out in autumn 1899 was 'Milner's war', George had played a crucial supporting role through his access to the Conservative press and defence of the war effort in the House of Commons.[39]

The year 1895 gave George not just a new cause but a new aptitude. For the first time, his letters began to describe successes as a platform orator, speaking to the crowds of thousands who attended political functions at this time. After an appearance at Manchester during the election campaigns in July, he told his wife, 'I spoke third. Felt weak at first (temp nearly a degree above normal) but steadily warmed to work and gained strength, so that in the end made the best speech of all I have made – about an hour and five minutes, during which I held them in my hand.'[40] Later he would define his 'immense power over mobs' in terms that implied the self-annihilation of the sexual act:

They listen & believe. I have not always got it to the full. It fluctuates.
But when I am really magnetic I can sweep crowd after crowd. It
is not oratory. Because, when I have it, they do not wait for me to
finish my sentences … It is almost frightening to be so intimate with
so many. I know the symptoms. But they made me gasp at the end.
They mobbed up to the platform and made me sign my name on
cards and tickets and bits of torn paper till my hand ached, & then
dragged me around town.[41]

However fascinated he was by Renaissance perspectives on dissimulation and endless manoeuvring, George never inhabited the
Machiavellian persona comfortably. When he tried, he struck parliamentary insiders as a man of bustling self-importance, performing for imaginary audiences and prone to magnify his centrality to
events.[42] But leading 'the people' to understand the importance
of the Anglo-Saxon mission and the competitive dangers it faced
gave George his pathway into the tumultuous world of mass politics and allowed him to feel himself what he most admired and
wanted to be – the 'functional man' living fully immersed and unselfconsciously in moments of heightened experience.[43]

One biographer argues that George was 'merely conforming to
the romantic Conservative imperialism of his generation' in his
embrace of Britain's global mission. But H. G. Wells was accurate
in noting that men like George were trying to create a more 'subtle and intricate' modern life that would be able to incorporate
'monumental emotionality' into political action.[44] George became a follower of Joseph Chamberlain's grand vision for empire
consolidation. The challenges and opportunities of building the
Anglo-Saxon world would unite conflicting classes at home, allow aristocratic virtues of daring, courage and high emotion to
come forward, justify the subterfuges of leadership and annihi-
late self-consciousness. As the new century developed, George's
speeches would become blunter and more urgent and his private
visions more willing to court violence and bloody sacrifice. By the
time that H. H. Asquith became Liberal prime minister in 1908,
George was quietly breaking from Arthur and turning himself
into a leader of the 'radical right' wing of the Conservative Party.
Parliamentary politics, he told his wife, were *not* a game at which
he could play, nor would he 'put his trust in princes'.[45] Wars, not
games, legitimised the deep emotional engagement and 'excitable
speech' that always came more naturally to Wyndham.[46]

*

In another mysterious conjunction of events, 1895 proved a turning point for Mary Elcho as well. The two years before are surprisingly undocumented in the correspondence, but her diaries reveal that they were full of unhappiness. Her health and spirits had seemed to recover in 1892, when the birth of Hugo's son with Hermione Leinster gave her a kind of psychological independence in relation to her husband. Then, in December, three-year-old Colin died of scarlet fever during the family's Christmas holiday at Clouds. Mary's diary shows how severely this tragedy affected her. Deeper involvement in the lives of her offspring and continuous worries about them began at this time – an extremely anxious Cynthia slept in Mary's bed for months, and ill or distraught youngsters did so periodically through the years that followed.[47] She spent good portions of 1893 on the Continent with the children.

Six months after Colin's death, Hugo and eight-year-old Guy both came down with a fever so high that Hugo nearly died. Mary remembered 'frightful' scenes caused by Hermione Leinster's 'excruciating anxiety … and the wild almost killing passion of relief and joy when he was better'.[48] The normal autumn social rounds resumed in 1894, but Arthur Balfour was absorbed by a self-imposed deadline to finish *Foundations of Belief* before the collapse of Rosebery's government would bring him into office again. Meanwhile, Hugo was receiving increasingly dire news about Hermione's illness. He left to stay with her at Monte Carlo and then Mentone during her final winter. In December 1894 when Mary embarked on a trip to Egypt – with governess, maid and three children – to visit the Wilfrid Blunt family, she had not seen Hugo for nearly two months.

Mary's brief Egyptian fling with her cousin Wilfrid, twenty-two years older and notorious for his sexual unrestraint, was sensitively revealed by his biographer in 1979.[49] The complications were many, for Mary got pregnant almost immediately after she reached Blunt's compound at Sheykh Obeydh in January 1895. A month later, Hugo joined the party on a visit full of awkward episodes that nevertheless provided an explanation for the baby who was born in October.[50] Blunt suffered several months of torment at the failure of what he called the '*grande passion*' of his life, before resuming his old ways with women.

Hugo and Mary reached a kind of reconciliation after this event that included an intentional pregnancy and the birth of a son exactly a year after Wilfrid and Mary's daughter arrived. The reactions of Arthur to some unavoidable conclusions have usually been dismissed with Mary's cryptic remark to Wilfrid that Arthur was not jealous – 'you know he is not like other men'.[51] Nevertheless, he could not disguise an unusual despondency at the events. 'I couldn't bear to see you sitting back in that chair more depressed than if the Education Bill had gone wrong instead of me', Mary wrote, 'with a horrid unplumbed gulf between us, bridged over by a feeble finger clasp.'[52]

Mary could be secretive and misleading, but she was not promiscuous, either in emotional or physical attachments. That she allowed herself the indulgence with Wilfrid Blunt demonstrated to the two men who knew her best, Arthur and Hugo, some need for escape, if not complete revision of the life she had been leading. Hugo told Mary that he could have understood if the pregnancy had been with Arthur, rather than Wilfrid, whom he blamed for taking advantage of her unhappiness. Hugo would continue to succumb to spells of absence, anger and score-settling. It did not help that he lost his parliamentary seat in the 1895 election, through years of inattention to his Ipswich constituents, and was out of parliament until he inherited the earldom in 1914. But Mary no longer had to pretend with him that Arthur meant no more to her than did other 'tame' bachelors who haunted these circles. In return, Hugo's current loves, unlike Hermione Leinster, were invited to Stanway, where Mary was usually able to make them personal friends who shared the challenge of distracting her moody, unpredictable and easily bored spouse.

For his part, Arthur must have had a new realisation of what Mary meant to him and the fact that he could not take her forbearance for granted. In 1894 he had been unusually dismissive of her endless planning, requests for assurance and concerns that he found other women, especially Ettie Grenfell, more amusing company. By late autumn, however, he seems to have been genuinely alarmed that Mary might transfer her emotional attachment to someone who would give her more consistent assurance that she was valued. 'All the things I really want to say are unsayable', he wrote to her in Egypt, 'so that if you wish to know them you must imagine them for yourself. Think of what you would like best to hear and have faith that that is what I should like to speak.'[53] There would be one other period in their lives when Mary paid Arthur back for causing her intense anxiety over her importance to him. In July 1901, after he briefly showed enjoyment in the non-threatening company of George Curzon's wife, Mary conceived her last child, generally assumed by her biographers to have been Hugo's.[54]

With less need to hide from Hugo, Arthur's letters to Mary became more personal in their reassurances, gossip and admonishments. Mary in turn could let herself write about wishing that they had got married in 1883 – and could make enough coded allusions to sexuality to suggest that Margot was incorrect in thinking that the couple had no intimate life, only a passion of the 'soul'.[55] Like a married couple, they were capable of bickering and miscommunicating, especially when time apart and two heavily scheduled lives raised the importance of every letter – 'regarded as a channel of intercourse between soul and soul pens and paper are perfectly idiotic', as Arthur wrote.[56] But the usual picture of Balfour as only slightly invested in the relationship can go too far. There is no other correspondent in the records with whom he showed the same degree of psychological intimacy or shared so many secrets, so that the question of what Mary provided both to him and to their fin de siècle milieu needs to be explored.

Mary's diffuse, stream-of-consciousness letters can give a misleading picture of her mind, as do the somewhat stilted reminiscences that she wrote late in life.[57] What comes across in her discourse is a trait often gendered as feminine – a minuteness of observation and story-telling moments that resist either Margot's blunt assertions or the consciously shaping hand. Perhaps surprisingly, Arthur enjoyed these. 'Your letter really was magnificent! Nobody expresses better the passing biography of the hour, the actual living impression of the trifles that make life tolerable. This is the true art of letter writing. N.B. I haven't got it', he wrote, noting at another time how refreshing he found them after 'cabinets, defence committees, addresses, speeches and all night sittings!'[58] Eileen Gilhooly argues that since the time of Rousseau, women have been described as better at seeing life as a 'fragile', 'minutely tangled skein of human relations rather than as a socioeconomic construction of pressing political consequence'.[59] Female strategies of understatement, convoluted phrasing, self-deprecation, 'epistolary wittiness' and privately transmitted communication all characterised Mary's letters. They gave Arthur gossip and information, but also, as his days were increasingly consumed by contentious policy issues, a narrative

escape into small-scale social worlds he could enjoy without needing to see them as his responsibility.

In these letters, Mary's stance – quite unlike Margot's – was comedic rather than admonitory. Osbert Sitwell remembered her
humour late in life as essentially astringent.[60] It made no demands
for action, and when her stories and images spiralled out of control, she would close a section with a self-deprecating disclaimer
– 'what rot I am talking; I'm glad I don't have to read it' or 'there,
I've had a blow out'. Many of her stories were against herself:

> I was caught out smoking on the train and had to throw my just
> lit and much needed cigarette away. The porter dressed like a fat
> policeman looked very sympathetic but shook his head in a most
> reproving way! I laughed and he laughed. The whole carriage was
> wreathed in smoke when the accursed train stopped unexpectedly at
> Clapham Junction and two still more accursed people … got in! and
> I was discovered looking most ladylike amidst the fumes! … You are
> so conventional in some ways, you would not have liked it but luckily
> you are not responsible for me in public though you think yourself
> 'missioned' to chastise me in private. However if I were your wife I
> should never put you to shame. I can always assume virtue which is
> something.[61]

Other letters described the eccentric types of Stanway village life or
the equally comic behaviour of colleagues wondering who would
be in the next cabinet: 'politically everyone is excited (except me!)
but I am amused, and I long to tell you lots of funny little things,
everybody is behaving more like themselves than ever, which they
always do in times of *crisis*!'[62] That her gimlet eye targeted government ministers and great ladies as well as rustic bumpkins was part
of her appeal. 'Everything nice and funny and odd is always hap-
pening to me', she wrote, possibly because she had a 'penchant
for fools' that exasperated her family, made inconvenient devotees
of her servants and added spice to her Stanway entertainments.[63]

Laughter that is self-deprecating, sympathetic and diffuse carries its own value structures. The stance of wry amusement and
tolerance of eccentricity involved a distancing of engagement –
an avoidance, Mary admitted, of 'all the things in life that *I* (for
sanity's sake) keep shut off'.[64] She admitted to using Arthur as 'a
sink' for her grievances, because '*you* are the only person I go to in
distress, so you think me moody and peevish and idiotic'. In general, however, her tendency was to 'consume my own smoke', so

that other people came to *her* for help and advice, thinking 'I am calm and generous and wise'.[65] 'I was much amused at the space occupied in your letters to me by the repeated flatteries showered on you by your friends!' Arthur teased, 'and indeed by the highly appreciative estimate of your character and performances which you contribute on your own account! The worst of it is that they really are all true. You *have* a very peculiar genius for making people around you happy and on easy terms.'[66]

The problem was how difficult this was for her. Mary's internal reactions were more intense than what she conveyed openly. Dismissing servants, dealing with the emotional turmoil of her husband's 'lady loves', trying to run the Stanway household in the face of Hugo's roller-coaster finances, dealing with sick or unhappy children, placating critical friends and in-laws, competitive socialising in London and the country house – all left her drained and often ill. Mary was a wide reader in the psychological literature of her day, an interest she shared with Arthur more than any political passions. She diagnosed herself as using over-commitment to fend off facing inner pain. 'Dr Keitley came in a.m. He gave me a long psychological lecture. I see what he means and I affirm it all … but it seems too hard for me to do. I've got in the habit of living externally and cannot find my own soul! I may rest some but it makes me too sad – to sink within myself.'[67]

This rare moment of candour – confided to her diary – shows how fully integrated she was into the structures of behaviour and responsibility of elite society. Mary did come to understand herself as bundle of psychic, familial and social forces – she did not attribute her depression and anxiety, as her brother did, to an inherited propensity for madness or breakdown.[68] But she felt she had few choices about her incompatible marriage or the planning, placating, performances and secrets that her life entailed.[69] Like almost all her friends, she did not envision a different future for her daughters or provide them an upbringing that might have offered alternatives to the prominent marriage that had been the dutiful achievement of her own adolescence.[70] From Arthur she learned that the things most within control were outward appearance and internal attitude. Mary's mix of fortitude and levity came to mirror his, as did the reticence, deceptions and strategic uses of charming vagueness that they both deployed.[71]

*

ALL-ROUND POLITICIANS. No. 2.—ARTHUR GOLFOUR.

Fig. 16 'Arthur Golfour' by Harry Furniss, *Punch*, 14 March 1891

In 1891, six months before Arthur became leader of the House of Commons, Harry Furniss made him the second subject of *Punch*'s new cartoon series 'All-Round Politicians' (see Fig. 16).[72] There are eleven depictions of Arthur on the single page, most of them paired. In the top left corner, a languid, willowy 'Saint Balfour' – reminiscent of the effete imagery of the decade before – presents the dove of peace and an olive branch to a burly, Ulster 'bogie man' Arthur primed for harsher measures in Ireland. Next to them sits the decorous, serious-minded political adjudicator, juxtaposed to the wily snoop and intriguer 'Paul Pry'.[73] At the bottom, Arthur might be an uppity equivocator or a great philosopher, a scribbling writer and 'nobody' or a substantial, enthroned heir apparent to Lord Salisbury himself. The only image that shows Arthur in a group has him as the 'lady killer' surrounded by adoring women.

Missing from this hodgepodge was one setting in which Arthur actually spent much of his time – the back corridors, quiet offices and insider circles where governance was carried out. One of Arthur's greatest strengths was his ability to work productively with the increasing number of 'faceless' functionaries of the state – secretaries, civil servants and political operatives. He had shown this in Ireland, where his quickness in making hard decisions coupled with unflinching support for underlings earned their loyalty. A few years later, officials who had seen only his parliamentary improvisation were struck by his grasp, efficiency, mental initiative and perpetual courtesy in meetings where substantive work had to be done. Arthur's success in the everyday life of governance rested on his ability to work within small circles of men for often quite technical legislative goals and reforms. It has always been a criticism of Arthur that these worlds were too cosy and filled with personal friends, from Hotel Cecil to all those Souls such as George Wyndham, St John Brodrick and Alfred Lyttelton who ended up in his cabinet. But Arthur was more important in accommodating the experts and outsider authorities of the new Britain than his uncle was, as is revealed in his cooperative relationships – some of them facilitated by the women in his life – with the Chamberlains, the Webbs and the Liberals Asquith and Haldane.[74]

The dominating depiction of 'Arthur Golfour', however, shows his solitary, sticklike figure as a golf club, seated on a remote pinnacle, pondering the tiny globe perched before him. Martha Banta notes a shift in cartoon imagery in the 1890s that this drawing previsions. About 1895, cartoons that placed important politicians in relationships with recognisable social groups or situations started to be replaced by strikingly simpler caricatures that isolated a stylised essence of the individual.[75] This fascination with iconic figures and the face as a public mask, Banta argues, supported a reader's half-intuitive sense of abstract power embodied in façades behind which might lurk 'hypocrisy, fakeness and false consciousness'.[76] It might also reflect the public's need to put a face to increasingly complex institutions of imperial governance over vast and remote regions of the globe. Soon artists were concentrating on the Balfour head – solemn eyes, high wise forehead, unsmiling gaze – captured in so many studio photographs of the era. The change in visual commentary is most apparent in the astounding imagery that Max Beerbohm began to produce in this year, focusing on Arthur's aloofness and disconnection from the gritty phenomena around him.[77]

Fig. 17 Arthur James Balfour as prime minister, 1903

   This was the persona captured in Sargent's portrait of 1908 and drawn again fictionally as late as 1931 in Vita Sackville-West's Lord Slane (*All Passion Spent*): 'he seemed to have touched life on every side, and yet never seemed to have touched life at all, by virtue of his proverbial detachment'. It was never the only persona. Discontented Conservatives, as well as opposition radicals, could be particularly vicious in attacking Arthur's lack of decisive public leadership, willingness to collaborate – or collude – with political adversaries and his fastidious sensibilities.[78] Nevertheless, in the complicated 'history of public fame' in Britain and the United States since the eighteenth century, Arthur was acquiring the charisma of the mysteriously self-contained, resting on a 'posture of reticence' and imperturbability that created a public aura even while disclaiming its importance.[79] By the early 1890s the public image of the imperial statesman was coming into focus. It would be all but set within the next decade (see Fig. 17).

Despite Arthur's hope for a quiet spell of domestic legislation after the tumult of the home rule venture, Salisbury's final years and the cabinet he bequeathed to his nephew were notable for the sheer number of imperial challenges that beset them. If Furniss had remade his Golfour cartoon a decade after the first one, the small images surrounding the pensive statesman might have been quite different. They could have included the 10,000 Sudanese perishing in the 1898 Omdurman assault against a British invading force that lost thirty soldiers in that engagement; villagers on the northwest frontier of India watching as their homes, fields and stores of food were destroyed in punitive raids of the Malakand Field Force; the piled corpses of India's millions of emaciated famine victims; and the tiny coffins of Boer children who died in the concentration camps of the South Africa War. Like the metropolitan cartoonists, Balfour's biographers have been largely silent about these episodes. In seventy pages devoted to the 1895–1900 years, Arthur's niece mentioned none of them. The most recent study of Arthur's life has two paragraphs on the British–French standoff at Fashoda.[80] As leader of the House of Commons, Arthur was not in charge of the relevant departments, and with his uncle's health declining, his time was absorbed by relations with great power rivals and select pieces of domestic and Irish legislation that he chose to shepherd through the Commons.

Arthur always argued that cabinets in London should defer as much as possible to 'men on the spot' who understood local conditions better than distant overseers ever could. Nevertheless, as a leading cabinet member and spokesman for the government, he contributed to all sorts of decisions in these years about societies that he, like cartoonists, knew very little about.[81] He relied on reifying assumptions about motivations and abilities, religions, cultural practices and civilisational propensities outside the European traditions – Edward Said used a Balfour speech to introduce his seminal work, *Orientalism*, on framing 'others' as unalterably alien.[82] Arthur tended to skewer his systematising adversaries in progressive communities for a methodological error like this, but he employed it rhetorically when useful. Writings such as *Foundations of Belief* and 'A Fragment on Progress' give some idea of the mental lenses through which he approached the intensifying problems of imperial capitalism that his political generation was encountering.[83]

Most commonly understood as defences of theism against a scientific-materialist worldview, Arthur's essays are also excursions into the history of humanity. He used science, social sciences, history, even aesthetic promptings to explain his always provisional assessments, carefully asserting the need to consider human feelings and social needs as at the heart of any exploration of where the modern world might be heading. But in writings like these, Arthur expressed a deep pessimism about the developmental prospects of peoples from non-European cultures and in other stages of social organisation. He doubted the likelihood of vastly different peoples being able to coexist amicably, much less understand one another's mental worlds. Couched in the tones of balanced and common-sense speculation that his reasonable fellow countrymen would surely agree to, his tentative conclusions were cautionary and dire, and not only in the 'there will be an ice age again' scale of reckoning that George Wyndham attributed to him. Well before 1914, British statesmen were pondering the deaths of millions through the workings of history, if not deliberate human intent.

Arthur knew full well the problems of selectivity, framing and levels of vision in every individual's construction of the world. In his understandings of statesmanship he gained perspective from the large and synthetic, the abstract and general, and even alluded to the emotional implications that this stance entailed. The 'aesthetic interest' of the long perspective on history, he wrote, is 'massive rather than acute'. 'Particular episodes may indeed raise the most poignant emotions. But, broadly speaking, the long-drawn story of man and his fortunes stirs feelings which … are great in quantity but of low intensity.'[84]

These feelings he could handle. These as much as possible he brought to his personal, social, political and administrative responsibilities. Pragmatic action and tempered response were the preferred way to navigate in Balfour's world. From his earliest years in authority, enthusiasm was the emotion he had most mistrusted; the grounds for hopefulness resided in other worlds, not this one. Arthur's was never a rigid personality, but it could be implacable. In this he did show the will that Margot Tennant had sought, but in a form appropriate to the defensive management of both the self and the traditional structures of power and authority he was in charge of in a dangerously uncertain world.

Epilogue

L ATE IN HIS LIFE, Arthur confided to his niece that while he might 'more or less' like being praised and was 'not very uncomfortable when being abused', he experienced 'moments of uneasiness when I am being explained'.[1] He surely knew he would not escape it. He had resided too long among the tiny elite at the top of Britain's political and administrative power structures to escape attention and, as he might have predicted, professionalisation of the discipline of history ensured interpreters and reinterpreters of his life.

This study has attempted to add to a long conversation about the nature and construction of elites in Balfour's era by exploring the mental and emotional worlds of this imperial actor and some of the people with whom he shared his most private moments. The stories told here inevitably constitute experiments in reconstruction from the fragmentary and disparate sources available for different individuals. Whether, in attempting to study the inner landscapes of subjects, these clues reveal 'true' emotional states and senses of self as opposed to performed ones will always be an open question. As both the historian and the theorist of biography observe, in the end it is 'impossible to differentiate the essence of the self from its manifestations'.[2] Nevertheless, the diaries, letters, shared anecdotes and public expressions of George Pembroke, George Wyndham, Laura and Margot Tennant, Arthur Balfour and Mary Elcho show individuals deep in conversation with themselves, with trusted others and with the world around them. Through the work of many scholars over the past decades, these self-renderings can be at least partially contextualised in terms of the messages, constraints and opportunities

facing the broadening British political elite in the fin de siècle
epoch.

For these subjects, the years of early adulthood show individual
identities powerfully shaped by expectations for gendered selves.
The women studied here, and their friends, faced lives dominated and determined by the 'marriage script'. They were not as
overwhelmed by reproductive biology as their mothers had been,
however, and given their resources they had more opportunities to
move beyond domestic spaces and relationships. The increasingly diverse venues of political action gave them new opportunities
for local influence and even leadership in national organisations
such as the Primrose League or the suffragist movement. They
were able to form sustaining friendships with men who were not
relations and, especially after the turn of the twentieth century,
to publish novels, essays or memoirs in their own names. These
new freedoms were countered by more subtle shaping forces of
sociability. In Balfour's world, unless women chose to be reclusive,
they found they not only could be, but needed to be, attractive,
amusing, funny and extraordinarily aware of the needs and intentions of men. A fairly explicit sexualising of male–female comradeship coexisted with the new opportunities for self-expression and
public activity.

Privileged men faced their own dilemmas of gendered self-con-
struction, even if they were not among those such as Oscar Wilde,
Lord Esher or William Harcourt's son Lewis who were pulled by
same-sex desire. Diffidence like Pembroke's, poetic interests like
Wyndham's, even Arthur's devotion to a 'selfish', individualistic
sport like golf were scrutinised for evidence of unmanly peculiar-
ity. Men in the public eye needed to demonstrate that they were
not only masterful but accessible to new constituencies, audiences
and colleagues. Like aristocratic women, lords and gentry were in
competition with foreigners and rising middle-class families such
as the Tennants who often brought greater resources and different
aptitudes to elite life. Even for aristocrats, secure in family identities and traditions, these challenges were unsettling.

In political and social worlds at these levels, the venues of
performance changed as well as the participants. Campaigning,
platform speaking and party organisation took more of a politician's time, especially if he had national ambitions. J. P. Cornford
observed that in these decades perhaps half of Conservative gentry parliamentarians from the 'withering … main trunk of the

old Tory party' abandoned such ambitions, and their individual decisions to decline long political careers made room for the business and professional men who increasingly filled the Commons benches.[3] Institutions of elite socialisation and sociability – from public schools to hunting fields, from the marriage market of the London season to the country house visit – also adjusted to greater competition and more external scrutiny than had been evident in earlier generations. The challenges of who to invite, how to entertain, where to go and who would be there fill the private writings of both sexes in these years, and it is not surprising that the Souls, as their circle became more ensconced in the public arena, gave the impression of retreating into select company in their personal lives. The friendships stayed intact for so long that twelve of the children born to this group in the 1880s and 1890s later married each other.[4]

Patterns of emotional expression changed as well for this generation. Many of the people in Arthur's circles commented on the stiffness and formal reserve of older relatives in the aristocratic households in which they grew up. Surprisingly often this had combined with passionate outbursts of discontent or despair conveyed within the intimacy of the family and even in front of outsiders when self-censorship collapsed: evidence lies in the explosive rages of Percy Wyndham and DD Balfour's father Archibald, the depressive withdrawals of the mothers of Balfour, Pembroke and the Wyndhams, even suicides by the fathers of Alfred Lyttelton and Tommy Ribblesdale and Hugo Elcho's older brother. These, like infidelities or abandonments, were part of the deep secrets that aristocratic families tried to hold close and eclipse from surviving records. Nevertheless, most families had relatives described as some variant of wilful, imperious, extravagant, passionate, vehement or unheeding, people who in the grip of intense feeling exposed surprising parts of the self to the observation of others.

These characteristics became less tolerable in the emotional regime modelled by Arthur Balfour. Personal expression indeed became more spontaneous, casual and apparently confiding. Contemporaries such as Doll Liddell, Alfred Lyttelton and St John Brodrick all commented on the warmth and sympathies that could now be expressed in society. Thoughts and feelings that their parents' generation would not have deliberately shared were encouraged in group games and private moments. But this was not in the confessional mode of the therapeutic societies produced after the arrival of psychoanalysis in the 1920s.[5] The Edwardian tone was playful and light-hearted but controlled, with a distancing of those destabilising feelings that might result in painful breakdown or self-exposure. Very deep unhappiness, like Mary's over the death of her child or the estrangements of her marriage, were dealt with alone or with the most trusted of friends, something Margot found herself unable to adjust to as the realities of her life became more complicated.

Slightly younger of Arthur's friends such as Evan Charteris and George Wyndham linked the changes to a new awareness of the self and its presentation to others: 'that sort of spontaneity is among the graces and amenities of life – the cold laziness ... belongs to a formal reserve which is out of date now! – people take nothing for granted nowadays, the affections like scientific phenomena must be examined ... But of course if it's not natural you can't compel it or if you do its artificial and not what you want.'[6] The question of what real feelings lurked behind bonhomie preoccupied the 1890s. It was possible to hide behind humour and cordiality as much as behind rules of etiquette and formal reserve.

In the end, perhaps this was easier for aristocrats to adjust to than for newcomers who brought greater expectations of candour and forthrightness to national circles. Lords and eldest sons already knew something about playing roles in public. Assuming they continued to have the resources, they and their kin might adjust the lifestyle of the dandy, roué, sportsman or eccentric to performances rewarded in the emerging entertainment and celebrity culture. For those with aspirations towards public life it was different. They had to embody a face of power that was less flamboyant, more discerning and disinterested, in order to accommodate the many constituencies of democratic politics and imperial governance. Here too they had advantages, however, traditions of keeping secrets and separating external roles from inner life. They would help to form a successor imperial elite of gentlemanly professionals that combined assured composure with intellect and purpose in pursuit of duties beyond the daily concerns of most people.[7] Well into the twentieth century, men of this type would preoccupy the public imagination as custodians of insider knowledge, managers of intelligence and masters of the necessary act, projecting a charismatic control of self that justified the control of others.

Notes

1 Margot published this essay in her post-war memoirs, *An Autobiography*, two volumes (New York, 1920), II, pp. 84–8. Arthur's dictated reply of 2 January 1893 is in the National Archive of Scotland Balfour Papers (subsequently referred to as BPS) GD433/2/69, as well as the Margot Asquith Papers [Bodl.] MSS Eng. c.6670 (subsequently referred to as MAP). Balfour's position has a long tradition in conservative thought about man's ability to control the march of history, see J. C. D. Clark, *Our Shadowed Present: Modernism, Postmodernism, and History* (Stanford, 2004).

2 R. J. Q. Adams, *Balfour: The Last Grandee* (London, 2007).

3 Scholars who have influenced my understanding of these changes include Peter Marsh, *The Discipline of Popular Government: Lord Salisbury's Domestic Statecraft 1881–1902* (Sussex, 1978); T. A. Jenkins, *Parliament, Party, and Politics in Victorian Britain* (Manchester, 1996); Richard Shannon, *The Age of Salisbury 1881–1902: Unionism and Empire* (London, 1996); Brian Harrison, *The Transformation of British Politics, 1860–1995* (Oxford, 1996); E. H. H. Green, *The Crisis of Conservatism: the Politics, Economics and Ideology of the British Conservative Party, 1880–1914* (London, 1996). All studies of the aristocracy in the political world must begin with David Cannadine, *The Decline and Fall of the British Aristocracy* (New Haven, 1990), but see also Gregory D. Phillips, *The Diehards: Aristocratic Society and Politics in Edwardian England* (Cambridge, Massachusetts, 1979) and Andrew Adonis, *Making Aristocracy Work: The Peerage and the Political System in Britain, 1884–1914* (Oxford, 1993).

4 Fictional portraits of Balfour and his world can be found in Rudyard Kipling, 'Below the Mill Dam' (1902); John Buchan, *A Lodge in the Wilderness* (1906); H. G. Wells, *The New Machiavelli* (1911) and *Men Like Gods* (1923); G. B. Shaw, *Heartbreak House* (1919); Vita Sackville-West, *All Passion Spent* (1931).

5 For an assessment of the era's European and global transformations, see Eric Hobsbawm, *The Age of Empire, 1875–1914* (New York, 1987).

6 See the seminal work of Samuel Hynes, *The Edwardian Turn of Mind*

(Princeton, 1968) and Aaron Friedberg, *The Weary Titan: Britain and the Experience of Relative Decline, 1895–1905* (Princeton, 1988). Elaine Showalter contextualised the various manifestations of gender anxiety in *Sexual Anarchy: Gender and Culture at the Fin de Siècle* (New York, 1990), while Ryan Anthony Vieira insightfully places perceptions of change within the historiography of modernity in 'Connecting the New Political History with Recent Theories of Temporal Acceleration: Speed, Politics, and the Cultural Imagination of *Fin-de-Siècle* Britain', *History & Theory* 50 (October 2011): 373–89.

7 This study identifies aristocrats by the definition used in T. H. Hollingsworth's foundational study 'The Demography of the British Peerage', supplement to *Population Studies* 18 (London, 1965): 33, that is, being the spouse, child or the grandchild of a hereditary title holder. Balfour's maternal grandfather, for example, was the Marquess of Salisbury. The Wyndhams' was Lord Leconfield.

8 The estimate of Mike Davis, *Late Victorian Holocausts: El Nino Famines and the Making of the Third World* (New York, 2001), p. 7.

9 William C. Lubenow, *Liberal Intellectuals and Public Culture in Modern Britain: Making Words Flesh* (Woodbridge, 2010). For the impact of late-century change on ideas about international relations see Duncan Bell, *The Idea of Greater Britain: Empire and the Future of World Order, 1860–1900* (Princeton, 2007) and *Victorian Visions of World Order: Empire and International Relations in Nineteenth-Century Political Thought,* ed. Duncan Bell (Cambridge: 2007).

10 Joel Pfister and Nancy Schnog, eds, *Inventing the Psychological: Toward a Cultural History of Emotional Life in America* (New Haven, 1997).

11 For Balfour's range see Arthur James Balfour, *Essays and Addresses* (London, 1893) and *The Mind of Arthur James Balfour, Selections from his Non-Political Writings, Speeches and Addresses, 1879–1917,* ed. Wilfrid M. Short (London, 1918).

12 Arthur James Balfour, 'Bishop Berkeley's *Life and Letters*', *National Review* I (March 1883): 85–100, (April 1883): 299–313.

13 Viscount Chandos, *From Peace to War: A Study in Contrast 1857–1918* (London, 1968), p. 29.

14 For a discussion of Gladstone's pioneering efforts in this regard after 1870 see Ruth Clayton Windscheffel, 'Politics, Portraiture and Power: Reassessing the Public Image of William Ewart Gladstone', *Public Men: Masculinities and Politics in Modern Britain,* ed. Matthew McCormack (New York, 2007), pp. 93–122.

15 Roland Quinault, 'Golf and Edwardian Politics', *Landed Society in Britain, 1700–1914,* ed. N. Harte and R. Quinault (Manchester, 1996), pp. 191–210.

16 Critics of Balfour have attributed his success to nepotism, intelligence, disloyalty and ruthlessness. Admirers stress wide-ranging intelligence, hard work and public spiritedness. Judith Hughes, *Emotion and High Politics: Personal Relations at the Summit in Late Nineteenth-Century Britain and Germany* (Berkeley, 1983) was one of the first biographers to argue that the personal characteristics of men like Salisbury, Gladstone and

Balfour are revealing of the larger political culture, but she confined her analysis to their methods of dealing with small groups of insiders such as cabinet colleagues and office subordinates, see pp. 77–112, 198–209.

17 The foundational work is Leonore Davidoff, *The Best Circles: Society, Etiquette and the Season* (New Jersey, 1973). Also K. D. Reynolds, *Aristocratic Women and Political Society in Victorian Britain* (Oxford, 1998); Susan K. Harris, *The Cultural Work of the Late Nineteenth-Century Hostess* (New York, 2002).

18 Norman and Jeanne MacKenzie, eds, *The Diary of Beatrice Webb*, two volumes (Cambridge, Massachusetts, 1982), I, p. 204.

19 Alexander Star, review of *American Nietzsche* by Jennifer Ratner-Rosenhagen, *The New York Times Book Review*, 15 January 2012.

20 William R. Reddy, *The Navigation of Feeling: A Framework for the History of Emotions* (Cambridge, 2001).

21 Among many works by Erving Goffman see *Encounters: Two Studies in the Sociology of Interaction* (Indianapolis, 1961), especially the chapter 'Fun in Games'.

22 See, for example, G. J. Barker-Benfield, *The Culture of Sensibility: Sex and Society in Eighteenth-Century Britain* (Chicago, 1996); Dror Wahrman, *The Making of the Modern Self: Identity and Culture in Eighteenth-Century England* (New Haven, 2004); Richard Sennett, *The Fall of Public Man: On the Social Psychology of Capitalism* (New York, 1978); Christopher Lasch, *The Culture of Narcissism: American Life in an Age of Diminishing Expectations* (New York, 1978).

23 Daniel Bivona, *British Imperial Literature, 1870–1940: Writing and the Administration of Empire* (Cambridge, 1998), pp. 22–3. Bivona builds from Hannah Arendt, *The Origins of Totalitarianism* (New York, 1951) for his study of the construction of the bureaucratic personality in the late-Victorian empire.

24 Lionel Trilling, *Sincerity and Authenticity* (Cambridge, Massachusetts, 1972). Gesa Stedman studies mid-Victorian discourses about emotionality in *Stemming the Torrent: Expression and Control in the Victorian Discourse on Emotions 1830–1872* (Aldershot, 2002), while Stefan Collini's *Public Moralists: Political Thought and Intellectual Life in Britain, 1850–1930* (Oxford, 1991) shows how the understanding of character was changing by the late nineteenth century.

25 Peter Stansky, *On or About December 1910: Early Bloomsbury and its Intimate World* (Cambridge, Massachusetts, 1996), pp. 2–3.

26 It is not, for example, the kind of subject-by-subject window on the world through one man's perspective that Michael Bentley provides in *Lord Salisbury's World: Conservative Environments in Late Victorian Britain* (Cambridge, 2007).

27 Eugene Rasor, *Arthur James Balfour, 1848–1930: Historiography and Annotated Bibliography* (Connecticut, 1998).

28 *The Letters of Arthur Balfour and Lady Elcho, 1885–1917*, ed. Jane Ridley and Clayre Percy (London, 1992); Nicola Beauman, *Cynthia Asquith* (London, 1987); Cynthia Asquith, *Haply I May Remember* (London,

1950) and *Remember and Be Glad* (London, 1952); Claudia Renton, *Those Wild Wyndhams: Three Sisters at the Heart of Power* (London, 2014).

29 J. W. Mackail and Guy Wyndham, *The Life and Letters of George Wyndham*, two volumes (London, 1925); Max Egremont, *The Cousins* (London, 1977); Nancy W. Ellenberger, 'Constructing George Wyndham: Narratives of Aristocratic Masculinity in Fin-de-Siècle England', *Journal of British Studies* 39 (October 2000): 487–517.

30 Most cited here are Margot Asquith's *Autobiography*; Margot Oxford, *More Memories* [published in New York as *More or Less About Myself*, 1934] and *Octavia* (London, 1928).

31 A particularly good example of this form, focusing on men in the Iran-Contra affair of the 1980s, is Robert Timberg, *The Nightingale's Song* (New York, 1995). Others include Louis Menand, *The Metaphysical Club* (New York, 2001) and Patricia O'Toole, *Five of Hearts: An Intimate Portrait of Henry Adams and his Friends, 1880–1914* (New York, 2006).

32 Susan Pederson, 'What is Political History Now?' in *What is History Now?*, ed. David Cannadine (London, 2002), p. 46.

33 Lubenow, *Liberal Intellectuals and Public Culture*, pp. 1–7; Geoffrey Searle, *The Quest for National Efficiency* (Berkeley, 1971); John Tosh, *Manliness and Masculinities in Nineteenth-Century Britain* (Harlow, 2005), pp. 192–214.

34 Stephen Arata, *Fictions of Loss in the Victorian Fin de Siècle* (Cambridge, 1996), pp. 1–7. Arata analyses the role that fiction writers – some of them friends of Balfour, most of them read by him – played in shaping these cultural tendencies of the 1890s around tropes of bodily and national degeneration.

CHAPTER ONE

1 *Times*, 3 July 1871; *ILN*, 15 July 1871; Edith Olivier, *Without Knowing Mr. Walkley* (London, 1938), pp. 149–58. There is no biography of Pembroke, though his youthful exploits gained him an entry in the original *Dictionary of National Biography*.

2 Lord Ronald Gower, *My Reminiscences*, two volumes (London, 1883), I, p. 251.

3 David Cannadine, *The Decline and Fall of the British Aristocracy* (New Haven, 1990), pp. 710–11.

4 R. J. Q. Adams, *Balfour, The Last Grandee* (London, 2007), p. 22; Arthur James Balfour, *Chapters of Autobiography* (London, 1930), pp. 68, 89. The most thorough accounts of Balfour's life before Adams's recent work were by his niece, Blanche Dugdale, *Arthur James Balfour*, two volumes (London, 1936); Kenneth Young, *Arthur James Balfour* (London, 1963); Max Egremont, *Balfour* (London, 1980). For a review of the interpretations see Adams, pp. 461–2, as well as Eugene Rasor, *Arthur James Balfour 1848–1903: Historiography and Annotated Bibliography* (Connecticut, 1998).

5 Linda Colley, *Britons: Forging the Nation, 1707–1837* (New Haven, 2005), ch. 4.

6 K. Theodore Hoppen, *The Mid-Victorian Generation, 1846–1886* (New Haven, 1998), p. 34; John Bateman, *The Great Landowners of Great Britain and Ireland*, ed. David Spring (New York, 1971), pp. 23, 355.

7 David Spring, 'Aristocracy, Social Structure, and Religion in the Early Victorian Period', *Victorian Studies* 6 (1963): 263–80.

8 Sheila Gooddie, *Mary Gladstone, a Gentle Rebel* (Chichester, 2003), pp. 76–82.

9 For shift in models of manliness from the earnest, self-restrained Christian to the vigorous dominator of self and others see Jeff Hearn, *Men in the Public Eye: The Construction and Deconstruction of Public Men and Public Patriarchies* (London, 1992), pp. 100–28; George L. Mosse, *The Image of Man: The Creation of Modern Masculinity* (New York, 1996), ch. 5; Peter N. Stearns, *Be a Man! Males in Modern Society* (New York, 1990), pp. 132–52; Michael Roper and John Tosh, eds, *Manful Assertions: Masculinities in Britain since 1800* (New York, 1991), ch. 1.

10 Gregory D. Phillips, *The Diehards: Aristocratic Society and Politics in Edwardian England* (Cambridge, Massachusetts, 1979), p. 18.

11 Percentage calculated from the birth and succession dates of landowners in Bateman, *The Great Landowners of Great Britain and Ireland*. Andrew Adonis notes that another 15 per cent of peers inherited their titles by the age of thirty, *Making Aristocracy Work: The Peerage and the Political System in Britain, 1884–1914* (Oxford, 1993), p. 204.

12 The following assessment of Lady Blanche Balfour comes from the Rev. Dr James Robertson, *Lady Blanche Balfour* (London, 1897); Janet Oppenheim, 'A Mother's Role, a Daughter's Duty: Lady Blanche Balfour, Eleanor Sidgwick, and Feminist Perspectives', *Journal of British Studies* 34 (April 1995): 196–232; reminiscences of their mother by Balfour's sisters in BPS GD/433/2/145.

13 Lady Blanche Balfour to Emily Faithfull, BPS GD433/2/149–151.

14 David Hudson, *The Ireland that We Made* (Ohio, 2003), p. 54. Adams writes of Balfour's 'happy childhood' and 'remarkably painless education', *Balfour*, p. 23.

15 Young was the first to give this picture of the Balfour offspring, based on information provided by the next generation of the family, *Arthur James Balfour*, p. 11

16 Balfour, *Chapters of Autobiography*, p. 7.

17 For the religious context of Catholicism among the mid-century upper classes see Stewart J. Brown, *Providence and Empire: Religion, Politics and Society in the United Kingdom, 1815–1914* (New York, 2008), pp. 267–73; Michael Wheeler, *The Old Enemies: Catholics and Protestants in 19th Century England* (Cambridge, 2006), ch. 1.

18 Elizabeth Herbert is Lady St Jerome in Disraeli's *Lothair*, as well as Lady Chiselhurst in W. H. Mallock's *The Old Order Changes* (1885), see M. C. Rintoul, *Dictionary of Real People and Places in Fiction* (London 2014), p. 504. Elizabeth Herbert's own account of her conversion is in M. E. Herbert, *How I Came Home* (London, 1894).

19 Augustus Hare, *The Story of My Life*, six volumes (London, 1900), IV, pp. 51–5; Roger Fulford, ed., *Dearest Child: Letters between Queen Victoria and the Princess Royal* (London, 1976), p. 111.

20 *Times*, 24 January, 11 March 1863; William Gladstone to Lady Herbert of Lea, 9 April 1865 and Lady Herbert to Gladstone, 2 April 1865, 3 July 1868, Gladstone Papers BL44212; Gladstone to GP, 25 May 1873, Gladstone Papers BL44438. See also Lady Herbert to Gladstone, 24 May 1873, urging him to believe that she had not known of her daughter's plan to convert, Gladstone Papers BL44212.

21 Mary Elizabeth Herbert, *Anglican Prejudices against the Catholic Church* (London, 1866). Mallock describes Catholic society in London in the 1880s in *Memoirs of Life and Literature* (London, 1920), 130ff.

22 Gower, *Reminiscences*, I, p. 279; *Mary Gladstone: Her Diaries and Letters*, ed. Lucy Masterman (London, 1930), p. 25; *Times*, 30 November 1867.

23 Edith Lyttelton, *Alfred Lyttelton* (London, 1917), p. 13.

24 Regenia Gagnier, *Subjectivities: A History of Self-Representation in Britain, 1832–1920* (Oxford, 1991), ch. 4.

25 Balfour, *Chapters of Autobiography*, p. 4; Judith Hughes, *Emotion and High Politics: Personal Relations at the Summit in Late Nineteenth-Century Britain and Germany* (Berkeley, 1983), pp. 101–3.

26 GP journal, 25 June 1868, GPP.

27 GP journal, 16, 18 March 1870, GPP.

28 GP to Mary Gladstone, 20 December 1870, MGP BL46251. For long-standing imagery of the easy, unforced self-assurance of men in George's position see Phillips, *The Diehards*, p. 13.

29 James Brinsely-Richards, *Seven Years at Eton* (London, 1883), p. 52; A. G. C. Liddell, *Notes from the Life of an Ordinary Mortal* (London, 1911), ch. 3.

30 See Leo McKinstry, *Rosebery: Statesman in Turmoil* (London, 2005), pp. 24–7.

31 Eleanor Sidgwick and Arthur Sidgwick, eds, *Henry Sidgwick, a Memoir* (London, 1906), p. 311.

32 Bart Schultz, *Henry Sidgwick, Eye of the Universe* (Cambridge, 2004), ch. 2; James C. Livingston, *Religious Thought in the Victorian Age* (New York, 2006), pp. 13–20.

33 Sheldon Rothblatt, *The Revolution of the Dons: Cambridge and Society in Victorian England* (Cambridge, 1981); Reba Soffer, *Ethics and Society in England: The Revolution in the Social Sciences 1870–1914* (Berkeley, 1978).

34 Seven of those eventually examined in autumn 1869 received first-class honours. Balfour was at the top of the list of three second-class recipients, *Times*, 10 December 1869.

35 Dugdale, *Arthur James Balfour*, I, p. 28.

36 William C. Lubenow, *The Cambridge Apostles, 1830–1914* (Cambridge, 1998), p. 56.

37 D. A. Winstanley, *Later Victorian Cambridge* (Cambridge, 1947), pp. 185–90.

38 The selectees were Frank Anderson, Trinity, classical tripos; George Blakesley, King's College, classical tripos and mathematical tripos;

Charles Colbeck, Trinity, classical tripos; John Moulton, St John's, mathematical tripos; Marlborough Pryor, Trinity, mathematical tripos: see Lubenow, *Cambridge Apostles*, pp. 414–32. The first Apostle who read in Moral Sciences was the brilliant legal historian Frederic Maitland, elected four years after Balfour left the university.

39 For the anxieties and debates occasioned by the rising importance of competitive examinations see Sheldon Rothblatt, *The Modern University and its Discontents* (Cambridge, 1997); for Oxbridge becoming the preserve of the rising middle-classes, William C. Lubenow, *Liberal Intellectuals and Public Culture in Modern Britain* (Woodbridge, 2010).

40 Schultz, *Henry Sidgwick*, p. 38.

41 Schultz, *Henry Sidgwick*, p. 415; on Symonds, Stephen Arata, *Fictions of Loss in the Victorian Fin de Siècle: Identity and Empire* (Cambridge, 1996), pp. 80–4.

42 The phrase is used by McKinstry in *Rosebery*, p. 25, when he discusses Rosebery's possible relations with William Johnson at Eton. On this transformation in conceptions of male friendship see Linda Dowling, *Hellenism and Homosexuality in Victorian Oxford* (New York, 1994).

43 Paul Deslandes, *Oxbridge Men: British Masculinity and the Undergraduate Experience, 1850–1914* (Bloomington, 2005), p. 72.

44 Two-thirds of those who did attended either Christ Church or Balliol at Oxford or Trinity at Cambridge: Adonis, *Making Aristocracy Work*, p. 208.

45 James A. Secord, *Victorian Sensation: The Extraordinary Publication, Reception, and Secret Authorship of 'Vestiges of the Natural History of Creation'* (Chicago, 2000).

46 *Mary Gladstone: Her Diaries and Letters*, p. 26.

47 Dane Kennedy, *The Highly Civilized Man: Richard Burton and the Victorian World* (Cambridge, Massachusetts, 2005), ch. 7.

48 G. H. Kingsley, *Notes on Sport and Travel, with a memoir by Mary H Kingsley* (London, 1900). Katherine Frank, Mary Kingsley's biographer, finds it 'unlikely that George Kingsley put up much resistance to the obvious appeal and advances of these South Seas beauties', *A Voyager Out: The Life of Mary Kingsley* (Boston, 1986) p. 26. Pembroke said otherwise, see his letter to Edward Hamilton, 30 August 1870, Hamilton Papers BL48620.

49 I. C. Campbell, *A History of the Pacific Islands* (Berkeley, 1989), chs 3–6; also Doug Munro and Brij V. Lall, *Texts and Contexts: Reflections in Pacific Islands Historiography* (Honolulu, 2006).

50 GP journal, 26 June 1868, GPP. Charles Mitchell was a young servant/companion for Pembroke from the Wilton estate. He stayed in personal service to the family for the rest of George's life.

51 Jane Samson, *Imperial Benevolence: Making British Authority in the Pacific Islands* (Honolulu, 1998) has a compelling account of Royal Navy humanitarian activity in the South Pacific.

52 [Earl of Pembroke and George Kingsley], *South Sea Bubbles by the Earl and the Doctor* (New York, 1872), p. 100.

53 *South Sea Bubbles*, p. 12.

54 GP to Edward Hamilton, 30 August 1870, Hamilton Papers BL48620.

55 Samson, *Imperial Benevolence*, pp. 25–7; *South Sea Bubbles*, p. 118.

56 *South Sea Bubbles*, p. 130.

57 *South Sea Bubbles*, p. 225.

58 *South Sea Bubbles*, p. 227. The party learned later that their fears were 'needlessly great'. Their information was based on the travel book they had been using throughout the trip.

59 *South Sea Bubbles*, p. 61.

60 Nancy Armstrong, *Desire and Domestic Fiction: a Political History of the Novel* (New York, 1987), p. 258.

61 *South Sea Bubbles*, p. 256.

62 Beth Newman, *Subjects on Display: Psychoanalysis, Social Expectation and Victorian Femininity* (Ohio, 2004), p. 107.

63 *South Sea Bubbles*, pp. 245–6.

64 Leonore Davidoff, *The Best Circles: Society, Etiquette and the Season* (New Jersey, 1973).

65 Edward Henry Stanley, Earl of Derby, *The Diaries of Edward Henry Stanley, 15th Earl of Derby (1826–1893), between September 1869 and March 1878*, ed. John Vincent, Camden 5th series, volume 4 (London, 1994), p. 107.

66 Betty Askwith, *The Lytteltons: A Family Chronicle of the 19th Century* (London, 1975); Sheila Fletcher, *Victorian Girls, Lord Lyttelton's Daughters* (London, 1997).

67 *Mary Gladstone: Her Diaries and Letters*, pp. 59, 65, 62.

68 Mary Gladstone, memoir of Arthur Balfour, MGP BL46270.

69 Michael Steinberg, *Listening to Reason: Culture, Subjectivity, and Nineteenth Century Music* (Princeton, 2004).

70 For a recent account see Sheila Gooddie, *Mary Gladstone, A Gentle Rebel* (New Jersey, 2003), pp. 79–85.

71 Liddell, *Notes from the Life*, p. 79.

72 Daisy White diary, 29 June 1889, Nevins Papers, Butler Library, Columbia University.

73 Armstrong, *Desire and Domestic Fiction*, p. 190.

74 Askwith, *The Lytteltons*, ch. 13; Fletcher, *Victorian Girls*, ch. 10.

75 Adams has resisted this standard view of the importance of the May Lyttelton episode in Balfour's life. In his interpretation Arthur used the excuse of a lasting grief to protect himself from the emotional demands of other women, *Balfour*, pp. 29–33.

76 Gooddie, *Mary Gladstone*, p. 86.

77 Gooddie, *Mary Gladstone*, p. 92.

78 Mike Davis, *Late-Victorian Holocausts: El Nino Famines and the Making of the Third World* (London, 2001), ch. 1; Paul R. Brumpton, *Security and Progress: Lord Salisbury at the India Office* (Connecticut, 2002), ch. 3.

79 Arthur James Balfour, *A Defence of Philosophic Doubt: Being an Essay on the Foundations of Belief* (London, 1879), p. 245.

80 James C. Livingston, *Religious Thought in the Victorian Age: Challenges and Reconceptions* (New York, 2006), p. 18.

81 *Defence of Philosophic Doubt*, p. 55.

82 *Defence of Philosophic Doubt*, pp. 72, 77.

83 Sidney Herbert had been a caustic opponent of Disraeli after the break

up of the Tory party in the late 1840s, as well as a lifelong friend of Gladstone, so securing Pembroke for the Conservative cause was significant. Disraeli invited the young earl to Hughenden with the Bradfords and Wharncliffes, see George Buckle and W. F. Moneypenny, *The Life of Benjamin Disraeli*, five volumes (London, 1920), V, pp. 296, 312.

84 GP to Carnarvon, 2 March 1874, Carnarvon Papers BL60774.

85 Gathorne Gathorne-Hardy, *The Diary of Gathorne Hardy, later Lord Cranbrook, 1866–1892: Political Selections*, ed. Nancy E. Johnson (Oxford, 1981), p. 237. Gathorne-Hardy, war secretary in the Commons, noted earlier that 'Pembroke was not effective in reply and had no support whatever' after one episode in the Lords, but thought 'he will do well if he tries', pp. 217, 221.

86 GP to Edward Hamilton, 21 May, 28 May, early August 1874, Hamilton Papers BL 48620.

87 For the tendency to give anecdotes about Gertrude Pembroke more than her husband, see Kenneth Rose, *Superior Person: A Portrait of Curzon and his Circle in Late Victorian England* (New York, 1969), pp. 183–5.

88 *Morning Post*, 20 August 1874.

89 He was also there in June 1883, with a party that included Hugo Elcho, Edward Hamilton, *The Diary of Sir Edward Walter Hamilton, 1880–1885*, two volumes, ed. Dudley W. R. Bahlman (Oxford, 1972), II, p. 449.

90 See Dror Wahrman, *The Making of the Modern Self* (New Haven, 2004), pp. 286–7.

91 GP to Mary Gladstone, 12 September1881, MGP BL46251.

92 Sophia Andres, *The Pre-Raphaelite Art of the Victorian Novel: Narrative Challenges to Visual Gendered Boundaries* (Ohio, 2005), ch. 4, on 'George Eliot's Pre-Raphaelite Gendered Imperialism'. Arthur made a special trip to London to buy the picture before Sir William Agnew could purchase it, Frances Balfour to Alice Balfour, 12 April 1883, BPS GD433/2/296.

CHAPTER TWO

1 Percy Wyndham to Mary Wyndham, 15 March 1882, Mary Wyndham diary, 9 March and after, 1882, MEP; Caroline Dakers, *Clouds, The Biography of a Country House* (New Haven, 1993), p. 23.

2 For an overview of divorce laws, and their punitive effects for women before the twentieth century, see Lawrence Stone, *Road to Divorce: England, 1530–1987* (Oxford, 1995).

3 LT to ME, 18 March 1885, MEP; Jane Hunter, *How Young Ladies Became Girls: The Victorian Origins of American Girlhood* (New Haven, 2002), ch. 1.

4 LT diary, 19 November 1879, MAP d.3311/f173–75. Laura's diaries ended up in her sister Margot's papers in the Bodleian.

5 LT to ME, [December 1884], MEP; Claudia Renton, *Those Wild Wyndhams: Three Sisters at the Heart of Power* (London, 2014), p. 37.

6 Nancy Crathorne, *Tennant's Stalk: The Story of the Tennants of the Glen* (London, 1973); Simon Blow, *Broken Blood: The Rise and Fall of the Tennant Family* (London, 1987).

7 See the Tennants' childhoods in Margot's various memoirs, but also the greater detail in an essay from 1889: MAP d.3293.

8 See Hunter, *How Young Ladies Became Girls*, ch. 2; Leonore Davidoff, *Thicker than Water: Siblings and Their Relations, 1780–1920* (Oxford, 2012).

9 MT diary, 18 March 1879, MAP d.3198.

10 MT diary, 30 December 1876, MAP e.3256.

11 MT diary, 23 March 1879, MAP d.3198; Rosebery to Charles Tennant, [April 1886], MAP d.3313.

12 Mary Gladstone, 'Laura Lyttelton', MGP BL46270; LT diary, 1 January 1883, MAP d.3312/f5–8.

13 LT to Doll Liddell, 22 October 1884, MAP d.3309.

14 LT diary, 26 March 1880, MAP d.3311/f392.

15 MT diary, 10 August 1883, MAP d.3198; LT diary, 8 December 1883, MAP d.3312/f63.

16 LT diary, 27 March 1883, 29 October 1884, MAP d.3312/f37–39.

17 Hunter, *How Young Ladies Became Girls*, ch. 2.

18 LT diary, 27 October 1880, MAP d.3311; J. L. Altholz, 'The Warfare of Conscience with Theology' in *Religion in Victorian Britain: Volume IV Interpretations*, ed. Gerald Parsons (Manchester, 1988).

19 LT diary, 12 February, 20 July 1882, MAP d.3312; Mary Gladstone, 'Laura Lyttelton', MGP BL46270/37, 22; Margot Asquith, *An Autobiography*, two volumes (New York, 1920), I, pp. 59–63.

20 Deborah Gorham, *The Victorian Girl and the Feminine Ideal* (Bloomington, 1982), p. 113.

21 Mary Scott Morison to LT, 13 February, 11 March 1880, MAP d.3313.

22 Patricia Jalland, *Women, Marriage, and Politics 1860–1914* (Oxford, 1986), pp. 272–89.

23 LT diary, 1 April 1884, MAP d.3312. For Frances and Burne-Jones: Penelope Fitzgerald, *Edward Burne-Jones* (London, 1975); Judith Flanders, *A Circle of Sisters: Alice Kipling, Georgiana Burne-Jones, Agnes Poynter, and Louisa Baldwin* (New York, 2005), pp. 137–8; Fiona MacCarthy, *The Last Pre-Raphaelite: Edward Burne-Jones and the Victorian Imagination* (Cambridge, Massachusetts, 2012), pp. 276–8; Stephen Wildman and John Christian, *Edward Burne-Jones: Victorian Artist-Dreamer* (New York, 1998), pp. 244–5.

24 Frances Horner, *Time Remembered* (London, 1933), pp. 62, 185; Frances Horner to Violet Cecil, 29 September 1900, Viscountess Milner Papers, [Bodl.] MS. Eng. VM42/C368. Frances implied in her memoir that she was born in 1858, but evidence suggests that it was several years earlier. Frances was presented at court in 1871, which is too early if she was born in 1858, and she noted once that grief entered her life when she was eighteen, which would correspond with the 1872 death of her brother Rutherford, Arthur Balfour's rival for the hand of May Lyttelton.

25 LT diary, 1 April 1884, 12 February 1882, MAP d.3312.

26 Emma Tennant to LT, [September 1877], MAP d.3313.

27 LT diary, 13 February 1882, 20 March 1881, MAP d.3311.

28 Sharon Marcus, *Between Women: Friendship, Desire, and Marriage in Victorian England* (Princeton, 2007), pp. 64–72.

29 Catherine Robson, *Men in Wonderland: The Lost Girlhood of the Victorian Gentleman* (Princeton, 2001), p. 4; LT diary, Christmas night 1884, MAP d.3312; Flanders, *Circle of Sisters*, p. 181.

30 LT diary, 1 April 1884, MAP d.3312.

31 Blunt diary, 13 Feb. 1901, Wilfrid Blunt Papers, 369–1975; 'Percy Wyndham', *Times*, 14 March 1911. For the Wyndhams' country house milieu and patronage of the arts see Dakers, *Clouds,* passim. Renton's new account of Mary's girlhood is in *Those Wild Wyndhams*, chs 3–4.

32 Jessica Gerard documents the closeness of many country house families in the Victorian age, *Country House Life: Family and Servants, 1815–1914* (Oxford, 1994), ch. 3.

33 Mary Wemyss, *A Family Record* (privately printed, 1932), ch. 2; J. W. Mackail in *Life and Letters of George Wyndham*, two volumes (London, 1925), I, p. 32; Edith Olivier, *Four Victorian Ladies of Wiltshire* (London, 1945), pp. 85–101; Cynthia Asquith, *Haply I May Remember* (London, 1950), pp. 40–2.

34 ME diary, 7 August, 17 September 1880, reminiscences in 'Souls' file, MEP; Wemyss, *Family Record*, p. 18.

35 ME diary, December 1881, ME to Madeline Wyndham, 7 December 1880, MEP.

36 Percy Wyndham to ME, 10 October 1880, 28 March 1882, MEP.

37 'Society in the Eighties', 'The Souls' file, MEP.

38 ME diary, 3 September 1882, MEP.

39 ME diary, 8 Dec. 1880, MEP.

40 Edward Hamilton, *The Diary of Sir Edward White Hamilton, 1880–1885,* two volumes, ed. Dudley W. R. Bahlman (Oxford, 1972), I, pp. 90–2; ME diary, 23 August 1881, MEP.

41 ME diary, 25 May 1882, MEP.

42 ME diary, 20 April 1881, MEP.

43 ME diary, 1 July 1883, MEP.

44 ME to Madeline Wyndham, 3 October 1883, MEP.

45 ME diary, 1 January 1883, MEP.

46 ME diary, 6 September,1882, MEP.

47 Max Egremont, *Balfour* (London, 1980), p. 68; 'The Souls' file, MEP.

48 LT diary, 8 May 1883, MAP d.3312.

49 *ILN*, 22 September 1883; *Punch*, 22 September 1883. *Graphic*, 29 September 1883, has a drawing of lunch for the royalties on board the vessel. There is a long account of the voyage in Sir Algernon West, *Recollections 1832–1886* (London, 1900), pp. 330–40; Mary Gladstone published some of Laura's record in Mary Gladstone Drew, *Acton, Gladstone and Others* (New York, reprint edn. 1968), ch. 5.

50 LT diary, 9 November 1883, 20 March 1884, MAP d.3312; MT diary, 10 August 1884, MAP d.3198.

51 Drew, *Acton, Gladstone and Others*, p. 120; MT diary, 4 March 1877, MAP e.3257. Frances Balfour's first impression of Laura was also that she

'lacked refinement' in her comportment, Frances to AB, 23 November [1884], BPS GD433/2/164/7.

52 West, *Recollections*, p. 331; Richard A. Kaye, *The Flirt's Tragedy: Desire without End in Victorian and Edwardian Fiction* (Charlottesville, 2002), p. 154.

53 Lisle March-Phillipps and Bertram Christian, eds, *Some Hawarden Letters 1878–1913 written to Mrs. Drew* (London, 1917), p. 183.

54 Drew, *Acton, Gladstone and Others*, p. 122. Curzon on a visit he and Laura paid to the Tennysons after this voyage wrote: 'That brilliant child acted to us one thing after another of Sarah Bernhardt, with perfect imitation of style and gesture and, above all, voice', Kenneth Rose, *Superior Person: A Portrait of Curzon and His Circle in Late Victorian England* (New York, 1969), p. 165.

55 LT diary, 28 October 1883, MAP d.3312.

56 Margot Oxford, *More or Less About Myself* (New York, 1934), p. 275.

57 Drew, *Acton, Gladstone and Others*, p. 121.

58 MT diary, 28 October 1883, MAP d.3198. Lady Jebb agreed that Laura was 'too adaptable ... For the moment she thought in sympathy with her company whoever the company might be', M. R. Bobbitt, *With Dearest Love to All: the Life and Letters of Lady Jebb* (London, 1960), p. 222.

59 A. G. C. Liddell, *Notes from the Life of an Ordinary Mortal* (London, 1911), p. 226; LT to Doll Liddell, 23 December 1884, CP 6/1.

60 LT diary, 28 October 1883, MAP d.3312.

61 Attachment in Percy's hand to a letter to Mary Elcho, 12 August 1883, MEP.

62 Press cuttings file on Hugo in 1882, MEP.

63 ME to Hugo, 3 August 1881, 21 February 1882, Percy Wyndham to ME, [autumn 1881], MEP.

64 ME diary, 11 January 1881, MEP.

65 Percy Wyndham to ME, [fall 1881], MEP.

66 Anne Wemyss to Hugo, 5 August 1881, MEP. Also many early 1880s letters from Lady Wemyss to Hugo's sister Evelyn de Vesci in HPP DD/DRU/82.

67 Percy Wyndham to ME, 17 May 1881, MEP.

68 LAB, p. 218; Egremont, *Balfour*, p. 68.

69 Gerald Balfour to Frances Balfour, 5 October, 14 December, 22 December 1883, BPS GD433/2/296. Maysie Baring was mentioned in Mary's diary account of the Wilton party of December 1880. She was probably Mabel Baring, born a year before Mary and a daughter of Lt Gen. Charles Baring who served in the Coldstream Guards with Percy Wyndham during the Crimean War.

70 *Times*, 10 August 1883; Percy Wyndham to ME, 9 August 1883, MEP.

71 ME diary, 9 August 1883, MEP.

72 Maude Wyndham to Ettie Desborough, 3 March 1944, Desborough Papers; Blunt Papers, 34–1975/17; Anne Wemyss to Evelyn de Vesci, undated fragment from late 1880s, 16 August 1889, 28 May 1890, HPP DD/DRU/82.

73 ME to Madeline Wyndham, [1885], MEP.

74 Evan Charteris to Ettie Desboroush, 1898, Desborough Papers; Mary

Elcho fragments in 'The Souls' file, MEP; Dakers, *Clouds*, p. 11. On Hugo see Asquith, *Haply I May Remember*, p. 42.

75 ME to Guy Wyndham, [late August 1883], MEP.

76 Percy Wyndham to ME, 18 November 1884, MEP.

77 Viscount Chandos, *From Peace to War: A Study in Contrast 1857–1918* (London, 1968), pp. 58–9.

78 Laura's complicated love life in 1884 was described by Alfred's son Oliver Lyttelton, Viscount Chandos, in *From Peace to War*. His information was based on an unpublished account left by DD Balfour Lyttelton in the Chandos Papers at Churchill College, 'Interwoven', CP 6/1. Pat Jalland used Laura as one of her case studies in *Women, Marriage and Politics*, pp. 102–9. None of these accounts used Laura's diary.

79 LT diary, 12 January 1885, MAP d.3312.

80 Laura's letters to Doll Liddell are in three locations. Lucy Graham Smith transcribed some into a bound copybook in MAP d.3309. DD Balfour copied some into 'Interwoven', CP 6/1, and others are in CP II 2/2. Material here is from Laura to Doll, 2 January 1885, CP 6/1 and 26 January 1886, CP II 2/2.

81 LT diary, 28 October 1884, MAP d.3312. Liddell's diary shows her telling him this in nearly the same words probably during the meeting at Mells in late November, CP 6/1:4.

82 LT to Doll Liddell, 8 and 24 September 1884, MAP d.3309.

83 Liddell, *Notes from the Life*, p. 225; 'Interwoven', CP 6/1.

84 LT diary, 28 October and 24 December 1884, MAP d.3312.

85 A good many letters relating to this relationship can be found in BPS GD433/2/297–98 and GD433/2/164–65.

86 LT to Doll Liddell, 30 October 1884, MAP d.3309.

87 Quoted in Stephen Kern, *The Culture of Love: Victorians to Moderns* (Cambridge, Massachusetts, 1992), p. 126.

88 Frances wrote to Arthur that she suspected he had only ever shown Laura the 'mass of flippant cynicism' side of his character, 23 November [1884], BPS GD433/2/164/7.

89 LT diary, 22 November 1884, 12 January 1885, MAP d.3312.

90 Frances Balfour to MT, 5 October 1890, MAP c.6670; LT diary, 16 January 1885, MAP d.3312; LT to Alfred Lyttelton, [Mar. 1885], CP II 2/2.

91 ME diary, 23 November 1884, MEP.

92 Kenneth Young, *Arthur Balfour: The Happy Life of the Politician, Prime Minister, Statesman and Philosopher* (London, 1963), p. 81.

93 ME diary, 27 November 1884, MEP; LT to Doll Liddell, 28 November 1884, CP 6/1.

94 Young, *Balfour*, p. 82.

95 Poem by Godfrey Webb headed 'The Glen, 14 December 1883', MAP d.3313.

96 'The Souls' file, MEP.

97 LT to Doll Liddell, 23 November 1884, CP 6/1.

98 St John Brodrick to George Curzon, 27 November 1884, Curzon Papers MSS Eur F111:9.

99 LT to ME, 20 October 1884, MEP; Chandos, *From Peace to War*, p. 29.

100 LT diary, 3 January 1885, MAP d.3312.

101 LT to Doll Liddell, 26 January 1886, CPII, 2/2.

102 MT diary, 3 January 1885, MAP. Margot appears to have shared her disappointment with others, see Gerald to Frances Balfour, 6 March 1885, BPS GD433/2/297.

103 Compare the accounts in MT diary, 3 January 1885; Asquith, *Autobiography*, I, pp. 88–9; Edith Balfour, *Alfred Lyttelton: An Account of His Life* (London, 1917), p. 130. See Stephen Kern's study of the iconography of marriage proposals in *Eyes of Love: The Gaze in English and French Culture, 1840–1900* (New York, 1996), pp. 7–9.

104 DD Balfour on Doll in 'Interwoven', CP 6/1.

105 LT diary, 28 January 1885, MAP d.3312; LT to Mary Gladstone, 28 January 1885, MGP BL 46270; LT to Alfred Lyttelton, 31 January 1885 and to Doll Liddell, 30 January1885, CP 6/1.

106 Alfred Lyttelton to Sibella Lyttelton, 21 January 1885, CP 2/19; Kern, *The Culture of Love*, p. 39, also Julia Bush, *Edwardian Ladies and Imperial Power* (London, 2000), p. 21.

107 Alfred Lyttelton to LT, 30 January, 24 February 1885, CP 6/1; 16 January 1885, CP II:2/3.

108 LT to Jack Tennant in Mary Gladstone, 'Laura Lyttelton', MGP BL 46270; LT diary, 10 and 15 February 1885, MAP d.3312.

109 This is what Tennyson called her, and the subject of a verse by Godfrey Webb, Asquith, *Autobiography*, I, pp. 62–3.

110 Kali Israel presents a similar image of acculturation and access to 'cultural capital' provided by the right kind of marriage for Charles Dilke's first wife, see Israel, *Names and Stories: Emilia Dilke and Victorian Culture* (Oxford, 1999), pp. 72–3.

111 ME to Hugo Elcho, 15 December 1885, 15 January 1886, MEP.

112 ME to Madeline Wyndham, [1885], MEP.

113 ME diary, 13 February 1886, MEP.

114 William Lubenow, *Liberal Intellectuals and Public Culture: Making Words Flesh* (Woodbridge, 2010), p. 107.

CHAPTER THREE

1 *Times*, 22 May 1885; Edward Hamilton, *The Diary of Sir Edward White Hamilton, 1880–1885*, two volumes, ed. Dudley W, R, Bahlman (Oxford, 1972), II, p. 868; Elizabeth Longford, *A Pilgrimage of Passion: The Life of Wilfrid Scawen Blunt* (London, 1979), p. 218; Rosebery to Charles Tennant, [May 1886], MAP d.3313; Lewis Harcourt, *Loulou: Selected Extracts from the Journals of Lewis Harcourt, 1880–1895*, ed. Philip Jackson (New Jersey, 2006), p. 96.

2 For an introduction to historiography on the transformation of British elites in the late nineteenth century, and some data regarding the emerging plutocracy, see Nancy W. Ellenberger, 'The Transformation of London "Society" at the End of Victoria's Reign: Evidence from the Court Presentation Records', *Albion* 22 (Winter 1990): 633–53.

3 LT diary, 12 January 1885, MAP d.3312; Edith Lyttelton, *Alfred Lyttelton* (London, 1917), p. 122.

4 Gail Bederman, *Manliness and Civilization: A Cultural History of Gender and Race in the United States, 1880–1917* (Chicago, 1995), ch. 1, explains how the idea of greater differentiation of physical traits between the sexes became linked with theories of civilisational progress during the late nineteenth century.

5 Lyttelton to Mary Gladstone, 21 January 1885, MGP BL46234; Kenneth Rose, *Superior Person: A Portrait of Curzon and his Circle in Late Victorian England* (New York, 1969), pp. 164–5.

6 The reason the sanctimonious Lady Mount-Temple would not befriend her as she had Laura, MT diary, 14 October 1884, MAP d.3198.

7 MT diary, 17 September 1878, MAP d.3198; 26 January 1877, 19 May 1877, MAP e.3257.

8 MT diary, 6 February 1882, MAP d.3198.

9 Margot Asquith, *An Autobiography,* two volumes (New York, 1920), I, p. 51.

10 All quotes are from Margot's diary, 1877–79, when she was between thirteen and fifteen years old. She describes something of this atmosphere in *More or Less About Myself* (New York, 1934), pp. 14–16.

11 Lady Jebb, wife of the holder of the chair in Greek at University of Glasgow, counted among that number, Mary Bobbitt, *With Dearest Love to All: The Life and Letters of Lady Jebb* (London, 1960), p. 134; MT diary from 6 July, 14 August, November 1877, MAP e.3257.

12 MT diary, June 1877, MAP e.3257, 30 March, 15 May 1879, 15 September 1878, MAP d.3198.

13 MT diary, 15 September 1878, November 1879, MAP d.3198.

14 MT diary, 30 March 1879, MAP d.3198. Two recent scholars have studied the socially constructed dimensions of the acceptance of 'looks' between men and women and their relationship to women's provocation of seduction, see introductory chapters in Stephen Kern, *Eyes of Love: The Gaze in English and French Culture, 1840–1900* (New York, 1996) and Beth Newman, *Subjects on Display: Psychoanalysis, Social Expectation, and Victorian Femininity* (Ohio, 2004).

15 MT diary, 5 October 1880, MAP d.3198; Asquith, *Autobiography,* I:138–39.

16 Asquith, *Autobiography,* I:162–73.

17 MT diary, 30 September, 5 October, 28 October 1880, 6 January, 21 March, 4 November 1881, MAP d.3198.

18 Asquith, *Autobiography,* I, pp. 78–9.

19 MT diary, 21 March 1881, MAP d.3198; 'A Flirt,' MAP c.6699, f. 35.

20 Lord Carlingford, *'And Mr Fortescue': Diaries of Chichester Fortescue, Lord Carlingford, 1851–1862,* ed. Osbert Hewett (London, 1958), pp. 69, 85, 113, 173.

21 Stanley Weintraub, *Edward the Caresser: The Playboy Prince Who Became Edward VII* (New York, 2001), p. 257.

22 Anita Leslie, *The Marlborough House Set* (New York, 1973), p. 3.

23 Colin Clifford, *The Asquiths* (London, 2002), ch. 2; Daphne Bennett, *Margot* (London, 1984), ch. 2.

24 MT diary, 18 March 1880, MAP d.3198.

25 Asquith, *Autobiography*, II, pp. 138–49.

26 Frank Sherman Peer, *Cross Country with Horse and Hound* (London, 1902), pp. 232–33. Also Roger D. Williams, *Horse and Hound* (London, 1908), ch. 7; Simon Blow, *Fields Elysian: A Portrait of Hunting Society* (London, 1983); David Itzkowitz, *Peculiar Privilege: A Social History of English Foxhunting, 1753–1885* (Hassocks, 1977), pp. 55–8.

27 Brian Luke, 'Violent Love: Hunting, Heterosexuality, and the Erotics of Men's Predation', *Feminist Studies* 24 (fall 1998): 627–55.

28 MT diary, 2 February 1882, MAP d.3198.

29 Asquith [Oxford] *More or Less about Myself*, p. 146. The *Autobiography* says this dinner was in 1881, a year before Margot was presented at court, and that she was standing in for Laura, II, p. 30.

30 MT diary, 6 June 1882, MAP d.3198.

31 MT diary, 28 October 1880, MAP d.3198; Asquith [Oxford], *More or Less*, pp. 25–6. Jennifer Phegley discusses debates over 'improper reading' for women outside of the family setting in *Educating the Proper Woman Reader: Victorian Family Literary Magazines and the Cultural Health of the Nation* (Ohio, 2004), ch 3.

32 MT diary, 23 June 1882, MAP d.3198.

33 MT diary, January 1883, MAP d.3198.

34 Reginia Gagnier, *Subjectivities: A History of Self-Representation in Britain, 1832–1920* (Oxford, 1991), p. 171.

35 John Tosh, *A Man's Place: Masculinity and the Middle-Class Home in Victorian England* (New Haven, 1999).

36 An illuminating introduction to the English private boarding schools known as 'public schools' can be found in John Chandos, *Boys Together: English Public Schools 1800–1864* (New Haven, 1984). The classic negative account is Jonathan Gathorne-Hardy, *The Old School Tie: The Phenomenon of the English Public School* (New York, 1977).

37 Gilbert Coleridge, *Eton in the Seventies* (London, 1912), pp. 278–9; for a modern scholarly assessment, see Gail Savage, *The Social Construction: The English Civil Service and Its Influence, 1919–1939* (Pittsburgh, 1996), pp. 28–33.

38 J. A. Mangan, *Athleticism in the Victorian and Edwardian Public School: The Emergence and Consolidation of an Educational Ideology* (Cambridge, 1981) and *The Games Ethic and Imperialism* (New York, 1986).

39 Jonathan Rutherford, *Forever England: Reflections on Masculinity and Empire* (London, 1997), pp. 21–5.

40 Nancy W. Ellenberger, 'Constructing George Wyndham: Narratives of Aristocratic Masculinity in Fin-de-Siècle England', *Journal of British Studies* 39 (October, 2000): 487–517.

41 Winston Churchill, *My Early Life, A Roving Commission* (London, 1930), pp. 8–13. Also A. G. C. Liddell, *Notes from the Life of an Ordinary Mortal* (London, 1911), p. 17: 'This sudden change from a home where I was surrounded by love and affection to the indifference and occasional

rough usage of school overwhelmed me, the more because I had never imagined anything of the kind.'

42 Tosh, *A Man's Place*, ch. 8. Scholars who have begun to explore the psychodynamics and affective conditioning of Victorian male mono-cultures include Tosh, Michael Roper, Eve Kosofsky Sedgwick, William Lubenow and Barbara Black.

43 Blanche Dugdale, *Arthur James Balfour*, two volumes (London, 1937), I, pp. 21–3; R. J. Q. Adams, *Balfour: The Last Grandee* (London, 2007), pp. 11–12.

44 Lord Frederick Hamilton, *The Days Before Yesterday* (London, 1920), pp. 94–6; LLGW, I, p. 23.

45 Coleridge, *Eton in the Seventies*, ch. 2.

46 LLGW, I, p. 128; J. Brinsley-Richards, *Seven Years at Eton 1857–1864* (London, 1883), ch. 19.

47 Coleridge, *Eton in the Seventies*, ch. 1.

48 Simon Blow, *Broken Blood: Rise and Fall of the Tennant Family* (London, 1987), p. 78.

49 LLGW, I, p. 24.

50 LLGW, I, pp. 129–30.

51 Justin Accomando, 'Chronicle of an Imperial Education: knowledge and debate about empire in the British boarding school', unpublished honours paper, United States Naval Academy Nimitz Library, 2003.

52 LLGW, I, p. 25; ME diary, 20 March 1881, MEP.

53 See especially Harold Perkin, *The Rise of Professional Society in England since 1880* (New York, 1989).

54 Paul Deslandes, *Oxbridge Men: British Masculinity and the Undergraduate Experience, 1850–1920* (Bloomington, 2005).

55 LLGW, I, p. 25.

56 David Cannadine, *The Decline and Fall of the British Aristocracy* (New Haven, 1990), pp. 265–9.

57 Edward Spiers, *The Late Victorian Army* (Manchester, 1992), p. 98.

58 LLGW, I, pp. 135–8.

59 LLGW, I, p. 137.

60 David Roberts, 'The Paterfamilias of the Victorian Governing Classes' in *The Victorian Family*, ed. Anthony S. Wohl (London, 1978), pp. 73, 87.

61 MT diary, 17 March 1883, MAP d.3198.

62 Margot Oxford, *Octavia* (London, 1928), ch. 1.

63 MT diary, January 1883, MAP d.3198. For the 'erotic intimacy' of sleep-wear by the mid-nineteenth century see Alain Corbin, 'The Secret of the Individual' in *A History of Private Life*, ed. Michelle Perot, four volumes (Cambridge, Massachusetts, 1990), IV, p. 486.

64 Blow, *Broken Blood,* pp. 79–84.

65 MT diary, January 1883, MAP d.3198.

66 Beatrix Lister, *Emma, Lady Ribblesdale, Life and Letters* (privately printed), p. 49.

67 MT diary, 10 August 1884, MAP d.3198.

68 MT diary, 23, 24 September 1883, 14 October 1884, MAP d.3198.

69 MT diary, 3 April, 2 January 1883, MAP d.3198.

70 MT diary, 3 April, 10 August 1883, MAP d.3198.

71 *Times*, 9 June 1883 reports the results of the Wokingham Stakes; Asquith [Oxford], *More or Less about Myself*, pp. 219–23; MT diary, 10 August 1883, MAP d.3198.

72 'Women', MAP c.6699, fols 44–49.

73 MT diary, 2 August 1882, 10 August 1883, MAP d.3198.

74 'Women', MAP c.6699.

75 MT diary, 6 August 1885, MAP d.3198; LT to Doll, 20 June 1885, CP 6/1.

76 Weintraub, *Edward the Caresser*, pp. 274–6.

77 Weintraub, *Edward the Caresser*, p. 266; Christopher Hibbert, *The Royal Victorians: King Edward VII, His Family and Friends* (Philadelphia, 1976), p. 154.

78 Asquith to MT, 25 November 1896, MAP c.6688.

79 Edward Spiers reviews changes in the army during George's youth in *The Late-Victorian Army* (Manchester, 1992). A contemporary account of the implications for education at Sandhurst is in A. F. Mockler-Ferryman, *Annals of Sandhurst* (London, 1900).

80 Press cutting in Mary's diary, 13 January 1882, MEP; LLGW, I, p. 132. For controversy over the use of crammers to prepare for the entrance exams, see Ian Worthington, 'Antecedent Education and Officer Recruitment: the origins and early development of the public school-army relationship', *Military Affairs* 41 (December 1977): 183–9.

81 ME diary, 17 and 21 May 1882, MEP.

82 Gwyn Harries-Jenkins, *The Army in Victorian Society* (New York, 1977), p. 30.

83 Jeffrey Richards, 'Popular Imperialism and the Image of the Army in Juvenile Literature' in *Popular Imperialism and the Military, 1850–1950*, ed. John MacKenzie (Manchester, 1992), pp. 80–108.

84 Ronald Robinson and John Gallagher, *Africa and the Victorian: The Official Mind of Imperialism* (1961).

85 A. B. Theobald, *The Mahdiya: A History of the Anglo-Egyptian Sudan, 1881–1899* (London, 1951), p. 32; Gabriel Warburg, *Islam, Sectarianism and Politics in Sudan since the Mahdiyya* (Wisconsin, 2003), chs 4–6.

86 For a highly critical account of Wolseley's campaign, see Adrian Preston's introduction to *In Relief of Gordon: Lord Wolseley's Campaign Journal of the Khartoum Relief Expedition 1884–1885*, ed. Adrian Preston (London, 1967). I am grateful to my colleagues Dr Aaron O'Connell and Dr Wayne Hsieh for sharing their military expertise as this chapter was written.

87 The official history is H. E. Colvile, *History of the Sudan Campaign, 1884–1885*, two volumes (Nashville, 1996 [from the 1889 original]), II, pp. 180–241. For a recent study of the political turmoil within Gladstone's government caused by the Sudan problem, see Fergus Nicoll, *Gladstone, Gordon and the Sudan Wars: The Battle over Imperial Intervention in the Victorian Age* (Barnsley, 2013).

88 Brian Robson, *Fuzzy Wuzzy: The Campaigns of the Eastern Sudan 1884–85* (Tunbridge Wells, 1993), p. 88; Colvile, *History of the Sudan Campaign,*

II, pp. 182–3. George's Coldstream Guards battalion joined the 3rd Battalion of the Grenadier Guards and 2nd Battalion of the Scots Guards to form the Guards Brigade of about 2,500 men.

89 Wilfrid Scawen Blunt, *Gordon at Khartoum* (London, 1911), pp. 236, 275.

90 LLGW, I, pp. 29–30.

91 Robson, *Fuzzy Wuzzy*, p. 107.

92 LLGW, I, pp. 141–77.

93 Colonel C. E. Callwell, *Small Wars: Their Principles and Practice*, 3rd edn ([1906] reprint, 1996), p. 441.

94 LLGW, I, pp. 167, 149–50.

95 LLGW, I, pp. 154–5.

96 Robson, *Fuzzy Wuzzy*, pp. 116–17.

97 LLGW, I, p. 156. Callwell deplored this engagement, using it as an example of what not to do on campaign, because the enemy was only heartened by the army's withdrawal, S*mall Wars*, p. 101.

98 On the casualty figures see Robson, *Fuzzy Wuzzy*, pp. 136–7; H. C. Jackson, *Osman Digna* (London, 1926), p. 97.

99 LLGW, I, p. 157.

100 LLGW, I, pp. 158–9.

101 LLGW, I, p. 161. Eye-witness sketches of much of what George described can be found in *Graphic*, 13, 20, 27 March 1885.

102 LLGW, I, p. 165; Robson, *Fuzzy Wuzzy*, ch. 9.

103 The quoted phrase is from Stephen Arata, *Fictions of Loss in the Victorian Fin de Siècle: Identity and Empire* (Cambridge, 1996), p. 122.

104 LLGW, I, p. 157.

105 LLGW, I, p. 162.

106 LLGW, I, p. 170.

107 Jackson, *Osman Digna*, p. 98.

108 For the controversy over execution of the wounded on the battlefield see Robson, *Fuzzy Wuzzy*, p. 71.

109 LLGW, I, p. 175.

110 George Wyndham, 'A Remarkable Book: Stephen Crane's *The Red Badge of Courage*', *New Review* (January 1896): 30–40.

111 LLGW, I, p. 238. The family never published Wyndham's poetry, which I saw in a private collection in 1980.

112 Jay Winter, *Remembering War: The Great War in Memory and History in the 20th Century* (2006), pp. 52–4. On the developing field of the body's reactions to cross-cultural engagements with 'others', Andrew Rotter, 'Empires of the Senses: How Seeing, Hearing, Smelling, Tasting, and Touching Shaped Imperial Encounters', *Diplomatic History* 25 (January 2011): 3–19.

113 See 'A Week of General Election, July 1892' and 'Isherwood' in MAP d.3297.

114 Janet Oppenheim, *'Shattered Nerves': Doctors, Patients, and Depression in Victorian England* (New York, 1991), p. 141.

115 Jill L. Matus, *Shock, Memory and the Unconscious in Victorian Fiction* (Cambridge, 2009), pp. 47–52.

116 For a fascinating appraisal for the way that adventure narratives played out in the lives of individuals, see Graham Dawson, *Soldier Heroes: British Adventure, Empire and the Imagining of Masculinities* (New York, 1994).

INTERLUDE: 'THE PIVOT OF POLITICS'

1 Richard Shannon, *The Age of Salisbury, 1881–1902: Unionism and Empire* (London, 1996), pp. 58, 132–5.
2 Arthur James Balfour, *Chapters of Autobiography* (London, 1930), pp. 172–3; Janet Oppenheim, *The Other World: Spiritualism and Psychical Research in England, 1850–1914* (Cambridge, 1988), p. 125; Deborah Blum, *Ghost Hunters: William James and the Search for Scientific Proof of Life after Death* (New York, 2007), pp. 57–8; Alex Owen, *The Darkened Room: Women, Power and Spiritualism in Late Victorian England* (Philadelphia, 1990), pp. 230–1.
3 Shannon, *Age of Salisbury*, p. 81.
4 *The Wellesley Index to Victorian Periodicals*, ed. Walter E. Houghton, five volumes (Toronto, 1972), II, p. 527; Shannon, *Age of Salisbury*, pp. 53–4; Peter Gordon, introduction to *The Political Diaries of the Fourth Earl of Carnarvon, 1857–1890*, Camden 5th series, volume 35, ed. Peter Gordon (Cambridge, 2009), pp. 80–1. On the Conservative press in the early 1880s, see Stephen Koss, *The Rise and Fall of the Political Press in Britain: The Nineteenth Century* (Chapel Hill, 1981), pp. 243–53.
5 GP to Edward Hamilton, 1 July 1885, Hamilton Papers BL48620.
6 Gathorne Gathorne-Hardy, *The Diary of Gathorne Hardy, later Lord Cranbrook, 1866–1892: Political Selections*, ed. Nancy Johnson (Oxford, 1981), pp. 475–6. Gety Pembroke worried that Lady Salisbury did not like them, and she was probably right: Edward Hamilton, *The Diary of Sir Edward Walter Hamilton, 1880–1885*, ed. Dudley W. R. Bahlman, two volumes (Oxford, 1972), II, p. 901.
7 GP to Carnarvon, 6 May and 8 May 1882, Carnarvon Papers BL60774. On 1884, see Anthony Jones, *The Politics of Reform 1884* (Cambridge, 1972), p. 74; Andrew Adonis, *Making Aristocracy Work: The Peerage and the Political System in Britain 1884–1914* (Oxford, 1993), p. 120. Peter Marsh shows that Salisbury shared Pembroke's goal of alliance with the Whig aristocracy and the moderate middle-class voter, *The Discipline of Popular Government: Lord Salisbury's Domestic Statecraft 1881–1902* (Sussex, 1978), p. 105.
8 GP to Edward Hamilton, 27 January and 5 November 1883, 4 March 1884, 1 July 1885, Hamilton Papers BL48620.
9 *Diary of Sir Edward White Hamilton*, II, p. 901; GP to Hamilton, 1 July 1885, Hamilton Papers BL48620.
10 GP to Hamilton, [February 1883], Hamilton Papers BL 48620.
11 *Salisbury–Balfour Correspondence, 1869–1892*, ed. R. H. Williams (Hertfordshire Record Society,1988), p. 101; Frances Balfour to AB, [spring 1885], BPS GD433/2/164/3. See Frances Balfour's account of the Leeds election in *Ne Obliviscaris*, two volumes (London, 1930) II, pp. 33–43.

12 For the election of 1885 as the beginning of the 'End of the Patrician Polity', see David Cannadine, *The Decline and Fall of the British Aristocracy* (New Haven, 1990), pp. 31–46.

13 Shannon, *Age of Salisbury*, p. 178. For a thorough study of this election and the functioning of the new House of Commons that followed, see W. C. Lubenow, *Parliamentary Politics and the Home Rule Crisis: The British House of Commons in 1886* (Oxford, 1988).

14 Henry Pelling, *The Social Geography of British Elections, 1885–1910* (1967), p. 385; Adonis, *Making Aristocracy Work*, p. 244.

15 Shannon, *Age of Salisbury*, pp. 208–9; Marsh, *Discipline of Popular Government*, pp. 112–15.

16 Edward Stanley, *The Later Derby Diaries: Home Rule, Liberalism, and Aristocratic Life in Late Victorian England*, ed. John Vincent (Bristol, 1981), p. 50

17 Shannon, *Age of Salisbury*, p. 209.

18 Shannon, *Age of Salisbury*, p. 184.

19 Hawkins provides a succinct review of the development of historians' ideas about Gladstone's motivations in initiating a home rule programme and the impact it had on both political parties, *British Party Politics, 1852–1886* (London, 1998), pp. 254–60. Lubenow's *Parliamentary Politics and the Home Rule Crisis* is the definitive work on the importance of 1885–86 in terms of the governing elites.

20 For the sudden change in numbers of people trying to enter polite and political society in the late century, see Nancy W. Ellenberger, 'The Transformation of London "Society" at the End of Victoria's Reign: Evidence from the Court Presentation Records', *Albion* 22 (Winter 1990), pp. 633–53.

CHAPTER FOUR

1 MT manuscript on the sisters' childhood in MAP e.3285.

2 Manuscript by Margot headed 'Bournemouth, November 1888', MAP e.3285. Other accounts of this week can be found in Margot Asquith, *An Autobiography*, two volumes (New York, 1920), I, pp. 89–107; Edith Lyttelton, *Alfred Lyttelton* (London, 1917), pp. 143–8; Mary Gladstone, 'Memoir of Laura Lyttelton', MGP BL46270; Pat Jalland, *Women, Marriage and Politics 1860–1914* (Oxford, 1986), pp. 177–9; Kathleen Lyttelton to Mary Gladstone, 17 April 1886, MGP BL46235.

3 Emma Tennant to Margot, [16 Ap. 1886], MAP d.3286/73. Medical details from Lady Frederick Cavendish to Lady Frances Balfour, 26 April 1886, BPS GD433/2/298.

4 Judith Lewis, '"Tis a Misfortune to be a Great Ladie": Maternal Mortality in the British Aristocracy: 1558–1959', *Journal of British Studies* 37 (January 1998): 32–3 ; LT to Lucy Cavendish, 5 April 1886, CP 4/2.

5 See Pat Jalland, *Death in the Victorian Family* (Oxford, 1996), pp. 174–83.

6 Margot used this same phrase in a letter to Stanley Baldwin forty years later to describe her feelings of abandonment after her husband died,

Stanley Baldwin, *Baldwin Papers: A Conservative Statesman, 1908–1947*, ed. Philip Williamson and Edward Baldwin (Cambridge, 2004), p. 206.

7 Georgiana Burne-Jones to Frances Balfour, 26 April 1886, BPS GD433/2/298; ME to Madeline Wyndham, 26 April 1886, MEP; MT to ME, 3 May 1886, MEP; MT to Harry Cust, 21 Nov 1888, MAP d.3278; Anne Wemyss to MT, 6 May 1886, MAP e.3282.

8 AB to MT, 26 April 1886, MAP c.6670. Others also found Balfour at his moment of greatest empathy when a death occurred, Frances Balfour to Betty Balfour, letters of December 1891, BPS GD433/2/305.

9 See Janet Oppenheim, *The Other World: Spiritualism and Psychical Research in England, 1850–1914* (Cambridge, 1988), pp. 129–35.

10 A replica can be seen in the Victoria and Albert Museum. The translation was done by Edward Marsh for inclusion in a pamphlet that Frances Horner wrote about the Mells church.

11 [Frances Horner], 'The Veil of Maya', *Temple Bar* 93 (1891): 73–96; [Edith Balfour], 'Love in a Mist', *Longman's Magazine* 17 (1890): 155–66.

12 GP to Evelyn de Vesci, 28 April 1886, HPP DD/DRU/84.

13 Lady Jebb, *With Dearest Love to All: the Life and Letters of Lady Jebb,* ed. Mary Bobbitt (London, 1960), p. 222.

14 *Autobiography*, I, p. 89, where Margot says that Laura and Alfred married on 10 May, instead of 21 May. This view of Margot's obsession with Laura's life and death accords with the picture presented by Colin Clifford, *The Asquiths* (London, 2002), p. 27.

15 MT to Spencer Lyttelton, 17 June, 14 Oct 1886, MAP d.3281.

16 MT to Harry Cust, 21 Nov 1888, MAP d.3278.

17 MT to Mary Elcho, 11 Aug and [no date] 1886, MEP.

18 MT to Spencer Lyttelton, 1 July 1886, MAP d.3281.

19 MAP c.6675.

20 Alain Corbin, 'Intimate Relations' in *A History of Private Life: Vol IV From the Fires of Revolution to the Great War*, ed. Michelle Perrot (Cambridge, Massachusetts, 1990), pp. 596–7; Michele Plott, 'The Rules of the Game: Respectability, Sexuality, and the Femme Mondaine in Late-Nineteenth Century Paris', *French Historical Studies* 25 (Summer 2002): 531–56.

21 John Tosh, *Manliness and Masculinities in Nineteenth-Century Britain* (Harlow, 2005), p. 90.

22 For a contemporary discussion of friendship based on a self-sacrificing, other-regarding Christian love, see Henry Clay Trumbull, *Friendship the Master-passion* (New York, 1892). Sharon Marcus shows how Christian rhetoric infused and justified ideals of both hetero- and same-sex intimacy in the nineteenth century, *Between Women: Friendship, Desire, and Marriage in Victorian England* (Princeton, 2007), pp. 62–8.

23 LAB, p. 24.

24 MT diary, [New Year 1884], MAP d.3198. See especially the first meeting between Joe and Harrington, *An American Politician*, ch. 2.

25 Asquith, *Autobiography*, I, p. 184, II, pp. 16, 48; Mary King Waddington, *Letters of a Diplomat's Wife* (London, 1903), p. 334.

26 MT to AB, 26 May 1886, BP BL 49794; A. C. Benson (anon), *Memoirs*

of Arthur Hamilton (London, 1886), ch. 7; GP to MT, 17 January 1886, MAP c.6677.

27 MT to Spencer Lyttelton, letters of June, 1 July, 14 July, 23 October 1886, MAP d.3281.

28 MT to Harry Cust, 19 October 1887, MAP d.3278/fols 17–19.

29 Blunt's 'Secret Memoirs', 19 August 1892, Blunt Papers 32–1975.

30 On these 'outsider' women who were Pembroke's friends, see Nigel Nicolson, *Mary Curzon* (London, 1977); Hugh and Mirabel Cecil, *Imperial Marriage: An Edwardian War and Peace* (London, 2002); Donna M. Lucey, *Archie and Amelie: Love and Madness in the Gilded Age* (New York, 2006). For the reputation of Americans marrying into the British aristocracy, see Maureen Montgomery, *Gilded Prostitution: Status, Money, and Transatlantic Marriages, 1870–1914* (London, 1989).

31 Kenneth Rose, *The Later Cecils* (New York, 1975), p. 193.

32 Evan Charteris to Constance Wenlock, [Fall 1888], WP DDFA 3/5/9.

33 Jane Abdy and Charlotte Gere, *The Souls* (London, 1984) contains a good biographical and photographic introduction to individuals in the group. See also Angela Lambert, *Unquiet Souls: The Indian Summer of the British Aristocracy, 1880–1918* (London, 1984); Kenneth Rose, *Superior Person: A Portrait of Curzon and his Circle in Late Victorian England* (New York, 1969), pp. 176–90; Richard Davenport-Hines, *Ettie: The Intimate Life and Dauntless Spirit of Lady Desborough* (London, 2009), pp. 38–86. For a shorter treatment: Nancy W. Ellenberger, 'The Souls and London "Society" at the End of the Nineteenth Century', *Victorian Studies* 25 (Winter 1982): 133–60.

34 Henry James, *The Awkward Age* (1899), ch. 10.

35 Marc Brodie and Barbara Caine, 'Class, Sex, and Friendship: The Long Nineteenth Century' in *Friendship, A History*, ed. Barbara Caine (London, 2009), pp. 223–77. Joyce Appleby, *Inheriting the Revolution: The First Generation of Americans* (Cambridge, Massachusetts, 2000) describes this phenomenon in the settlements of the newly opened Ohio territories in the generation after the founding of the United States. Most recently, James Vernon has made the creation of large communities of strangers the definitive attribute of modernity in Britain and places the most jarring decades of transition in the late nineteenth century, *Distant Strangers: How Britain Became Modern* (Berkeley, 2014).

36 See the authors cited in Chapter 3, fn. 42.

37 Victor Luftig, *Seeing Together: Friendship between the Sexes in English Writing, from Mill to Woolf* (Stanford, 1993). Judith Walkowitz provides a case study of the problem in 'Science, Feminism and Romance: The Men and Women's Club, 1885–1889', *History Today* 21 (Spring, 1986): 37–59.

38 Mrs Hwfa Williams, *It Was Such Fun* (London, 1935), p. 215.

39 Peter Gay, *The Cultivation of Hatred* (London, 1993), ch. 5. For a good introduction to the history of theories and definitional categories about humour, see Jeffrey Goldstein, 'Introduction' in *The Psychology of Humor: Theoretical Perspectives and Empirical Issues*, ed. Jeffrey Goldstein and Paul McGhee (New York, 1972), ch. 1. For greater depth on individual

theorists: John Parkin, *Humour Theorists of the Twentieth Century* (New York, 1997).

40 Robert Bernard Martin, *The Triumph of Wit: A Study of Victorian Comic Theory* (Oxford, 1974), pp. 17, 27–8.

41 [Leslie Stephen, anon.], 'Feminine Humour', *Saturday Review* 32 (15 July 1871): 75–6. The expatriate British intellectual Christopher Hitchens provided close to the same opinions in 'Why Women Aren't Funny', *Vanity Fair*, 1 January 2007. Debate continues over whether women do indeed find different things funny than do men: Regina Barreca, *They Used to Call Me Snow White … But I Drifted: Women's Strategic Use of Humor* (New York, 1991).

42 Dawn T. Robinson and Lynn Smith-Lovin, 'Getting a Laugh: Gender, Status, and Humor in Task Discussions', *Social Forces* 80:1 (2001): 123–8.

43 Virginia Cowles, *Edward VII and His Circle* (London, 1956), p. 75; Diana Souhami, *Mrs Keppel and her Daughter* (New York, 1996), p. 33; Geoffrey Bennett, *Charlie B.* (London, 1968), p. 54.

44 Consuelo Balsan, *The Glitter and the Gold* (New York, 1952), p. 102.

45 Christopher Simon Sykes, *The Big House: The Story of a Country House and its Family* (New York, 2004), pp. 179–85.

46 Daisy, Princess of Pless, *From My Private Diary* (London, 1931), p. 92.

47 The phrase is from Max Egremont, *Balfour* (London, 1980), p. 39.

48 Lady Randolph Churchill, *Reminiscences* (New York, 1908), p. 36. See the extraordinary pranks reported by the Countess of Cardigan, *My Recollections* (London, 1909), pp. 61–3, 119. On Alexandra in these circles: Christopher Hibbert, *Edward VII* (London, 1976), pp. 150–1; Balsan, *The Glitter and the Gold*, p. 73; E. F. Benson, *As We Were* (New York, 1930), p. 75.

49 Leslie, *Marlborough House Set*, p. 1.

50 Annette Wheeler Cafarelli, 'What Will Mrs. Grundy Say?', *Criticism* 38 (1996), p. 70.

51 Quoted in Elizabeth Longford, *Eminent Victorian Women* (New York, 1981), p. 19, in a section on George Kingsley's daughter Mary, who admitted to a sense of humour that was broad enough to border on vulgarity.

52 G. W. E. Russell, *Collections and Recollections* (New York, 1903), p. 175. See also the peeresses described in Russell's *Portraits of the Seventies* (New York, 1916), pp. 446–63.

53 Virginia Woolf, *The Diary of Virginia Woolf, Vol. 4 1931–1935*, ed. Anne Oliver Bell (New York, 1982), p. 80; Sonia Keppel, *Edwardian Daughter* (London, 1958), p. 37.

54 Eileen Gilhooly, *Smile of Discontent: Humor, Gender, and Nineteenth-Century British Fiction* (Chicago, 1999).

55 Frances Balfour to Betty Balfour, 30 January 1890, BPS GD433/2/302.

56 ME diary, 23 and 30 June, 1 July 1888, MEP.

57 Betty Balfour to Gerald Balfour, 6 August 1889, BPS GD433/2/301. Michael Holroyd notes that the actress Ellen Terry 'shocked viewers' in the early 1880s when she insisted on touching men's arms on stage as part of her performance, but that this then began a change in the

habits of London society, *A Strange Eventful History: The Dramatic Lives of Ellen Terry, Henry Irving, and their Remarkable Families* (New York, 2008), pp. 152–3.

58 GP to Michael Herbert, 29 November 1889, GPP; ME diary, 14 September 1888, 22 June 1890, MEP.

59 Sybil Lubbock, *The Child in the Crystal* (London, 1939), pp. 135–6.

60 Frances Balfour to Betty Balfour [June 1889], BPS GD433/2/301, from a party at Mells.

61 Daisy White diary, 22–3 June 1889, Butler Library, Columbia University. Stephen Kern, *The Culture of Love, Victorian to Moderns* (Cambridge, Massachusetts, 1992), ch. 4, describes the social messages sent by women's bodies in unconventional activities like these. Ladies, he says, did not run, and rarely knew how to swim.

62 ME diary, 5 October 1886, 6 October 1888 MEP; Blanche Dugdale, *Family Homespun* (London, 1940), p. 70; MT to Harry Cust, 8 October 1887, MAP d.3278. For more on the Souls' games see Ellenberger, 'The Souls and London Society', pp. 146–51.

63 LT to ME, [23 December] 1884, MEP.

64 Emily Lutyens, *A Blessed Girl* (1953), p. 184.

65 Daisy White diary, 27 January 1889, Butler Library, Columbia University; Charty Ribblesdale to Harry Cust, 30 January 1889, MAP d.3278; Lord Ribblesdale, 'The Art of Conversation', *Nineteenth Century* 26 (August 1889): 273–9.

66 Paul Langford, *Englishness Identified: Manners and Character 1650–1850* (Oxford, 2000), p. 185.

67 AB to ME, 29 March 1890, MEP.

68 MT to George Curzon, 11 November 1889, originally seen at the India Office Library, Curzon Papers F111:12. Lady Wemyss found this dinner highly unusual and shocking, Lady Wemyss to ME, 10 October 1889, MEP.

69 Betty Balfour to Frances Balfour, 10 December 1889, BPS GD433/2/301.

70 All examples taken from Mary's diaries for 1888–91, MEP. Charteris's description of his parents' entertaining is in Mary Wemyss, *A Family Record* (privately printed, 1927), pp. 8–10.

71 MT to Harry Cust, 8 October 1887, MAP d.3278.

72 MT to Spencer Lyttelton, 19 September 1888, MAP d.3281; ME diary, 21 January 1891, MEP.

73 Asquith, *Autobiography*, II, pp. 17–24; Daisy White diary, 10 July 1889, Nevins Papers, Columbia University. Also Frances Balfour to Betty Balfour, 12 July 1889, BPS GD433/2/301: 'Arthur seems to have been in wild spirits, and the fun so loud it was almost impossible to hear anyone speak.'

74 Curzon's proclivity for masculine humour and adoring women is acknowledged by his biographers, Rose, *Superior Person*, pp. 149–51; David Gilmour, *Imperial Statesman* (New York, 1994), p. 102.

75 Esme Wingfield-Stratford, *Before the Lamps Went Out* (London, 1945), pp. 199, 241.

76 Asquith, *Autobiography*, II, p. 18.

77 Gathorne Gathorne-Hardy, *The Diary of Gathorne Hardy*, ed. Nancy John-
    son (Oxford, 1981), p. 652; Andrew Adonis, *Making Aristocracy Work:
    The Peerage and the Political System in Britain, 1884–1914* (Oxford, 1983),
    pp. 52–60.

78 GP to DD Balfour, 18 April 1889, CP5/18.

79 Edward Hamilton, *Diary of Sir Edward Hamilton*, two volumes, ed. Dudley
    W. R. Bahlman (Oxford, 1972), II, p. 733.

80 Alfred Lyttelton to Mary Gladstone Drew, 12 September 1889, MGP
    BL46234; Alfred Lyttelton to Lavinia Talbot, 8 September 1889, CP
    II 5/24. Charty Ribblesdale described this cruise as well, particularly
    Gety's reaction to the co-ed swimming, *Some Hawarden Letters* (London,
    1917), pp. 235–6.

81 Betty Balfour to Frances Balfour, 10 December 1889, BPS GD433/2/301.
    Frances Balfour presented a softer picture of the Pembrokes at Wilton
    in *Ne Obliviscaris*, two volumes (London 1930), I, pp. 441–5, but in 1887
    she wrote to Betty that Pembroke was 'one in a thousand. I do wish his
    wife were up to him', 18 August 1887, BPS GD433/2/299 and [June
    1889], BPS GD433/2/301.

82 GP to Ettie Grenfell, [12 April 1890], Desborough Papers DE/Rv/
    C1293.

83 Barbara Leckie, *Culture and Adultery: The Novel, the Newspaper, and the Law
    1857–1914* (Philadelphia, 1999), pp. 79–92. On the sensational Dilke
    trial, see David Nicholls, *The Lost Prime Minister: A Life of Sir Charles Dilke*
    (London, 1995, ch. 13; Kali Israel, *Names and Stories: Emilia Dilke and
    Victorian Culture* (New York, 1999), pp. 202–19. Lord Colin Campbell
    was Frances Balfour's brother. Two of her other siblings, Lorne and
    Archibald, also had irregular marriages.

84 Recorded by Lord Derby, whose diary for this year is full of scandalous
    family secrets among the highest in the land, see *The Later Derby Diaries:
    Home Rule, Liberal Unionism, and Aristocratic Life in Late-Victorian England*,
    ed. John Vincent (Bristol, 1981), p. 120. Also Roy Foster, *Lord Randolph
    Churchill* (Oxford, 1981), p. 270; Anne Sebba, *American Jennie: The Re-
    markable Life of Lady Randolph Churchill* (New York, 2007), pp. 143–9.

85 Anita Leslie, *The Marlborough House Set* (New York, 1973), ch. 12.

86 GP to Evelyn de Vesci, 7 December 1886, HPP DD/DRU/84.

87 GP to Frances Horner, 9 August 1889, FHP.

88 GP to Constance Wenlock, 16 September 1887, WP DDFA3/5/6. For
    George's unhappiness in 1886, GP to Hamilton, 19 December and
    [n.d., late December] 1886, Hamilton Papers BL48620 and letters to
    Evelyn de Vesci of 1886, HP DD/DRU/84. On Constance's scrutiny
    of unhappy marriage, see Richard Davenport-Hines, *Ettie: The Life and
    World of Lady Desborough* (London, 2008), pp. 63–4 .

89 GP to Evelyn de Vesci, 12 February 1886, HPP DD/DRU/84.

90 The quotes from George Pembroke that follow in this paragraph come
    from letters of GP to Constance Wenlock, 16 September, 4 October
    1887 and [undated, autumn 1887, marked 'keep this letter to your-
    self'], WP DDFA3/5/6. Gerald Balfour gave his sister-in-law Frances

nearly identical advice a few years earlier, see letters from late 1883 and early 1884, GD433/2/296–297.

91 Elaine Hadley points out that this idea is in J. S. Mill's *Autobiography* in *Living Liberalism: Practical Citizenship in Mid-Victorian England* (Chicago, 2010), p. 79.

92 GP to Violet Maxse, 24 April 1892,Viscountess Milner Papers, [Bodl.] MS. Eng.VM42/C345/f.1; *South Sea Bubbles*, p. 89.

93 Luftig, *Seeing Together*, p. 137.

94 GP to Constance Wenlock, n.d. and 20 March 1890, WP DDFA3/5/6; to Evelyn de Vesci, 26 January 1890, HPP DD/DRU/84. There is a typed copy of this short essay among the Frances Horner Papers at Mells.

95 MT to Spencer Lyttelton, [n.d. spring 1888], MAP d.3281.

96 GP to Frances Horner, [no date, late 1892?], FHP; Daisy White diary, 18 December 1888, Butler Library, Columbia University.

97 One of these women was Frances Balfour, whose deep emotional investment in male friends was the subject of cautionary letters between Lord Lytton and his daughter Betty after she married Gerald Balfour, see letters from autumn 1888 in BPS GD433/2/300.

98 John Tosh, *Manliness and Masculinities in Nineteenth-Century Britain* (London, 2005), ch. 4. Ben Griffin has recently provided a nuanced account of a 'domestic ideology' that encompassed both the upper and middle strata of the Victorian 'governing classes' resting on a normative paradigm of male patriarchal authority over wives and children, *The Politics of Gender in Victorian Britain: Masculinity, Political Culture and the Struggle for Women's Rights* (Cambridge, 2012), ch. 2.

99 Kelly Cannon, *Henry James and Masculinity: The Man at the Margins* (New York, 1994), p. 19.

100 Doll Liddell to Constance Wenlock, 27 December 1887, WP DDFA3/5/3.

101 Rose, *Superior Person*, pp. 147–57.

102 Quote in Davenport-Hines, *Ettie*, p. 45; Doll Liddell to DD Balfour, 8 February 1889, CP II:3/7.

CHAPTER FIVE

1 Henry Asquith to MT, 16 October 1893, MAP c.6685.

2 Blanche Dugdale, *Arthur James Balfour*, two volumes (London, 1936), I, pp. 58, 72–3.

3 John Morley, *The Life of William Ewart Gladstone*, three volumes (New York, 1903), III, p. 364.

4 Salisbury to Commons leader W. H. Smith in Viscount Chilston, *W H Smith* (London, 1965), p. 264; Edward Stanley, Lord Derby, *The Later Derby Diaries: Home Rule, Liberal Unionism, and Aristocratic Society in Late Victorian Britain*, ed. John Vincent (Bristol, 1981), p. 82.

5 Richard Shannon, *The Age of Salisbury 1881–1902 Unionism and Empire* (London, 1996), pp. 280–1; Eugenio Biagini, *British Democracy and Irish Nationalism, 1876–1906* (Cambridge 2007) on the importance of the

Irish political movement to British radical and labour politics. From the Irish perspective see Stephen Howe, *Ireland and Empire: Colonial Legacies in Irish History and Culture* (Oxford, 2000), ch. 5.

6 Peter Marsh, *The Discipline of Popular Government: Lord Salisbury's Domestic Statecraft 1881–1902* (Sussex, 1978), pp. 173–4; David Steele, *Lord Salisbury: A Political Biography* (1999), ch. 9.

7 See the *Evening Capital* (Annapolis, Maryland), 23 February, 22 March, 3 September 1889. My thanks to my colleague Dr Fred Harrod for showing me the attention that Balfour attracted even in Maryland.

8 Gerald Balfour to Frances Balfour, 3 August 1883, BPS GD433/2/296 and [autumn 1887], BPS GD433/2/299; Eleanor Sidgwick to Alice Balfour, 6 September 1918, BPS GD433/3/80.

9 Max Egremont, *Balfour* (London, 1980), p. 121.

10 Kenneth Young is the only biographer who hints at a connection between Arthur's new masculine vitality in 1887 and his relationship with Mary, *Arthur Balfour: The Happy Life of the Politician, Prime Minister, Statesman and Philosopher* (London, 1963), p. 102.

11 LT to Frances Balfour, 8 October 1885, BPS GD433/2/477. See Claudia Renton's fuller narrative of these events, including Madeline Wyndham's distress, in *Those Wild Wyndhams: Three Sisters at the Heart of Power* (London, 2014), pp. 65–9.

12 Alfred Lyttelton to LT, 10 December 1884, BPS GD433/2/297.

13 LAB, pp. 354, 34; note Queen Victoria's mention of a Fenian 'plot to kill Mr. Balfour' in summer of 1888, *Letters of Queen Victoria*, ed. George Buckle, 3rd series, three volumes (London, 1930), I, p. 435.

14 Anne Wemyss to Evelyn de Vesci, 28 May 1890, HPP DD/DRU/82; Henry Asquith to Frances Horner, 14 August 1893, FHP.

15 ME to AB, 26 November, 1899, 28 October 1901, MEP.

16 Charles Gatty, *George Wyndham, Recognita* (London, 1917), pp. 38, 45.

17 Gerald Balfour to Frances Balfour, 19 October 1889, BPS GD433/2/301.

18 Antony Taylor, *Lords of Misrule: Hostility to Aristocracy in Late Nineteenth- and Early Twentieth-Century Britain* (Basingstoke, 2004); Len Platt, *Aristocracies in Fiction: The Idea of Aristocracy in Late-Nineteenth-Century and Early-Twentieth-Century Literary Culture* (Connecticut, 2001). For actions of peers in combating these stereotypes, see Andrew Adonis, *Making Aristocracy Work: The Peerage and the Political System in Britain, 1884–1914* (Oxford, 1993).

19 For an extended exploration of this socially constructed type, see Alan Sinfield, *The Wilde Century: Effeminacy, Oscar Wilde and the Queer Moment* (New York, 1994), chs 2–3. Ben Griffin describes the difficulties that other members faced in 'performing masculinities in the House of Commons', *The Politics of Gender in Victorian Britain* (Cambridge, 2012), ch. 6.

20 Winston Churchill, *Lord Randolph Churchill*, two volumes (New York, 1906), I, p. 134. Du Maurier cartoons in *Punch*, 22 May, 5 June, 19 June 1880; *New Review* 6 (November 1889): 572–84. My thanks again to Fred Harrod for finding *Punch* as the source of the Postlethwaite nickname for Balfour. L. P. Curtis in summarising Balfour's pre-Ireland reputation

explicitly mentioned concerns about his ability to function in 'a man's world', *Coercion and Conciliation 1880–1892: A Study in Conservative Unionism* (Princeton, 1963), p. 175. Ian Malcolm says that the Parnellite MP Swift McNeill coined the term 'Fanny' for Balfour to indicate his delicate appearance, and that Henry Lucy was responsible for 'Prince Arthur', 'the best and last nickname that was attached to him in public life', *Lord Balfour, a Memory* (London, 1930), p. 9.

21 *United Ireland*, 19 March 1887.

22 L. P. Curtis, *Apes and Angels: The Irishman in Victorian Caricature* (Washington DC, 1997), ch. 1; Stephen Arata, *Fictions of Loss in the Victorian Fin de Siècle: Identity and Empire* (Cambridge, 1996), pp. 19–21.

23 *Graphic*, 19 November 1887.

24 E. T. Raymond echoed this assessment in 1920 when he said that Balfour was only really mobilised to action when motivated by 'almost feminine obstinacy and dislike of admitting defeat', *Mr. Balfour* (London, 1920), p. 2. Raymond used the terms 'effeminate', 'blue stocking' and 'ladylike' about Balfour.

25 Marsh, *Discipline of Popular Government*, p. 156.

26 Gail Bederman, *Manliness and Civilization: A Cultural History of Gender and Race in the United States 1880–1917* (Chicago, 1995), ch. 1; John Tosh, *Manliness and Masculinities in Nineteenth-Century Britain* (Harlow, 2005), pp. 193–8. S*pectator* commented explicitly on this concern in 1888, but gave Gladstone's leadership of 'the revolutionary spiritual change in attitudes toward the Irish' as an example that manly passion still existed among the English, 21 January 1888.

27 Gesa Stedman, *Stemming the Torrent: Expression and Control in the Victorian Discourse on Emotions 1830–1872* (Aldershot, 2002). An excellent summary of the literature on manliness and emotional control can be found in Joseph Valente, 'The Manliness of Parnell', *Eire-Ireland* 41 (2006): 64–69. For the parliamentary impression Parnell made: Pauric Travers, 'Reading Between the Lines: The Political Speeches of Charles Stewart Parnell' in *The Ivy Leaf: Parnell Remembered*, ed. Donald McCartney and Pauric Travers (Dublin, 2006), ch. 4; Winston S. Churchill, *Great Contemporaries* (Chicago, 1973), p. 352.

28 *Punch*, 18 March 1887; Curtis, *Coercion and Conciliation*, p. 182; George Curzon, *Parliamentary Eloquence* (London, 1911), pp. 43–4; Earl of Oxford and Asquith, *Memories and Reflections, 1852–1927*, two volumes (Boston, 1928), I, p. 131; Raymond, *Mr Balfour*, p. 44.

29 *Punch*, 4 July 1887; *Graphic*, 2 April, 2 July 1887.

30 *Punch*, 7 June 1887.

31 *Graphic*, 1 October 1887.

32 *Punch*, 25 February 1888. Also *Annual Register for the Year* 1888, pp. 32–36; *Spectator*, 18 and 25 February 1888; *Graphic*, 25 February 1888.

33 *Saturday Review*, 18 February 1888.

34 *Graphic*, 25 February 1888. Edward Hamilton diary, 23 February 1888, Edward Hamilton Papers BL48647.

35 Eibhear Walshe, 'The First Gay Irishman? Ireland and the Oscar Wilde Trials', *Eire-Ireland* 40 (Fall/Winter 2005): 40–1.

36 *Saturday Review*, 31 March 1888; L. Perry Curtis, 'The Battering Ram and Irish Evictions, 1887–90', *Eire-Ireland* 42 (Fall/Winter, 2007): 240–4.

37 Justin M'Carthy, *Mr. Balfour's Rule in Ireland* (London, 1891), ch. 5.

38 Joseph Meisel, *Public Speech and the Culture of Public Life in the Age of Gladstone* (New York, 2001), p. 8.

39 LAB, p. 41.

40 *Spectator*, 22 February 1890; Arthur Balfour, *The Mind of Arthur James Balfour*, ed. Wilfred Short (New York, 1918), p. 306; *ILN*, 21 May 1891.

41 See Patrick Dunleavy et al., 'Leaders, Politics and Institutional Change: The Decline of Prime Ministerial Accountability to the House of Commons, 1868–1990', *British Journal of Political Science* 23 (July 1993).

42 See *Graphic*'s description of the difficulties in capturing the emotional ambience of the House of Commons, 23 April 1887; also William C. Lubenow, *Parliamentary Politics and the Home Rule Crisis: The British House of Commons in 1886* (Oxford, 1988), pp. 1, 325–31.

43 Extract from Evelyn Rayleigh diary, BPS GD433/2/6; John Morley, *Recollections*, two volumes. (New York, 1917), I, p. 227.

44 *Annual Register for 1889*, pp. 28–9, 193; *ILN, Punch, Graphic*, 17 August 1889.

45 *Spectator*, 5 May, 12 May 1888; *Graphic*, 28 April 1888; Smith to Queen Victoria in *Letters of Queen Victoria*, I, p. 299.

46 *Graphic*, 25 February, 14 April, 21 July 1888.

47 *ILN*, 8 June 1889.

48 See the episode on 30 April 1888 after which Morley sent a personal note of apology to Balfour for words that one press cutting (*Spectator*, 5 May 1888) thought would result in 'a personal embitterment' between the two men, Morley diary 30 April, 1 May 1888, Morley Papers [Bodl.] MS. Eng. d.3443. Morley wrote that 'Balfour replied in a style that made me very unhappy all the rest of the aftn: sorry that I had not made my attack more delicately.' The apology is in BP BL49778, dated 1 May 1888.

49 *Punch*, 26 May 1888.

50 Michael Holroyd, *A Strange Eventful History: The Dramatic Lives of Ellen Terry, Henry Irving and their Remarkable Families* (New York, 2008), p. 356; J. P. Waller, 'Laughter in the House: A Late Nineteenth and Early Twentieth Century Parliamentary Survey', *Twentieth Century British History* 5 (1994): 10.

51 Betty Balfour to Alice Balfour, 11 May 1892, BPS 433/2/306.

52 Geoffrey Searle, *A New England? Peace and War 1886–1918* (Oxford, 2004), pp. 156–9.

53 *Pall Mall Gazette, The New House of Commons* (London, 1895); Shannon, *Age of Salisbury*, p. 261.

54 Virginia Crossman, *Politics, Law and Order in Nineteenth Century Ireland* (New York, 1996), p. 162

55 Curtis, *Coercion and Conciliation*, pp. 223–6.

56 *Annual Register of 1888*, p. 172; Arthur's speech in the *Times*, 2 October 1888; Laurence M. Geary, 'John Mandeville and the Irish Crimes Act of 1887,' *Eire-Ireland* 25 (Winter 1983).

57 Andrew Roberts, *Salisbury, Victorian Titan* (London, 1999), p. 452; Dugdale, *Arthur James Balfour*, I, p. 113.

58 R. J. Q. Adams's statement that Balfour 'never showed any enthusiasm for the judicial commission' [*Balfour* (London, 2007), p. 92] needs to be qualified by Balfour to Iwan Muller, 17 February, 1 March 1890; to John Ross, 24 February 1890, BP BL49828. On Salisbury's role: Margaret O'Callaghan, *British High Politics and a Nationalist Ireland: Criminality, Land and Law under Forster and Balfour* (New York, 1994), p. 112; Alvin Jackson, *Home Rule: An Irish History 1800–1900* (New York, 2003), pp. 72–3; Roberts, *Salisbury*, p. 452; *Letters of Queen Victoria*, I, pp. 431–2.

59 Salisbury to Queen Victoria in *Letters of Queen Victoria*, I, p. 454; Jon Lawrence, *Electing Our Masters: The Hustings in British Politics from Hogarth to Blair* (Oxford, 2009), pp. 41, 53. Meisel makes it clear that Salisbury was more or less right. Gladstone gave an average of 1.3 extra-parliamentary public speeches between 1833 and 1859, but 10.2 per year from 1860–96, with the numbers skewed to the years after 1878, Meisel, *Public Speech and the Culture of Public Life*, p. 241.

60 *Punch*, 12 October 1889; *Saturday Review*, 24 November 1888; *Graphic*, 8 December 1888; *Annual Register of 1888*, p. 172. Grant Duff complained to Kimberley in 1887 about the new tendency of Commons members to make speeches on the floor that were directed to audiences outside, Mountstuart Grant Duff, *Notes from a Diary, 1886–1888* (London, 1900), p. 77.

61 AB to ME, 26 January 1889, MEP.

62 Letters between AB and Ridgeway, BP BL49826–49830. Carnarvon reported that Randolph Churchill was trying to put together a power base to challenge Balfour's policies, and presumably the man himself; see the introduction to *The Political Diary of the Fourth Earl of Carnarvon, 1857–1890*, ed. Peter Gordon, Camden 5th series, volume 35 (Cambridge, 2009), pp. 76–7.

63 Shannon, *Age of Salisbury*, p. 257; Biagini, *British Democracy and Irish Nationalism*, pp. 80–1.

64 Crossman, *Politics, Law and Order*, p. 170.

65 David Gilmour, *Curzon* (London, 1994), pp. 45–7, 60–1.

66 LLGW, I, p. 200.

67 LLGW, I, pp. 212–19.

68 *Annual Register of 1888*, pp. 118–22.

69 O'Callaghan, *British High Politics and Nationalist Ireland*, p. 118.

70 LLGW, I, p. 234; *Annual Register of 1890*, pp. 65, 82.

71 Dugdale, *Balfour*, I, p. 95.

72 *Scenes from the Triumph of 'Law and Order' in Ireland under the Last and Worst Coercion Act as Administered by the 'Brave Mr Balfour'* (Dublin, 1889). On Irish political cartoons in these decades, see Elisabeth Tilley, 'Irish Political Cartoons and the New Journalism', *Ireland and the New Journalism*, ed. Karen Steele and Michael de Nie (New York, 2014), pp. 81–98.

73 Dugdale, *Balfour*, I, p. 95.

74 These and other examples can be found in A. J. Balfour and George

Wyndham, *Lies and Replies: An Exposure of Some of the Commoner Gladstonian Fallacies* (London, 1892), pp. 32, 71, 35, 40.

75 Sir Henry Robinson, *Memories: Wise and Otherwise* (New York, 1923), p. 92.

76 *Times,* 2 October 1888.

77 O'Callaghan, *British High Politics and Nationalist Ireland*, ch. 5.

78 Bernard Porter describes the creation and expansion of the 'Special Branch' during the years of Balfour's Irish administration in *Plots and Paranoia: A History of Political Espionage in Britain, 1790–1988* (Boston, 1989), ch. 6. See also Roberts, *Salisbury, Victorian Titan*, p. 451, and the discoveries in Christy Campbell, *Fenian Fire: The British Government Plot to Assassinate Queen Victoria* (London, 2003).

79 Dugdale, *Balfour,* I, pp. 115–22; Balfour to George Pembroke, January 1889, BP BL49827. For operation of the syndicate, see Earl of Midleton, *Records and Reactions* (New York, 1939), p. 227.

80 Myles Dungan, *The Captain and the King* (Dublin, 2009), p. 329; Campbell, *Fenian Fire*, p. 352.

81 Shannon, *Age of Salisbury*, pp. 261–2; Thomas J. Spinner, *George Joachim Goschen* (Cambridge, 1973), p. 155.

82 Pam Morris, *Imagining Inclusive Society in 19th Century Novels: The Code of Sincerity in the Public Sphere* (Baltimore, 2004), pp. 10–14. This discussion is indebted to Morris's work, as well as Elaine Hadley, *Living Liberalism: Practical Citizenship in Mid-Victorian England* (Chicago, 2010).

83 D. A. Hamer, 'Gladstone: The Making of Political Myth', *Victorian Studies* 22 (Autumn 1978): 41.

84 Hamer's assessments of Gladstone's personal and political psychology seems to have emerged as a scholarly consensus, see Ian St John, *Gladstone and Logic of Victorian Politics* (London, 2010), pp. 365–6, 387, 400–3; James Thompson, *British Political Culture and the Idea of 'Public Opinion', 1867–1914* (Cambridge, 2013), ch. 1, section on 'The Thinking Public'.

85 AB to Mary Gladstone Drew, 19 May 1891, in *Some Hawarden Letters*, ed. Lisle March-Phillipps and Bertram Christian (London, 1917), p. 248.

86 Daisy White diary, 17 December 1888, Nevins Papers, Butler Library, Columbia University. This may have been a truism about the difference between the two men. In 1928 O. F. Christie wrote that 'Disraeli probably understood Disraeli, but did even Gladstone understand Gladstone?', *The Transition from Aristocracy, 1832–1867* (New York, 1928), p. 275.

87 Edward Hamilton, *The Diary of Sir Edward Walter Hamilton, 1885–1906*, ed. Dudley W. R. Bahlman (Hull, 1993), p. 63. For an introduction: David Runciman, *Political Hypocrisy: The Mask of Power, from Hobbes to Orwell and Beyond* (Princeton, 2008).

88 Morris, *Imagining Inclusive Society*, p. 42.

89 See Leo McKinstrey's discussion of Rosebery's speaking in *Rosebery, Statesman in Turmoil* (London, 2003), pp. 165–71.

90 AB to Frances Balfour, 4 April 1893, BPS GD433/6; speech to the Royal

Literary Society, 26 April 1893 in Balfour, *The Mind of Arthur James Balfour*, p. 306.

91 *Saturday Review*, 14 April 1888. On Gladstone's inability to use humour in promoting the Irish cause, see Joseph Meisel, 'The Importance of Being Serious: The Unexplored Connection between Gladstone and Humour', *History* 84 (April 1999): 297.

92 Norman Vance, *Sinews of the Spirit: The Ideal of Christian Manliness in Victorian Literature and Religious Thought* (Cambridge, 1985), pp. 183–4.

93 Hamilton, *Diary of Edward Hamilton*, p. 145; also Lubenow, *Parliamentary Politics and the Home Rule Crisis*, pp. 330–1.

<h2 style="text-align:center">CHAPTER SIX</h2>

1 ME to AB, 23 January 1889, MEP. This reconstruction of the Stanway party relies on the diary for 1888–89 of Margaret Rutherford White, Nevins Papers, Butler Library, Columbia University; diary entries of A. G. C. Liddell and unpublished memoir of Edith Balfour Lyttelton, CP 6/1; Gladys de Grey to Michael and Belle Herbert, [January 1889], GPP; George Curzon to St John Brodrick, 22 January 1889, Midleton Papers BL 50073. For the country house entertaining of Mary Elcho, see Cynthia Asquith, *Remember and Be Glad* (London, 1952), pp. 3–23.

2 R. Gill, *Happy Rural Seat: The Country House and the Literary Imagination* (London, 1972); Adeline R. Tintner, *The Cosmopolitan World of Henry James: An Intertextual Study* (Baton Rouge and London, 1991), ch. 1. Novels of the types mentioned here: Ouida, *The House Party* (1887), Henry James, *The Sacred Fount* (1901), H. H. Munro, 'Reginald on House-Parties' [1904] in *The Penguin Complete Saki* (New York, 1976), pp. 20–2, Vita Sackville West, *The Edwardians* (1930). Novels modelled on Stanway: Angela Thirkell, *Wild Strawberries* (1934), Edith Wharton, *The Buccaneers* (1938), L. P. Hartley, *The Go-Between* (1953).

3 Leonore Davidoff, *The Best Circles: Women and Society in Victorian England* (New Jersey, 1973); Mark Girouard, *Life in the English Country House* (New Haven, 1978).

4 Nancy Armstrong, *Desire and Domestic Fiction: A Political History of the Novel* (London and New York, 1987); Patricia Meyer Spacks, *Gossip* (New York, 1985) and *Boredom: The Literary History of a State of Mind* (Chicago, 1995).

5 These important changes in elite social life as a genuinely national elite emerged in Britain can be charted in Girouard, *Life in the English Country House*, chs 7–8; Linda Colley, *Britons: Forging a Nation, 1707–1837* (New Haven, 1992), ch. 4; Judith Schneid Lewis, *In the Family Way: Childbearing in the British Aristocracy, 1760–1860* (New Jersey, 1986); G. J. Barker-Benfield, *The Culture of Sensibility: Sex and Society in Eighteenth-Century Britain* (Chicago, 1992); Michael Morgan, *Propriety and Position: A Study of Victorian Manners* (New York, 1987).

6 Mark Girouard, *A Country House Companion* (New Haven, 1987), p. 49.

7 *Habits of Good Society* (London, 1859). On visiting and hospitality far

from the metropolis in earlier periods, Susan E. Whyman, *Sociability and Power in Late-Stuart England: The Cultural World of the Verneys, 1660–1720* (Oxford, 1999); Amanda Vickery, *The Gentleman's Daughter: Women's Lives in Georgian England* (New Haven, 1998).

8 Dorothy Nevill, *Reminiscences of Lady Dorothy Nevill*, ed. Ralph Nevill (London, 1906), p. 7; Lady Cardigan, *My Recollections* (London, 1909), pp. 51–2.

9 A. L. Kennedy, ed., *'My Dear Duchess': Social and Political Letters to the Duchess of Manchester, 1858–1869* (London, 1956), p. 166; *Manners and Rules of Good Society by a Member of the Aristocracy* (London, 1894), pp. 173–4. See Lord Derby in 1873 at Alnwick: 'we found a large party, none known to us before: it is the custom of the Duke and Duchess [of Northumberland] not to invite parties made up beforehand, but to ask all their friends to stay with them in passing: a hospitable and convenient custom, but which is apt to make a dull house, as it is left to chance whether the guests are or are not congenial', Edward Stanley, Earl of Derby, *A Selection from the Diaries of Edward Henry Stanley, 15th Earl of Derby*, ed. John Vincent (London, 1994), p. 145.

10 Norbet Elias and G. Dunning, *The Quest for Excitement: Sport and Leisure in the Civilizing Process* (London, 1986), pp. 68–70.

11 *Habits of Good Society*, pp. 353–7; Frances Horner to DD Balfour, 30 December 1890, CP 5/9.

12 Christopher Hibbert, *Edward VII, A Portrait* (New York, 1976), ch. 5; Virginia Cowles, *Edward VII and his Circle* (London, 1956), p. 331.

13 Georg Simmel, *The Sociology of Georg Simmel*, trans. and ed. Kurt Wolff (Illinois, 1950), pp. 40–57; Elias and Dunning, *Quest for Excitement*, pp. 68–70

14 *Habits of Good Society*, p. 28.

15 Edward Marsh, *A Number of People* (London, 1939), pp. 200–4.

16 Girouard, *Life in the English Country House*, ch. 10.

17 By late in the century, *Manners of the Aristocracy by One of Themselves* (London, 1881) and *Manners and Rules of Good Society* (London, 1894) had added entire chapters of guidance specifically for this type of country house visit.

18 For the Whites' social life, Allan Nevins, *Henry White: Thirty Years of American Diplomacy* (New York, 1930), ch. 7.

19 Graham Dawson, *Soldier Heroes: British Adventure, Empire and the Imagining of Masculinities* (New York, 1994), ch. 3 on the characteristics of this genre. Mary Elcho's daughter – fifteen months old at the time of this party – described the anxieties of trips to visit a country house when she was a young debutante, Asquith, *Remember*, pp. 164–5.

20 In 1896, Balfour shocked Gladstone by pedalling himself to and from the station on a visit to Hawarden, Arthur James Balfour, *Chapters of Autobiography* (London, 1930), pp. 76, 82.

21 H. G. Wells commended Mary for the kind way in which she instructed a novice in the correct attire for these occasions, Osbert Sitwell, *Laughter in the Next Room* (Boston, 1948), p. 114.

22 James Jolliffe, *Raymond Asquith: Life and Letters* (London, 1980),

pp. 78–9. Mary's informality was becoming acceptable. In the early 1890s Lady Colin Campbell noted that 'breakfast and lunch do not require a punctual attendance', but that failing to assemble in time for dinner constituted a 'grave offense against social law', *Etiquette of Good Society* (London, 1893), p. 73.

23 *Manners of the Aristocracy*, p. 11; *Etiquette, Social Ethics, and Dinner Table Observances* (London, 1860), p. 48.

24 *Etiquette for Gentlemen* (London, 1857), p. 86.

25 *Etiquette for Ladies in Public and Private* (London, 1894), p. 81.

26 Augustus Hare, *The Story of My Life*, six volumes (London, 1896–1900), 2, p. 275; Frederick Ponsonby, *Recollections of Three Reigns* (London, 1951), p. 200.

27 Erving Goffman, *Behavior in Public Places* (New York, 1963), p. 25, ch. 3.

28 AB to Ettie Grenfell, [n.d.], Desborough Papers DE/Rv/C132.

29 Spenser Theyre-Smith, *The Happy Pair* (London, 1868; Boston, 1890).

30 Gladys de Grey to Michael and Belle Herbert, [January 1889], GPP. W. G. Wills's *Olivia* based on *The Vicar of Wakefield* was a popular theatrical production during this decade, see Ellen Terry, *The Story of My Life* (London, 1908), pp. 141, 235.

31 *Manners and Rules of Good Society*, p. 194.

32 On these important changes in cultural expression: Terry Castle, *Masquerade and Civilization: The Carnivalesque in Eighteenth-Century English Culture and Fiction* (Stanford, 1986), ch. 8; Nina Auerbach, *Private Theatricals: The Lives of the Victorians* (Cambridge, Massachusetts, 1990), pp. 4–10; Richard Sennett, *The Fall of Public Man: On the Social Psychology of Capitalism* (New York, 1978), pp. 150–74; Davidoff, *Best Circles*, p. 66.

33 J. Jeffrey Franklin, *Serious Play: The Cultural Form of the Nineteenth-Century Realist Novel* (Philadelphia, 1999), ch. 2; Ilse Hayden, *Symbol and Privilege: The Ritual Context of British Royalty* (Arizona, 1987), ch. 6.

34 Valerie Steele, *Fashion and Eroticism: Ideals of Feminine Beauty from the Victorian Age to the Jazz Age* (New York, 1985), p. 134; Stephen Kern, *The Culture of Love, Victorians to Moderns* (Cambridge, Massachusetts, 1992), p. 65; Maureen E. Montgomery, *Displaying Women: Spectacles of Leisure in Edith Wharton's New York* (New York, 1998), ch. 5.

35 MT to Curzon, 29 August 1888, Curzon Papers Eur F 111/12, seen originally at India Office Library.

36 Nancy W. Ellenberger, 'The Souls and London "Society" at the End of the Nineteenth Century', *Victorian Studies* 25 (Winter, 1982), pp. 149–51.

37 MT to DD Balfour, [undated], CP 5/1.

38 AB to ME, 26 January 1889, MEP. Lady Colin Campbell wrote that 'the more complete the transformation the greater the fun – gentlemen dressed as ladies, children metamorphosed into adults, thin people made up into stout ones – any change, in fact, but that of ladies donning male attire', *Etiquette of Good Society*, p. 178.

39 This generalisation is too broadly stated, of course. See Christopher Breward, *The Hidden Consumer: Masculinities, Fashion and City Life 1860–1914* (Manchester, 1999), ch. 3.

40 George Curzon to DD Balfour, [January 1889], CP 5/5; Carole Edelsky,

'Who's Got the Floor?', *Gender and Conversational Interaction*, ed. Deborah Tannen (Oxford, 1993), pp. 189–227.

41 Daisy White diary, 14 August 1888, 26 November 1888, Nevins Papers, Butler Library, Columbia University.

42 Gladys de Grey to Michael and Belle Herbert, 10 January 1889, GPP. Hilda Brodrick to George Curzon, 4 January 1887, Curzon Papers Eur F 111/9; Hilda Brodrick to Ettie Grenfell, 3 January 1888, Desborough Papers DE/Rv/C210.

43 For other examples of Curzon's 'relish for more boisterous pleasures than parodies and paper games', see Kenneth Rose, *Superior Person: A Portrait of Curzon and His Circle in Late Victorian England* (New York, 1969), pp. 188–9.

44 *Manners and Rules of Good Society*, p. 192.

45 ME to AB, 30 October 1912, MEP.

46 Gertrude Pembroke to ME, 22 January 1889, MEP.

47 Robert Blake, *Disraeli* (New York, 1967), p. 410; Claudia Renton, *Those Wild Wyndhams: Three Sisters at the Heart of Power* (London, 2014), p. xix.

48 ME to Frances Balfour, 21 January 1889, MEP.

49 *Manners of the Aristocracy*, p. 25. See Maureen E. Montgomery, '"The Fruit that Hangs Highest": Courtship and Chaperonage in New York High Society, 1880–1920', *Journal of Family History* 21 (1996): 172–91.

50 DD Balfour Lyttelton, 'Interwoven', CP 6/1. Letters with Curzon in CP 5/5. The realisation that she was being talked about and called a prig is in DD Balfour to Kathleen Lyttelton, 5 March 1889, CP II 3/14. Curzon had told Daisy White in January that he would have to marry into money, but that he would not marry without love. In February, Daisy thought that he was smitten with DD, Daisy White diary, 17 February 1889, Nevins Papers, Butler Library, Columbia University.

51 Beth Newman, *Subjects on Display: Psychoanalysis, Social Expectation, and Victorian Femininity* (Ohio, 2004), p. 104.

52 See DD Balfour to Doll Liddell, letters from summer and autumn 1888, CP 5/13.

53 Doll Liddell to DD Balfour, 25 January [1889], CP II 3/7.

54 DD and her sister were not allowed to visit Glen, because her mother 'hears stories and unkind things about Margot and though I do not know that she believes them, she has taken fright about our becoming intimate with her', DD to Doll Liddell, 17 September 1888, CP 5/13.

55 Andrew St George, *The Descent of Manners: Etiquette, Rules and the Victorians* (London, 1993), p. 95; Castle, *Masquerade and Civilization*, pp. 32–35.

56 Clive Aslet places Stanway among the late-Victorian 'romantic houses', along with Frances Horner's Mells in Frome and St Fagan's in Cardiff, the home of the Windsors, *The Last Country Houses* (New Haven and London, 1982), ch. 1.

57 More than two decades later, Liddell acknowledged to DD that he had been wrong to urge her to keep up the physical relationship when he knew she would not marry him – they met in his rooms when DD was supposed to be on her charity visits, Liddell to DD Lyttelton, 9 January 1911, CP II:3/7.

58 ME to Hugo Elcho, 16 August 1887, MEP.

59 Liddell to DD Balfour, 23 January 1889, CP 6/1.

60 MT to ME, 9 October 1887, MEP.

61 Letters between Mary Elcho and Lord Ribblesdale, 1887 and 1888, MEP; Curzon to Daisy White, 8 November 1886, Library of Congress White Papers (Family 6); Charty Ribblesdale to George Curzon, 6 June 1885, in Rose, *Superior Person*, p. 160; Nicola Beauman, *Cynthia Asquith* (London, 1987), p. 13; Daisy White diary, 24 August 1888, Nevins Papers, Butler Library, Columbia University.

62 St John Brodrick to George Curzon, 8 December 1889, Curzon Papers Eur F 111:9.

63 Daisy White diary, 14 August 1888, 12 May 1889, Nevins Papers, Butler Library, Columbia University. On DeGrey: Rose, *Superior Person*, p. 66.

64 Liddell to Constance Wenlock, [December 1889], WP DDFA3/5/3.

65 Daisy White diary, 22 November 1888, Nevins Papers, Butler Library, Columbia University.

66 ME diary, 16 November 1891, MEP; ME to Evelyn de Vesci, 29 November 1891, HPP DD/DRU/87.

67 DD Balfour Lyttelton to ME, 16 February 1932, MEP; DD Balfour to Doll Liddell, 13 September 1888, CP 5/13.

68 Michael Mason, *The Making of Victorian Sexuality* (Oxford, 1994), pp. 109–33. Joan Perkin argues by anecdote that infidelity for married aristocratic women was constant throughout the century, just more discreet, *Women and Marriage in Nineteenth-Century England* (London, 1989), ch. 4. Lewis provides the most nuanced account of how guilt about infidelity as a violation of private moral standards was internalised among elite women during the first half of the nineteenth century, *In the Family Way*, pp. 38–47, 227–8. For the concerns of contemporaries see 'Young Married Women', *Saturday Review*, 23 July 1887.

69 Kali Israel, *Names and Stories: Emilia Dilke and Victorian Culture* (Oxford, 1999), p. 131.

70 The Honorable Mrs Gell, *Under Three Reigns* (London, 1927), p. 206. One modern historian concludes that this was true of high society in 1890s Paris: Michele Plott, 'The Rules of the Game: Respectability, Sexuality, and the Femme Mondaine in Late-Nineteenth Century Paris', *French Historical Studies* 25 (Summer 2002): 531–56.

71 The host and hostess of Ouida's *A House Party* (1887) discuss this practice at length, with the husband disparaging a custom of which he himself takes advantage.

72 Herbert Sussman, *Victorian Masculinities: Manhood and Masculine Poetics in Early Victorian Literature and Art* (Cambridge, 1995), p. 144. Daisy White diary, 14 January 1889, Nevins Papers, Butler Library, Columbia University.

73 Simmel, *Sociology of George Simmel*, pp. 50–1; Davidoff, *The Best Circles*, pp. 90–3. The view was shared by E. C. Greville Murray, who devoted thirteen chapters to discussing the 'flirt' in *Side-Lights on English Society*, two volumes (London, 1881), 1, pp. 9–148.

74 See for example, Patricia Jalland, *Women, Marriage and Politics,*

1860–1914 (Oxford, 1986), where infidelity is not mentioned. M. Jeanne Peterson, *Family, Love, and Work in the Lives of Victorian Gentlewomen* (Indiana, 1989), pp. 78–9 describes some incompatible marriages among upper-middle-class families, but without mentioning affairs. Julia Bush notes discrete liaisons on the part of some women she studies, but on the basis of their self-writings concludes that 'the difficulties of marriage' were 'more than compensated for by its advantages' in terms of access to important people and activities, *Edwardian Ladies and Imperial Power* (London, 2000), p. 24.

75 Cowles, *Edward VII*, p. 331.

76 ME to AB, 19 January, 1904, MEP.

77 ME to AB, 23 January 1889, MEP.

78 Ettie Grenfell to Constance Wenlock, 8 December 1892, WP DDFA3/5/13; ME to AB, [undated] and 17 January, 5 June, 8 June 1894, MEP.

79 Rhoda Broughton, *Dr Cupid* (London, 1886).

80 Anne Wemyss to Evelyn de Vesci, undated, HPP DD/DRU/82.

81 ME to Percy Wyndham, 6 December 1887, MEP; ME to Evelyn de Vesci, 8 March 1889, HPP DD/DRU/87; Frances Balfour to Betty Balfour [June 1889], BPS GD433/2/301.

82 Renton, *Those Wild Wyndhams*, p. 126.

83 Richard Davenport-Hines, *Ettie: The Intimate Life and Dauntless Spirit of Lady Desborough* (London, 2008), p. 71; Hugo to ME, 31 Sep. 1888, MEP.

84 Hines, *Ettie*, p. 54; ME diary, 15 Dec 1890, MEP.

85 Hugo to Belle Herbert, [undated, from Stanway], GPP; Hugo to Ettie Grenfell in Nicholas Mosley, *Julian Grenfell: His Life and the Times of his Death, 1888–1915* (New York, 1976), p. 16, and letters from 1890 in Desborough Papers DE/Rv/C474.

86 ME to AB, 13 August 1890, MEP.

87 On Hermione Leinster, see her friend Elizabeth, Countess of Fingall, *Seventy Years Young* (London, 1938), pp. 175–85. The account that follows differs from Renton's in *Those Wild Wyndhams*, pp. 139–41, in taking Mary's ill health in these years more seriously, as caused by illnesses such as typhoid and influenza, and in seeing the crisis caused by Hugo's relationship with Hermione Leinster as potentially more destabilising of Mary's life. Hermione's letters to Evelyn are in HPP DD/DRU/90.

88 Harry White to Daisy White, 13, 22, 26, 29 March 1890, Library of Congress White Papers (Family 6).

89 Anne Wemyss to Evelyn de Vesci,16 August 1889, 28 May 1890, 3 June 1890, HPP DD/DRU/82.

90 Anne Wemyss to ME, 30 September 1894, MEP.

91 Frances Horner to DD Balfour, undated, CP 5/9.

92 GP to Constance Wenlock, April 1892, WP DDFA3/4/5; confirmed by Frances Horner to DD Balfour, [April 1892], CP 5/9.

93 Wilfrid Blunt diary, 13–15 August 1892, Blunt Papers 31–1975.

94 Lady Angela Forbes, *Memories and Base Details* (New York, 1921), p. 99.

95 Peter Raby quoted in Nicholas Freeman, *1895: Drama, Disaster and Disgrace in Late Victorian Britain* (Edinburgh, 2011), p. 46.

96 H. H. Asquith to Frances Horner, 25 October 1893, FHP; E. F. Benson, 'Country House Parties', *New Review* 11 (October 1894): 355–65.

97 Duke of Sutherland, *Looking Back* (London, 1958), p. 43; LAB, p. 124.

98 Frances Balfour, *Ne Obliviscaris*, two volumes (London, 1930), I, p. 148. See David Cannadine, 'After the Horse: Nobility and Mobility in Modern Britain' in *Land and Society in Britain, 1700–1914*, ed. Negley Harte and Ronald Quinault (Manchester, 1996), pp. 211–34.

99 Auerbach, *Private Theatricals*, p. 4. Lady Cowper, who knew the Souls well, also thought that the new expressiveness in social life was eradicating inner privacy and depth, though she admitted that it allowed for greater warmth and sympathy than the rigid self-suppression of her upbringing, 'The Decline of Reserve among Women', *Nineteenth Century* 27 (January, 1890): 65–7.

100 Emily Lutyens, *A Blessed Girl, Memoirs of a Victorian* Girlhood (London, 1989), p. 115.

101 Frances Balfour to Betty Balfour, June 1889, BPS GD433/2/301; Richard Kaye, *The Flirt's Tragedy: Desire without End in Victorian and Edwardian Fiction* (Virginia, 2002), p. 179.

102 Freeman, *1895*, p. 46.

103 Jolliffe, *Raymond Asquith*, p. 98.

104 James Vernon, *Distant Strangers: How Britain Became Modern* (Berkeley, 2014), ch. 1.

105 Plott, 'The Rules of the Game', p. 539.

106 ME to AB, 20 November 1895, MEP.

INTERLUDE: FIN DE SIÈCLE:

1 Arthur James Balfour, *A Fragment on Progress* (Edinburgh, 1892).

2 Blanche Dugdale, *Arthur James Balfour*, two volumes (London, 1936), I, p. 29.

3 *Pall Mall Gazette*, 15 February 1895.

4 Stephen Arata, *Fictions of Loss in the Victorian Fin de Siècle: Identity and Empire* (Cambridge, 1996), pp. 68–70.

5 Arthur James Balfour, *Essays and Addresses* (Edinburgh, 1893), p. 4

6 Quotes from *Fragment on Progress*, pp. 1, 8–9. Within a decade this would be the consensus of those knowledgeable about the biological sciences and a guiding conviction of the eugenics movement, G. R. Searle, *Eugenics and Politics in Britain, 1900–1914* (Leyden, 1976), pp. 3, 46.

7 *Fragment on Progress*, p. 52.

8 The best study of the intersection between Balfour's philosophical inquiries and his political stance is Jason Tomes, *Balfour and Foreign Policy: The International Thought of a Conservative Statesman* (Cambridge, 1997), chs 2–3. For a study of some of the social thinkers that Balfour was refuting, see Jeffrey Paul von Arx, *Progress and Pessimism: Religion, Politics,*

and History in Late Nineteenth Century Britain (Cambridge, Massachusetts, 1985).

9 *Fragment on Progress*, pp. 55, 52–3, 68–9.

10 *Fragment on Progress*, 70–3.

11 The *Dundee Courier*, 27 November 1891 and *Derby Mercury*, 2 December 1891 – and other provincial newspapers – ran a short press-release blurb of this speech; the *Evening Telegraph*, 27 November 1891, summarised the reactions of the major metropolitan dailies, while the *Leeds Mercury* and *Birmingham Daily Post* of 27 November gave long and fairly accurate summaries of the talk itself.

12 The version used here is published in Arthur James Balfour, *Essays and Addresses* (Edinburgh, 1893), pp. 1–38.

13 Margot told George Curzon that this address was 'skillful, rather thin, all got up at Stanway, not a good place for work', 15 December 1887, seen originally in Curzon papers India Office Library, Eur. F111. Mary admitted that 'Notes on Progress' was also written in about a week at Stanway, ME to Evelyn de Vesci, 1 November 1891, HPP DD/DRU/87.

14 'The Pleasures of Reading', p. 4.

15 'The Pleasures of Reading', pp. 31–2.

16 'The Pleasures of Reading', pp. 8–10.

17 "The Pleasures of Reading', pp. 17–18.

18 *Spectator*, 17 December 1887.

19 Balfour developed this argument more thoroughly in *Foundations of Belief* (London, 1895), pp. 276–8.

20 Holbrook Jackson, *The Eighteen Nineties* (London, 1913); Nicholas Freeman, *1895: Drama, Disaster and Disgrace in Late Victorian Britain* (Edinburgh, 2011), p. 46.

21 Arata, *Fictions of Loss*, pp. 99–101, 107–11.

22 *Fragment on Progress*, pp. 18–19.

23 My thoughts on these developments have been helped by the recent works of James Vernon, *Distant Strangers: How Britain Became Modern* (Berkeley, 2014) and James Thompson, *British Political Culture and the Idea of 'Public Opinion', 1867–1914* (Cambridge, 2013).

24 Alfred Lyttelton to MT, 26 August 1886, MAP c.6697. For Arthur's many club affiliations: William C. Lubenow, *Liberal Intellectuals and Public Culture in Modern Britain, 1815–1914* (Woodbridge, 2010), p. 107.

CHAPTER SEVEN

1 ME to Daisy White, 12 August 1890, MEP.

2 For the mechanics of travel: Marjorie Morgan, *National Identities and Travel in Victorian Britain* (New York, 2001), ch. 1; on women's travel abroad: Maureen Montgomery, *Displaying Women: Spectacles of Leisure in Edith Wharton's New York* (New York, 1998), pp. 108–16.

3 Margot published this disjointed journal in *More or Less about Myself* (New York, 1934), pp. 106–27.

4 Richard Davenport-Hines, *Ettie: The Intimate Life and Dauntless Spirit of Lady Desborough* (London, 2008), pp. 68–9.

5 DD Balfour to Kathleen Lyttelton, 6 March 1891, CP5/16.

6 Seth Koven, *Slumming: Sexual and Social Politics in Victorian London* (London, 2006).

7 For the politics of British agriculture in general, see Avner Offer, *Property and Politics, 1870–1914: Landownership, Law, Ideology and Urban Development in England* (Cambridge, 1981); E. H. H. Green, *The Crisis of Conservatism: The Politics, Economics and Ideology of the British Conservative Party, 1880–1914* (London, 1995); Paul Readman, *Land and Nation in England: Patriotism, National Identity, and the Politics of Land, 1880–1914* (Woodbridge, 2008). For peers and landed gentry: Gregory D. Phillips, *The Diehards: Aristocratic Society and Politics in Edwardian England* (Cambridge, Massachusetts, 1979), ch. 3, F. M. L. Thompson, *English Landed Society in the Nineteenth Century* (London, 1963), pp. 292–326.

8 Speeches and letters to the editor in LSGP, II, pp. 3–100.

9 Offer, *Property and Politics*, p. 208.

10 LSGP, II, pp. 98–9.

11 The great achievement of Wyndham's career, while serving as chief secretary for Ireland in Arthur's cabinet, was overseeing passage of the 1903 Irish Land Act paying the immediate purchase price to landowners who wished to sell, while establishing government mortgages on low-interest terms for peasant purchasers of land. The principle had been tried ineffectively for almost twenty years, but this act was finally successful in creating the 'Ireland that we made' of small, native-Irish farmers after more than two centuries of Protestant ascendancy, see David Hudson, *The Ireland that We Made: Arthur and Gerald Balfour's Contribution to the Origins of Modern Ireland* (Ohio, 2003) and Andrew Gailey, *The Death of Kindness: The Experience of Constructive Unionism, 1890–1905* (Cork, 1987).

12 Andrew Adonis, *Making Aristocracy Work: The Peerage and the Political System in Britain, 1884–1914* (Oxford, 1993), p. 244. For Pembroke's alarm in 1881, see Edward Hamilton, *The Diary of Sir Edward Hamilton, 1880–1885*, ed. Dudley W. R. Bahlman, two volumes (Oxford, 1972), I, p. 210. The obituary of George's brother-in-law Lord Brownlow noted apologetically that he had inherited too many landed properties for him to fulfil responsibilities to them all: *Times*, 18 March 1921.

13 LSGP, I, p. 65.

14 See Lord Derby's activities in January 1887 in Edward Stanley, Earl of Derby, *The Later Derby Diaries*, ed. John Vincent (Bristol, 1981), p. 50.

15 Offer, *Property and Politics*, ch. 2, on the creation of this large class of 'white collar' professionals who specialised in serving the landed interest.

16 The *Times*, 28 July 1871, said that the Dublin areas brought in £71,000 per year, though the New Domesday survey conducted five years later reported half that, with £70,000 being closer to Pembroke's total yearly income.

17 James Caird, *The Landed Interest and the Supply of Food* (London, [1878],

1967), pp. 56–8. Caird lays out the duties of each of the three groups in the farming community and compares this unique system with those of other countries, chs 5–6.

18 For discussion of peers in relation to their rural estates. see Phillips, *The Diehards*, ch. 4.

19 LSGP, II, pp. 325, 343.

20 *Western Gazette*, 10 May 1895.

21 Martin Pugh, *The Tories and the People, 1880–1935* (New York, 1985), pp. 102, 221.

22 LSGP, I, p. 45; GP to Lord Wemyss, 18 March 1886, MEP; Adonis, *Making Aristocracy Work,pp.* 248–50.

23 LSGP, I, pp. 175, 123.

24 Joseph Meisel, *Public Speech and the Culture of Public Life in the Age of Gladstone* (New York, 2001), pp. 225–7.

25 Betty Balfour to Frances Balfour, 28 May and 19 August 1891, BPS GD433/2/304.

26 Edward Hamilton noted that George tried to provide monetary assistance and promise of employment to encourage Wilton emigrants to Tasmania, but no one took the offer, diary for 4 January 1888, Hamilton Papers BL48647.

27 GP to DD Balfour, 19 April 1889, CP 5/18; GP to Constance Wenlock, 10 November 1890, WP DDFA/3/5/6.

28 GP to Violet Maxse, 27 September 1893, Viscountess Milner Papers [Bodl.] MS. Eng. VM42/C345/fol. 21.

29 Gety Pembroke to Constance Wenlock, [late 1880s], WP DDFA3/5/6; GP to Violet Maxse, 20 July 1892, Viscountess Milner Papers [Bodl.] MS. Eng.VM42/C345/fol. 4.

30 A. G. C. Liddell, *Notes from the Life of an Ordinary Mortal* (London, 1911), pp. 259–60. The news that Hugo had lost this election came on Thursday of the week of the house party, perhaps accounting for some of his ill-humour.

31 MT to DD Balfour, [1889], CP 5/1.

32 GP to Ettie Grenfell, 1 April 1891, Desborough Papers DE/Rv/C1293.

33 K. D. Reynolds notes how many of the activities that George engaged in might be undertaken by aristocratic wives, depending on the circumstances of particular families, *Aristocratic Women and Political Society in Victorian Britain* (Oxford, 1998), pp. 42–73.

34 Betty Balfour to Frances Balfour, 13 December 1889, BPS GD433/2/301.

35 GP to DD Balfour, 18 April 1889, CP/18; William C. Lubenow, *Liberal Intellectuals and Public Culture in Modern Britain, 1814–1914: Making Words Flesh* (Woodbridge, 2010), ch. 3.

36 GP to Michael Herbert, 18 February 1894, GPP.

37 See, for example, Countess of Cowper, *Lord Cowper* (privately printed, 1911) or Lord Ribblesdale, *Impressions and Memories* (London, 1927). John Morley observed this sense of melancholy when visiting Cowper at Panshanger, diary for 29 June 1889, Morley Papers [Bodl.] MS. Eng. d.3444.

38 Andrea Geddes Poole, *Stewards of the Nation's Art: Contested Cultural Authority, 1890–1939* (Toronto, 2010).

39 David Spring, 'Willoughby de Broke and Walter Long: English Landed Society and Political Extremism, 1912–1914', *Land and Society in Britain, 1700–1914*, ed. Negley Harte and Roland Quinault (Manchester, 1996), pp. 176–7.

40 GP to Violet Maxse, 24 April 1892, Viscountess Milner Papers [Bodl.] MS. Eng. VM42/C345/fol. 1.

41 GP to Evelyn de Vesci, 4 August 1886, HPP DD/DRU/84; for context that confirms Pembroke's view, see Ben Griffin, *The Politics of Gender in Victorian Britain: Masculinity, Political Culture and the Struggle for Women's Rights* (Cambridge, 2012), ch. 6, section 'Anxious Masculinities and the Politics of Complicity'.

42 Ruddock F. Mackay, *Balfour: Intellectual Statesman* (Oxford, 1985), p. 43.

43 *Spectator,* 4 March 1893.

44 GW to ME, 29 January 1906, MEP. Lubenow, *Liberal Intellectuals and Public Culture*, p. 89. Hugo Elcho's brother-in-law St John Brodrick described this group of aspiring aristocrats in Earl of Midleton, *Records and Reactions* (London, 1939), p. 49.

45 *Whitehall Review,* 4 July 1896; T. S. Escott, *Society in the New Reign* (London, 1904), p. 99; *Western Times,* 3 April 1893.

46 LLGW, I, p. 234; Max Egremont, *The Cousins* (London, 1977), pp. 145–6.

47 Kali Israel, 'French Vices and British Liberties: Gender, Class and Narrative Competition in a Late-Victorian Sex Scandal', *Social History* 22 (1997): 12–13.

48 LLGW, I, pp. 190–1.

49 Charles Gatty, *George Wyndham, Recognita* (London, 1917), pp. 111, 230.

50 Ben Griffin calls the subjective worlds of late-Victorian political men a 'terra incognita', *Politics of Gender in Victorian Britain*, ch. 6, while Michael Roper and John Tosh argue that with men in general 'subjective experiences are left unexplored', introduction in *Manful Assertions: Masculinities in Britain since 1800* (London, 1991), p. 8.

51 H. G. Wells, *The New Machiavelli* (Thirsk, reprint edn, 2002), pp. 298–9.

52 Quote from an *Observer* article in a letter from Lady Wemyss to Evelyn de Vesci, 28 February 1892, HPP DD/DRU/81; GW to Sibell Grosvenor, 20 [April] 1890, 2 February 1891, GWP.

53 GW to Sibell Grosvenor, 1 March 1893, GWP; Gatty, *George Wyndham*, pp. 133–4.

54 GW to Sibell Grosvenor, 12 March and 30 June 1893, GWP.

55 GW to Ettie Grenfell, 26 December 1897, Desborough Papers DE/Rv/C/2800; *Outlook,* 3 May 1924.

56 *The Wellesley Index of Victorian Periodicals, 1824–1900*, ed. Walter Houghton, five volumes (Toronto, 1966–89), III, pp. 303–7.

57 Jonathan Rose, *The Edwardian Temperament 1895–1919* (Ohio, 1986), pp. 169–71.

58 GW to Sibell Grosvenor, 8 March 1889, 2 April 1892, GWP; LLGW, I,

p. 49; *Letters of George Wyndham*, ed. Guy Wyndham, two volumes (privately printed, 1915), I, p. 2.

59 L. P. Curtis, *Coercion and Conciliation in Ireland 1880–1882: A Study in Conservative Unioniism* (Princeton, 1963), pp. 355–74 ; Blanche Dugdale, *Arthur James Balfour*, two volumes (London, 1937), I, pp. 174–80; Virginia Crossman, 'The Charm of Allowing People to Manage their Own Affairs': Political Perspectives on Emergency Relief in Late Nineteenth-Century Ireland', *Ireland in Transition, 1867–1921*, ed. G. R. Boyce and Alan O'Day (London, 2004).

60 Curtis notes that the term 'congested district' was a misnomer. The post-famine landscapes of the western coast were sparsely populated, but without the economic diversification that would raise the inhabitants out of subsistence. Balfour's preferred solution was emigration, see Curtis, *Coercion and Conciliation*, pp. 355–62.

61 These and the quotes that follow are from GW to Sibell Grosvenor, 24, 25, 28, 30 October 1890, GWP; see also Egremont, *The Cousins*, pp. 146–8.

62 LLGW, II, p. 450; Nigel Nicolson, *Mary Curzon* (New York, 1977), p. 151; Curtis, *Coercion and Conciliation*, p. 356 for Wyndham's private response to a similar trip in 1901.

63 Richard Shannon, *The Age of Salisbury, 1881–1902* (London, 1996), pp. 307–32, 419–21.

64 LLGW, I, pp. 240–1.

65 Gatty, *George Wyndham*, p. 139; Gerald Balfour to Betty Balfour, 9 January 1891, BPS GD433/2/303; also similar reactions of Herbert Gladstone in Frances Balfour to Betty Balfour, [June 1889], BPS GD433/2/301.

66 LLGW, I, p. 247.

67 Jon Lawrence, *Electing Our Masters: The Hustings in British Politics from Hogarth to Blair* (Oxford, 2009), pp. 77–8.

68 Ed Cohen quoted in Ruth Robbins, 'A Very Curious Construction: Masculinity and the Poetry of A D Housman and Oscar Wilde' in *Cultural Politics at the Fin de Siècle*, ed. Sally Ledger and Scott McCracken (Cambridge, 1995), pp. 141–3.

69 Curtis, *Coercion and Conciliation*, p. 356; ME to GW, 18 October 1898, GWP; Egremont, *The Cousins*, pp. 194–8.

70 Wyndham's unsigned editorial 'Youth in Politics', *Outlook*, 12 February 1898; Charles Boyd, *George Wyndham* (London, 1913), p. 15.

71 GW to his wife, 2 April 1892, GWP, and 1 April 1893, *Letters of George Wyndham*, I, p. 303.

72 John Tosh, *Manliness and Masculinities in Nineteenth-Century Britain* (Harlow, 2005), p. 110.

73 T. S. Eliot, *The Sacred Wood* (London, 1920), pp. 24–32.

74 The pioneering work was done by Leonore Davidoff, *The Best Circles: Society, Etiquette and the Season* (New Jersey, 1973); Pat Jalland, *Women, Marriage, and Politics, 1860–1914* (Oxford, 1986) and M. Jeanne Peterson, *Family, Love, and Work in the Lives of Victorian Gentlewomen* (Indiana, 1989), followed by Reynolds, *Aristocratic Women*; Julia Bush, *Edwardian Ladies and Imperial Power* (New York, 2000); Susan K. Harris, *The Cultural*

Work of the Late Nineteenth-Century Hostess: Annie Adams Fields and Mary Gladstone Drew (Basingstoke, 2002).

75 Frances Balfour, *Ne Obliviscaris*, two volumes (London, 1930), I, pp. 47–50, 55–8.

76 Reynolds, *Aristocratic Women*, pp. 178–9. Sarah Richardson makes the point that letter-writing could extend the political reach of elite women, as did the well-established *salon*, '"Well-Neighboured Houses": The Political Networks of Elite Women, 1780–1860' in *Women in British Politics, 1760–1860: The Power of the Petticoat*, ed. Kathryn Gleadle and Sarah Richardson (London, 2000), pp. 56–68.

77 Jalland, *Women, Marriage and Politics*, pp. 189–204; Lawrence, *Electing Our Masters*, pp. 83–7. Joseph Meisel sees Catherine Gladstone and Jennie Churchill, starting in the late 1870s, as the first political wives to appear so visibly in election settings, *Public Speech and the Culture of Public Life*, pp. 260–2. Lady Cowper, who was born in 1845, confirmed how suddenly women began to appear in print, on platforms and doing committee work, another example of the 'Decline of Reserve among Women', *Nineteenth Century* 27 (January 1890): 69–70.

78 Frances Balfour to Alice Balfour, 12 December 1882, BPS GD433/2/296; Balfour, *Ne Obliviscaris*, II, p. 33.

79 See Margot's draft 'A Week of General Election, July 1892' in MAP d.3297. Judith Walkowitz and Maureen Montgomery describe the mixes of freedom and danger resulting from women's new access to public space and consumer opportunities that began in the last third of the century: Judith Walkowitz, *City of Dreadful Delight: Narratives of Sexual Danger in Late-Victorian London* (Chicago, 1992), Montgomery, *Spectacles of Leisure*, pp. 88–96.

80 *Graphic*, 19 August 1893.

81 Edward Hamilton diary, 15 October 1891, Hamilton Papers BL 48655. Eliza Lynn Linton also blasted these infractions in 'The Partisans of the Wild Women', *Nineteenth Century* 31 (March 1892): 455–64. Griffin has pointed out how the presence of women would change the dynamics of constructing masculine identity in the Commons, *Politics of Gender*, ch. 6, section 'Women in Parliament'.

82 See Bush, *Edwardian Ladies*, ch. 2.

83 Davenport-Hines, *Ettie*, p. 57.

84 Morley diary, 13 March, 14 May, 15 June 1888, Morley Papers [Bodl.] MS. Eng. d.3443.

85 Lubenow, *Liberal Intellectuals and Public Culture*, ch. 4.

86 Frances Horner to Ettie Grenfell, 23 December 1890, Desborough Papers DE/Rv/C1346.

87 Morley diary, 18 July 1888, Morley Papers [Bodl.] MS. Eng. d.3443

88 Frances Balfour to Gerald Balfour, 9 October 1887, BPS GD433/2/283.

89 Morley diary, 30 June 1889, Morley Papers [Bodl.] MS. Eng. d.3444.

90 Charty Ribblesdale to Harry Cust, [autumn 1887] and 15 September 1888, MAP d.3278.

91 Morley diary, 24 July 1892, Morley Papers [Bodl.] MS. Eng. d.3447.

92 ME to AB, 18 February 1907, MEP.

93 'A Week of General Election, July 1892', MAP d.3297.

94 Both women play a large role in Bush's *Edwardian Ladies* for their part in founding and guiding the Victoria League.

95 Lawrence, *Electing Our Masters*, pp. 85–6.

96 This assessment generally accords with the conclusions of Bush, *Edwardian Ladies* and Martin Pugh, *The March of the Women, A Revisionist Analysis of the Campaign for Women's Suffrage, 1866–1914* (Oxford, 2000).

97 Asquith, *Autobiography*, II, pp. 81–7.

98 Barbara Onslow describes how these were the typical subject areas where women were allowed to enter the field of journalism in the late nineteenth century, *Women of the Press in Nineteenth-Century Britain* (New York, 2000), pp. 56–60.

99 Julia Bush, *Women against the Vote: Female Anti-Suffragism in Britain* (Oxford, 2007), pp. 141–56.

100 See the House of Commons dinner at which Asquith and Haldane pitted Margot and Frances Horner against Beatrice Webb and Alice Stopford Green, R. B. Haldane to Elizabeth Haldane, 31 October 1892, Haldane Papers. Asquith reported similar dinners to Margot, 4 April, 23 November 1892, MAP c.6686.

CHAPTER EIGHT

1 Gety Pembroke to Belle Herbert, 2 April 1890, GPP.

2 Daisy Warwick, *Afterthoughts* (London, 1931), p. 126; Gladys de Grey to ME, [undated], MEP.

3 *World*, 16 July 1890; *Pall Mall Gazette*, 18 Feb 1891.

4 *ILN*, 7 March 1891.

5 *Times*, 31 January 1884.

6 David Reed, *The Popular Magazine in Britain and the United States, 1880–1960* (Toronto, 1997), pp. 27–49; Matthew Rubery, *The Novelty of Newspapers: Victorian Fiction after the Invention of the News* (Oxford, 2009), pp. 102–3.

7 Barbara Black, *A Room of His Own: A Literary-Cultural Study of Victorian Clubland* (Ohio, 2012), p. 113.

8 Reed, *The Popular Magazine*, p. 44.

9 Reed, *The Popular Magazine*, pp. 99–100.

10 *Spectator*, 1 November 1890.

11 Daniel Boorstin, *The Image: A Guide to Pseudo Events in America* (New York, [1962] 1972 [Atheneum edn]), p. 57.

12 Margot to Ettie Grenfell, 19 January 1890, Desborough Papers DE/Rv/C71.

13 *Dundee Advertiser*, 7 February 1890; AB to ME, 5 March 1890, MEP.

14 AB to ME, 9 February 1890, MEP.

15 *Pall Mall Gazette*, 4 June 1890; Michael Herbert to GP, 4 December 1891, GPP.

16 *England*, 19 November 1892.

17 Margot to Spencer Lyttelton, 2 December 1892, MAP d.3281.

18 The best account of this event, written from private papers of the Benson family, is Brian Masters, *The Life of E F Benson* (London, [1991] 1993 [Pimlico edn]), pp. 99–106. References to *Dodo* that follow come from the three-volume collection of Benson's 'Dodo' books, copyrighted by Kenneth S. P. McDowall (New York, 1978).

19 Advertisements in *Pall Mall Gazette*, 14 July 1893; *Spectator*, 17 June 1893.

20 Margot Asquith, *An Autobiography*, two volumes (New York, 1920), I, p. 252. Harcourt told John Morley of Balfour's rejoinder when the rumour first appeared, Morley's diary, 12 June 1890, Morley Papers [Bodl.] MS. Eng. d.3445.

21 Asquith to MT, 1 June 1891, MAP c.6685.

22 Masters, *Benson*, p. 99.

23 *Punch*, 14 October 1893.

24 Asquith to MT, 12 October 1891, MAP c.6685.

25 *Spectator*, 17 June 1893.

26 Emily Lutyens, *A Blessed Girl: Memoirs of a Victorian Girlhood* (London, reprint edn, 1989), pp. 204–7.

27 *Spectator*, 17 June 1893; *Graphic*, 15 July 1893.

28 Stephen Arata, *Fictions of Loss in the Victorian Fin de Siècle: Identity and Nation* (Cambridge, 1996), p. 12.

29 MTA diary, [January] 1893. MAP d.3199.

30 See Michele Plott, 'The Rules of the Game: Respectability, Sexuality, and the Femme Mondaine in Late-Nineteenth Century Paris', *French Historical Studies* 25 (Summer 2002): 531–56. Plott describes a social milieu very much like what Margot observed, but does not discuss, as Margot did, the men who participated.

31 In a letter to Betty Balfour, quoted in Lutyens, *Blessed Girl*, p. 207. In November she wrote that 'it stuns me to find intelligent people calling it a clever book', MT to Spencer Lyttelton, 18 November 1893, MAP d.3281.

32 MT diary, 6 April 1894, MAP d.3199.

33 MT diary 11 January 1894, MAP d.3199, reproduced with some editing in Asquith, *Autobiography*, II, p. 206.

34 Margot Asquith, *Off the Record* (New York, 1944), p. 96. Probably an episode reported in the diary, 30 December 1892, about the prior spring when Margot had a scene with her sister in which 'Charty put a finger on a naked throbbing nerve and I felt my whole being turn into stone and my voice came from someone else as I asked her to leave the room', MAP e.3280.

35 Evan Charteris to MT, 5 August 1893, MAP e.3280; Liddell to Constance Wenlock, 12 November 1892, Wenlock MSS DDFA3/5/3 letter 58.

36 E. F. Benson, 'A Question of Taste', *Nineteenth Century* 34 (September 1893): 458–69.

37 Richard Kaye, *The Flirt's Tragedy: Desire without End in Victorian and Edwardian Fiction* (Charlottesville, 2002).

38 On Cust: Ronald Storrs, *Orientations* (London, 1937), pp. 31–40; Anita Leslie, *The Marlborough House Set* (New York, 1972), pp. 241–8; Jane Abdy and Charlotte Gere, *The Souls* (London, 1984), pp. 69–81.

39 *Lincolnshire Echo,* 16 May 1893.

40 For Cust's importance to the 'new journalism' of the 1890s, see Jonathan Rose, *The Edwardian Temperament* (Ohio, 1986), pp. 169–71; J. W. Robertson Scott, *The Life and Death of a Newspaper* (London, 1952), pp. 360–90.

41 Philip Ziegler, *Diana Cooper* (New York, 1983), pp. 15–16, 39; Catherine Bailey, *The Secret Rooms* (New York, 2013) is a new study of Violet Granby, though with less on Harry Cust than might be expected given his importance in her life.

42 David Gilmour, *Curzon* (London, 1994), pp. 105–11. On Milner: Thomas Pakenham, *The Boer War* (New York, 1979), pp. 27–8.

43 Evan Charteris to Constance Wenlock, [no date], WP DDFA3/5/9.

44 Fawcett to AB, 19 March 1894, BPS GD433/2/482; Claudia Renton, *Those Wild Wyndhams: Three Sisters at the Heart of Power* (London, 2014), p. 410.

45 Renton covers the Pamela portion of the story in *Those Wild Wyndhams,* chs 12–13.

46 GP to Violet Maxse, 8 December 1893, Viscountess Milner Papers [Bodl.] MS. Eng. VM42/C345/25.

47 GW to Ettie Grenfell, 27 September 1893, Desborough Papers DE/Rv/C2800/38. His account of the sudden journey to Scotland is in LLGW, I, pp. 276–7.

48 Peter Jackson, ed., *Loulou: Selected Extracts from the Journals of Lewis Harcourt, 1880–1895* (New Jersey, 2006), p. 96.

49 Harry White told his wife this as early as 30 March 1890, Library of Congress, White Papers (family 6).

50 Charles Welby to AB, 3 Nov 1893, BPS GD433/2/482.

51 MT to G. Curzon, 16 December 1893, MAP.

52 Frances Horner to DD Lyttelton, [summer 1894], CP II3/5; DD to Kathleen Lyttelton, 10 February 1894, CP II3/14.

53 GP to Violet Maxse, 12 October, 8 December 1893, Viscountess Milner Papers [Bodl.] MS. Eng. VM42/C345/22, 25.

54 GP to Constance Wenlock, 8 October 1894, WP DDFA3/5/6.

55 Asquith to Frances Horner, 11 October 1892, FHP; Hugo Elcho to Evelyn de Vesci, nd, HPP DD/DRU/90.

56 Ben Griffin, *The Politics of Gender in Victorian Britain: Masculinity, Political Culture and the Struggle for Women's Rights* (Cambridge, 2012), ch. 3.

57 GP to Violet Maxse, 8 December 1893, Viscountess Milner Papers [Bodl.] MS. Eng. VM42/C345/25.

58 Sybil Lubbock, *The Child in the Crystal* (London, 1939), pp. 131–2

59 Lyttelton to Lavinia Talbot, 8 September 1889, CP II 5/24. Charty Ribbledale admonished Cust for fawning over Constance Wenlock in public in the way Alfred described, Charty Ribblesdale to Harry Cust, 15 September 1888, MAP d.3278.

60 Charty Ribblesdale's daughter described Cust flirting casually with the governess, Barbara Wilson, *Dear Youth* (London, 1937), pp. 177–8; Scott, *Life and Death of a Newspaper,* pp. 366–7, 384–5 on his high spirits around men.

61 Daisy White diary, 14 August 1888, Nevins Papers, Butler Library, Columbia University.

62 Arata, *Fictions of Loss*, pp. 28–30. Arata would argue that Wilde's Dorian Gray is one of them, pp. 60–1.

63 GP to Ettie Grenfell, 7 January 1891, Desborough Papers DE/Rv/C/1293/11.

64 This mirrors Kali Israel's reconstructions of the narratives surrounding Charles Dilke and his wife. See Kali Israel, *Names and Stories: Emilia Dilke and Victorian Culture* (Oxford, 1999).

65 Beth Newman, *Subjects on Display: Psychoanalysis, Social Expectation, and Victorian Femininity* (Ohio, 2004), p. 100.

66 MT diary, 30 December 1892, MAP d.3199.

67 MT to AB, 18 November 1891, BP BL49794.

68 For the Frewen-Churchill milieu Margot might have entered if she married Peter, see Elisabeth Kehoe, *The Titled Americans: Three American Sisters and the British Aristocratic World into Which They Married* (New York, 2005). Margot wrote about the 'Dark Lady' – Jennie Churchill – who begged her to either marry Peter or set him free, in *Autobiography*, II, pp. 181–9.

69 Peter's letters from August and September 1891, MAP c.6675, ff.113–23.

70 MT diary, January 1893, MAP d.3199.

71 Without the aid of either Evan's letters or Margot's diaries, Daphne Bennett incorrectly made Milner the love interest who diverted Margot from Asquith for so long, *Margot: A Life of the Countess of Oxford and Asquith* (London, 1984), pp. 94–104.

72 MT to ME, 30 August 1893, MEP; MT to Ettie Grenfell, 22 October 1891, Desborough Papers DE/Rv/C71. Margot's published writings hint that she considered Arthur essentially sexless, hence suited for a moral and intellectual, rather than physical, love.

73 MT diary, [Glen 1892], MAP d.3199.

74 She laid out to herself this dichotomy in the diary entry of 8 March 1893, MAP d.3199, but Asquith had raised the 'two natures' image in a letter two years before. It is hard to know whether Margot wrote into her diaries descriptions of herself that men gave her or if they repeated things that she had said to them.

75 On Evan: Cynthia Asquith, *Haply I May Remember* (London, 1950), pp. 76–8; Nicholas Mosley, *Julian Grenfell* (New York, 1976), pp. 54–9; Richard Davenport-Hines, *Ettie: The Intimate Life and Dauntless Spirit of Lady Desborough* (London, 2008), pp. 75–7.

76 *Northampton Mercury*, 14 November 1902. According to the newspaper, Peter died of infection after a broken rib punctured his lung. Ribblesdale attended the funeral, and one wreath came from a Mary A. Asquith.

77 Colin Clifford, *The Asquiths* (London, 2002), p. 57.

78 MT diary, 19 October 1893, MAP d.3199.

79 Charteris to MT, 27 October 1893, MAP e.3280.

80 Blunt diary, 31 August 1893, Blunt Papers 33–1975.

81 Anne Wemyss to MT, 18 May 1888, MAP e.3282.

82 Nicholas Mosley, *Julian Grenfell: The Life and Times of His Death* (New York, 1976), ch. 8.

83 Charteris to MT, 5 August 1893, MAP e.3280. One of Evan's flings was with Jennie Churchill, who had earlier been in love with Peter Flower, prompting Margot's comment that Jennie always went after her men, MT to AB, 18 November 1891, BP BL49794.

84 Charteris to MT, [autumn 1893], MAP e.3280, f. 107.

85 Anne Wemyss to MT, 20 December 1893, MAP e.3282.

86 Charteris to MT, 5 August 1893, MAP e.3280; GP to Violet Maxse, 24 December 1893, Viscountess Milner Papers [Bodl.] MS. Eng. VM42/345/27. Evan, who was barely thirty and did not marry until the end of his life, might have seemed like the professional males whom John Tosh describes from this generation as fleeing domesticity, either through prolonged bachelorhood or long absences from family, see *A Man's Place: Masculinity and the Middle Class Home in Victorian England* (New Haven, 1999), ch. 8, and *Manliness and Masculinities in Nineteenth-Century Britain* (London, 2005), pp. 205–6.

87 Ettie Grenfell to Constance Wenlock, 13 October 1892, WP DDFA3/5/13; Arata, *Fictions of Loss*, pp. 58–62.

88 MT diary, [early 1892], MAP d.3199.

89 *The Letters of John Addington Symonds*, ed. Herbert Schueller and Robert Peters, three volumes (Detroit, 1969), III, pp. 272, 734. For Symonds's complicated relationship to his own sexual identity and yet embrace of 'conventional' moral values, see Arata, *Fictions of Loss*, pp. 84–9.

90 Historians see the 'emotional revolution' – occasioned by the integration of psychological models of the self into popular consciousness – occurring in the generation after the people studied here, see Joel Pfister, 'Glamorizing the Psychological', *Inventing the Psychological: Toward a Cultural History of Emotional Life in America*, ed. Joel Pfister and Nancy Schnog (New Haven, 1997), pp. 167–9.

91 Asquith to MT, 22 May 1891, MAP c.6685.

92 Doll Liddell to Constance Wenlock, 12 November 1892, WP DDFA3/5/3.

93 Introduction to Margot Asquith, *Margot Asquith's Great War Diary 1914–1916: The View from Downing Street*, ed. Michael Brock and Eleanor Brock (Oxford, 2014), p. xli.

94 *Graphic*, 12 May 1894; *Burnley Gazette*, 12 May 1894.

95 *Leeds Times*, 30 March 1895.

96 *New York Herald Tribune*, 25 February 1894.

97 John Garrard, review of Anna Clark, *The Sexual Politics of the British Constitution* (Princeton, 2004) in *Reviews in History* (31 May 2005) at http://www.history.ac.uk/reviews.

98 John B. Thompson, *Political Scandal: Power and Visibility in the Media Age* (Cambridge, 2000).

99 Michael Foldy, *The Trials of Oscar Wilde: Deviance, Morality, and Late-Victorian Society* (New Haven, 1997), pp. 24–7 argues that Rosebery's nervous collapse in 1895 arose from his panic over being exposed during the Wilde trials; see also Richard Dellamora, *Masculine Desire: The Sexual*

Politics of Victorian Aestheticism (Chapel Hill, 1990), ch 10. Leo McKinstry does his best to refute the long-standing speculations about Rosebery's sexual preferences, *Rosebery: Statesman in Turmoil* (London, 2005), ch. 12.

100 BPS GD433/2/482. The exchanges between Balfour and Millicent Fawcett are in the Fawcett Papers as well, though not the letters that others sent to Arthur during this period. Unless stated otherwise, all letters quoted in the Cust discussion are from the Balfour file.

101 Arthur implied to Mary that it was Cust, not he, who had told the Manchester authorities that Harry had nothing to account for except Nina's pregnancy, 14 March 1894, MEP.

102 Cust to MTA, 1 November 1909, MAP d.3278.

103 Barbara Caine, *Victorian Feminists* (Oxford, 1992), pp. 231–3; David Rubinstein, *A Different World for Women: The Life of Millicent Garrett Fawcett* (Ohio, 1991), pp. 87–9.

104 The announcement that Harry was withdrawing his candidacy 'on the ground of ill-health' came several months later, *Sheffield Evening Telegraph*, 22 September 1894.

105 GP to Constance Wenlock, 20 June 1894, WP DDFA3/5/6.

106 *Lincolnshire Echo*, 30 November 1893; *Edinburgh Evening News*, 30 November 1893, included the rumour that Cust had been engaged to Pamela Wyndham, but retracted it the next week, 9 December 1893. The joke is from Jackson, *Loulou*, p. 97.

107 Ben Griffin, *The Politics of Gender in Victorian Britain: Masculinity, Political Culture and the Struggle for Women's Rights* (Cambridge, 2012), ch. 6, section 'Performing Parliamentary Masculinities'.

108 Griffin, *The Politics of Gender*, ch. 3.

109 Harry White diary, late January 1894, Library of Congress, White Papers.

110 Scott, *Life and Death of a Newspaper*, pp. 376–7.

111 Daisy White diary, 2 March 1889: 'I got a sort of blackmailing letter from an ex-footman … who says he destroyed a letter of mine to a gentleman given him by a fellow servant and on the strength of which service he wants money from me!', Nevins Papers, Butler Library, Columbia University; on cheating at cards, Betty to Gerald Balfour, 9 June 1891, GD433/2/304.

112 Gilmour, *Curzon*, pp. 105–11.

113 *Sheffield Evening Telegraph*, 16 June 1893; *Sheffield Daily Telegraph*, 21 July 1893; *The Star*, 27 July 1893; Charles Gatty, *George Wyndham, Recognita* (London, 1917), p. 114. For the growing use of campaign posters and flyers, and the rise of character assassination in elections, see Jon Lawrence, *Electing Our Masters: The Hustings in British Politics from Hogarth to Blair* (Oxford, 2009), pp. 57, 78–80.

114 Henry Vane, *An Affair of State: A Biography of the 8th Duke and Duchess of Devonshire* (London, 2004), pp. 182–3.

115 Fawcett to AB, 19 March 1894, reporting what Frances Balfour had told her in February.

116 See Judith Walkowitz, *City of Dreadful Delight: Narratives of Sexual Danger in Victorian London* (Chicago, 1992).

117 James Thompson, *British Political Culture and the Idea of 'Public Opinion', 1867–1914* (Cambridge, 2013), ch.1.

118 AB to ME, 6 September 1893, MEP.

119 Andrew Adonis, *Making Aristocracy Work: The Peerage and the Political System in Britain 1884–1914* (Oxford, 1993), ch. 7. After home rule decimated their ranks among the aristocracy, Liberals often filled these spots with law peers or other recently ennobled professionals. The point was that a minister who himself sat in the Commons would need an undersecretary counterpart to be spokesperson in the Lords.

120 Andrew Roberts, *Salisbury: Victorian Titan* (London, 1999), pp. 504–5. The threat of public exposure partly accounts for the political marginalisation of another rising Tory in these years, Lord Charles Beresford, as does his alienation from the Prince of Wales, again over a sex scandal.

121 Fawcett to Balfour, 26 March 1894. Her position was by no means universal. Eliza Lynn Linton wrote that seduction was entirely the fault of women, either as adults who should have known better, or as mothers who had not protected their daughters. See her articles on 'Wild Women' as politicians and social insurgents in *The Nineteenth Century* 30 (July and October 1891): 79–88, 596–605, as well as 'Partisans of the Wild Women', *The Nineteenth Century* 31 (March 1892): 455–64.

122 Martin Jay, *The Virtues of Mendacity: On Lying in Politics* (Charlottesville, 2010), p. 7.

123 David Cannadine, *The Decline and Fall of the British Aristocracy* (New Haven, 1990), p. 214.

124 Arata, *Fictions of Loss*, pp. 60–1.

CHAPTER NINE

1 AB to ME, 30 January 1895, MEP.

2 Nicholas Freeman, *1895: Drama, Disaster and Disgrace in Late Victorian Britain* (Edinburgh, 2011).

3 Freeman, *1895*, pp. 113, 46. Useful here is Michael Foldy, *The Trials of Oscar Wilde: Deviance, Morality, and Late-Victorian Society* (New Haven, 1997).

4 GP to Constance Wenlock, 7 April 1895, WP DDFA3/5/6.

5 GP to Evelyn De Vesci, 7 April 1894, HPP DD/DRU/84; Lady Herbert of Lea to Belle Herbert, 17 June [1895], GPP; Tresham Lever, *The Herberts of Wilton* (London, 1967), pp. 228–9.

6 Gety Pembroke to Eddie Hamilton, [1895], Hamilton Papers BL48620; Janet Oppenheim, *'Shattered Nerves': Doctors, Patients, and Depression* (New York, 1991), ch. 5.

7 GP to MT, [1895], MAP c.6677.

8 *Taunton Courier and Western Advertiser,* 15 May 1895.

9 Lady Herbert implied as much in a letter to Eddie Hamilton, 13 May 1895, Hamilton Papers BL48620.

10 GP to 'Pollywogs', 9 March 1895, GPP.

11 GP to Violet Maxse, [n.d. 1892], Viscountess Milner Papers [Bodl.] MS. Eng. VM42/C345/6.

12 GP to 'Pollywogs', 9 March 1895, GPP.

13 *Western Gazette*, 10 May 1895.

14 GP to MT, 17 January 1886, MAP c.6677; to Evelyn de Vesci, 5 February 1886, 6 April 1887, HPP DD/DRU/84.

15 R. L. Stevenson, *The Letters of Robert Louis Stevenson*, ed. Bradford Booth and Ernest Mehew (New Haven, 1994), p. 223; Stephen Arata, *Fiction of Loss in the Victorian Fin de Siècle* (Cambridge, 1996), pp. 43–9. For mixed reactions to *Prince Otto* see *Robert Louis Stevenson, the Critical Heritage*, ed. Paul Maixner (London, 1981), pp. 176–98.

16 Edith Olivier, *Without Knowing Mr. Walkley* (London, 1938), p. 156.

17 Edward Hamilton diary, 9 October 1892, Hamilton Papers BL48659.

18 *Cornishman*, 27 July 1895; F. M. L. Thompson, *English Landed Society in the Nineteenth Century* (London, 1963), p. 314; M. J. Daunton, 'The Political Economy of Death Duties: Harcourt's Budget of 1894' in *Land and Society in Britain, 1700–1914*, ed. N. Harte and R. Quinault (Manchester, 1996), pp. 137–71. The current web page for Wilton House describes an agricultural acreage one-third the size of George's Wiltshire holdings.

19 *Taunton Courier and Western Advertiser*, 23 May 1900. Gilbert is best known as the creator of the winged Anteros figure at the centre of Picadilly Circus, London. For an image of the statue, see humphreysfamilytree.com/Herbert.

20 Betty Balfour to Frances Balfour, 13 December 1889, BPS GD433/2/301.

21 For a recent analysis of this marriage, see Michael Brock's introduction to *Margot Asquith's Great War Diary 1914–1916* , ed. Michael Brock and Eleanor Brock (Oxford, 2014), pp. xxxvi–xli, xlv–lv.

22 Asquith to MT, 11 November 1891, MAP c.6685.

23 Patrick Joyce, *Democratic Subjects: The Self and the Social in Nineteenth-Century England* (Cambridge, 1994), pp. 179–80.

24 Margot Oxford, *Lay Sermons* (London, 1927), passim.

25 Asquith to MT, 11 September 1892, MAP c.6686.

26 See the description by Joseph Chamberlain's daughter of Margot in the Ladies Gallery in 1904 'dancing round in a frantic state and more intolerable than usual', Peter T. Marsh, *The Chamberlain Literary: Letters Within a Governing Family from Empire to Appeasement* (London, 2010), p. 72

27 Ben Griffin *The Politics of Gender in Victorian Britain: Masculinity, Political Culture and the Struggle for Women's Rights* (Cambridge, 2012), ch. 2.

28 Nigel Nicholson, *Mary Curzon* (New York, 1977), p. 146.

29 Martin Pugh, *The March of the Women: A Revisionist Analysis of the Campaign for Women's Suffrage, 1866–1914* (Oxford, 2000), p. 139. Michael Brock revealed the most famous of these attachments in *H H Asquith: Letters to Venetia Stanley* (Oxford, 1983).

30 R. C. K. Ensor, *England, 1870–1914* (Oxford, 1936), pp. 220–1, 610–11.

31 Phyllis Rose, *Parallel Lives: Five Victorian Marriages* (New York, 1983), p. 5.

32 Nancy W. Ellenberger, 'Constructing George Wyndham: Narratives of Aristocratic Masculinity in Fin-de-Siècle England', *Journal of British Studies* 39 (October 2000): 487–93. The Wyndham introduction to North's Plutarch used here is in George Wyndham, *Essays in Romantic Literature*, ed. Charles Whibley (London, 1919), pp. 115–236.

33 Wyndham, *Essays in Romantic Literature*, p. 164.

34 GW to Sibell Grosvenor, 22 March 1893, GWP.

35 For context on Blunt's thinking, see Gregory Claeys, 'The "Left" and the Critique of Empire, c. 1860–1900', *Victorian Visions of Global Order: Empire and International Relations in Nineteenth-Century Political Thought*, ed. Duncan Bell (Cambridge, 2007), pp. 244–51.

36 Wyndham's toast to the annual meeting of the association, *Times*, 22 May 1908; Andrew S. Thompson, 'The Language of Imperialism and the Meaning of Empire: Imperial Discourse in British Politics, 1895–1914', *Journal of British Studies* 36 (April 1997), pp. 147–55.

37 LLGW, I, p. 60; GW to ME, 1 February 1907, MEP; Arata, *Fictions of Loss*, p. 158; John M. MacKenzie, *Propaganda and Empire: The Manipulation of British Public Opinion, 1880–1960* (Manchester, 1984).

38 For a review of the scholarly literature on Rhodes, Chamberlain and the Jameson affair, see Robert L. Rothberg, *The Founder: Cecil Rhodes and the Pursuit of Power* (Oxford, 1988), ch. 19.

39 Thomas Pakenham, *The Boer War* (London, 1979), p. 87.

40 GW to Sibell Grosvenor, 22 July 1895, GWP.

41 LLGW, II, pp. 540, 537. Joseph Meisel's indispensable study of public speaking in Victorian political culture describes the fatigue that such performances brought on, but not much about the emotionality of the experience for the speaker himself.

42 Even those close to him could see these qualities, see his secretary Mark Sykes's impression in Roger Adelson, *Mark Sykes* (London, 1975), p. 97; Evan Charteris to ME, [1915], MEP. Evan thought that George's letters showed he had a modern, reflexive self-consciousness: 'Life was a stage with a mirror in the distance on the far side of the audience – that gave him his force and activity – he was always out pouring his exuberant mental fire not only for the benefit of the audience but for the mirror also.'

43 Charles Gatty, *George Wyndham: Recognita* (London, 1917), pp. 116, 119.

44 Max Egremont, *The Cousins* (London, 1977), p. 189; H. G. Wells, *The New Machiavelli* (Thirsk, reprint edn, 2002), p. 283.

45 For a fuller development of this interpretation see Ellenberger, 'Constructing George Wyndham', pp. 509–16.

46 Judith P. Butler, *Excitable Speech: A Politics of the Performative* (New York, 1997).

47 Lady Wemyss, *A Family Record* (privately printed, 1932), passim.

48 MT to AB, 20 November 1895, MEP.

49 Elizabeth Longford, *A Pilgrimage of Passion: The Life of Wilfrid Scawen Blunt* (London, 1979), ch. 16. Her account is based not only on Blunt's 'secret diaries' but Mary's letters to him later. Claudia Renton, *Those*

Wild Wyndhams: Three Sisters at the Heart of Power (London, 2014), chs 16–17 adds details to the story, especially from Hugo's point of view.

50 In an effort to keep her daughter's paternity a secret, Mary told a relative that all her children tended to arrive early, ME to Evelyn de Vesci, 5 November 1895, HPP DD/DRU/87.

51 Max Egremont, *Balfour* (London, 1980), pp. 118–19.

52 ME to AB, 6 June 1896, MEP.

53 AB to ME, 27 February 1895, MEP.

54 An uncharacteristic picture of Mary showing distress openly and Arthur's embarrassment at this emerges from the account that Curzon's wife wrote to him in India, see Nigel Nicolson, *Mary Curzon* (New York, 1977), pp. 147–8.

55 ME to AB, 11–12 June 1896, 15 October 1900, 25 June 1905, 1 February 1906, 14 February 1907, MEP. Margot's views on Balfour and Mary: Blunt diary, 4 July 1891 and 23 August 1892, Blunt Papers 31/32–1975.

56 AB to ME, 27 February 1903, MEP.

57 *A Family Record* and drafts of 'The Souls', MEP. Claudia Renton describes the despair of Evan Charteris and Edmund Gosse over the inadequacy of these writings, *Those Wild Wyndhams*, pp. 371–3.

58 LAB, p. 245; AB to ME, 11 August 1904, MEP.

59 Eileen Gilhooly, *Smile of Discontent: Humor, Gender, and Nineteenth-Century British Fiction* (Chicago, 1999), p. 68.

60 Osbert Sitwell, *Laughter in the Next Room* (Boston, 1948), p. 102.

61 ME to AB, 31 October 1898, MEP.

62 ME to AB, 19 January, 15 October 1900, 20 September 1904, MEP.

63 Her children recorded the 'dotty or potty friends who invest Stanway. In the summer they visited us in considerable numbers', including a group of spiritualists and mediums in 1912, *A Family Record*, p. 216.

64 ME to Hugo Elcho, 24 August 1896, MEP.

65 ME to Ettie Grenfell, 28 October 1900, Desborough Papers DE/Rv/C477; ME to AB, 30 July 1901, February 1906, MEP.

66 AB to ME, 16 June 1901, MEP.

67 ME diary, 19 April 1905, MEP.

68 Renton's work has shown that Madeline Wyndham was prone to depression and nervous exhaustion, which the family kept well hidden, see *Those Wild Wyndhams*, pp. 148, 152–3. George feared that he had inherited this 'special neurotic' temperament, see J. S. Sandars to AB, 5 March 1905, MEP. These were some of the 'shameful' deviations from the normal and acceptable that Deborah Cohen has shown as constituting the hidden realities of domestic relations at all levels of British society, *Family Secrets: The Things We Tried to Hide* (New York, 2013).

69 T. H. Hollingsworth shows that only one in thirty marriages contracted by Mary's age cohort of aristocrats ended in divorce. In their children's era, after the Matrimonial Causes Act of 1907 liberalised the grounds for marital dissolution, the number would leap to one in eight. For children born between 1900 and 1925, it would be one in four, see T. H. Hollingsworth, 'The Demography of the British Peerage', supplement to *Population Studies* 18 (London, 1965): 24.

70 This lack of guidance about any real alternatives for daughters of privilege continued for at least another half century, see the women interviewed by Anne de Courcy, *Debs at War: 1939–1945, How Wartime Changed Their Lives* (London, 2005), chs 2–3.

71 'In conversation she was like a butterfly that would never quite settle', a late-in-life acquaintance recalled; 'One remembers little things: the sometimes startling abruptness of her speech and manner': Lady Cynthia Asquith, *Diaries 1915–1918*, foreword by L. P. Hartley (New York, 1969), p. ix.

72 *Punch*, 14 March 1891. Furniss did similar graphics on Gladstone, 21 February, and Salisbury, 30 May 1891.

73 It was typical of *Punch*'s cosy, inside-the-family humour that readers could be expected to recognise an allusion to John Poole's farce *Paul Pry* (1825), which went out of popular performance in the 1870s, Arthur Prager, *The Mahogany Tree: An Informal History of Punch* (New York, 1979), pp. 140–51.

74 In this regard see Geoffrey Searle, *The Quest for National Efficiency: A Study in British Politics and Political Thought, 1899–1914* (Berkeley, 1971).

75 Daniel Bivona describes a late-century 'public discourse saturated with' metaphors symptomatic of the contradiction between individual distinctiveness and group identification and loyalty, *British Imperial Literature, 1870–1940: Writing and the Administration of Empire* (Cambridge, 1998), p. 197.

76 Martha Banta, *Barbaric Intercourse: Caricature and the Culture of Conduct, 1841–1936* (Chicago, 2006), pp. 43–53.

77 Max Beerbohm, *Max's Nineties, Drawings 1892–1899*, intro. Osbert Lancaster (London, 1958), plate 13; also N. John Hall, *Max Beerbohm Caricatures* (New Haven, 1997), pp. 152–4.

78 Vita Sackville-West, *All Passion Spent* (New York, 1931), pp. 5–6. Lord Slane has some characteristics of Rosebery, such as winning the Derby and gaining the cabinet at an 'astonishingly early age', but his 'charm, his languor, and his good sense', his ability to 'cast his eye over a report and pick out its heart and its weakness before another man had had time to read it through' are Balfour. For a critique of Arthur and other politicians during the Boer War, note Harold Begbie and M. H. Temple, *Clara in Blunderland: A Political Parody based on Lewis Carroll's Wonderland* (London, 1902) where Arthur is redrawn by J. S. Ransome as John Tenniel's Alice, complete with pinafore, tights and tentative, little-girl postures. The work was reissued by Michael Everson in 2010.

79 Leo Braudy, *The Frenzy of Renown: Fame and Its History* (Oxford, 1988), pp. 392–3.

80 Blanche Dugdale, *Arthur James Balfour*, two volumes (London, 1936), I, pp. 223–89; R. J. Q. Adams, *Balfour: The Last Grandee* (London, 2007), pp. 156–7. Balfour's official responses to several of these episodes can be followed in the specialised study by Denis Judd, *Balfour and the British Empire* (London, 1968).

81 Jason Tomes is enlightening on this point in his discussion of

'imperialism', *Balfour and Foreign Policy: The International Thought of an Imperial Statesman* (Cambridge, 1997), ch. 3.

82 Edward Said, *Orientalism* (New York, 1978), pp. 31–6.

83 For the many intellectuals and parliamentarians who shared Balfour's understandings, see *Victorian Visions of Global Order: Empire and International Relations in Nineteenth-Century Political Thought,* ed. Duncan Bell (Cambridge, 2007).

84 Arthur James Balfour, *Theism and Humanism* (New York, 1915), p. 95.

EPILOGUE

1 Kenneth Young, *Arthur James Balfour* (London, 1963), p. xi.

2 Frederick Kirchhoff, discussing the work of Henry Kohut, in *William Morris: The Construction of a Male Self, 1856–1872* (Ohio, 1990), p. xii.

3 J. P. Cornford, 'The Parliamentary Foundations of the Hotel Cecil', *Ideas and Institutions in Victorian Britain,* ed. R. Robson (London, 1967), pp. 281–3.

4 See Jeanne MacKenzie, *The Children of the Souls: A Tragedy of the First World War* (London, 1986).

5 Deborah Cohen, *Family Secrets: The Things We Tried to Hide* (London, 2014) pp. 241–53.

6 Evan Charteris to Constance Wenlock, [undated], WP 3/5/9.

7 Len Platt, *Aristocracies of Fiction: Aristocracy in Late-Nineteenth-Century and Early-Twentieth-Century Literary Culture* (New York, 2001), pp. 8–15; Gail Savage, *The Social Construction of Expertise: The English Civil Service and Its Influence, 1919–1939* (Pittsburgh, 1996), ch. 1.

Bibliography

MANUSCRIPT COLLECTIONS

Margot Asquith Papers (University of Oxford, Bodleian Library Special Collections and Western Manuscripts)
Balfour Papers (British Library, Additional Manuscripts)
Balfour Papers [Whittingehame] (National Archives of Scotland)
Battersea Papers (British Library, Additional Manuscripts)
Wilfrid Scawen Blunt Archives (University of Cambridge, Fitzwilliam Museum)
Carnarvon Papers (British Library, Additional Manuscripts)
Chandos [Lyttelton] Papers (University of Cambridge, Churchill Archives Centre)
G. N. Curzon Papers (British Library, Asia, Pacific and Africa Collections)
Desborough Papers [Ettie Grenfell] (Hertfordshire Archives and Local Studies)
Mary Elcho Papers (Stanway House, Gloucestershire)
Mary Gladstone [Drew] Papers (British Library, Additional Manuscripts)
William Gladstone Papers (British Library, Additional Manuscripts)
Edward White Hamilton Papers (British Library, Additional Manuscripts)
W. E. Henley Papers (Pierpont Morgan Library, New York City)
Herbert of Pixton Papers [Evelyn de Vesci] (Somerset Heritage Centre)
Frances Horner Papers (Mells Manor House, Somerset)
Viscount Midleton Papers (British Library, Additional Manuscripts)
Viscountess Milner Papers [Violet Maxse] (University of Oxford, Bodleian Library, Western Manuscripts)
Morley Papers (University of Oxford, Bodleian Library, Western Manuscripts)
Pembroke Papers (Wiltshire and Swindon History Centre)
Edward Stanhope Papers (Kent History and Library Centre)
Wenlock Papers (Hull History Centre, University of Hull Archives)
Henry White Papers (Library of Congress)
Margaret Rutherford White Diary (Nevins Papers, Columbia University Libraries)
George Wyndham Papers (private collection)

CONTEMPORARY SOURCES: COMMENTARY,
DIARIES, LETTERS, MEMOIRS, NOVELS, CONDUCT BOOKS

Asquith, Cynthia, *Haply I May Remember* (London, 1950)

Asquith, Cynthia, *Remember and Be Glad* (London, 1952)

Asquith, Margot, *Autobiography*, two volumes (New York, 1920)

Asquith, Margot, *Margot Asquith's Great War Diary 1914–1916: The View from Downing Street*, ed. Michael Brock and Eleanor Brock (Oxford, 2014)

Asquith, Margot [as Margot Oxford], *More or Less About Myself* (New York, 1934)

Asquith, Margot [as Margot Oxford], *Octavia* (London, 1928)

Balfour, Arthur James, *A Defence of Philosophic Doubt: Being an Essay on the Foundations of Belief* (London, 1879)

Balfour, Arthur James, *Chapters of Autobiography* (London, 1930)

Balfour, Arthur James, *Essays and Addresses* (London, 1893)

Balfour, Arthur James, *The Foundations of Belief* (London, 1895)

Balfour, Arthur James, *The Mind of Arthur James Balfour, Selections from his Non-Political Writings, Speeches and Addresses, 1879–1917*, ed. Wilfrid M Short (London, 1918)

Balfour, Lady Frances, *Ne Obliviscaris*, two volumes (London, 1930)

Balsan, Consuelo, *The Glitter and the Gold* (New York, 1952)

Bateman, John, *The Great Landowners of Great Britain and Ireland*, ed. David Spring (New York, 1971)

Benson, A. C. (published anonymously), *Memoirs of Arthur Hamilton, B A of Trinity College, Cambridge* (London, 1886)

Benson, E. F., *As We Were* (New York, 1930)

Benson, E. F., *Dodo: A Detail of the Day* (London, 1893)

Blunt, Wilfrid Scawen, *My Diaries, 1888–1914*, two volumes (New York, 1922)

Blunt, Wilfrid Scawen, *The Land War in Ireland* (London, 1912)

Bobbitt, Mary Reed, *With Dearest Love to All: The Life and Letters of Lady Jebb* (London, 1960)

Bonham Carter, Violet, 'The Souls', *Listener*, 30 October 1947

Broughton, Rhoda, *Dr Cupid* (London, 1886)

Buckle, George Earle, ed., *The Letters of Queen Victoria*, 3rd series, volume one (London, 1930)

Callwell, Colonel C. E., *Small Wars: Their Principles and Practice*, 3rd edn (London, [1906] 1996)

Campbell, Lady Colin, *Etiquette of Good Society* (London, 1893)

Carnarvon, Henry Herbert, 4th Earl of, *The Political Diaries of the Fourth Earl of Carnarvon, 1857–1890*, Camden 5th series, volume 35, ed. Peter Gordon (Cambridge, 2009)

Churchill, Lady Randolph, *Reminiscences* (New York, 1908)

Churchill, Winston S., *Great Contemporaries* (London, 1937)

Churchill, Winston S., *Lord Randolph Churchill*, two volumes (New York, 1906)

Crawford, David Lindsay, Earl of, *The Crawford Papers: The Journals of David Lindsay, Twenty-Seventh Earl of Balcarres, 1871–1940: During the Years 1892–1940*, ed. John Vincent (Manchester, 1984)

Crawford, Marion, *An American Politician* (New York, 1885)

Curzon, George N, *Parliamentary Eloquence* (London, 1911)

Derby, Edward Henry Stanley, *The Diaries of Edward Henry Stanley, 15th Earl of Derby (1826–1893), between September 1869 and March 1878*, Camden, 5th series, volume 4, ed. John Vincent (London, 1994)

Derby, Edward Henry Stanley, *The Later Derby Diaries: Home Rule, Liberal Unionism, and Aristocratic Life in Late Victorian England*, ed. John Vincent (Bristol, 1981)

Dugdale, Blanche, *Arthur James Balfour*, two volumes (London, 1936)

Dugdale, Blanche, *Family Homespun* (London, 1940)

Escott, T. H. S., *Social Transformations of the Victorian Age* (London, 1897)

Escott, T. H. S., *Society in the Country House* (London, 1907)

Etiquette for Gentlemen (London, 1857)

Etiquette for Ladies in Public and Private (London, 1894)

Fingall, Elizabeth, Countess of, *Seventy Years Young* (London, 1938)

Forbes, Lady Angela, *Memories and Base Details* (New York, 1921)

Gathorne-Hardy, Gathorne, *The Diary of Gathorne Hardy, later Lord Cranbrook, 1866–1892: Political Selections*, ed. Nancy Johnson (Oxford, 1981)

Gatty, Charles, *George Wyndham, Recognita* (London, 1917)

Gladstone, Mary (Mrs Drew), *Acton, Gladstone and Others* (New York, reprint edn, 1968)

Gladstone, Mary (Mrs Drew), *Mary Gladstone: Her Diaries and Letters*, ed. Lucy Masterman (New York, 1930)

Gower, Lord Ronald, *My Reminiscences*, two volumes (London, 1883)

Habits of Good Society (London, 1859)

Haldane, R. B., *Autobiography* (London, 1929)

Hamilton, Sir Edward Walter, *The Diary of Sir Edward Walter Hamilton, 1880–1885*, ed. Dudley W. R. Bahlman, two volumes (Oxford, 1972)

Hamilton, Sir Edward Walter, *The Diary of Sir Edward Walter Hamilton, 1885–1906*, ed. Dudley W. R. Bahlman (Hull, 1993)

Hamilton, Lord George, *Parliamentary Reminiscences and Reflections, 1868–1885* (New York, 1917)

Harcourt, Lewis, *Loulou: Selected Extracts from the Journals of Lewis Harcourt (1880–1895)*, ed. Patrick Jackson (New Jersey, 2006)

Horner, Frances, *Time Remembered* (London, 1933)

James, Henry, *The Awkward Age* (London, 1899)

James, Henry, *The Sacred Fount* (London, 1901)

James, Henry, *What Maisie Knew* (London, 1897)

Letters of Arthur Balfour & Lady Elcho, 1885–1917, ed. Jane Ridley and Clayre Percy (London, 1992)

Letters of Queen Victoria, ed. George Buckle, 3rd series, three volumes (London, 1930)

Liddell, A. G. C., *Notes from the Life of an Ordinary Mortal* (London, 1911)

Lubbock, Sybil, *The Child in the Crystal* (London, 1939)

Lucy, Henry W., *Diary of the Salisbury Parliament, 1886–1892* (London, 1892)

Lutyens, Emily, *A Blessed Girl: Memoirs of a Victorian Girlhood* (London, [1953] 1989)

Lyttelton, Edith, *Alfred Lyttelton: An Account of His Life* (London, 1917)

Mackail, J. W. and Guy Wyndham, *Life and Letters of George Wyndham*, two volumes (London, 1925)

Mallock, W. H., *Memoirs of Life and Literature* (London, 1920)

Manners and Rules of Good Society by a Member of the Aristocracy (London, 1894)

Manners of the Aristocracy by One of Themselves (London, 1881)

March-Phillipps, Lisle and Bertram Christian, eds, *Some Hawarden Letters* (London, 1917)

M'Carthy, Justin, *Mr. Balfour's Rule in Ireland* (London, 1891)

Morley, John, *Recollections*, two volumes (New York, 1917)

Morley, John, *The Life of William Ewart Gladstone*, three volumes (London, 1903)

Olivier, Edith, *Without Knowing Mr. Walkley* (London, 1938)

Oxford and Asquith, Earl of, *Memories and Reflections, 1852–1927*, two volumes (Boston, 1928)

Paget, Lady Augusta, *In My Tower*, two volumes (London, 1924)

[Pembroke, Earl of and George Kingsley], *South Seas Bubbles by the Earl and the Doctor* (New York, 1872)

Political Letters and Speeches of George, 13th Earl of Pembroke and Montgomery, two volumes (London, 1896)

Ponsonby, Frederick, *Recollections of Three Reigns* (London, 1951)

Raymond, E. T., *Mr Balfour* (London, 1920)

Ribblesdale, Lord, *Impressions and Memories* (London, 1927)

Robinson, Sir Henry, *Memories: Wise or Otherwise* (New York, 1923)

Salisbury-Balfour Correspondence, 1869–1892, ed. R. H. Williams (Hertfordshire Record Society,1988)

Sitwell, Osbert, *Laughter in the Next Room* (Boston, 1948)

Webb, Beatrice, *The Diary of Beatrice Webb*, two volumes, ed. Norman and Jeanne MacKenzie (Cambridge, Massachusetts, 1982)

Wells, H. G., *The New Machiavelli* (Thirsk, reprint edn, 2002)

Wemyss, Lady, *A Family Record* (privately printed, 1932)

Wilson, Barbara, *Dear Youth* (London, 1937)

Wyndham, George, *Essays in Romantic Literature*, ed. Charles Whibley (London, 1919)

Wyndham, George, *Letters of George Wyndham*, ed. Guy Wyndham, two volumes (privately printed, 1915)

Wyndham, George and Arthur Balfour, *Lies and Replies: An Exposure of Some of the Commoner Gladstonian Fallacies* (London, 1892)

SECONDARY BIOGRAPHICAL WORKS

Abdy, Jane and Charlotte Gere, *The Souls* (London, 1984)

Adams, R. J. Q., *Balfour: The Last Grandee* (London, 2007)

Askwith, Betty, *The Lytteltons: A Family Chronicle of the Nineteenth Century* (London, 1975)

Beauman, Nicole, *Cynthia Asquith* (London, 1987)

Bennett, Daphne, *Margot: A Life of the Countess of Oxford & Asquith* (London, 1984)

Blow, Simon, *Broken Blood: The Rise and Fall of the Tennant Family* (London, 1987)

Chandos, Lord, *From Peace to War: A Study in Contrast, 1857–1918* (London, 1968)

Clifford, Colin, *The Asquiths* (London, 2002)

Crathorne, Nancy, *Tennant's Stalk: The Story of the Tennants of the Glen* (London, 1973)

Dakers, Caroline, *Clouds: The Biography of a Country House* (New Haven, 1993)

Davenport-Hines, Richard, *Ettie: The Life and World of Lady Desborough* (London, 2008)

Egremont, Max, *Balfour: A Life of Arthur James Balfour* (London, 1980)

Egremont, Max, *The Cousins: The Friendship, Opinions and Activities of Wilfrid Scawen Blunt and George Wyndham* (London, 1977)

Ellenberger, Nancy W., 'Constructing George Wyndham: Narratives of Aristocratic Masculinity in *Fin de Siècle* England', *Journal of British Studies*, 39 (October 2000): 487–517

Flanders, Judith, *A Circle of Sisters: Alice Kipling, Georgiana Burne-Jones, Agnes Poynter and Louisa Baldwin* (New York, 2005)

Fletcher, Sheila, *Victorian Girls, Lord Lyttelton's Daughters* (London, 1997)

Foster, Roy, *Lord Randolph Churchill* (Oxford, 1981)

Gilmour, David, *Curzon* (London, 1994)

Gooddie, Sheila, *Mary Gladstone, A Gentle Rebel* (Chichester, 2003)

Hudson, David, *The Ireland That We Made: Arthur and Gerald Balfour's Contribution to the Origins of Modern Ireland* (Ohio, 2003)

Hughes, Judith, *Emotion and High Politics: Personal Relations at the Summit in Late Nineteenth-Century Britain and Germany* (Berkeley, 1983)

Jenkins, Roy, *Asquith: Portrait of a Man and an Era* (New York, 1966)

Judd, Denis, *Balfour and the British Empire* (London, 1968)

Kennedy, Dane, *The Highly Civilized Man: Richard Burton and the Victorian World* (Cambridge, Massachusetts, 2005)

Koss, Stephen, *Asquith* (New York, 1976)

Lambert, Angela, *Unquiet Souls: The Indian Summer of the British Aristocracy, 1880–1918* (London, 1984)

Leslie, Anita, *The Marlborough House Set* (New York, 1973)

Longford, Elizabeth, *A Pilgrimage of Passion: The Life of Wilfrid Scawen Blunt* (London, 1979)

MacCarthy, Fiona, *The Last Pre-Raphaelite: Edward Burne-Jones and the Victorian Imagination* (London, 2011)

MacCarthy, Fiona, *William Morris: A Life for Our Time* (New York, 1995)

Mackay, Ruddock, *Balfour: Intellectual Statesman* (Oxford, 1985)

MacKenzie, Jeanne, *The Children of the Souls: A Tragedy of the First World War* (London, 1986)

Marsh, Peter, *Joseph Chamberlain, Entrepreneur in Politics* (New Haven, 1994)

Masters, Brian, *The Life of E. F. Benson* (London, 1991)

McKinstry, Leo, *Rosebery, Statesman in Turmoil* (London, 2005)

Mosley, Nicholas, *Julian Grenfell: His Life and the Times of his Death, 1888–1915* (New York, 1976)

Nicolson, Nigel, *Mary Curzon* (New York, 1977)

Renton, Claudia, *Those Wild Wyndhams: Three Sisters at the Heart of Power* (London, 2014)

Roberts, Andrew, *Salisbury, Victorian Titan* (London, 1999)

Rose, Kenneth, *Superior Person: A Portrait of Curzon and His Circle in Late Victorian England* (New York, 1969)

Rubinstein, David, *A Different World for Women: The Life of Millicent Garrett Fawcett* (Ohio, 1991)

Schultz, Bart, *Henry Sidgwick: Eye of the Universe* (Cambridge, 2004)

Souhami, Diana, *Mrs Keppel and Her Daughter* (New York, 1996)

Steele, David, *Lord Salisbury, A Political Biography* (London, 1999)

Sykes, Christopher Simon, *The Big House: The Story of a Country House and Its Family* (London, 2004)

Vane, Henry, *Affair of State: A Biography of the 8th Duke and Duchess of Devonshire* (London, 2004)

Weintraub, Stanley, *Edward the Caresser: The Playboy Prince Who Became Edward VII* (New York, 2001)

Young, Kenneth, *Arthur Balfour: The Happy Life of the Politician, Prime Minister, Statesman and Philosopher* (London, 1963)

OTHER SECONDARY SOURCES

Adams, James Eli, *Dandies and Desert Saints: Styles of Victorian Masculinity* (New York, 1995)

Adonis, Andrew, *Making Aristocracy Work: The Peerage and the Political System in Britain, 1884–1914* (Oxford, 1993)

Arata, Stephen, *Fictions of Loss in the Victorian Fin-de-Siècle: Identity and Empire* (Cambridge, 1996)

Arendt, Hannah, *The Origins of Totalitarianism* (New York, 1951)

Armstrong, Nancy, *Desire and Domestic Fiction: A Political History of the Novel* (New York, 1987)

Auerbach, Nina, *Private Theatricals: The Lives of the Victorians* (Cambridge, Massachusetts, 1990)

Auerbach, Nina, *Woman and the Demon: The Life of a Victorian Myth* (Cambridge, Massachusetts, 1982)

Banta, Martha, *Barbaric Intercourse: Caricature and the Culture of Conduct, 1841–1936* (Chicago, 2003)

Bederman, Gail, *Manliness and Civilization: A Cultural History of Gender and Race in the United States, 1880–1917* (Chicago, 1995)

Belcham, John and James Epstein, 'The Nineteenth-Century Gentleman Leader Revisited', *Social History* 22 (May, 1997): 174–93

Bell, Duncan, *The Idea of Greater Britain: Empire and the Future of World Order, 1860–1900* (Princeton, 2007)

Bell, Duncan, ed., *Victorian Visions of Global Order: Empire and International Relations in Nineteenth-Century Political Thought* (Cambridge, 2007)

Bentley, Michael, *Lord Salisbury's World: Conservative Environments in Late Victorian Britain* (Cambridge, 2007)

Biagini, Eugenio F., *British Democracy and Irish Nationalism, 1876–1906* (Cambridge, 2007)

Bivona, Daniel, *British Imperial Literature, 1870–1940: Writing and the Administration of Empire* (Cambridge, 1998)

Black, Barbara, *A Room of His Own: A Literary-Cultural Study of Victorian Clubland* (Ohio, 2012)

Breward, Christopher, *The Hidden Consumer: Masculinities, Fashion and City Life 1860–1914* (Manchester, 1999)

Brown, Stewart J., *Providence and Empire: Religion, Politics and Society in the United Kingdom, 1815–1914* (New York, 2008)

Bush, Julia, *Edwardian Ladies and Imperial Power* (London, 2000)

Bush, Julia, 'Ladylike Lives? Upper Class Women's Autobiographies and the Politics of Later Victorian and Edwardian Britain', *Literature and History* 10 (Autumn 2001): 42–61

Bush, Julia, *Women Against the Vote: Female Anti-Suffragism in Britain* (Oxford, 2007)

Butler, Judith P., *Excitable Speech: A Politics of the Performative* (New York, 1997)

Cain, P. J. and A. G. Hopkins, *British Imperialism, 1688–2000* (London, 2002)

Caine, Barbara, ed., *Friendship, A History* (London, 2009)

Campbell, Christy, *Fenian Fire: The British Government Plot to Assassinate Queen Victoria* (London, 2002)

Cannadine, David, *Aspects of Aristocracy: Grandeur and Decline in Modern Britain* (New Haven, 1994)

Cannadine, David, *The Decline and Fall of the British Aristocracy* (New Haven, 1990)

Cannon, Kelly, *Henry James and Masculinity: The Man at the Margins* (New York, 1994)

Chandos, John, *Boys Together: English Public Schools 1800–1864* (New Haven, 1984)

Clark, J. C. D., *Our Shadowed Present: Modernism, Postmodernism, and History* (Stanford, 2004)

Coetzee, Frans, *For Party or Country: Nationalism and the Dilemmas of Popular Conservatism in Edwardian England* (Oxford, 1990)

Cohen, Deborah, *Family Secrets: The Things We Tried to Hide* (New York, 2013)

Coles, Robert, *Privileged Ones: The Well-Off and Rich in America* (Boston, 1977)

Collini, Stefan, *Public Moralists: Political Thought and Intellectual Life in Britain, 1850–1930* (Oxford 1991)

Crossman, Virginia, *Politics, Law and Order in Nineteenth Century Ireland* (New York, 1996)

Curtis, L. P., *Apes and Angels: The Irishman in Victorian Caricature* (Washington DC, 1997)

Curtis, L. P., *Coercion and Conciliation in Ireland, 1880–1892: A Study in Conservative Unionism* (Princeton, 1963)

Curtis, L. P., 'The Battering Ram and Irish Evictions, 1887–90', *Eire-Ireland* 42 (Fall/Winter, 2007): 207–48

Davidoff, Leonore, *The Best Circles: Society, Etiquette and the Season* (New Jersey, 1973)

Davis, Mike, *Late-Victorian Holocausts: El Nino Famines and the Making of the Third World* (London, 2001)

Dawson, Graham, *Soldier Heroes: British Adventure, Empire and the Imagining of Masculinities* (London, 1994)

Dellamora, Richard, *Masculine Desire: The Sexual Politics of Victorian Aestheticism* (Chapel Hill, 1990)

Deslandes, Paul, *Oxbridge Men: British Masculinity and the Undergraduate Experience, 1850–1920* (Bloomington, 2005)

Dixon, Thomas, *From Passions to Emotions: The Creation of a Secular Psychological Category* (Cambridge, 2003)

Ellenberger, Nancy W., 'The Souls and London "Society" at the End of the Nineteenth Century', *Victorian Studies* 25 (Winter 1982): 133–60

Ellenberger, Nancy W., 'The Transformation of London "Society" at the End of Victoria's Reign: Evidence from the Court Presentation Records', *Albion* 22 (Winter 1990): 633–53

Foldy, Michael, *The Trials of Oscar Wilde: Deviance, Morality, and Late-Victorian Society* (New Haven, 1997)

Franklin, J. Jeffrey, *Serious Play: The Cultural Form of the Nineteenth-Century Realist Novel* (Philadelphia, 1999)

Freeman, Nicholas, *1895: Drama, Disaster and Disgrace in Late Victorian Britain* (Edinburgh, 2011)

Friedberg, Aaron, *The Weary Titan: Britain and the Experience of Relative Decline, 1895–1905* (Princeton, 1988)

Gagnier, Regenia, *Subjectivities: A History of Self-Representation in Britain, 1832–1920* (Oxford, 1991)

Gailey, Andrew, *Ireland and the Death of Kindness: The Experience of Constructive Unionism, 1890–1905* (Cork, 1987)

Gathorne-Hardy, Jonathan, *The Old School Tie: The Phenomenon of the English Public School* (New York, 1977)

Geary, Laurence, 'John Mandeville and the Irish Crimes Act of 1887', *Irish Historical Studies* 25 (November 1987): 358–75

Geary, Laurence, *The Plan of Campaign, 1886–1891* (Cork, 1986)

Gilhooly, Eileen, *Smile of Discontent: Humor, Gender, and Nineteenth-Century British Fiction* (Chicago, 1999)

Goffman, Erving, *Behavior in Public Places: Notes on the Social Organization of Gatherings* (New York, 1963)

Goffman, Erving, *Encounters: Two Studies in the Sociology of Interaction* (Indianapolis, 1961)

Gray, F. Elizabeth, ed., *Women in Journalism at the Fin de Siècle: Making a Name for Herself* (New York, 2012)

Green, E. H. H., *The Crisis of Conservatism: The Politics, Economics and Ideology of the British Conservative Party, 1880–1914* (London, 1995)

Griffin, Ben, *The Politics of Gender in Victorian Britain: Masculinity, Political Culture and the Struggle for Women's Rights* (Cambridge, 2012)

Gross, Daniel, *The Secret History of Emotion: From Aristotle's Rhetoric to Modern Brain Science* (Chicago, 2006)

Habermas, Jurgen, *The Structural Transformation of the Public Sphere: An Inquiry into a Category of Bourgeois Society*, trans. Thomas Burger and Frederick Lawrence (Cambridge, Massachusetts, 1989)

Hadley, Elaine, *Living Liberalism: Practical Citizenship in Mid-Victorian England* (Chicago, 2010)

Hampton, Mark, *Visions of the Press in Britain, 1850–1950* (Illinois, 2004)

Harris, Jose, *Private Lives, Public Spirit: Britain, 1879–1914* (Oxford, 1993)

Harris, Susan K., *The Cultural Work of the Late Nineteenth-Century Hostess* (Basingstoke, 2002)

Harrison, Brian, *The Transformation of British Politics, 1860–1995* (Oxford, 1996)

Harte, Negley and Roland Quinault, eds, *Land and Society in Britain, 1700–1914* (Manchester, 1996)

Hunter, Jane, *How Young Ladies Became Girls: The Victorian Origins of American Girlhood* (New Haven, 2002)

Hynes, Samuel, *The Edwardian Turn of Mind* (Princeton, 1968)

Israel, Kali, *Names and Stories: Emilia Dilke and Victorian Culture* (Oxford, 1999)

Jackson, Alvin, *Home Rule, An Irish History 1800–2000* (Oxford, 2003)

Jalland, Patricia, *Women, Marriage, and Politics, 1860–1914* (Oxford, 1986)

Jay, Martin, *The Virtues of Mendacity: On Lying in Politics* (Charlottesville, 2010)

Jenkins, T. A., *Parliament, Party, and Politics in Victorian Britain* (Manchester, 1996)

Joyce, Patrick, *Democratic Subjects: The Self and the Social in Nineteenth-Century England* (Cambridge, 1994)

Kaye, Richard A., *The Flirt's Tragedy: Desire without End in Victorian and Edwardian Fiction* (Charlottesville, 2002)

Kern, Stephen, *Eyes of Love: The Gaze in English and French Culture, 1840–1900* (New York, 1996)

Kern, Stephen, *The Culture of Love, Victorians to Moderns* (Cambridge, Massachusetts, 1992)

Koss, Stephen, *The Rise and Fall of the Political Press in Britain: The Nineteenth Century*, two volumes (Chapel Hill, 1981)

Koven, Seth, *Slumming: Sexual and Social Politics in Victorian London* (London, 2006)

Lammers, Joris, Diederik A. Stapel and Adam D. Galinsky, 'Power Increases Hypocrisy: Moralizing in Reasoning, Immorality in Behavior', *Psychological Science* 21 (May 2010): 737–44

Langford, Paul, *Englishness Identified: Manners and Character 1650–1850* (Oxford, 2000)

Larson, Jil, *Ethics and Narrative in the English Novel, 1880–1914* (Cambridge, 2001)

Lawrence, Jon, 'Class and Gender in the Making of Urban Toryism, 1880–1914', *English Historical Review* 108 (July, 1993): 629–52

Lawrence, Jon, *Electing Our Masters: The Hustings in British Politics from Hogarth to Blair* (Oxford, 2009)

Lawrence, Jon, *Speaking for the People: Party, Language and Popular Politics in England, 1867–1914* (Cambridge, 1998)

Leckie, Barbara, *Culture and Adultery: The Novel, the Newspaper, and the Law 1857–1914* (Philadelphia, 1999)

Ledger, Sally and Scott McCracken, eds, *Cultural Politics at the Fin de Siècle* (Cambridge, 1995)

Lewis, Judith Schneid, *In the Family Way: Childbearing in the British Aristocracy, 1760–1860* (New Jersey, 1986)

Linstrum, Erik, 'The Making of a Translator: James Strachey and the Origins of British Psychoanalysis', *Journal of British Studies* 3 (July 2014): 685–704

Livingston, James C., *Religious Thought in the Victorian Age: Challenges and Reconceptions* (New York, 2006)

Lubenow, W. C., *Liberal Intellectuals and Public Culture in Modern Britain, 1815–1914: Making Words Flesh* (Woodbridge, 2010)

Lubenow, W. C., *Parliamentary Politics and the Home Rule Crisis: The British House of Commons in 1886* (Oxford, 1988)

Lubenow, W. C., *The Cambridge Apostles, 1820–1914: Liberalism, Imagination and Friendship in British Intellectual and Professional Life* (Cambridge, 1998)

Luftig, Victor, *Seeing Together: Friendship between the Sexes in English Writing, from Mill to Woolf* (Stanford, 1993)

MacKenzie, John M., *Popular Imperialism and the Military, 1850–1950* (Manchester, 1992)

MacKenzie, John M., *Propaganda and Empire: The Manipulation of British Public Opinion, 1880–1960* (Manchester, 1984)

Mangan, J. A., *Athleticism in the Victorian and Edwardian Public School* (Cambridge, 1981)

Mangan, J. A., *The Games Ethic and Imperialism* (New York, 1986)

Marcus, Sharon, *Between Women: Friendship, Desire, and Marriage in Victorian England* (Princeton, 2007)

Marsh, Peter, *The Discipline of Popular Government: Lord Salisbury's Domestic Statecraft 1881–1902* (Sussex, 1978)

Mason, Michael, *The Making of Victorian Sexuality* (Oxford, 1994)

Martin, Clancy, ed., *The Philosophy of Deception* (Oxford, 2009)

McClintock, Anne, *Imperial Leather: Race, Gender, and Sexuality in the Colonial Conquest* (New York, 1995)

McCormack, Matthew, ed., *Public Men: Masculinity and Politics in Modern Britain* (New York, 2007)

Meisel, Joseph S., *Public Speech and the Culture of Public Life in the Age of Gladstone* (New York, 2001)

Meisel, Joseph S., 'The Importance of Being Serious: The Unexplored Connection between Gladstone and Humour', *History* 84 (April, 1999): 278–300

Meisel, Joseph S. and Gareth Cordery, *The Humours of Parliament: Harry Furniss's View of Late Victorian Political Culture* (Ohio, 2014)

Montgomery, Maureen, *Displaying Women: Spectacles of Leisure in Edith Wharton's New York* (New York, 1998)

Montgomery, Maureen, *Gilded Prostitution: Status, Money, and Transatlantic Marriages, 1870–1914* (London, 1989)

Morris, Pam, *Imagining Inclusive Society in 19th-Century Novels: The Code of Sincerity in the Public Sphere* (Baltimore, 2004)

Newman, Beth, *Subjects on Display: Psychoanalysis, Social Expectation, and Victorian Femininity* (Ohio, 2004)

O'Callaghan, Margaret, *British High Politics and a Nationalist Ireland: Criminality, Land, and Law under Forster and Balfour* (New York, 1994)

Offer, Avner, *Property and Politics, 1870–1914: Landownership, Law, Ideology and Urban Development in England* (Cambridge, 1981)

Onslow, Barbara, *Women of the Press in Nineteenth–Century Britain* (New York, 2000)

Oppenheim, Janet, 'Shattered Nerves': Doctors, Patients, and Depression in Victorian England (New York, 1991)

Oppenheim, Janet, The Other World: Spiritualism and Psychical Research in England, 1850–1914 (Cambridge, 1985)

Owen, Alex, The Darkened Room: Women, Power and Spiritualism in Late Victorian England (Philadelphia, 1990)

Perkin, Harold, The Rise of Professional Society in England since 1880 (New York, 1989)

Perkin, Joan, Women and Marriage in Nineteenth–Century England (London, 1989)

Pfister, Joel and Nancy Schnog, eds, Inventing the Psychological: Toward a Cultural History of Emotional Life in America (New Haven, 1997)

Phegley, Jennifer, Educating the Proper Woman Reader: Victorian Family Literary Magazines and the Cultural Health of the Nation (Ohio, 2004)

Phillips, Gregory D., The Diehards: Aristocratic Society and Politics in Edwardian England (Cambridge, Massachusetts, 1979)

Porter, Bernard, Plots and Paranoia: A History of Political Espionage in Britain, 1790–1988 (Boston, 1989)

Pugh, Martin, The March of the Women: A Revisionist Analysis of the Campaign for Women's Suffrage, 1866–1914 (Oxford, 2000)

Reddy, William R, The Navigation of Feeling: A Framework for the History of Emotions (Cambridge, 2001)

Reed, David, The Popular Magazine in Britain and the United States, 1880–1960 (Toronto, 1997)

Reynolds, K. D., Aristocratic Women and Political Society in Victorian Britain (Oxford, 1998)

Roper, Michael and John Tosh, eds, Manful Assertions: Masculinities in Britain since 1800 (New York, 1991)

Rose, Jonathan, The Edwardian Temperament, 1895–1918 (Ohio, 1986)

Rubery, Matthew, The Novelty of Newspapers: Victorian Fiction after the Invention of the News (Oxford, 2009)

Rubinstein, W. D., Men of Property: The Very Wealthy in Britain since the Industrial Revolution (New Jersey, 1981)

Rutherford, Jonathan, Forever England: Reflections on Masculinity and Empire (London, 1997)

Savage, Gail, The Social Construction of Expertise: The English Civil Service and Its Influence, 1919–1939 (Pittsburgh, 1996)

Schneer, J., London 1900: The Imperial Metropolis (New Haven, 1999)

Scott, J. W. Robertson, The Life and Death of a Newspaper (London, 1952)

Searle, G. R., Eugenics and Politics in Britain, 1900–1914 (Leyden, 1976)

Searle, Geoffrey, The Quest for National Efficiency (Berkeley, 1971)

Sedgwick, Eve Kosofsky, Epistemology of the Closet (Berkeley, 1990)

Sennett, Richard, The Fall of Public Man: On the Social Psychology of Capitalism (New York, 1978)

Shannon, Richard, The Age of Salisbury, 1881–1902: Unionism and Empire (London, 1996)

Showalter, Elaine, Sexual Anarchy: Gender and Anarchy at the Fin de Siècle (New York, 1990)

Smith, Beverly A., 'William O'Brien, Mr. Balfour's Prisoner', *Eire-Ireland* 18 (Winter 1983): 72–96

Spacks, Patricia Meyer, *Gossip* (New York, 1985)

Spiers, Edward, *The Late Victorian Army* (Manchester, 1992)

St John, Ian, *Gladstone and Logic of Victorian Politics* (London, 2010)

Stansky, Peter, *On or About December 1910: Early Bloomsbury and its Intimate World* (Cambridge, Massachusetts, 1996)

Stedman, Gesa, *Stemming the Torrent: Expression and Control in Victorian Discourses on Emotions, 1830–1872* (Aldershot, 2002)

Steele, Karen and Michael de Nie, eds, *Ireland and the New Journalism* (New York, 2014)

Steele, Valerie, *Fashion and Eroticism: Feminine Beauty from the Victorian Age to the Jazz Age* (New York, 1985)

Taylor, Anthony, *Lords of Misrule: Hostility to Aristocracy in Late Nineteenth Century and Early Twentieth Century Britain* (New York, 2004)

Taylor, Charles, *Sources of the Self: The Making of Modern Identity* (Cambridge, Massachusetts, 1989)

Thompson, F. M. L., *English Landed Society in the Nineteenth Century* (London, 1963)

Thompson, James, *British Political Culture and the Idea of 'Public Opinion', 1867–1914* (Cambridge, 2013)

Thompson, John B., *Political Scandal: Power and Visibility in the Media Age* (Cambridge, 2000)

Tomes, Jason, *Balfour and Foreign Policy: The International Thought of a Conservative Statesman* (Cambridge, 1997)

Tosh, John, *A Man's Place: Masculinity and the Middle-Class Home in Victorian England* (New Haven, 1999)

Tosh, John, *Manliness and Masculinities in Nineteenth-Century Britain* (Harlow, 2005)

Trilling, Lionel, *Sincerity and Authenticity* (Cambridge, Massachusetts, 1972)

Vernon, James, *Distant Strangers: How Britain Became Modern* (Berkeley, 2014)

Walkowitz, Judith, *City of Dreadful Delight: Narratives of Sexual Danger in Victorian London* (Chicago, 1992)

Waller, J. P., 'Laughter in the House: A Late Nineteenth and Early Twentieth Century Parliamentary Survey', *Twentieth Century British History* 5 (1994): 4–37

Walshe, Eibhear, 'The First Gay Irishman? Ireland and the Wilde Trials', *Eire-Ireland* 40 (Fall/ Winter 2005): 38–57

Warwick-Haller, Sally, *William O'Brien and the Irish Land War* (Dublin, 1990)

Index

References to illustrations are shown in *italics*. References to notes consist of the page number followed by the letter 'n' followed by the number of the note, e.g. 326n57 refers to note no. 57 on page 326.